.5
3-90

D0225641

534375

NOTABLES OF THE RIGHT

NOTABLES OF THE RIGHT

The Conservative Party and Political Mobilization in Germany, 1876–1918

JAMES N. RETALLACK

University of Toronto

Boston
UNWIN HYMAN
London   Sydney   Wellington

CENTRAL MISSOURI
STATE UNIVERSITY
Warrensburg,
Missouri

© James N. Retallack, 1988
This book is copyright under the Berne Convention. No reproduction
without permission. All rights reserved.

Allen & Unwin Inc.,
8 Winchester Place, Winchester, Mass. 01890, USA

Published by the Academic Division of
Unwin Hyman Ltd
15/17 Broadwick Street, London W1V 1FP, UK

Allen & Unwin (Australia) Ltd,
8 Napier Street, North Sydney, NSW 2060, Australia

Allen & Unwin (New Zealand) Ltd in association with the
Port Nicholson Press Ltd,
60 Cambridge Terrace, Wellington, New Zealand

First published in 1988

Library of Congress Cataloging-in-Publication Data

Retallack, James N.
  Notables of the right.
Bibliography: p.
Includes index.
1. Deutsch – Konservative Partei – History.
2. Conservatism – Germany – History.
3. Germany – Politics and government – 1871–1918.
I. Title.
JN3946.K66R48 1988 324.243′02 87–15285
ISBN 0–04–900038–1 (alk. paper)

British Library Cataloguing in Publication Data

Retallack, James N.
  Notables of the right: the Conservative Party and
  political mobilization in Germany, 1876–1918.
1. Deutsch-Konservative Partei – History
I. Title
324.243′04 JN3970.D3/
ISBN 0–04–900038–1

Typeset in 10 on 12 point Garamond by
Computape (Pickering) Ltd, North Yorkshire
and printed in Great Britain by
Biddles of Guildford

JN
3946
K66
R48
1988

To My Parents

534375

Contents

Abbreviations

CONTEMPORARY NEWSPAPERS AND JOURNALS

BadLp	*Badische Landpost*
BadP	*Badische Post*
BayrLb	*Bayrischer Landbote*
BBC	*Berliner Börsen-Courier*
BNN	*Berliner Neueste Nachrichten*
BT	*Berliner Tageblatt*
CC	*Conservative Correspondenz*
DtAgrarKorr	*Deutsche Agrarkorrespondenz*
DtAgrarZ	*Deutsche Agrarzeitung*
DtRp	*Deutsche Reichspost*
DTZ	*Deutsche Tageszeitung*
DAB	*Deutsches Adelsblatt*
DtTbl	*Deutsches Tageblatt*
DtWbl	*Deutsches Wochenblatt*
DresdN	*Dresdner Nachrichten*
FkZ	*Frankfurter Zeitung*
FsZ	*Freisinnige Zeitung*
Ger	*Germania*
HN	*Hamburger Nachrichten*
HannP	*Hannoversche Post*
HannTN	*Hannoversche Tages-Nachrichten*
KJ	*Kasseler Journal*
KVZ	*Kölnische Volkszeitung*
KnZ	*Kölnische Zeitung*
KM	*(Allgemeine) Konservative Monatsschrift*
KWbl	*Konservatives Wochenblatt*
KdBdl	*Korrespondenz des Bundes der Landwirte*
LeipNN	*Leipziger Neueste Nachrichten*
LeipZ	*Leipziger Zeitung*
MecklN	*Mecklenburger Nachrichten*
Mitteilungen	*Mitteilungen aus der konservativen Partei*
MdDVP	*Mitteilungen der Deutschen Vaterlands-Partei*
MAZ	*(Münchener) Allgemeine Zeitung*
NZ	*National-Zeitung*
NeueDtland	*Das neue Deutschland*

KZ	*Neue Preußische (Kreuz-) Zeitung*
NWVZ	*Neue Westfälische Volkszeitung*
NAZ	*Norddeutsche Allgemeine Zeitung*
OstprZ	*Ostpreußische Zeitung*
PommRp	*Pommersche Reichspost*
PrJbb	*Preußische Jahrbücher*
Rb	*Der Reichsbote*
SchlMZ	*Schlesisches Morgenzeitung*
SchlZ	*Schlesische Zeitung*
SchlMbl	*Schlesische Morgenblatt*
SchwMerkur	*Schwäbischer Merkur*
StaatsbgZ	*Staatsbürger Zeitung*
SCC	*Süddeutsche Conservative Correspondenz*
SddLp	*Süddeutsche Landpost*
SddZ	*Süddeutsche Zeitung*
TR	*Tägliche Rundschau*
Vk	*Das Volk*
Vw	*Vorwärts*
VossZ	*Vossische Zeitung*

OTHER ABBREVIATIONS

a.D./z.D.	*außer Dienst/zum Dienst*, inactive or retired
ADV	Pan-German League
BAK	Bundesarchiv Koblenz
BA-MA	Bundesarchiv-Militärarchiv Freiburg i.B.
BdL	Farmers' League
CSP	Christian Social Party
CvdI	Central Association of German Industrialists
DKP	German Conservative Party
DOV	German Society for the Eastern Marches
DVP	German Fatherland Party
FKP	Free Conservative Party
GLA	Generallandesarchiv
GStA	Geheimes Staatsarchiv
Kl. Erw.	Kleine Erwerbungen
LT	Landtag
NDB	*Neue Deutsche Biographie*
NL	Nachlaß
NL F	Nachlaß Fechenbach (BAK)
NLP	National Liberal Party
PA AA	Political Archive of the German Foreign Office, Bonn
PAH	Prussian House of Deputies

Pb	Prussian League
PHH	Prussian Herrenhaus
PVV	Prussian People's Association
Rkz.	Files of the Reich Chancellory
RLB	Reichslandbund
RT	Reichstag
RvgSD	Imperial League against Social Democracy
SBR	*Stenographische Berichte über die Verhandlungen des Reichstages*
Sg F	Sammlung Fechenbach (BAK)
SPD	German Social Democratic Party
St. Min.	Prussian State Ministry meeting protocols
VdSWR	Association of Tax and Economic Reformers
WV	Economic Union
ZSg	Zeitgeschichtliche Sammlung
ZStA I	Zentrales Staatsarchiv I, Potsdam
ZStA II	Zentrales Staatsarchiv II, Merseburg

Note: Dates in the endnotes are listed according to the European convention of day-month-year. Thus 8.12.92 is 8 December 1892.

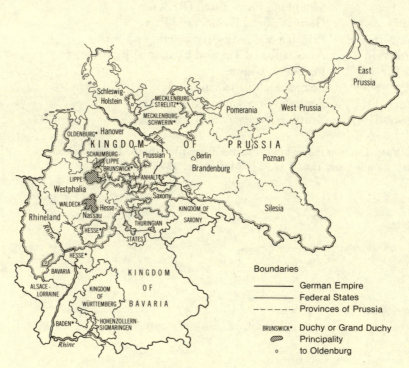

The German Empire, 1871–1918

Acknowledgements

I am happy to have the opportunity to thank the groups and individuals who provided travel grants, archival assistance, scholarly discussion and general encouragement during the many stages of this project.

For financial assistance for travel and research in Germany I am indebted to St John's College, Oxford, in particular its former President, Sir Richard Southern; and to the Rhodes Trust, Oxford, and the two wardens of Rhodes House during my days in Oxford, Sir Edgar Williams and Robin Fletcher. My debt to the Social Sciences and Humanities Research Council of Canada is especially great, for doctoral and post-doctoral fellowships from 1980 to 1984 and for a research grant to return to German archives in the summer of 1984. I have also received generous funding from the University of Alberta.

The personnel of the various libraries and archives I visited in England, Germany, the United States and Canada played a large role in whatever success I achieved in locating useful evidence for my study. Worthy of special mention here is the staff of the Bundesarchiv in Koblenz, particularly Dr Real, Herr Fischer and Frau Marschall-Reiser. At Stanford my work was considerably advanced by the kindness and expertise of Peter Frank at the Green Library and Agnes Peterson at the Hoover Institution.

A number of individuals permitted me to use unpublished material in private collections, for which I am grateful. These include the Fürstlich von Bismarck'sches Privatsekretariat, Friedrichsruh, for permission to use the Bismarck Nachlaß; Dr Friedrich Freiherr Hiller von Gaertringen, who provided me with a copy of the Heydebrand–Westarp correspondence; Wolfgang von Loebell, who gave me access to the Nachlaß of his father, Friedrich Wilhelm von Loebell; to Frau Toni von Goßler, who allowed me to use the Nachlaß of Alfred von Goßler in Freiburg; and to J. von Hugo-Graf Knyphausen, who permitted me to use the Nachlaß of Edzard Fürst zu Innhausen und Knyphausen in the Staatsarchiv Aurich.

My many scholarly debts extend from my undergraduate days at Trent University in Peterborough, Ontario, where my work was directed most closely by Stuart Robson and the late Brian Heeney. At Oxford, the guidance of my doctoral supervisor, Hartmut Pogge von Strandmann, was the largest single influence in the development of my understanding of Imperial German history; he saw me faithfully through the ordeal of learning 'that awful German language' in my first year, and gently but uncompromisingly pushed me to take the first plunge into German archives in 1979. My two thesis examiners, John Röhl and Peter Pulzer, both provided useful advice at early stages of my research, and their comments during my oral examination helped inaugurate the thesis revisions that followed. Other people who provided advice and comradeship during my years in England and Germany were David Blackbourn, Gary Bonham, Hans Horn, Michael John, Philippa Maddern, Ross McKibbin, Rosemary Orthmann, Robert Ridenour and the Schilfert family.

At Stanford I profited from the advice of many colleagues but from none more than James Sheehan, who took time to sponsor my various research activities as a post-doctoral fellow and consistently provided thoughtful comment on my work. The Junior Faculty Research Group at Stanford offered many useful suggestions on ways to refine my hypotheses, as did the members of the History Colloquium at the University of Alberta. For their comments on my work and other assistance since I left England I am also grateful to Robert Berdahl, David Blackbourn, Dieter Fricke, Hans-Jürgen Kremer, James Murray, Hans-Jürgen Puhle, Dirk Stegmann and Hans-Ulrich Wehler. In its penultimate form the manuscript of this book was read by Geoff Eley, Robert Moeller, Hartmut Pogge, James Sheehan and Ulrich Trumpener, all of whom deserve special thanks. For the drawing of the map I am indebted to Inge Wilson; for the index, to Hans Neumann. Jane Harris-Matthews at Unwin Hyman has offered first-rate assistance in bringing this study to press. These friends and colleagues have provided personal support and scholarly encouragement over the past eight years. Any errors of substance or flaws of argument which may be found in what follows are, of course, my responsibility alone.

My wife, Helen Graham, played many roles during the life of this project, from reading painfully dense chapter drafts to finding the umlauts I knew resided somewhere in my computer. I hope her many sacrifices and her faith in this book will be repaid. My final and greatest debt of gratitude is to my parents. As a necessarily inadequate acknowledgement of their support, this book is dedicated to them.

Edmonton, Alberta
December 1986

1

Introduction:
The Dilemmas of German Conservatism

It is remarkable how long the political history of German Conservatism has been defined negatively. In the early 1960s intellectual history seemed to provide the appropriate key to unlock the mystery of Germany's political culture. In the 1970s, critical social history, as exemplified in the works of Hans-Ulrich Wehler, studied the internal structure and working of the imperial establishment, partly to see what effect Germany's authoritarian heritage had on its anti-democratic development in the 1920s and 1930s. Because it concentrated on the manipulatory schemes of Bismarck and leading élites, this approach was referred to (albeit somewhat misleadingly) as history 'from the top down'.[1] In the late 1970s and early 1980s this style of historical writing was in turn subjected to critical review. The activities and ideals of the German masses became no longer merely the *object* of historical inquiry that concentrated on established élites; the common man – and woman – moved at least a step closer to centre stage. This approach has been referred to as history 'from the bottom up' (again not without confusion).[2] It is itself presently giving way to even more sophisticated analyses that integrate both approaches. Recent contributions to the political history of the *Kaiserreich* have rightly emphasized the importance of regional diversity in determining political attitudes, the impact of economic modernization and social upheaval on political structures at various levels, and the inability of manipulative élites to retain many of their privileges in a hostile political world.[3] Yet still the social and political development of German Conservatism has not been thoroughly integrated into these historiographical currents. There remains a general predilection for defining Conservatism in terms of what it *prevented* from happening in Germany, as the persistent paradigm of 'illiberalism' illustrates.[4] This general approach also characterizes past treatments of the German Conservative Party (Deutsch-Konservative Partei, or DKP) specifically. Aspects of the party's history have been written mainly by those concerned with agrarian interest politics,[5] nationalist pressure groups[6] and the emergence of a radical 'proto-fascist' Right in the last decade of the Second Empire.[7]

While great advances have been made on all these fronts, a new approach is necessary. This study for the first time offers a sustained analysis of the party's institutional development, leading personnel, social and regional composition, ideological foundation, propaganda network and legislative record. At the same time it advances theses designed to further discussion about the long-term development of the German Right, about the contours of the imperial party system and about the wider process of political modernization after 1871. The aim is to combine a survey history of the Conservative Party, needed by advanced students, non-specialist and specialist readers alike, with a deeper analysis of how Conservatives reacted to, and in turn influenced, German political development. The present availability of sources does not permit as full a discussion of every feature of party life as would be wished, particularly at the local level. There are none the less other deficits of Conservative history that are arguably more pressing than the need to provide detailed analyses of associational life on a micro scale. Outlining the general contours of the party's structure and development, while at the same time proceeding beyond the simple history of a political party *qua* party, seems a particularly appropriate way to confront the larger political dilemmas confronting Conservatives in the Second Reich.

Three major themes of Conservative history merit special attention. The first is certainly the most complex. It concerns the Conservatives' capacity to reconcile the conflicting demands of what may be termed 'political exclusivity' (or élitism) and 'mass inclusion' (or democracy). The second theme is the Conservative Party's place within German political society. The third is the effect of factional disputes and regional diversity on the evolution of the party. The degree of interconnection between these themes can hardly be overemphasized; but it may help to outline them separately.

Conservatives almost everywhere have recognized that survival depends on the ability to adapt to new political forms and to turn the path of radical change in a non-revolutionary direction. Some Conservatives have enjoyed considerable advantages in waging this struggle. In England the decline of the aristocracy, for many reasons, has been largely a story of reason, compromise and the preservation of the 'pleasing draperies of life' from a bygone age. But for Conservatives in post-1871 Germany, survival did not mean a long and comfortable twilight of prosperity and privilege. Rather, it necessitated a determined and even ruthless resistance against the combined threats of rapid social, economic and political change. In erecting these barriers to change, Conservatives had to contend with an unfamiliar and seemingly 'unconservative' constitutional structure designed by Bismarck, the White Revolutionary. The introduction of universal manhood suffrage at the birth of the Reich, and the subsequent expansion of political participation, communication and activism at the local level, confronted traditional élites with what has rightly been described as 'politics in a new key'[8] after 1871. As turn-out for Reichstag elections and the number of run-off ballots increased dramatically, as publishing enterprises expanded, as transport opportunities were extended to the common man and as regional awareness of national issues grew, the character of politics in Germany was transformed. This quantum leap in participation threatened the Conservatives' (and others') traditional pre-rogatives in the sphere of decision-making. Within the constituencies of all parties, and in the state as a whole, new political demands were registered for inclusion in the circles of influence. Early in the history of the Reich, the central question of mass politics became: participation on whose terms? The implications of this question were extremely large, whether for the party or the nation. In fact the many political dilemmas faced by Conservatives paralleled those confronting the political establishment of Imperial Germany as a whole. In the state, newly enfranchised groups struggled to wrest democracy and social justice from the élites, but those élites worked to retain their exclusivity by adapting to political circum-stances in a number of more or less conservative ways. The same conflicts were recreated at the party level. The questions of popular mobilization and participatory politics were inextricably linked; therefore, they must be studied together.

One way to investigate how Conservatives responded to these questions is to picture the Conservative Party suspended between 'high' and 'low' politics. This does not mean that the DKP was middle class or that its policies placed it in the middle of the political spectrum. Rather it means the party was forced to respond to political forces acting upon it both from above and from below. It can therefore be studied most appropriately by using both the 'politics from above' and the 'politics from below' approaches mentioned earlier. Such a rough methodological synthesis cannot illuminate all the colours of the rainbow between the ultraviolet of one method and the infra-red of the other. However, conceiving the Conservatives' political predicament in these terms is another way to break the constraints of party history narrowly defined.

What follows is largely a tale of woe, of challenges unmet. All too often Conservatives were inspired by motives that failed to rise above economic self-interest, social haughtiness and political intransigence. Of course the Conservatives had no monopoly on these faults, and a major point of this study is to highlight the *possibilities* that existed for reforming the ideology and 'style' of Conservative politics. For the Conservative Party contained within itself a vital potential for a more enlightened, realistic, 'up-to-date' brand of Conservatism. But in the end, no major campaign to provide Conservatives with a positive perspective on change or to make the party truly popular proved successful.

Is this, then, a tale signifying nothing? Not at all. Poor marks in achievement do not necessarily reflect lack of effort. First, the success of the radical nationalists and other right-wing groups in generating a mass following after 1890, often at the expense of the DKP, cannot adequately be explained without defining the causes of Conservative isolation. The 'self-marginalization' of the DKP after 1909 is a critical ingredient in the story of why new anti-Socialist initiatives emerged on the Right just before and during the First World War. It may be true that nothing resembling the ideological materials generated by the radical nationalist groups ever surfaced within the Conservative Party. The legacies of Prussianism, agrarianism and anti-intellectualism imposed burdens on the party that were too heavy to permit the flights of fancy engaged in by Pan-Germanists and others in the right-wing vanguard. But it is important to define the reasons why traditionalism and caution suppressed the radical nationalist agenda within the party and sent its advocates elsewhere. Only then can a final conclusion be reached on the overall adaptability of the German Right.

Second, an unwillingness to pursue radical nationalist campaigns did not mean that Conservatives had not been pondering other important aspects of right-wing mobilization for some time before 1914. In fact a plethora of initiatives had arisen even in the 1870s and 1880s which aimed to redefine the party's programme and agitational style, to diminish the authority of the DKP leadership in Berlin, to discard traditions of governmentalism and (most generally) to educate Conservatives about the urgencies of mass recruitment and organization in a new political age. These proposals, for various reasons, failed to fire the imagination of most party leaders in Berlin, and with Bismarck's aid they were actively suppressed in the 1880s. But at the regional level quite a different response was evident. Calls for party reform fuelled a rebellion against the Berlin leadership which by 1892 threatened to redefine Conservative allegiances fundamentally. The failure of this rebellion – finally decided only in 1896 – was certainly not inevitable.

Third and most significantly for the long-term development of the German Right, the Conservatives' greatest triumphs in the realm of political mobilization were contributed not by the more moderate or politically 'generous' members of the party but by the resolutely anti-democratic leaders of the DKP's auxiliary interest group, the Farmers' League (Bund der Landwirte, or BdL).[9] The agrarians' awareness of new political realities after 1890 allowed them to mobilize a mass constituency; but the direction in which these masses were led was not conducive to rational compromise with the forces of liberal democracy. Instead the agrarians rallied the bulk of Germany's Protestant rural sector behind campaigns to preserve the social, economic and political privileges of the class which, after all, *did* constitute the backbone of the Conservative Party: aristocratic landowners on the vast grain-growing estates east of the Elbe river. Thanks to the new organizational, agitational and propaganda techniques developed by the Farmers' League, the Conservative Party's electoral decline was far less precipitous than it might have been otherwise. However, the dominance in Conservative Party affairs which the Farmers' League's agitational 'savvy' gave it did not go unopposed. Throughout the period 1893 to 1918 there were loud and impassioned voices raised condemning the influence of the agrarians within the DKP and arguing in favour of more lofty goals for Conservatism than the defence of narrow economic interests. These voices were continually challenged and over-ruled but they were never completely silenced. Along the way opportunities arose for Conservative leaders, if they had wished, to disavow agrarian chauvinism. Such a course might have brought the party back to its 'natural' place alongside the government, and thus might have placed decisive political forces at the service of German chancellors struggling to find a middle path between the forces of revolution and reaction. The fate of reformism in the Reich could not be divorced from the fate of reformism within the Conservative Party.[10]

The outcome of the struggle for the Conservative Party, for all these reasons, is hardly an uplifting tale. The 'success' of the radical agrarians most particularly held the seed of later disasters. As Alexander Gerschenkron and Hans Rosenberg argued long ago, there were serious liabilities inherent in the preservation of a traditional élite whose economic interests and political ideals diverged fundamentally from the common good.[11] Gerschenkron postulated in the 1940s that the price of bread was related to the price of democracy in Germany. Rosenberg showed that the 'pseudo-democratization' of the landowning class contributed to the effectiveness of the Conservatives' rearguard action against mass democracy. Other historians have since refined these theses. They have illustrated how the anti-Semitic, anti-liberal and anti-democratic ideals shared by the radical agrarians and most Conservatives seriously weakened traditions of liberty in Germany. But always one comes back to this problem of political exclusivity and mass inclusion. By helping others on the Right learn to be *responsive* to the wishes of the masses but not *responsible* to them, the Conservatives played a crucial role in Germany's political misdevelopment in the twentieth century.

The second theme concerns the DKP's middle position in a political hierarchy running from the Kaiser and his government at the top to 'the people' at the bottom. The Conservatives faced the triple task of retaining influence with the Kaiser and his ministers, of allying with the other parliamentary groups to pass right-wing legislation and of mobilizing a new constituency to broaden the popular base of the party. The way party members confronted or avoided their uncomfortable choices revealed a great deal about their most basic political ideals. Campaigns to gain influence with political groups at one end of the political hierarchy always presented Conservatives with difficult compromises and made them consider the relative merits and liabilities of alienating groups at the other end. Therefore, a study of the ebb and flow of Conservative allegiances can tell us something of how contemporaries regarded the relative balance between 'popular' and 'élitist' forces in the Second Empire.

The Conservative Party's relations to three broad groups in this political hierarchy must be examined. First, it is necessary to reconsider past assertions of a basic unanimity between Conservatives and the German 'establishment'. Studies of the Prussian army, court and bureaucracy have generally asserted rather than demonstrated the benefits which accrued to the Conservative Party directly as a result of its close proximity to these service élites. A new approach must determine which members of the ruling strata were willing to support 'their' party, the DKP, in a tangible way, and why they did so. The goal is to move beyond imprecise statements about a 'Conservative hegemony' in society and politics, to consider not only why Conservative popularity declined but also why the party *continued* to attract the allegiance of powerful individuals in government, business and society. How did the party convince these men that it best reflected their political philosophy and was worthy of their allegiance? Why did successive chancellors never seriously contemplate a full break from the Conservative Party?[12]

The second main group in the political hierarchy includes the right-wing political parties and interest groups in the empire. In many cases the forces of attraction or repulsion within the right-wing milieu are inexplicable without deeper analysis of how internal DKP developments affected ties between Conservatives and their political allies. Changes in Conservative Party leadership, organization, regional strength, agitational strategies and electoral fortunes all played an important part in determining on whose terms any political alliances on the Right would be forged.

Third, what was the relationship between the Conservative Party and German society? Given the impossibility of apprehending this relationship completely, smaller investigations can consider the problem with different degrees of precision and comprehensiveness, as with studies of Conservative initiatives to win the votes of city dwellers, women and young people. With these approaches it is possible to discuss the Conservatives' attempt to broaden their social base without recourse to simple explanatory concepts like 'deference' and 'manipulation' or reliance on the Gotha Genealogical Handbook. At the same time it is necessary to keep in view the larger story of the Conservative Party's relation to 'the people' (*das Volk*). We must analyse how and why Conservative politicians sought to fashion their party as a *Volkspartei* (people's party) and how these efforts reflected their attitudes to parliamentarism. In short, our aim is to examine how a dynamic political party outgrew its wish to be 'small and mighty'[13] and sought, like all other parties, to be large and mighty – that is, popular and influential. The quest for 'popularity' (*Volkstümlichkeit*) coloured the changing relationships between the DKP and all other political groups in the Second Reich.

The third theme concerns the factional divisions and regional variations within the Conservative Party. Throughout its history the party was caught between the demands of ideological and interest politics (*Ideen- und Interessenpolitik*). Rather than undergoing a linear progression from a 'party of ideals' to a 'party of interests',[14] the DKP's development was shaped by a *continuing* conflict of ideals and interests. This conflict also determined the DKP's place in political society. The Conservatives enjoyed considerable agreement with the government, the Free Conservatives and the National Liberals on many issues, such as anti-Socialism, and yet became estranged from them on many other issues, such as a defence of agriculture. The political manoeuvring undertaken by DKP leaders to hold together the strands of their own programme and to reconcile differences of outlook between themselves and their allies revealed how they believed they could best defend the political status quo.

A study of political Conservatism in its regional diversity offers other new insights. It illustrates, first, why it is unwise to identify all the failures of leadership in Berlin with the 'party at large'. The most vocal members of the party outside Berlin – the editors of local party newspapers, rank-and-file party functionaries and regional chairmen – tended to be those who most clearly articulated and analysed the political challenges facing the party. Before the DKP's organization and ideology can be properly explained on the national level, it is necessary to study the attitudes and aspirations of these party members.

Second, earlier studies of German Conservatism from a purely Prussian vantage-point have unnecessarily narrowed our historical perspective. Thumbnail sketches of the Conservative Party now often refer to it simply as the party of 'Prussianism' – as the most well-connected party, representing 'throne and altar' and made up exclusively of those élites which stood atop the local social, economic and political hierarchies (especially in the six eastern provinces of Prussia).[15] But not all Conservatives in Germany found the same sources of political support as the backwoods Junkers. Not all of them dined at the Kaiser's table or counted their assets in millions of marks; not all of them enjoyed the legal advantages of police powers on their estates, the economic advantages of protective tariffs, or the political advantages that rested on the bayonets of the local Prussian garrison. In fact in Bavaria, Württemberg, Baden and many other non-Prussian regions, notions of Junker 'hegemony' in Germany might have aroused more astonishment than fear.

This argument must not be overstated. The power of Prussia provided many barriers to democratization in Germany. When the spectre of left-wing majorities in the Reichstag threatened the DKP with political isolation or even extinction, Conservatives always looked with nostalgia (but also with good reason) to the political institutions of Prussia for support. They looked to the Prussian Herrenhaus, filled with the personal appointees of the monarch, and to the Prussian House of Deputies, where a plutocratic three-class franchise provided a strong phalanx of Conservative seats out of all proportion to the number of ballots cast for Conservative candidates. On a broader scale the Conservatives looked to the Prussian court and government ministries; to the continued respect accorded the Prussian reserve officer class and militarist values in general; to the prevailing conservative mentality of the Prussian *Landräte* (county councillors) and other sectors of the Prussian administration; to the anti-revolutionary catechisms read from Prussian pulpits or taught in Prussian schools; and to the obvious election-rigging undertaken with the active or tacit approval of the state. Many other elements can be included in what has been called the 'matrix of authoritarian society', through which the Conservatives allegedly controlled Prussia and, by extension, Germany.[16]

The precise ways in which these Prussian structures and habits of mind determined the Conservatives' attitude towards 'politics in a new key' have yet to be determined. There is no doubt that Prussian circumstances had a profound influence on the political development of the nation as a whole, and continued to do so long after the political caesura of 1871. That is something that we, like contemporaries in the Second Reich, forget only at our peril. Nevertheless, as the Conservatives turned their eyes with increasing desperation to these traditional bastions of authority in Prussia, they found that Prussia itself was being transformed. Perhaps most disquieting of all was the shrinking economic foundation of Prussian Conservatism. As the structural crisis of east-Elbian agriculture deepened after the mid-1870s, the financial situation of the Junkers became more uncertain, and the network of social relationships in the rural east became more brittle. Growing estate indebtedness, spreading social unrest and the gradual disappearance of political deference were all aspects of modernization that tended to reduce the status of those who made up the bulk of the Conservative constituency. Just as Germany could not escape being 'Prussianized', so Prussia was not completely immune from 'Germanization'. In more than one sense, then, the Prussian Conservatives after 1871 were strangers in a strange land. Their social and economic predicament coloured their larger perspective on the tasks of Conservatism in the new Reich. Conservatives knew they had brought along some comforting baggage on their historical journey. Prussian soil clung firmly to their boots as they entered the Reich edifice. But decline had already set in before the German Conservative Party was born.

The contrasting situation of Conservatives in Prussia and Germany helps explain why a fuller appreciation of the 'Conservative experience' in the *Kaiserreich* has become imperative. It was the *diversity* of Conservative movements and the *breakdown* of habits of deference that forced the Conservative Party to develop its most innovative adaptive strategies. Battles for political power were often waged more fiercely in Stuttgart than in Stettin; Conservatives often coveted parliamentary seats more keenly in Karlsruhe than in Königsberg. It is therefore understandable why past portraits of the Conservative Party as monolithic or exclusively Prussian have failed to describe adequately how it was changed by the challenge of mass politics. The peculiarities rather than the uniformity of social, economic and political circumstances in the different regions of Germany affected how Conservatives approached the hateful business of 'politicking'. Historians of other regional party movements have illustrated how the tension between politics from above and politics from below had its analogue in the conflict between the centre and the periphery. They have shown how the need to co-ordinate politics on the local, regional and national levels gave rise to internal party tensions that directly affected the conduct of policy in Berlin. What follows complements these studies by analysing the same tensions within the Conservative Party.

Third, the factional nature of the DKP coloured contemporary perceptions of the possibilities for reforming the party. Various individuals and groups outside the party supported one faction or the other in hopes of bringing the DKP as a whole into line with particular ideals of Conservatism. Therefore the persistence of factional disputes helped nourish hopes within the broader conservative community that the DKP could be enlightened, or at least that it could achieve a 'healthy' balance between reactionary and progressive forces. The list of those who declared an allegiance to, or wished to work with, 'reasonable' Conservatism is a very long one indeed. In particular, the lingering tension between radical agrarians and other Conservatives after 1893 led certain figures in government to believe that the party's trend towards an anti-governmental position could be reversed. The line of chancellors who sought to detach moderate Conservatives from their intransigent party colleagues extends unbroken from Bismarck to Bethmann Hollweg.

The problems of factionalism and regionalism are important, then, because they help us investigate Conservatives' efforts to reconcile their principles and interests, their actions in Berlin and in other parts of the Reich and their inclinations to compromise with the government or to remain resolute in opposition. The varieties of Conservatism encouraged many Germans not to 'lose faith' with the DKP; they therefore help explain the ability of the party to survive throughout the *Kaiserreich*.

In the end the Conservatives failed to reconcile the conflicting demands of élitism and mass mobilization. That failure meant that the Conservative Party was swept away when the Second Empire itself collapsed in

November 1918. Before it expired, however, the party had contributed to the volatile mixture of anti-democratic values and revolutionary means that made a reconstructed Right so disloyal, and dangerous, to the Weimar Republic.

NOTES

1 See Wehler, *German Empire*; the present author must count himself among those who used these rather crude categories; see my 'Social History' for a guide to further literature.
2 Cf. Evans (ed.), *Society and Politics*, 'Introduction'.
3 See among many possible examples Blackbourn, *Class*; White, *Splintered Party*; O'Donnell, 'National Liberalism'; Bacheller, 'Class'; Blackbourn and Eley, *Peculiarities*.
4 Cf. Stern, *Failure of Illiberalism*; Jarausch, 'Illiberalism and Beyond'.
5 Puhle, *Agrarische Interessenpolitik*, and other works by this author listed in the Bibliography; Flemming, *Landwirtschaftliche Interessen*; Schumacher, *Land und Politik*.
6 Eley, *Reshaping*, and other works; Chickering, *We Men*.
7 Stegmann, *Erben*, and other works; Peck, *Radicals*. Typical appeals for a fuller history of Conservative politics are found in Stern, 'Prussia', p. 67; Puhle, 'Conservatism', pp. 689–92; Moeller, *Peasants and Lords*, p. 15; Kennedy, 'Pre-War Right', pp. 1–3, 9, 12–13. The recent collection by Stegmann, Wendt and Witt (eds.), *Deutscher Konservatismus*, has not yet achieved the impact it deserves; forthcoming works by Robert Berdahl, Jens Flemming, Dieter Fricke, Klaus Saul, Hans-Jürgen Puhle and Wolfgang Schwentker promise to expand the field of analysis further.
8 This phrase has been taken from Schorske, 'Politics in a New Key'.
9 The standard work is Puhle, *Interessenpolitik*.
10 I have developed this argument further in my essay 'Road to Philippi'.
11 Gerschenkron, *Bread*; Rosenberg, 'Pseudodemokratisierung'; cf. Dahrendorf, *Politics*.
12 Cf. Retallack, 'Conservatives *contra* Chancellor'.
13 See Wagener, *Die kleine aber mächtige Partei*.
14 As postulated in Neumann, *Stufen*; Allen, 'From Romanticism to *Realpolitik*'; Martin, 'Weltanschauliche Motive'; and other studies.
15 See, for example, Sagarra, *Introduction*, p. 152: 'The commitment of these people to what they chose to identify as "the Prussian tradition"; the preservation of a social structure and hierarchy, of habits of mind and a kind of life which was *totally* that of a pre-industrial society, was *absolute*. It was *invariably* presented in moral terms. Deviation from the pattern was regarded as an affront' (emphasis added). One must appreciate that writers of such surveys can seldom include more sophisticated analysis due to limits of space.
16 See especially Wehler, *German Empire*, pp. 118 ff.

PART I

The Young Party, 1876–90

2

The Birth of the
German Conservative Party

Prussian Conservatives had tried more than once before the 1870s to develop a popular programme and an effective organization, with little success. A fundamental reorientation of Conservative politics in another direction was necessary between 1866 and 1876 in order to follow Bismarck on his nationalist course. The 'New Conservatism' that emerged in this period abandoned many older Conservative ideals. Its proponents applied the lessons of *Realpolitik* to the task of leading the party out of the political wilderness to which 'principled Conservatism' had consigned it.[1] However, even the founding of the German Conservative Party in July 1876 hardly represented a full break with past traditions.

Agrarian interest politics in the modern sense may be said to date from the Junkers' successful action to undercut the Stein–Hardenberg reforms in the second decade of the nineteenth century. They were given more concrete form in the revolutionary year of 1848, with the advent of the short-lived Association for the Protection of the Interests of Land-ownership and the Well-Being of All Classes.[2] In the early 1860s the Prussian People's Association (Preußischer Volks-Verein, or PVV) launched a massive campaign to rally urban artisans and other social groups to a defence of the established order, with equally episodic results.[3] The growth of Reich institutions after 1871 hardly assuaged Conservative fears about losing ground to the Left. The leading Conservative news-paper, the *Neue Preußische Zeitung* (known as the *Kreuzzeitung*), attacked the Reichstag in particular, arguing that the universal franchise rendered the national parliament a 'motley jumble of notabilities, the consequence of head-count polls'.[4] Other Conservative spokesmen pointed fearfully to Bismarck's preference for the Free Conservative Party (FKP) and the National Liberal Party (NLP), founded in 1866 and 1867 respectively, as the bulwarks of his new national state.[5] Even an appeal to traditional Conservative principles failed to maintain the reputation of the Prussian Conservative Party. Old-guard Conservatives like Ludwig von Gerlach and Hans von Kleist-Retzow found that such appeals led their party further down the road to electoral defeat, parliamentary isolation and opposition to Bismarck.[6]

13

534375

The deep bitterness Bismarck felt towards the Conservatives in the early 1870s is clear from his memoirs.[7] The sources of conflict between them were many. They included the war with Austria in 1866, since it overturned the Conservative principle of legitimacy; the *Kulturkampf* against the Catholic Church, since it seemed to threaten the Protestant Church as well; and the reform of local government in Prussia (the *Kreisordnung*) in 1872, since it aimed to reduce the local administrative powers of Junker estate owners in the Prussian east. By December 1872 the Prussian Conservative Party was in total disarray. Around this time a leading Conservative parliamentarian, Moritz von Blanckenburg, wrote to the Minister of War that the Conservatives were being 'forced to drink the liberal cup to the dregs'.[8]

The events that led to the founding of the DKP in 1876 began when a cadre of parliamentarians, led by Wilhelm von Rauchhaupt, Friedrich Wilhelm von Limburg-Stirum and Otto von Helldorff-Bedra,[9] stepped forward in 1872–3 to resurrect the splintered party. Forty-five of 116 Conservatives in the Prussian House of Deputies split from their caucus colleagues to constitute themselves as a New Conservative faction in the House. These men recognized their political affinity with Reichstag allies who already went by this name. They also recognized that the personal dominance of Bismarck and the avenues of power still open to men of wealth and position in the Reich argued for a new approach. As even the *Kreuzzeitung* wrote in January 1873, the Conservatives had 'to learn the party struggle from our opponents, from the ground up'.[10] Over the next two years Helldorff and other New Conservatives tried to mute the extreme anti-liberal arguments of their more reactionary colleagues, the Old Conservatives, and to re-establish close ties with Bismarck. However, in 1875 their efforts were dealt a severe blow by the appearance of a sensational series of articles in the *Kreuzzeitung*.

The Old Conservative editor of the *Kreuzzeitung*, Philipp von Nathusius-Ludom,[11] had commissioned an obscure (and at first anonymous) journalist to write on 'The Era Bleichröder–Delbrück–Camphausen and the New-Fangled German Economic Policy'.[12] The author of these articles was Dr Franz Perrot – a one-time railroad expert, a former captain in the army and general secretary of the Congress of German Farmers. In the 'Era' articles Perrot linked Bismarck, his leading liberal ministers and his Jewish banker to the speculation and subsequent scandals of the Second Empire's founding years.[13] He charged that these men's *Judenpolitik* had made Germany a ready victim for economic disaster. On 9 February 1876 Bismarck launched a vitriolic attack on the *Kreuzzeitung* in the Reichstag, charging that anyone who subscribed to the paper was indirectly participating in its slander. The Old Conservatives replied with a declaration of their own in the *Kreuzzeitung* on 26 February 1876. In the following weeks, many more Conservatives added

14

their names to the list of *Deklaranten*, including some of Bismarck's oldest Pomeranian associates.[14] It was a hard test for the nerves of an old man, Bismarck later wrote, suddenly to break with so many old Junker colleagues.

Bismarck also found his suspicion of orthodox Christian politicians confirmed by the events of 1875–6. Protestant pastors, always tending to the Old Conservative faction of the party, were strongly represented among the *Deklaranten*. This prompted Bismarck to remark in his memoirs that their opposition had increased his distrust of 'politicians who wear long robes, whether female or priestly'.[15] Finally, Bismarck felt that the Conservatives' opposition had illustrated how political parties in Germany 'pursued their policies as if they were alone . . . isolated on their caucus islands'. The conflict with the *Deklaranten* was a crucial motive behind Bismarck's overriding concern in the 1880s to fashion an electoral and parliamentary 'Kartell' of German Conservatives, Free Conservatives and National Liberals, to act as a firm alliance of parties willing to support government policy.

Just at the height of the controversy over the 'Era' articles, the practical organizing effort of the New Conservatives was bearing its first fruit, in the form of a new agrarian interest group. German agriculture had not been entirely unrepresented since 1848. In 1866 a Farmers' Club had been founded in Berlin, and two years later the Congress of North German Farmers was established.[16] Martin Anton Niendorf's newspaper, the *Deutsche Landes-Zeitung*, had a respectable though hardly overwhelming circulation of about 5,000. However, these efforts were recognized as insufficient by 1875, when Niendorf and other Prussian estate owners provided the impetus to establish an Association of Tax and Economic Reformers (Vereinigung der Steuer- und Wirtschaftsreformer, or VdSWR).[17] The *Deutsche Landes-Zeitung* published a founding proclamation (*Aufruf*) for the VdSWR with 127 signatures. Just seven days after representatives of heavy industry had founded the Central Association of German Industrialists (Centralverband deutscher Industrieller or CvdI), the Tax and Economic Reformers met for their constituent assembly on 22–4 February 1876. The statement of purpose issued by the new Association suggested not only how the Conservatives sought to refashion a closer relationship with Bismarck but also how they sought to become popular: 'If we want to win over to Conservatism wider circles, we must go along with the times. Indeed, we cannot betray our principles, but must at the same time follow the trends that move the people. We live in an age of material interests.'[18] The VdSWR's programme concentrated on efforts to relieve the indebtedness of agriculture; on measures to tax 'mobile capital' and otherwise disadvantage 'un-Christian' elements in German economic life; and, as one of the VdSWR's leaders put it in 1878, on means to return to the 'patrimonial or partriarchal state'. Ties to the protectionist CvdI were quickly established and nurtured.

The landed nobility from the six eastern provinces of Prussia thoroughly dominated the Association's executive organs. The VdSWR allegedly numbered 481 members when it was founded (total membership probably never exceeded seven hundred). A remarkable 450 of these members owned large estates. More detailed figures provided after the general assembly of 1877 indicated a total of 683 members, of whom over five hundred were large or medium estate owners. This total included 45 counts and 74 barons, with nobles (420) far outnumbering commoners (263) overall. Reserve officers and higher officials were strongly represented, especially among the ranks of estate owners, in contrast to the twenty or thirty members from the learned professions and other middle-class groups. In 1877 there were two Tax and Economic Reformers who sat in the Prussian House of Deputies (in 1894, when total VdSWR membership was 580, there were thirty-five); one member sat in the Reichstag (1894; forty-five); and no fewer than twelve members sat in the Herrenhaus (1894; forty-five). The Prussian orientation was also strongly marked; 47 Saxon and south German members faced 630 colleagues from Prussia, of whom only 50 came from territories west of the Elbe.

It was typical of Conservative organizations at this time that the greatest possible number of VdSWR members were taken into the Association's executive, whose membership numbered twenty initially but quickly rose to roughly sixty. The chairman of the executive committee was Count Udo zu Stolberg-Wernigerode, lord of three entailed estates (*Fideikommisse*) in Silesia.[19] In 1876 Stolberg stood at the outset of a political career that included membership in both the Reichstag and Herrenhaus, as well as a career in the Prussian bureaucracy, where he rose from *Landrat* to provincial governor of East Prussia in 1891. The VdSWR's vice-chairman was Count Werner von der Schulenburg-Beetzendorf, owner of the entailed estate of Beetzendorf and other estates totalling over 3,000 hectares in the Prussian province of Saxony.[20] Schulenburg sat in the Herrenhaus after 1872, one of a number of forums he used to pursue his special interest in aristocratic associations; he was also a member of the Order of the Knights of St John, and in the 1880s he served as chairman of the German Society of Nobles (Deutsche Adelsgenossenschaft, or DAG).[21] Second vice-chairman of the VdSWR was Baron Karl von Thüngen-Roßbach, a Bavarian estate owner who would later be instrumental in establishing the Franconian Farmers' Association. Another prominent member of the executive was Baron (later Count) Julius von Mirbach-Sorquitten, also beginning a long career in the top echelons of the Conservative Party, where he was regarded as the principal spokesman of agrarian interests and the confidant of Bismarck. Mirbach was soon to become chairman of the VdSWR, a post in which he served from 1879 to 1919. Arnold von

Frege-Abtnaundorf, an owner of estates in the Kingdom of Saxony totalling close to 2,000 hectares, was another original executive member who reappeared often in Conservative history; he combined duties in the Reichstag and in the upper chamber of the Saxon Landtag. Free Conservative leaders such as Oktavio von Zedlitz-Neukirch were represented in the VdSWR executive, but not in the same numbers as German Conservatives.

The personalities involved in the founding of the Association of Tax and Economic Reformers in February 1876 – and in the founding of the German Conservative Party five months later – were hardly ones to ease Bismarck's fears about continued Conservative opposition to his policies. One founder of the VdSWR had been involved in commissioning the 'Era' articles for the *Kreuzzeitung*, while others were prominent *Deklaranten*. Anti-Semitic conservative journalists in the new agrarian interest group shocked Bismarck even more. These included Nathusius-Ludom, Perrot, Niendorf, Baron Wilhelm von Hammerstein-Schwartow (the later editor of the *Kreuzzeitung* and leader of the so-called '*Kreuzzeitung* group')[22] and Carl Wilmanns, whose anti-Semitic views had already won him a national reputation. Stolberg, Mirbach and other high-ranking Tax and Economic Reformers, it is true, were loyal Bismarckians. But the high profile of Perrot, Niendorf and the controversial Thüngen-Roßbach in the VdSWR's subsequent assemblies perpetuated Bismarck's concerns.[23]

Many of these VdSWR leaders gathered again in June and July 1876 to act as midwives at the birth of the German Conservative Party. Significantly, the Conservative Party was founded by proclamation. An enunciation of general aims was circulated by Helldorff among an allegedly 'large number' of Conservatives in late 1875 and then discussed at a meeting in Berlin the next spring. A second meeting of Conservatives in Frankfurt am Main on 7 June 1876 issued a 'Proclamation for the Formation of a German Conservative Party'.[24] This proclamation of six main points then became the official DKP programme, which remained in effect until it was revised in December 1892. Declaration in favour of these six points was enough to make one an official member of the new party. At the same time, however, the *Wahlverein* (electoral association) of German Conservatives was also established. The exact relationship between the Conservative *Wahlverein* and the 'party' is patently unclear. It appears that virtually all official aspects and functions of the party were initially set upon the *Wahlverein*, in order to comply with the laws of association in Prussia. The party as such, however, was taken to be the general body of parliamentary deputies and all other individuals who adhered, however informally, to the German Conservative cause.

The Conservative *Wahlverein* alone had an eight-point list of statutes. These stated that it was the purpose of the *Wahlverein* to rally all conservative forces in the Reich, 'irrespective not only of the particular position of the government to the Conservative Party' but also of 'various party nuances and the momentary composition of parliamentary groups'. The clear intent was to end as quickly as possible the factional disputes of previous years. The statutes also stipulated that *Wahlverein* members were obliged to contribute at least 2 marks per year, but that wealthier members were expected to contribute 10 marks annually; that general assemblies would not be held; and that periodically a news-sheet would be distributed to inform members of the activities of the executive. The first *Wahlverein* executive comprised the twenty-seven signatories of the DKP's founding proclamation, and was to enlarge itself through co-optation. To facilitate the collection of dues and to distribute communiqués and propaganda material, an office was established in Berlin. This office was apparently first presided over by Wilmanns and Niendorf of the VdSWR, but then came under the direction of the Reichstag and Landtag deputy, Hermann von Busse-Neustettin.[25] With this bare minimum of formal organization, the *Wahlverein* of German Conservatives, together with the new party for which it acted, was designed to bring a degree of coherence and party discipline to the Conservative cause.

In selecting their *Wahlverein*'s first executive committee the Conservative leaders were clearly attempting to convince the population at large that the DKP represented diverse regions and interests. To be sure, thirteen of the twenty-seven original members came from Prussia, including many of the most important leaders in the party; Helldorff and Rauchhaupt both came from the Province of Saxony, Baron Helmuth von Maltzahn-Gültz represented Nearer Pomerania, and Baron Wilhelm von Minnigerode-Rositten owned estates in East and West Prussia. But five came from Bavaria, and three each came from the Kingdom of Saxony and the Grand Duchies of Hesse and Baden. These regional representatives were by no means of uniform background. They included established notables – such as Baron Ernst August Göler von Ravensburg and Dr Karl Mühlhäußer from Baden, or August Luthardt from Bavaria – who resisted efforts to reform the Conservative Party in the early 1880s. But also on the executive were more independent figures, such as Count Friedrich zu Solms-Laubach and Max Rieger from Hesse, and Carl Ott-Fürth from Bavaria, who displayed a powerful commitment to expanding the party's popular capability. There was also a markedly higher proportion of non-landowners in the *Wahlverein*'s executive than in the VdSWR leadership.

Contemporaries understood clearly that the Conservatives were organizing and displaying their popular credentials largely with upcoming elections in mind. And as election results showed in the years 1876 to 1881, Conservative fortunes improved dramatically, not only nationally but also in elections to the Prussian Landtag[26] and other regional parliaments. (See Appendices 5 and 6.) These gains must be interpreted in the light of other factors aiding the DKP, including electoral mispractice, anti-Socialist excitement and closer Conservative–government co-operation. Taking account of these factors, however, one sees why the top Conservative parliamentarians around Helldorff might have felt satisfied with the organizational structure of the Conservative Party in 1876. The rejuvenation of the party at the polls could indeed be presumed to have followed as a direct result of their initial organizing effort.

The leaders of the DKP also recognized that decisive steps were needed to muzzle the *Deklaranten*. Nathusius-Ludom was 'persuaded' to step down as editor of the *Kreuzzeitung* in May 1876. He was replaced by a colourless bureaucrat, Benno von Niebelschütz, who administered the post for the next five years. But the Old Conservatives could not be silenced completely. Before his resignation Nathusius-Ludom published a tract enunciating the oppositional views of those Conservatives who found Helldorff's draft programme too 'national' and 'unchurchly'.[27] He also tried to mobilize south German and Saxon Conservatives against Helldorff, and reconciled himself to the party only when this attempt failed. In late July 1876 Kleist-Retzow, who had been even less willing than Nathusius to participate in the founding of the DKP, warned the new *Wahlverein* executive that it must not simply support Bismarck indiscriminately. 'If the party does not wish to be untrue to its principles,' he wrote, 'it cannot swim with the government; rather, it must be an arrow in the flesh, an awakening of the conscience.'[28]

Because Helldorff had proved himself unable to overcome these liabilities, Bismarck was at first very unimpressed with his effort in founding the DKP. What Bismarck wanted was precisely the kind of governmental *Mittelpartei* Kleist-Retzow feared, a party like the Free Conservatives.[29] As the more moderate or 'left-wing' party of conservatives, the FKP was well placed to work closely with the National Liberals. It also attracted leading members of the German establishment who wanted to display their conservative pedigree without endorsing the particular policies of the German Conservative Party. For example, when the chancellor's oldest son, Herbert von Bismarck, sought election to the Reichstag in 1878, he was outraged that 'lies' labelled him a member of the DKP or even in sympathy with it. It was this kind of prejudice against the DKP that the respective chairmen of the VdSWR and the DKP, Stolberg and Helldorff, tried to break down. They sought to build a relationship of personal trust and common interests with the chancellor, like that which linked Bismarck to the Free Conservative leader, Wilhelm von Kardorff. Some time in late 1876 Bismarck began to recognize the DKP's potential as a true 'state-supporting' (*staatserhaltend*) party, just as he was growing wary of the National Liberals' demands for greater influence on national policy. Bismarck continued to advise Stolberg to accommodate the National Liberals as far as possible on the large political issues of the day; as the chancellor put it, he did not want to 'throw out dirty water' before there was clean water to replace it.[30] But on strictly economic questions Bismarck advised Stolberg to be 'as agrarian' as possible. He also suggested that the *Kulturkampf* might be dismantled as soon as the government was assured of steady support.

After the Conservatives increased their Reichstag caucus from twenty-two to forty members in the elections of January 1877, Bismarck and the leading Conservatives pursued their personal reconciliation further. However, they encountered immediate embarrassment when Nathusius-Ludom and Kleist-Retzow joined the Conservative caucus in the Reichstag. Bismarck eventually withdrew his objections to these men.[31] But the unhappy marriage of Old and New Conservatives in the Reichstag had a number of important consequences, particularly in the destabilizing effect it had on Conservative–government relations in the 1880s. Bismarck was referring to his failure to eliminate this rump of bloody-minded Old Conservatives when he wrote in 1879 that 'the first mistake lay in the fusion of the Conservatives – in every extreme party (*Flügelpartei*) the leadership always falls to the most radical elements'.[32] These were prescient words indeed. As long as the Old Conservatives found a hearing within the Conservative Party for their views – which included strongly anti-capitalist, anti-National-Liberal and pro-Centre arguments – Bismarck's grand strategy for erecting a truly hegemonic Kartell could never be achieved. The same could be said of the diversity of interests among the German Conservative, Free Conservative and National Liberal parties themselves. As a leading Conservative journalist, Rudolf Meyer, put it at the time, reconciling these parties' ideological, confessional and economic interests would be as easy as 'making lemonade from oil and water.'[33] Partly because the Conservative Party could not be 'homogenized' ideologically at its inception, Bismarck chafed under what he called 'the theoretical caucus groupings – these kinds of parliamentary joint-stock companies' – which complicated the job of mustering a Reichstag majority. Helldorff's greatest service to the chancellor lay in his campaign to de-emphasize the differences that distinguished the Conservatives from their allies on the Right.[34] But the fact that his assistance was needed at all was a sign that something was still rotten in Bismarck's state of the 1880s.

NOTES

1 As Bismarck once said in conversation: 'If I had to go through life with principles, I would feel as though I had to walk a narrow path in the woods and carry a long pole in my mouth.' Cited in Vossler, 'Bismarcks Ethos', p. 267.
2 See Becker, *Reaktion*; Klatte, 'Anfänge', pp. 281 ff.; Jordan, *Entstehung*; Canis, 'Verein zur Wahrung'; Schult, 'Partei'; Fischer, 'Konservatismus'.
3 See ZStA I, NL Wagener, 1, f. 191, Heinrich Leo to Hermann Wagener, 23.1.62; Müller, 'Preußischer Volks-Verein'; Herz, 'Preußischer Volks-Verein'.
4 *KZ*, 6.1.71.

5 On the FKP see Aandahl, 'Free Conservatism'; Viebig, *Entstehung*; Wolfstieg, 'Anfänge'; Fricke, 'Reichs- und freikonservative Partei'; on the NLP see Seeber and Hohberg, 'Nationalliberale Partei'.

6 Cf. Hesse, 'Haltung Gerlachs'; Ritter, 'Konservativen'; Petersdorff, *Kleist-Retzow*.

7 For Bismarck's remarks cited below, except where noted, see Bismarck, *Gedanken*, Vol. 2, pp. 142–61. Bismarck wrote to Albrecht von Roon on 13.12.72 that the Conservatives had attacked him 'with a bitterness and fanaticism' equalling that of any enemy of the state; cited in Stürmer (ed.), *Bismarck*, p. 58.

8 Blanckenburg to Albrecht von Roon, cited in Aandahl, 'Free Conservatism', p. 264; cf. Berdahl, 'Transformation'; Berdahl, 'Conservative Politics'; Schröder, 'Junkertum'.

9 Cf. biographical details in Chapter 3.

10 *KZ*, 9.1.73.

11 Not to be confused with his father, Philipp von Nathusius, the former editor of the *Volksblatt für Stadt und Land*, or with his brother, Martin von Nathusius, editor of the *KM*.

12 *KZ*, 29.6.75–3.7.75.

13 Cf. Stern, *Gold and Iron*, pp. 187–92.

14 See Witte, 'Bismarck'; Kardorff, 'Beziehungen', p. 34.

15 Cf. ZStA II, Rep. 90a, B III, 2 b, Nr. 6, Vol. 99, state ministry protocols, 10.1.87 and 15.3.87, where Bismarck expressed fear of 'the rule of priests' (*Priesterherrschaft*) in Germany.

16 Renamed the Kongress deutscher Landwirte in 1870; cf. Gottwald, 'Kongress'.

17 For the following, see 'Statut der Steuer- und Wirthschafts-Reformer' (1876); Stephan, *25jährige Tätigkeit*; Parisius, *Parteien*, pp. 215–21; Bueck, *Centralverband*; Gottwald, 'Vereinigung'; Böhme, *Deutschlands Weg*, pp. 400–9.

18 Cited in Lambi, *Free Trade*, p. 138.

19 Biographical data in this chapter and Chapter 3 are derived mainly from the sources on the VdSWR listed above, from Reichstag and Landtag handbooks and from Poschinger, *Bismarck*, Vols. 1–3, *passim*.

20 See Müller, *Großgrundbesitz*, pp. 104 ff.

21 See Chapter 5.

22 See Chapter 3.

23 Cf. Stephan, *25jährige Tätigkeit*, *passim*.

24 'Unsere Aufgabe', 'Aufruf zur Bildung einer deutschen conservativen Partei' (with signatures) and *Wahlverein* statutes are found in the 'Flugblatt des Wahlverein der deutschen Conservativen' (July 1876); the 1876 party programme is printed in the works edited by Mommsen, Salomon and Treue.

25 Nipperdey, *Organisation*, p. 252.

26 Conservative representation in the Prussian House of Deputies (1870–1918) was:

Year	Total deputies	DKP deputies	Remarks
1870	432	114	(70 Old and 44 New Conservatives)
1873	432	30	(6 Old and 24 New Conservatives)
1876	433	41	(10 Old and 31 New Conservatives)
1879	433	110	
1882	433	122	
1885	433	133	
1888	433	129	
1893	433	144	
1898	433	145	
1903	433	143	
1908	443	152	
1913	443	148	
1918	437	147	

27 Nathusius-Ludom, *Conservative Position* (1876), pp. 7 ff.; cf. Nathusius-Ludom, *Conservative Partei und Ministerium*, pp. 3 f., 56.

28 Letter of 31.7.76, cited in Petersdorff, *Kleist-Retzow*, pp. 463 f.

29 For this and the following see Stern, *Gold and Iron*, pp. 191, 199; Kardorff, *Kardorff*; Kardorff, *Vier Vorträge*, pp. 62 ff.
30 See Poschinger, *Bismarck*, Vol. 2, pp. 236 ff., 328 f., and Vol. 3, pp. 262 ff.
31 BAK, NL Bismarck, Bestand B, 62, Kleist-Retzow to O. von Bismarck, 19.9.78, and Kleist-Retzow to H. von Bismarck, 6.8.82; cf. Kardorff, *Vier Vorträge*, pp. 35 f. The weakness of the DKP at this time was also revealed in Hermann Wagener's belief that its founding had proved a 'complete failure'; BAK, NL Bismarck, Bestand B, 120, f. 1183 ff., Wagener to O. von Bismarck, 18.1.77.
32 For this and the following see Bismarck to Robert Lucius von Ballhausen, 3.11.79, in Bismarck, *Gesammelte Werke*, Vol. 14, p. 1621; and Bismarck to Christoph von Tiedemann, 22.11.79, ibid., Vol. 6 c, p. 170.
33 Meyer, *Hundert Jahre*, p. xiv; on continuing conflicts between Bismarck and the *Deklaranten* in the 1880s, cf. Poschinger, *Bismarck*, Vol. 3, pp. 49 ff., and Chapter 4 below.
34 Cf. H. R. von U., *Das Recht auf Arbeit* (1884), pp. 4 f.: 'Any ministry with Prince Bismarck at its head can just as easily be called liberal as conservative. In fact, in the obliteration of these colourless, trivial labels, which are manipulated by party mania, lies one of the greatest services of this statesman [Bismarck] and his colleagues.'

3

'Firmly Organized throughout the Entire Monarchy'

In 1861, shortly after the founding of the Prussian People's Association, Blanckenburg had linked the Conservatives' effort in the popular arena with the need to stand firm against a 'liberal' government. 'Now', Blanckenburg wrote, 'we are firmly organized throughout the entire monarchy, and I think this will be of use to us not *only* for the elections, but otherwise too, if the crown should completely ride roughshod over us.'[1] The near demise of the Prussian Conservative Party in the early 1870s, when it stood in opposition to Bismarck, showed how wrong Blanckenburg had been. In 1876 a new start was made. By the late 1880s, however, the failure to extend organizational roots downwards and continued reliance on Bismarck revealed how little had changed in Conservative affairs. The traditional sources of Conservative influence continued to provide artificial buoyancy to party fortunes, but these foundations of Conservative strength were already being severely undermined before Bismarck's fall from power in 1890.

There were numerous early signs that the long-standing deficiencies in Conservative recruitment, organization and propaganda had not been made good simply by proclaiming the movement's renaissance in 1876. The Prussian orientation of Conservatism remained obvious, as did its agrarian basis. Even in their first official communiqué, the *Wahlverein* leaders had to acknowledge the particular difficulties of establishing the party in more liberal, non-Prussian areas.[2] Fearing economic or social boycott should their membership in the party of Prussian reaction become known, south-western Conservatives had expressed 'partly legal, partly practical reservations' about the extension of the *Wahlverein*'s organization into their territories. The party leadership, therefore, decreed that non-Prussian Conservatives need not have their names printed in the membership lists. They also emphasized that all German states would be represented in the *Wahlverein* executive – as far as possible. Yet at least one observer writing in the *Preußische Jahrbücher* noted that the inclusion of 'a couple of orthodox names' from south-west Germany could not dissuade the people that 'the Junker party, like the agrarian movement, does not extend beyond the Main'.[3] Subsequent elections bore out this assertion, as a continued high proportion of large estate owners in the

DKP's Reichstag caucus belied the Conservatives' claim to be a party of all interests and classes. That proportion declined only slightly between 1874 and 1890, averaging roughly 50 to 60 per cent.[4] (See Appendix 2.)

Quite apart from these doubts about the overall political reorientation of Conservatism in 1876, many instances of neglect within the structure and working of the DKP were also readily apparent. For example, the *Wahlverein* statutes were meant to provide for some uniformity of party organization at the local level, in that they suggested of what basic ingredients a *Verein*'s structure and activity might consist. Yet the amazing diversity of local *Verein* statutes indicates that Conservatives had widely differing views of how 'the principle of authority'[5] should be translated into practical organizational form.[6] Some placed special emphasis on the official party programme, others on organization. Some listed *Verein* executive or ordinary members; others did not. Some local *Vereine* printed the 1876 programme in their statutes; others provided their own interpretation of it and defended their right to do so. Further variations included regulations regarding membership qualifications, composition and election of executive organs, summoning and procedural points of assemblies, disciplinary measures, support of the local press, finances, fees, honorary memberships, action committees, and so on. Despite such radical departures from the plan of the original *Wahlverein* statutes – and very rarely were other statutes so concise – the Berlin party leadership almost never expressed disapproval of other statutes or, indeed, took any notice of them at all.

The minimal extent to which a firm DKP structure had been erected by the early 1880s was revealed by a meeting between *Wahlverein* leaders and some three hundred local party delegates in Berlin on 17 January 1882.[7] At this meeting Helldorff noted that further organizational plans and the continuing activity of local *Vereine* were needed. He declared that Conservatives could not afford to move into action only at election time, 'because they may not employ demagogic means'. Furthermore, since Prussian law prohibited the formal organization of political *Vereine* at the national level, a line of communication had to be established between local Conservative groups and the central *Wahlverein*. The original articulation of party *Vereine* 'from above to below', Helldorff continued, had been necessary because 'the organizational basis from below was lacking'. But now the aim was to ensure contact between the local elements and the top leadership. In the ensuing discussion various objections were raised to Helldorff's remarks. A delegate from East Prussia, noting the recent establishment of a provincial organization there, doubted whether all local members could be persuaded to join the *Wahlverein*. Two Silesian delegates noted that Conservatives in their region did not like the emphasis on *German* Conservative *Vereine* (that is, excluding the Free Conservatives and other nationalist parties). In the end, no clearer definition of the relationship between party and *Wahlverein* emerged, and no mechanism was established for the election of delegates to the *Wahlverein* or its executive.

Hammerstein spoke next on the financial needs of the *Wahlverein*'s central office. He proposed that a 'party tax' be levied, based roughly on the Prussian income tax system. This would ensure a steady flow of revenue and serve to provide a sense of 'solidarity' among party members. In the discussion a general lament was raised that Conservatives had less money than liberals, and various delegates advanced strong objections to the idea of a party tax. Eventually an impatient Helldorff declared that the Berlin leaders did not want to impose their ideas on the local *Vereine*, but that the principle of financial support for the party's central office had to be established. Referring to the cost of maintaining a party news-sheet and press, he said the practice of living from hand to mouth could not continue. Minnigerode reiterated this point as he outlined the duties of the *Wahlverein*'s central office and defended its scope of activity in the face of criticism from various quarters. The delegates in turn argued for more local contributions to the party news-sheet, especially from southern Germany. Again, however, there were few prospects of concrete action on these proposals.

Characteristically, more than a year elapsed before the *Wahlverein* executive issued its new 'organizational plan'. This plan was based on, but by no means limited by, the discussions of January 1882.[8] On paper, these reforms would have introduced important changes in the workings of the party. At last the new plan defined the *Wahlverein*'s central body (*Centralstelle*) as comprising the *Wahlverein*'s executive committee, which had by that time grown to forty-nine members (seventy by 1887), together with the delegates of the various German states. In fact, however, this stipulation clarified nothing, because the number of state delegates was not established, no mention was made of Conservative delegates from the individual Prussian provinces, and in any case the previous executive had included both provincial and state leaders. The activities of local and regional leaders were laid out in even more detail. To them fell the responsibility for such party activities as the collection of membership dues, expanding the local press, holding regional congresses and supplying party rallies with speakers familiar with the local political terrain. It was emphasized that every Conservative who joined a local Conservative club automatically became a member of both the regional Conservative *Verein* and the national *Wahlverein*. This maximized the number of members obligated to abide by the *Wahlverein*'s statutes.

This 'organizational plan' was especially revealing in that it compromised the principle of decentralized authority within the party in a number of ways. For instance, the central office now claimed the right to appoint local delegates from Berlin, in direct contradiction to Helldorff's statement in January 1882 that this had been necessary only in the early days of the party. Also, candidate selection difficulties were to be worked out by calling in the regional delegate or, in the second instance, the *Wahlverein* executive; but it was laid down in bold type that 'by principle no agreements may be reached with other parties without the involvement of the *Wahlverein* executive'. A corollary to this was found in a reform of party propaganda, which had been initiated by a *Wahlverein* executive meeting of 5 September 1882. Previously, local *Vereine* had been encouraged to look to the central office to co-ordinate the distribution of party leaflets and other propaganda at election time. For the Conservative leaders understood that it was 'impossible to produce Conservative pamphlets for all social groups and all provinces which are equally appropriate and understandable'. In the new system this responsibility devolved on to regional and local *Vereine*. However, the *Wahlverein* leaders did not want to relinquish their influence over the *content* of party propaganda. So they decreed that all requests for the drafting of leaflets from local committees be directed through the central office. The aim was clearly to maintain the control but reduce the work (and expense) of the executive.

This emphasis on regional inequalities was intended to diminish the impression of a dominating central leadership. On the one hand, because the *Wahlverein* insisted on appointing local constituency delegates, it could determine which men performed the important function of liaison between the party rank and file and the *Wahlverein* executive. On the other hand, despite assurances that local *Vereine* would continue to name their own candidates, the *Wahlverein* wished to have *de facto* control over the general direction of the Conservative campaign, by virtue of its exclusive right to conclude electoral alliances with other parties. Again, except in so far as particularly prominent candidates might offend National Liberal or Free Conservative allies, the *Wahlverein* leaders realized that local *Vereine* were better placed than they were to select a suitable candidate for a specific district. For the horse-trading of candidacies necessary to maintain alliances throughout the Reich, however, as with the drafting of the party's official election platform, the *Wahlverein* could claim with some justification that it alone possessed the larger view necessary to co-ordinate party strategy.

The Tax and Economic Reformers were similarly willing to consider amending their organization and agitation after February 1876. When the VdSWR's executive met for the first time in late March 1876, it discussed the Association's structure, its preparations for upcoming Landtag elections, its press and its relationship with other agricultural societies. It paid particular attention to the need to influence the small local newspapers known as *Kreisblätter*, which traditionally not only carried government announcements but also represented conservative opinion in the countryside.[9] In subsequent meetings, the executive established a fund to support the ailing *Deutsche Landes-Zeitung*, and it changed the annual membership fee of 10 marks, until that time mandatory for all members, to one mark for those members earning less than 3,000 marks per year. In 1879 and 1885 the agrarians fine-tuned the VdSWR's programme, in accordance with their shift to protectionism and the fulfilment of some of their demands. Between 1883 and 1885 they also considered amalgamating with the Congress of German Farmers and other agrarian interest groups, but then decided that the time was not yet ripe. Instead, they concentrated on staging their general assemblies every February in Berlin, seeking to ensure that Bismarck did not waver from his protectionist course.

These attempts at organizational reform are especially significant in the light of what we know about the DKP's activities at this time. Clearly the need for reform had grown imperative by the early 1880s. It is impossible to ascertain exactly how many Germans were members of formal Conservative *Vereine*. In the Reichstag elections of 1881 about 831,000 Germans voted for Conservative candidates. Only the Centre Party and the combined left-liberal parties won more votes in that year. By contrast, only slightly over 1,800 people officially made financial contributions of any kind to the Conservative *Wahlverein* in 1882.[10] No matter what criteria are used for determining who was an official *Wahlverein* member, it is plausible that total membership in 1882 numbered somewhat fewer than 2,000, taking account of donations made secretly and of non-contributory members. There was also considerable overlap in the memberships of the DKP and the VdSWR.

Official contributions in 1882 totalled 37,250 marks. Ninety people contributed 100 marks or more, contributing together 11,985 marks, or almost one-third of the *Wahlverein*'s income from personal contributions. Of these ninety individuals, only four were non-noble. Fourteen *Wahlverein* supporters donated 200 marks or more, totalling 4,100 marks. The single largest contribution was 800 marks, exactly double the second largest figure.[11] Since the 1882 report lists the total *Wahlverein* income as 59,369 marks, approximately 22,000 marks came either from secret donations or, more probably, from regional *Vereine*. Yet state, provincial and local *Vereine* must have retained for their own activities significant proportions of the funds they collected. For the *Wahlverein* provided only a fraction of the financial support given to Conservative Landtag candidates and the DKP provincial press in 1882. It funded agitation in only forty-three electoral districts, although 122 Conservative candidates were elected in November 1882, and many more undertook campaigns. The *Wahlverein* also provided financial support for only seventeen Conservative newspapers in 1882. As of February 1883, the Conservatives had even had to suspend publication of their own *Conservative Correspondenz* temporarily through lack of funds. This however did not prevent the new

Wahlverein secretary, retired Major Baron Leo von Seckendorff, from continuing to try to find vacant editorial posts for Conservative editors whose newspapers had not survived.

Whatever the authority with which the anonymous authors of the 1883 'organizational plan' issued their recommendations for reform, one thing is certain: throughout the 1880s the top DKP parliamentarians who might have come out firmly in favour of these proposals were either unwilling or unable to do so. There is no evidence that this plan was implemented in any concrete way. Instead, leaders like Helldorff and Rauchhaupt casually dismissed the inadequacies of DKP organization, because to overcome them would have required the kind of sustained effort in which they had little interest. As a consequence the practices of previous decades persisted. *Ad hoc* Conservative committees continued to nominate candidates accustomed to the congenial atmosphere of *Honoratioren* politics (or, more often, they renominated a current member of parliament who, it was hoped, would weather the electoral storm once again). Reliance on government favour persisted. Financial uncertainty and a weak press continued to undercut party efforts. And most importantly of all, efforts to exert personal influence in Berlin continued to bring tangible economic and political rewards. At least for the first decade of the party's history, the political successes scored by Helldorff and his small band of party comrades determined the political profile of the Conservative Party far more than any effort to make the DKP truly popular.

The Conservatives' reintegration into the Bismarckian fold was a very complex and uncertain process. It was, moreover, a process which illustrated the degree to which Bismarck was politically adrift in the years 1874–9, when he was no longer certain of the National Liberal Party's support but still unwilling to trust the Conservatives. Although these developments can be followed only in outline, an understanding of the personalities and tactics involved is as useful as knowledge about the party's organization and programme. We have already encountered some of the leading agrarians and DKP parliamentarians, with Helldorff most prominent among them. But who really led the day-to-day affairs of the Conservative Party after 1876? What talents assured Helldorff the right to represent (and interpret) the Conservative programme? To what degree were his successes dependent on good relations with Bismarck and other right-wing parties?

In 1877 Helldorff had four colleagues on the Conservative Reichstag caucus executive. His closest associate was Count Conrad von Kleist-Schmenzin, an estate owner who represented Pomerania in the Reichstag and who remained loyal to Helldorff even after he was deposed as party chairman in 1892. Otto Theodor von Seydewitz, a Silesian estate owner, was the titular head of the caucus. In May 1879 he became the first German

Conservative president of the Reichstag, at which time he gave up his position as chairman of the Conservatives' caucus, being replaced by Helldorff. Carl Ackermann was a lawyer in the Kingdom of Saxony who held many high-ranking positions, honorary and otherwise, in Dresden's business circles. He was a member of the Saxon lower house, and also served as second vice-president in the Reichstag during the 1881–4 session. After 1881 he was a common speaker for the DKP on social issues, but he was singled out for ridicule by the Socialists; they labelled him one of the renowned 'house-emptiers' among the Conservatives, because his speeches were so devoid of interest that they emptied the benches of the Reichstag.[12] Field Marshal Count Hellmuth von Moltke, Chief of the Prussian General Staff, sat as a figurehead in the Conservative caucus from 1867 until his death in April 1891, only occasionally rising to defend the interests of the Prussian army. Other influential Conservatives in the Reichstag through the 1880s included Mirbach, Bernhard von Puttkamer-Plauth (the brother of Prussia's Minister of the Interior) and Albert von Levetzow, president of the Reichstag (with interruptions) in the 1880s and early 1890s.[13]

In the Prussian Herrenhaus, Kleist-Retzow resumed his unchallenged position among the Conservatives after his reconciliation with Bismarck. He devoted special attention to issues like Sunday rest and the independence of the Protestant Church in the 1880s. But he still regarded himself in a two-front war: against the liberals, because he sought to dismantle the *Kulturkampf*; and against the Centre Party, because he defended the Protestant Church against what he regarded as overweening Catholic ambitions. In the Prussian House of Deputies the diversity of Conservative views was more pronounced. Here Minnigerode, Rauchhaupt and Limburg held the most prominent positions. Although all three generally managed to reconcile occasional divergences from Kartell policies with continued support for the chancellor, each placed different weight on his relationship to Bismarck. Minnigerode was one of the most frequent Conservative speakers in the Landtag, despite his alleged preference for backstairs negotiation. But he never won real influence for himself in the top ranks of the party. Among those Conservatives who remained close to the chancellor, Limburg can be considered *primus inter pares*, since this relationship persisted even after 1890.[14] Limburg chaired the DKP's House of Deputies caucus after 1893, and he later sat in the party's Committee of Twelve. Rauchhaupt, who chaired the DKP's House of Deputies caucus until Limburg replaced him in 1893, tended to complicate Bismarck's relations with the DKP by virtue of his ambiguous positions in parliament. Like Kleist-Retzow, in the 1880s he often found himself on the side of the Kartell's most determined enemy, Hammerstein.[15] To these three names must be added those of Hammerstein and Court Preacher Adolf Stöcker; both dominated the list of Conservative deputies in the

Landtag who addressed social and church issues in the 1880s. By 1883 these men were already acknowledged as two of the most gifted speakers in Conservative ranks.[16]

A later DKP chairman, Ernst von Heydebrand und der Lasa, noted in his memoirs that in these years there was virtually no conscious co-ordination of policy between the party's three most important caucuses in the Reichstag and Landtag; they each more or less went their own way.[17] The Conservatives often claimed that the independence of their deputies was one of their great strengths, as was their refusal to regard the DKP programme as a party shibboleth. These attitudes hampered the consolidation of party institutions, but at the same time they provided Helldorff great latitude in the conduct of Conservative policy. As the Free Conservative leader, Kardorff, once remarked, Helldorff was able to hold the party 'in bridles'.[18] After 1876 Helldorff was the arbiter not only between Bismarck and the DKP but also between the rival Conservative factions themselves. Bismarck may well have been referring to Helldorff when he wrote in his memoirs that 'in our caucuses the real point of crystallization was not a programme, but rather a person, a parliamentary *condottiere*'.[19]

Helldorff was born into an old noble family in 1833, near Merseburg in the Prussian province of Saxony.[20] After completing his law studies at four German universities, Helldorff (like his father) became a *Landrat*. In 1873 he retired to manage Bedra and the family's three other estates. In the meantime he had entered the first German Reichstag in 1871, where he sat until 1893, except for interruptions in 1874–7 and 1881–4. After 1890 he also sat in the Prussian Herrenhaus. Helldorff first met Bismarck in 1867, but a personal relationship did not develop until Helldorff entered parliament and began to gather a following of New Conservatives. The details of Helldorff's early leadership remain obscure. For all the times they met on Bismarck's estates at Varzin and Friedrichsruh to discuss parliamentary strategy, and for all the parliamentary dinners Helldorff attended – often as the only Conservative representative – neither Bismarck nor Helldorff left behind more than a few veiled remarks about how their relationship developed. They both indicated, however, that the older style of politics still practised by so many other Conservative notables, together with the fear of another break between the party and the government, left them considerable room to manoeuvre politically. Bismarck wrote that the 'lack of industriousness among the majority greatly eased the task of leading a Conservative caucus . . . From my experience the dependence of the Conservative caucuses on the command of their leadership was at least as strong as, and perhaps stronger than, on the extreme Left.' None the less, he noted, even Conservative leaders were sensitive to the charge 'of being ministerial', that is, being excessively pro-government.

What remains of Helldorff's correspondence with Bismarck documents the many advantages the Conservative leader derived from this relationship. Helldorff's activity during the 1881 Reichstag election campaign offers a useful example.[21] Helldorff discussed DKP propaganda in detail with Bismarck and his aides, sometimes changing only the odd word in the chancellor's drafts. In fact he was obsequious in emphasizing the need to identify the Conservative programme completely with Bismarck's own policies. As he wrote at one point to Bismarck's son-in-law, Count Kuno von Rantzau: 'With the other flyers it is above all a matter of presenting the convincing policies and brilliant speeches of the chancellor. The rest of the text is secondary . . . The authority and popularity of your father-in-law is of the greatest importance – and therefore everything depends on faithfully bringing his own words to the masses.' Helldorff did not estimate the intellectual capacity of those masses highly. 'A whole page of reading-matter scares them off,' he observed. Thus he wanted only four themes reiterated in Conservative propaganda, the most successful of which were 'the protection of national work' and the desperate situation of German agriculture.[22]

When Helldorff drew up a more comprehensive report for the chancellor later in the campaign, he outlined the party's other efforts in the selection of candidates, the collection of money and the editing of a last-minute election manifesto. Helldorff hoped with this report to illustrate that the Conservative leadership was not inactive, as Bismarck apparently might have thought. In all these facets of the Conservatives' campaign, Helldorff's pre-eminent position (even allowing for some self-substantiation) is clear. He named only Minnigerode and the *Wahlverein*'s secretary, Seckendorff, among the other Conservatives assisting in the campaign. But even Minnigerode's job supervising the party press was about to be passed on to Helldorff, so that virtually all policy questions would go, as Helldorff put it, 'mainly through my hands'. This did not mean, however, that Helldorff expected he could conduct a successful campaign on his own. He claimed he suffered from no illusions about the DKP's popularity or the strength of its press. He also complained that he was fighting an uphill battle against the party rank and file in the countryside, who were 'unbelievably lazy, indolent and stingy'. The level of their contributions to the party's war chest during the campaign was completely unpredictable, he wrote. This attitude led to an unfortunate diffusion of energy and 'much discouragement' in the wake of unsuccessful undertakings. In any case, the party's main electoral activity remained under the guidance of 'the local constituencies, which we may be able to motivate but whose own efforts we cannot replace'. For these reasons, therefore, Helldorff's most immediate goal was to secure financial support from Bismarck. If the chancellor had any doubts about how the government might profit from such expenditure, Helldorff noted that these funds could help defray the costs of the Conservatives' brochure entitled 'Prince Bismarck and his Economic Policy'. This brochure had already been distributed to constituency delegates as a *Hilfsbuch* to guide them in their speeches.

This example of one Conservative's relationship with Bismarck, and the practical political benefits that accrued to the DKP because of it, could be multiplied many times for the 1880s.[23] What it illustrates is the degree to which the Conservatives' personal relationship to Bismarck shaped their very concept of their party in the years 1876 to 1890. Given their reliance on Bismarck's good will, they had little choice but to accede to his desire for a minimum of differentiation between the three right-wing parties of the Kartell. Mirbach probably reflected the Conservatives' attitude best when he described his own thoughts on what the 'party' meant to him:[24] 'I never use the word "conservative" in the sense of narrow partisan politics, for which I perceive there is very little enthusiasm. Rather I understand it to be a standpoint which seeks to strengthen and secure the authority of the state.'

With this understanding of what motivated Conservative parliamentarians to set their course firmly with Bismarck and his Kartell, it becomes clearer why these party notables neglected the task of grass-roots organization after 1876. But we must remember that the parliamentary equation of the late 1880s, dominated by Bismarck's Kartell, required considerable time to take shape. In fact the National Liberals found themselves among the political 'outs' in 1879, largely because Bismarck had decided to weaken the left wing of the party and, as eventually happened in 1880, to prompt its defection. Bismarck was aware of prominent voices in government and court circles calling for a return to 'conservative' policies at this time; he was also aware that the National Liberals could not be persuaded to abandon their quest indefinitely for individual liberties and ministerial responsibility.[25] The occasion Bismarck used to break with the National Liberals was the campaign for protective tariffs, which had been mounting since the depth of the depression had first become apparent in the mid-1870s. By 1879 Bismarck, heavy industrialists and agrarian Conservatives had agreed on a programme of substantial revisions to the duties Germany charged on the import of certain industrial and agricultural goods.[26] Because the National Liberals were unable to follow the chancellor and the conservative parties in this sudden renunciation of free trade, they voted against the final bill. The Centre, by contrast, after receiving hints that the *Kulturkampf* would eventually be dismantled, moved into the government majority and helped pass the new duties. These duties were revised upwards in 1881, 1885 and 1887.

Other factors tending to bring the Conservatives back into the Bismarckian fold included the growing fear of Socialism, which came to a head after two attempted assassinations of Kaiser Wilhelm I in 1878.

Bismarck used these incidents to pass his anti-Socialist laws – in force from 1878 to 1890 – which the government and the right-wing parties hoped (in vain) would halt the growth of the Social Democratic Party (Sozial-demokratische Partei Deutschlands, or SPD).[27] Debate on the Anti-Socialist Bill of 1878 allowed the Conservatives to display the full measure of their patriotic, monarchist, anti-Socialist and anti-democratic ideals.[28] Speaking for the party in the debates of 16–17 September 1878, Helldorff advocated a revision of the universal franchise and a lengthening of legislative periods, since 'too frequent use' of their right to vote had undermined the Germans' sense of authority.[29] Along the way Helldorff also revealed how strongly the Conservatives were committed to using parliamentary means to meet the challenges of mass politics.

> You, gentlemen, have all just emerged from an election campaign. I ask you on all sides [of the house]: have you enjoyed the electoral game (*Wahltreiben*)? I must say, gentlemen, this game, where everyone is more or less forced to reckon with the prejudices of the masses and to speculate with their passions, this game is a most dangerous one, and we have the most obvious cause to consider whether means against it are possible.

When the Conservatives helped pass the anti-Socialist legislation in 1878 and the new Reich tariffs in 1879 there was perhaps reason to say that a 'second founding of the Reich' had taken place, this time more on the Conservatives' terms than on the National Liberals'.[30] There were, however, ominous storm clouds already on the political horizon. In the early 1880s these became darker as Socialists and left-liberals made strong gains in the Reichstag elections of 1881; as the Centre Party seemed determined to align itself with the Reichstag opposition to Bismarck whenever possible; and as the ascension of Crown Prince Friedrich – who held well-known (if highly ambiguous) liberal views – became more immediate.

These developments worried others as much as they did the Conservatives. In particular, the need to construct a united front against the Socialist threat and to preserve the economic benefits of high import tariffs allowed certain *Realpolitiker* in the National Liberal Party to copy the Conservatives' about-face of 1876 and resurrect their ties to Bismarck. Partly on the basis of the Heidelberg Programme of 1884, Johannes Miquel, Rudolf von Bennigsen and others engineered a *rapprochement* with Bismarck and the two conservative parties. From that time on contemporaries began to speak of the DKP–FKP–NLP alliance as a 'Kartell' of anti-Socialist forces, even though this Kartell emerged in full bloom only during the Reichstag election campaign of February 1887. The Kartell's dominance in the Reichstag provided Bismarck and the Conservatives the means they had long sought to contain the emancipatory aspirations of all those groups who remained 'enemies of the Reich' – Poles, Danes, Socialists, the Centre Party and left-liberals. None the less these threats forced Bismarck to divert public attention from constitutional issues towards social insurance programmes, colonial affairs and foreign crises. On many of these issues the Conservatives followed Bismarck with considerable prevarication and bad grace. On other issues, like army increases, Polish rights and the continued curtailment of civil liberties, they came much closer to living up to their growing reputation as a Bismarckian party *sans phrase*.[31] The future costs for the party, however, were substantial on both counts. Bismarck's Kartell strengthened the Conservatives at the polls, and in parliament it allowed them to translate some of their Christian, national and authoritarian ideals into practical policy. But at the same time reliance on the Kartell hindered the development of more effective means to mobilize the masses. Although the Bismarckian orientation of the Conservative Party brought Helldorff many tangible successes, it also laid the groundwork for momentous upheavals in the 1890s.

NOTES

1 Blanckenburg to Ludwig von Gerlach, 11.8.61 (original emphasis), cited in Diwald (ed.), *Von der Revolution*, Vol. 2, pp. 1083 f.
2 'Flugblatt des Wahlvereins der deutschen Conservativen' (1876).
3 *PrJbb*, 38 (2), 1876, pp. 209–16.
4 Executive listed in *NWVZ*, 19.1.87.
5 Cf. Nipperdey, *Organisation*, p. 245.
6 The following comments are based on a wide selection of local *Verein* statutes dating from the 1860s to 1914; they are listed in my 'Reformist Conservatism', p. 57.
7 Reports in *NAZ*, 19.1.82; *Wahlverein* 'Mitteilungen' (1883), p. 1.
8 *Wahlverein* 'Mitteilungen' (1883), pp. 4–6.
9 Details in Stephan, *25jährige Tätigkeit*, pp. 20, 74–6 and *passim*.
10 Following details calculated from the 'Quittung über die im Jahre 1882 dem Verein zugegangenen Beiträge', 'Gesellschäftliche Mitteilungen' and 'Vereins-Tätigkeit', in the *Wahlverein*'s 'Mitteilungen' (1883), pp. 1 ff. *MAZ*, 25.3.91, put the membership of the *Wahlverein* at roughly 1,400, estimating that about one-half of all DKP PAH members did not belong to the *Wahlverein*.
11 The 800 marks came from the wealthy Conservative patron, Count Adolf von Hohenthal-Dölkau, who owned five estates (four entailed) in Prussian Saxony, totalling over 1,000 hectares.
12 *Neues Sündenregister der Konservativen*, pp. 9–10.
13 Cf. Deuerlein (ed.), *Reichstag*, pp. 105–7; Arnim and Below (eds.), *Aufstieg, passim*.
14 Limburg-Stirum, *Aus der konservativen Politik*.
15 Arnim and Below (eds.), *Aufstieg*, pp. 251–6.
16 Cf. DKP, *Die konservative Partei im Abgeordnetenhaus. Session 1882/83*; Heydebrand, 'Beiträge', pp. 500 ff.; and Chapter 4 below.
17 Heydebrand, 'Beiträge', p. 499.
18 Kardorff to his wife, 26.5.87, cited in Kardorff, *Kardorff*, p. 198.
19 Bismarck, *Gedanken*, Vol. 2, pp. 159 f.; for Bismarck's further appraisals of DKP leaders cf. BAK, Kl. Erw. 329 (Abegg), 1, 'Bismarck und die Konservativen', MS; Limburg-Stirum, *Aus der konservativen Politik*, p. 65.

20 See *NDB*, Vol. 8, pp. 474–5; Arnim and Below (eds.), *Aufstieg*, pp. 243–6; Poschinger, *Bismarck*, Vol. 2, pp. 154 ff.

21 For the following, BAK, NL Bismarck, Bestand A, 16, 'Reichstagswahlen 1878–81', Helldorff to Kuno von Rantzau, 29.9.81 and 7/13/18.10.81, and Helldorff to [Herbert] von Bismarck, n.d. [1881]. These letters were all directed to the chancellor.

22 See the 'Flugblätter des Wahlvereins der Deutsch-Konservativen', IV, 'Die Sorge für die Arbeiter' (1881). Cf. the strikingly similar vocabulary and tactics in Herbert von Bismarck to Tiedemann, 6.7.81, printed in Stürmer, *Bismarck*, pp. 174 f.

23 See, for example, BAK, NL Bismarck, Bestand B, 69, 'Limburg-Stirum', including many letters from 1880 on foreign policy, and Rantzau to Limburg, 8.10.80, supplying the *Kreuzzeitung* with articles but wishing to avoid giving them an 'official character'; Bestand B, 62, 'Kleist-Retzow', discussing the *Kulturkampf* and the workers' question; Bestand B, 79, 'Mirbach-Sorquitten', especially Mirbach to [Herbert] von Bismarck, 17.8.81 and 30.10.81, discussing Mirbach's uphill electoral battle in East Prussia and asking that railway and forestry workers be given free time to vote on election day; Bestand B, 117, letter from various *Deklaranten*, December 1879, seeking reconciliation with Bismarck; Bestand B, 120–1, 'Wagener', especially f. 1183 ff.; ZStA I, NL Wagener, 2, Stolberg to Wagener, 16.2.78, discussing the reconciliation with Bismarck; BAK, NL Rottenburg, 10, f. 517 ff., Stolberg to Franz von Rottenburg, 5.3.86.

24 BAK, NL Bismarck, Bestand B, 79, Mirbach to [Herbert] von Bismarck, 17.8.81.

25 Cf. BAK, NL Bismarck, Bestand B, 117, Tiedemann to Bismarck, 26.12.77 and 4.8.78; Lucius to Bismarck, 2.7.76, cited in Stern, *Gold and Iron*, p. 190; in the Saxon LT elections of 1877, DKP gains provided an effective majority against the united liberals for the first time; *Schultheß' Geschichtskalender* (1877), p. 143.

26 See Stephan, *25jährige Tätigkeit*, p. 27 f.; Lambi, 'Agrarian-Industrial Front'; Lambi, *Free Trade*; Webb, 'Agricultural Protection'; Perkins, 'Agricultural Revolution'; Böhme, *Deutschlands Weg*; Stürmer, *Regierung*.

27 For the full history of Bismarck's anti-Socialist laws, see Pack, *Ringen*; a summary in English is provided in Craig, *Germany*, pp. 93–6, 144 ff.

28 In February 1879 Thüngen-Roßbach called protectionist tariffs 'the correlate of the [anti-] Socialist laws, which without them would remain a dead letter'. See Rathmann, 'Bismarck', p. 936; Wallraf, 'Vereinigung', p. 778.

29 Speech printed in Kuhn, *Parlamentsdebatten*, Vol. 1, p. 89.

30 This is not the place to enter the historical controversy about the significance of these events. Cf. Anderson and Barkin, 'Myth'; Retallack, 'Social History'; Blackbourn and Eley, *Peculiarities*, for guides to the debate.

31 See the works by Karl von Fechenbach listed in the Bibliography.

4

The Kreuzzeitung Group and Christian Socialism

A counter-movement within the Conservative Party opposed the efforts of Bismarck and Helldorff during the 1880s. Comprising both the *Kreuzzeitung* group and the Christian Social Party, this movement was 'reformist' in a number of ways. It sought, first, to allow those party members outside Helldorff's inner circle to exert more influence on policy formation within the DKP. Here it suggested that neither Helldorff's political style nor his willingness to ally with Bismarck and the National Liberals was beneficial to the Conservative cause. It attempted, second, to attract new social groups to the Conservative Party, particularly Protestant workers and the threatened *Mittelstand*. This inclined it towards starkly anti-liberal and anti-capitalist positions. Its third main goal was to strengthen the Christian faith and to make the Protestant Church a more decisive factor in political affairs. This led its leaders to argue for increased co-operation between the Conservatives and the Catholic Centre Party, for the exclusion of Jews from positions of public authority and for a paternalist programme of social reform as announced in the Kaiser's proclamation (*Botschaft*) of 17 November 1881. For all their sound and fury, these dissidents could not realize their ambition to make the Conservative Party a *Volkspartei*. Throughout the decade, they had to operate within the constraints which circumstances (and in particular Bismarck) imposed on their agitation. None the less, their radical anti-liberal programme and their formulas for popular mobilization signified something very important for later and more successful agitators on the Right.

Perhaps no other political figure from the 1880s except Bismarck has aroused such extremes of acclaim and condemnation as Adolf Stöcker, leader of the Christian Social Party (CSP). 'One could hate Stöcker or one could love him,' wrote Hellmut von Gerlach, but 'no one could remain indifferent to him.'[1] Kurt von Wilmowsky, the husband of Barbara Krupp, recalled many heated debates in his youth assessing this 'new apostle'; to some Stöcker was a 'second Luther', to others he was a 'demagogue and corrupter of the people'.[2]

Historical obscurity still shrouds many of the personalities and political currents within the Christian Social Party. Yet even the barest outline of the 'Stöcker movement', as it was called, suffices to suggest its profound impact on the Conservative Party.[3] Adolf Stöcker, the son of a prison warder and blacksmith, was born in 1835 in the Harz mountain region of central Germany. Stöcker's childhood and education fostered in him both a faith in his own ability to overcome social antagonisms and a preference for contacts in the social classes above him. In the summer of 1874 he first came to Berlin to take up an appointment as court preacher to Kaiser Wilhelm I. He was appalled by the misery, irreligion and corruption he saw, and his social conscience awakened to the mission of political involvement. In early 1877 he became head of the Berlin City Mission, which placed him in the tradition of some of the most prominent social reformers and publicists of the era. On 3 January 1878 Stöcker was involved in the famous 'Eiskeller' incident, where he rose in the midst of a Social Democratic rally to proclaim the founding of a Christian Social Workers' Party. Within a month this new party had published its programme, which demanded factory legislation, old-age and invalid insurance schemes, economic representation by occupational estates (*Stände*), progressive taxation and regulation of stock-exchange dealings and usury mispractices. Stöcker seemed to have found the popular vehicle to translate his Christian and social ideas into political practice. However, when Bismarck's anti-Socialist campaign prompted Reichstag elections in July 1878, Stöcker's young party suffered a resounding defeat at the polls, gathering a mere 1,422 votes. By late 1879 Stöcker had changed the tone of the party's appeal. With his speech of 19 September 1879, entitled 'Our Demands of Modern Judaism', he embraced anti-Semitism, although with the emphasis on Christian ethics and social reform, not on racism as such. He also began to speak directly to the demands of the old *Mittelstand*, advocating legislation for artisans and small shopkeepers allegedly oppressed by Jewish money capital. Stöcker's argument was that, for the Berlin lower middle classes, the Jewish question *was* the social question. When the dropping of the term 'Workers' from the party name signalled a further change of emphasis, Stöcker found his party was more attractive to the Conservatives, who had never had any success in Berlin. The 'Conservative Central Committee' (CCC) was formed to co-ordinate the many Christian Social and Conservative *Bürgervereine* (burgher associations) that sprang up in the capital.[4] By the end of the 1880s Stöcker's followers had displaced the former liberal majority on the Berlin City Synod, an achievement which Stöcker later regarded as among his most significant.[5]

Stöcker achieved national recognition when a petition to the Prussian Landtag prompted a 'Jewish debate' in parliament on 22–4 November 1880. At this time more radical anti-Semitic leaders[6] began their campaign – which continued through the decade and beyond – to steer anti-Jewish agitation into more anti-establishment and racist streams. By contrast, Stöcker still professed to address 'the Jewish question as a social-ethical and social-political issue'.[7] Gradually he turned his attention to rallying recruits from other parts of Germany. Here his ambitions began to merge more directly with those of other Conservative Party reformers dissatisfied with Helldorff's policies. Stöcker was able to ride the crest of the anti-Semitic wave as it flowed into Hesse, Saxony, Westphalia and other areas. This added force to his argument that Christian Social reform and anti-Semitism provided the popular appeal the Conservatives needed to win these districts from the National Liberals. By 1884 Bismarck's banker, Gerson von Bleichröder, complained to the Kaiser that some of the Conservative leaders 'already call the worst anti-Semitic agitators "their dear and esteemed friends"'.[8] Stöcker's main success in incorporating anti-Semitism into Conservative politics was not to come until the next decade. But what brought Stöcker to such prominence within the Conservative Party when other radical anti-Semites seemed to lose the attention of the nation after 1885? Any answer must address, first, contemporaries' subjective assessments of Stöcker's talents and, second, the roots of the Conservatives' belief that he could, in fact, bring their message to new social groups.

The so-called *Kreuzzeitung* group around Hammerstein was a far more nebulous entity than Stöcker's Christian Social Party. Indeed, it was considered by many contemporaries to include Stöcker and his followers. Hammerstein's background was a much more typically Conservative one than Stöcker's, as he came from an ancient and respected family in Mecklenburg. Born the son of an estate owner in 1838, Hammerstein's rise to prominence included forestry service, the management of an estate (Schwartow) in Pomerania and election to the Prussian House of Deputies and the Reichstag in 1876 and 1881 respectively. The particular brand of high-church piety which Hammerstein learned in the home of his forest master inclined him to ally with the remnants of the Old Conservative faction within the DKP. As one of the *Deklaranten*, Hammerstein made his peace with Bismarck after the passage of the agrarian tariffs in late 1879. He even consulted the chancellor in November 1881 before taking over from Niebelschütz as editor of the *Kreuzzeitung*. Until 1884 Hammerstein remained on more or less cordial terms with Bismarck socially.[9]

In his discussions with Bismarck in November 1881, Hammerstein had sought assurances of government patronage for the *Kreuzzeitung*, but he was unsuccessful. Consequently he set out to tap new sources of support; as Heydebrand later observed, 'Hammerstein had a conscious image of the nature of an independent Conservative Party.' This support and Hammerstein's influence were certainly not unfluctuating, but they can perhaps best be described in terms of concentric rings of sympathy centring on the *Kreuzzeitung* itself. As Hammerstein worked to reverse the decline of his newspaper he relied heavily on two leading members of his staff. One was Baron Eduard von Ungern-Sternberg, a member of the Tax and Economic

Reformers' original executive committee. As the writer of the weekly reviews for the *Kreuzzeitung*, and as co-editor of both the *Conservative Correspondenz* and the *Konservative Monatsschrift*, Ungern became one of the most prolific Conservative journalists between 1880 and 1914. Hammerstein's other close aide was Hermann Kropatschek, who eventually succeeded Hammerstein as editor in 1895. By the middle of the 1880s the *Kreuzzeitung* had regained its unchallenged position as the dominant Conservative organ, which it never lost again. As the Conservatives were always quick to point out, the *Kreuzzeitung*'s inability to rival the readership of the liberal and non-partisan newspapers – some of which enjoyed circulations of over 200,000 – did not reduce its significance as the mouthpiece of very powerful interests. The *Kreuzzeitung* remained the best source of news on social engagements, military promotions, agricultural prices, patents of nobility and palace intrigues. Thus, through the next tortuous decade, Hammerstein's editorials continued to be read by all Conservatives who needed their 'court reporter'. The *Kreuzzeitung*'s pre-eminent position did not cause Hammerstein to lose touch with the rapidly expanding DKP provincial press in the 1880s. In fact, the phalanx of independent editors leading these enterprises, along with the corpus of social, religious and political ideas they represented, came to be regarded as very much integral elements of the *Kreuzzeitung* group itself.

The second main element of the *Kreuzzeitung* group was the cadre of Old Conservatives – also called the High Conservatives or 'Ultras' – who sat in parliament. Most of these sat in the Prussian House of Deputies, and there they regarded Hammerstein and Stöcker, not their own nominal caucus chairmen, as their real leaders.[10] Reichstag deputies under Helldorff, on the other hand, had to deal with economic, military and social bills requiring a greater degree of flexibility; they were therefore more mindful of Kartell requirements due to the relative weakness of their caucus.

The third element, which eventually gave the *Kreuzzeitung* group its most tangible form, was the network of party activists scattered across Germany who wished to steer their regional party organizations in the same 'Christian' and 'social' directions in which Hammerstein and Stöcker were trying to impel the Conservative Party as a whole. These men demanded the right to speak out in favour of party reform. They justified their action by pointing to their own independent efforts to move beyond the traditional limits of Conservative agitation. As Helldorff and the *Wahlverein* leadership in Berlin settled into comfortable Kartell politics after 1884, these dissidents worked through the *Bürgervereine* in Berlin and the established Conservative *Vereine* in the countryside to keep alive the grass-roots desire for independence from government influence. Over time, as Hammerstein and the editors who followed him grew more critical of Helldorff's Kartell orientation and his apparent disregard for party organization, these activists acquired a sense of belonging to what contemporaries called the '*Kreuzzeitung* party'.

Finally, a line of nominal '*Kreuzzeitung*' ministers and generals ran from Edwin von Manteuffel, Leopold von Gerlach and Albrecht von Roon at mid-century to Robert von Puttkamer, Gustav von Goßler (Minister of Cultural and Ecclesiastical Affairs) and Alfred von Waldersee (Chief of the Prussian General Staff) in the 1880s. The danger presented by these high-placed men was very real. The Prussian Minister of Justice, Heinrich von Friedberg, once said of Puttkamer that 'he rules wholly in line with the extreme *Kreuzzeitung* party'.[11] On 12 June 1888 Robert Lucius von Ballhausen, the Prussian Minister of Agriculture, wrote to Bismarck about a cabinet shuffle explicitly calculated to meet 'the danger of a development of internal politics in the *Kreuzzeitung*–Stöcker direction'.[12] Eight days later the death of Kaiser Friedrich III prompted Friedrich Nietzsche to remark that 'Now the rule of *Stöcker* begins.'[13]

Thus, through the *Kreuzzeitung* and its affiliated provincial press, through the corps of Conservative Ultras in the Prussian Landtag, through the agitation of regional Conservative *Vereine*, and through the influence of state ministers or Prussian officers who felt an affinity for their cause, Hammerstein and Stöcker found a number of important means for exerting their influence on the DKP. They wished to see the *scope* of Conservative politics enlarged into a popular movement or *Volkspartei*. This they believed would transform the party into a decisive agent for the breaking of the political mould which they described as the 'liberal era'. They wished to see the *direction* of Conservative politics realigned to provide for the reacquisition of the full rights of their church, as well as for the reincorporation of the middle and lower classes into a socioeconomic order of hierarchical relationships. In both scope *and* direction, Conservative politics were to break with liberal influences, no matter with what authority they were draped. To the Conservative constituency of *Kreuzzeitung*-group dreams there were few limits indeed.

The charismatic qualities and propagandist talents which Stöcker and Hammerstein possessed gave their followers a crusading zeal hitherto unknown in Conservative circles. It was, in turn, that sense of embarking on a new political journey that prompted *Kreuzzeitung*-group hopes for a transformation of the DKP into a *Volkspartei*.

Stöcker could speak in an equally comfortable (and compelling) manner whether he found himself in Berlin high society, in meetings of the Supreme Protestant Church Council, or in the most tumultuous political rally.[14] Aristocratic Berliners who saw him tending to such mundane tasks as organizing bazaars for the Inner Mission would fill the galleries of parliament or the Berlin cathedral just to hear him speak.[15] Rumours circulated that at one time Stöcker had taken lessons from an actor. Many observers also noted Stöcker's incredible capacity for work and travel.[16] But it is Stöcker's talents as a speaker and his ability to elicit unparalleled commitment from his followers which seem to provide the key to his charisma. As co-editor of the Christian Socials' leading newspaper, *Das Volk*, and as Stöcker's electoral agent in Siegen, Hellmut von Gerlach came into contact with Stöcker almost every day after 1885. 'Whenever I began to waver,' Gerlach wrote, 'I was set straight by the infatuation of his speeches . . . I adhered to Stöcker with limitless devotion . . . Enchanted, I remained on the magic mountain.'

Certainly this picture of Stöcker as the greatest Conservative speaker in the 1880s was not universally held. Bismarck, his advisers and most adherents of the Kartell were negatively impressed, especially when Stöcker trespassed on the chancellor's own terrain in parliament. Christoph von Tiedemann, for instance, was appalled by Stöcker's Landtag speech during the anti-Semitic debates of 22 November 1880. He predicted that with another such speech Stöcker would be 'parliamentarily dead, despite the frenetic applause of the extreme Right, which really had something hysterical about it'.[17] But rather than denying the popular talents of the court preacher, Bismarck and others condemned the uses to which he put them. Count Kuno zu Rantzau wrote that Stöcker was merely 'fishing for popularity at the cost of the workers'.[18] The Kaiser thought Stöcker's activities inappropriate for a court preacher.[19] And Bismarck and Bleichröder both complained that Stöcker appeared to be turning the struggle against the Jews into a social crusade against property as such. 'For me,' wrote the chancellor, '*the Socialist element* in his speeches and agitation is far more decisive *than the anti-Semitic*.'[20] Later in the decade Bismarck offered a rather different assessment of Stöcker and the influence he had won in the Conservative Party. Bismarck declared that he was amazed by Stöcker's 'bold and eloquent' agitation; 'he has a tongue like a sword'.[21] Like the Kaiser, however, Bismarck did not consider this talent appropriate for a court preacher.

Hammerstein completely lacked Stöcker's enthusiasm for mass rallies, almost never speaking before such audiences; he preferred to avoid the dust of the people's meeting. But many Germans regarded Hammerstein's pen as mightier than Stöcker's tongue, or at least its natural complement. Stöcker's biographer, Walter Frank, wrote that Hammerstein used his unparalleled literary talents at the writing-desk in order to make up for the Conservatives' inferiority in the sphere of propaganda – just as Stöcker did for their 'rhetorical' inferiority.[22] Hammerstein's idiosyncrasies and his impassioned crusades were undoubtedly the secret of his rejuvenation of the *Kreuzzeitung*. As the *Kölnische Volkszeitung* put it in 1891, 'However little tendency to opposition the Conservative nobility may have, it still loves to see in its press the turn for independence and a salty style.'[23] When the *Kreuzzeitung*'s theatre critic, Rudolph Stratz, first met Hammerstein, he was immediately impressed; Stratz stood before a man with 'a fox head atop a bull neck', sporting a moustache and imperial beard, displaying his coat of arms (a hammer) on a tie-pin, 'rattling deeply in an east-Elbian voice' and exhibiting 'a sly look' that nevertheless seemed to lack self-assurance. To match his appearance and penmanship, Hammerstein's early career as a forester gave him the reputation of being a sure shot – 'a very convincing argument', Stratz wrote, for any who might have challenged him 'in this world of blue-blooded satisfaction'.

Hammerstein's political talents were not overshadowed by his journalistic gifts and arrogant manner; rather, all meshed perfectly. Hellmut von Gerlach regarded Hammerstein as 'the realization of my party-political ideal'. He also recognized, however, that for its editor the *Kreuzzeitung* was 'only a means to make himself master of the Conservative Party, and to raise this party, independent of crown and chancellor, to the first order of power in Prussia-Germany'. Stratz agreed. 'The Junker versus the *Oberjunker*' was how he described Hammerstein's campaign against Bismarck.

Stöcker and Hammerstein, then, were clearly something different from the average Conservative parliamentarian. In the 1880s Stöcker was already being labelled a 'people's tribune'. In the next decade, after he was forced to resign as court preacher, his title in retirement was rendered as 'Preacher to All Germans'.[24] But which Germans 'flocked' to the Christian Social banner, and which actually read Hammerstein's editorials in the *Kreuzzeitung*? Unfortunately, the lack of CSP membership lists and the absence of readership surveys makes a definitive answer impossible. Of the *Kreuzzeitung*'s circulation, little more can be said than that it rose from about 2,000 in the late 1870s to a high point of roughly 10,000 in the period 1887–90. Other Conservative newspapers, however, helped bring *Kreuzzeitung*-group views to a less exclusive audience.

Stöcker's following, especially in Berlin and in certain Protestant areas of Westphalia, can be assessed with somewhat more precision. Stöcker's first attempt at political organization and propaganda was very small in scale. In 1877 the Central Association for Social Reform numbered around nine hundred members, made up mainly of pastors, lower officials and teachers. By contrast, the Christian Social Workers' Party allegedly had some 3,000 followers in mid-1878, that is, half a year after it was founded. Four years later, as the Social Democratic propagandist Franz Mehring wrote, Stöcker was apparently still speaking 'in obscure phrases' about his 'three or four thousand' followers.[25] But Gerlach claimed that free beer, military music and parades on national holidays added to the sense of commitment felt by these Conservatives and increased the appeal of the party in Berlin generally.[26] So, too, did the occasional brawl and, for some, the burning of a synagogue in 1881.

Contested membership figures reveal little about the occupational background of the Berlin *Bürgervereine* or about the regularity of their political activity.[27] According to one Berlin police report from 1878, early CSP members were divided between two main groups: the poor and unemployed on the one hand, and workers and artisans on the other. Of the latter, many already belonged to Christian youth and men's associations.[28] In other words, Stöcker's earliest supporters in Berlin were already long acquainted with the benefits of the Protestant Church and the Prussian state, or hoping for material advantages from them in the future. Returns from elections to the Berlin city council in 1883 also indicate that the CSP did well among the third (least affluent) class of voters, comprised mainly of the lower middle and lower classes.[29] But Stöcker's refusal to endorse social revolution prevented him from recruiting to his cause more than perhaps 150 or 200 workers in Berlin.[30] After four years of agitation, as Mehring wrote, the CSP's 'trills of hope and sounds of jubilation' still sought to 'demolish and plunder' the proletariat.

The Christian Social Party's agitation outside Berlin embraced more than just anti-Semitic speeches, and it addressed issues beyond those that interested voters in the capital. The special targets were hard-pressed small farmers. The synagogue burning of 1881 was never attributed to the CSP directly; however, as the local provincial governor wrote to Puttkamer, it reflected the 'deep bitterness' which small landowners felt towards Jewish usurers who exploited indebtedness in the countryside for their own ends.[31] That bitterness was felt as well by the independent retailers and skilled workers in the small villages, who resented Jewish big business. Finally, to these lower-middle-class adherents of Stöcker can be added certain members of the educated *Mittelstand*, principally retired officers, lower officials, pastors and academic youth. The last group is most consistently mentioned in the memoirs of Stöcker's associates. Reinhard Mumm, a later leader of the CSP, recalled that there existed a division in student ranks: the 'Christian social line and the "pure" German line'. The first group brought many recruits to Stöcker's side. But the more starkly anti-Semitic and nationalist tendency among German students gained the upper hand in the 1880s, as it did among the leaders of the influential German National Commercial Employees' Union, who had originally represented Stöcker's views in Hamburg and elsewhere.[32]

When considering these nationalists and other members of the CSP constituency it is necessary to differentiate as far as possible between geographic areas of support. Even between three regions in central Germany – the districts of Siegen and Minden-Ravensberg, both in Westphalia, and Kassel in Hesse-Nassau – there existed profound differences in the sociological make-up of Stöcker's supporters and in their political outlook.[33] In Siegen, where Stöcker won election to the Reichstag for a quarter-century, pastors were an almost negligible force in the CSP following, in contrast to Minden-Ravensberg, where they were crucial in providing Stöcker with his seat in the Prussian Landtag. A contemporary portrait of the CSP as a crusading pastor galloping through Westphalian villages and commanding the populace to vote for Stöcker 'in the name of God' would be out of place in Siegen. Also, anti-Semitism was among the least useful of Stöcker's appeals. Instead, the district's long history of independent, lay Protestantism (the *Gemeinschaftsbewegung*) provided the organizational basis of the movement. Social distinctions were as important as religious ones. Stöcker's support in Siegen, as elsewhere, derived largely from elements of the lower *Mittelstand*, as the membership lists of his various electoral committees document. But the relatively harmonious relations between workers and employers in Siegen and its environs produced Stöcker's greatest success among workers, in stark contrast to Berlin.

Stöcker's ability to appeal to a broad range of social groups and political leanings was also aided by the development of subsidiary, quasi-political organizations. The precise relationship between the DKP and these religious, occupational, charitable, or anti-Semitic groups was often obscure. But these organizations clearly added to the local appeal of the Christian Social cause, especially among workers. One of the CSP members who chose to sit in the DKP's Reichstag caucus, Gustav Hüpeden, discussed such organizations in his retrospective account, 'How I Became Conservative'.[34] After 1886 Hüpeden was secretary for the Inner Mission in Kassel. There he established close relations with a prominent social reformer, Pastor Ludwig Weber of Mönchen-Gladbach, who founded the Protestant workers' movement in western Germany and who figured prominently in the history of Christian Socialism after 1890.[35] Hüpeden also founded a branch of the Protestant League (Evangelischer Bund) in Kassel in 1889. His greatest effort, however, was reserved for the Protestant Workers' Association, which he founded in Kassel in April 1890. The Inner Mission and the Protestant League provided a secure cadre of adherents, and the association grew slowly from three hundred to about eight hundred members. According to Hüpeden, the association was comprised of one-third officials, one-third artisans and small business men and one-third factory workers. For many, 'the main attraction was the biblical sermon'. In June 1893 Hüpeden was advanced as a joint candidate of the Protestant League, the anti-Semites and the Conservative Party. Due to their independent campaign of 1891, the anti-Semites in the Kassel area already possessed a good organization; they had delegates in all the rural towns and large villages. 'This the Conservative Party lacked. They had financial patrons, but no speakers and agitators ... The Conservative Party bore the costs of the campaign, and the anti-Semitic party provided the speakers for working the localities; it was they who had the eager youth.' This combination of forces sent Hüpeden to the Reichstag.

These models of the Stöcker movement can only suggest the broad matrix of factors which contributed to the Christian Social Party's success. But Siegen, Minden-Ravensberg and Kassel were not areas where Stöcker conjured up a political following out of thin air. Rather they were areas where Stöcker was able to tap already existing sources of support and make his movement an influential factor in local political affairs. Stöcker's movement was the beneficiary of particular social, religious and economic relationships found in many parts of Germany but nowhere in quite the same combination.

Any final observations on the 'mass appeal' of the *Kreuzzeitung* group should point less to the actual achievements of Stöcker, Hammerstein and the CSP, and more to their ability to produce among their followers a fervent *belief* that their efforts were producing a new, independent, dynamic political organization. Stöcker's charisma, a rejuvenated Conservative press, a willingness to expand the Conservative constituency and the *sense* of a new beginning immeasurably increased the significance of the CSP and its patron, the *Kreuzzeitung*, within the Conservative Party. Gerlach best presented the goals for which the faithful fought under the *Kreuzzeitung* banner.[36] He wrote:

A Conservative Party – in the sense of a solid organization extending throughout the country, with *Vereine* and secretaries – did not exist at all . . . The current wind from the government determined the course and the strength of the party . . . That appeared to me an unacceptable situation. I wanted a party based on the trust of the people, who themselves made policy rather than having policy made by using them. The party was to be Christian, monarchist, agrarian, militarist and social, but above all independent, no Bismarckian party.

The elements of the *Kreuzzeitung* group's anti-liberal ideology included anti-capitalism and anti-Semitism, the defence of church rights, co-operation between Protestant and Catholic conservatism, *Sozialpolitik*, anti-Socialism, *Mittelstand* politics, opposition to Helldorff, opposition to the Kartell and opposition to Bismarck. Each of these elements was closely related to the task of fashioning a new, vibrant, broadly based Conservative *Volkspartei*.

It is true that *Kreuzzeitung*-group dissidents shared a certain degree of anti-liberalism and, more specifically, anti-capitalism with their majority colleagues in the Conservative Party. The first Conservative programme of 1876 had expressed the party's antipathy to 'limitless economic freedom'. Conservatives in general believed that this 'freedom' had swept across Germany when Bismarck and the National Liberals had worked out a new economic policy for the Reich between 1867 and 1873, and that its worst features were found in the Industrial Code of 1869. They also believed that liberal freedoms were responsible for a myriad of social ills afflicting the nation in the depression. The financial scandals identified by Perrot, the atomization of society, the ruthlessness of economic competition and the alienation of the lower orders from the church and the state – all these evils of modern society were laid by most Conservatives at the door of the liberals. A majority of the party, furthermore, consistently advocated some action to limit stock-exchange dealings, the exploitation of workers and other features of modern economic life associated with liberal (or Jewish) capitalism. However, the *Kreuzzeitung* group believed that the requirements of Kartell politics (and in particular the personal dominance of Bismarck) had blinded Helldorff and other DKP leaders to the need to press this anti-liberal campaign vigorously in the 1880s. When Helldorff declared in the Reichstag in January 1885 that 'the interests of agriculture are no longer separable from those of industry and commerce', he may have been referring to the logic of his own *Realpolitik*.[37] But to Hammerstein and Stöcker the policies supported by Helldorff and other pro-Kartell Conservatives attested to the abandonment of Conservative principles which the *Kreuzzeitung* group, like the Old Conservatives before them, was dedicated to preserving. In questioning the socio-economic premises of the capitalist system, dissidents from Helldorff's line were prone to use arguments that had an eschatological ring to them. Often these arguments bore a remarkable similarity to those used by the Socialists. As Hammerstein wrote in a *Kreuzzeitung* article from January 1888, 'In many respects we stand much closer to the Socialists than we do to heartless, mammonistic Manchesterism.'[38]

The banner of Christianity, too, could be raised equally well by the *Kreuzzeitung* group in battles against left-liberals who sanctioned the Jewish influence in German commerce, against National Liberals as representatives of large-scale industry oppressing 'the little man' and against liberals of all ilks who had launched the *Kulturkampf*. The ideal of the 'Christian state' had long been a basic element of German Conservatism.[39] Its appearance in the DKP programme of 1876 may have prompted Johann Caspar Bluntschli, a contemporary liberal political scientist, to write: 'In our day "the Christian state" has become a conservative slogan.'[40] However, the Christian critique of liberalism was used by Hammerstein and Stöcker in ways not sanctioned by the party leadership. First, they interpreted Christian principles in a more reactionary way than most of their party colleagues. Under their influence, the term 'Christian' signified, more than ever, 'non-Jewish'. Thus, when they argued for the reform of marriage laws, school regulations and other elements of civil life, in accordance with Christian–German traditions, they were arguing for the exclusion of Jewish influence in these areas. They also insisted that the people must be imbued with a greater respect for authority and a more profound feeling of piety.[41] Second, the *Kreuzzeitung* group leaders sought to attract as allies for the DKP other parties that had reason to oppose Bismarck's apparent disregard of Christian principles. Of foremost importance here was the Centre Party. Third, Hammerstein and Stöcker, like their forerunners in the Old Conservative faction, were willing to antagonize the chancellor in their pursuit of more power and independence for the Protestant Church.

With the Kleist–Hammerstein proposals of 1886–7 the *Kreuzzeitung* group registered its determination to free the Protestant Church establishment from the influence of parliament and bureaucrats. As Stöcker had put it some years earlier, the 'state church' (*Staatskirchentum*) the Ultras were opposing had been erected largely during the *Kulturkampf* of the 1870s; it was 'no longer cloaked in the purple mantle of the monarchy but in the toga of constitutionalism'.[42] Exactly the same view was represented in a pamphlet entitled *Lay Thoughts on the Kulturkampf*, written and sent to Bismarck in 1879 by Baron Wilhelm von der Reck. Reck was a Landtag deputy elected from the Westphalian constituency of Minden; he was renowned as one of the most reactionary members of the Conservative Party's executive committee and an advocate of the *Kreuzzeitung* group.[43] In his *Lay Thoughts*, Reck appealed to Bismarck and the Kaiser to recognize the dangers of increased parliamentary influence if the liberal course which spawned the *Kulturkampf* were maintained. He advocated nothing less than 'a complete change of system'. Typical, too, was the view of the chairman of the Silesian Conservative *Verein*, Baron Hans Heinrich von Durant-Baranowitz, who wrote in 1881 that the DKP must stress the 'identification of liberalism with disbelief'.[44] Hammerstein agreed but went further. For him, a Conservative 'people's church' (*Volkskirchentum*) was the corollary to a Conservative *Volkspartei*. He sought a greater separation of church and state so that Protestant pastors, independent of government patronage and control, could – like their Catholic counterparts – agitate for their political party, if necessary in opposition to the government. However, the Kleist–Hammerstein proposals illustrated the limits of *Kreuzzeitung*-group influence. They were rejected not only by Bismarck but by a majority of Conservatives in the Landtag.[45]

As party antagonisms sharpened in the wake of left-liberal advances in the Reichstag elections of 1881, Hammerstein spoke more and more often of the 'bond of positive Christianity' uniting orthodox Protestants and Catholics in the face of a worldly, Jewish-liberal, anti-cultural *Zeitgeist*.[46] In his programmatic lead article after taking control of the Conservative organ in late 1881, Hammerstein wrote that a 'true and conservative' solution to Germany's problems was possible only through co-operation between the two Christian parties. He subsequently emphasized the idea of a 'Christian-social alliance' without regard to party or confession: 'It is very probable that in twenty-five years we will have only two parties left: a Christian-social and a social-revolutionary party.'[47] Bismarck would certainly have endorsed this anti-revolutionary strain in Hammerstein's argument. But because of his earlier conflict with the Old Conservatives and his antipathy towards 'politicians in robes', the chancellor was unusually sensitive to Hammerstein's overtures to the Centre. As he wrote to Wilhelm II when the latter seemed to be moving closer to the *Kreuzzeitung* group in 1887–8: 'The Protestant priest, as soon as he feels himself strong enough, tends towards a theocracy just as much as the Catholic, and is thereby more difficult to deal with, since he has no pope over him.'[48] As it happened, Helldorff's influence and Protestant–Catholic antagonisms precluded the 'Black–Blue' alliance Bismarck feared. One of his successors was not to be so lucky.

On matters relating to the welfare of workers and the protection of the *Mittelstand*, it is virtually impossible to separate the politics of the Conservative Party and those of the Christian Social Party.[49] Members of the DKP in both the Reichstag and Landtag often allowed Stöcker to speak for them on such questions. However, only a systematic breakdown of house divisions through the decade would indicate to what degree (but not with what motivation) they endorsed his statements. Both the DKP and the CSP professed a commitment to solving 'the social question', but here ambiguity and ambivalence abounded. Some Conservatives felt they had to put as good a face as possible on the Kaiser's proclamation of 1881 and on Bismarck's subsequent interpretation of it. Others agreed with Stöcker that Wilhelm's words proved that Germany (and the Conservative Party) had overcome the darkest hour before the dawn of a new age. However, the very term *Sozialpolitik* meant something narrower to contemporaries than 'social policy'. Instead it signified the response to the workers' question, and involved legislation pertaining to the protection of wage-earners and the 'raising' of the working classes into the social and political order of the *Kaiserreich*.[50] The Conservatives and Christian Socials diverged in both the hopes and the fears they entertained for the success of this campaign. But a leading Conservative publicist in the decades before 1876, Hermann Wagener, was probably correct in noting that very few of the benefits of support for social insurance schemes accrued to either party's account. 'It is a futile hope . . . to win the sympathy of the masses for the government and for Conservative *Sozialpolitik* as long as one persists in treating them as second-class Germans and subjecting them to exceptional laws.'[51]

Mittelstandspolitik, too, meant different things to different people. In a state of flux during the 1880s and 1890s, independent organizations representing the interests of the *Mittelstand* were becoming as unpredictable as their dissatisfaction was vocal.[52] Some of these groups saw the CSP as the best vehicle for their agitation; *Kreuzzeitung*-group rhetoric against the liberal economic system in general struck a responsive chord. Others, however, believed that Ackermann's conspicuous efforts in the Reichstag, representing the DKP as a whole, were more sincere and effective. For in wooing these groups, Hammerstein and Stöcker could only barely outbid Ackermann, the Tax and Economic Reformers and other mainstream Conservatives, who themselves spoke in favour of the protection of 'honest' work against the onslaught of 'big-city trade capital'. Ackermann in April 1877 declared that the Conservatives were committed to the hope that the occupational estate of artisans 'should recover its golden age'.[53] Not surprisingly, the bonds of sympathy between *Mittelstand* groups and the DKP fluctuated considerably during the 1880s. The long-term trend probably produced more alienation than friendship, since the Kartell included the main representatives of big business, the National Liberals, and was directed against Protestant and Catholic social reformers. But that sympathy also depended on whether parliament passed the artisans' most determined demand: an amendment to the Industrial Code giving local authorities the right to restrict the training and employment of apprentices to guild members. Hopes for this legislation, sponsored by Ackermann in the Reichstag, rose and fell throughout the decade. In any case, the Conservatives could be sure that any legislation which seriously undermined the economic system upon which the Reich had been built would be boycotted by the government or vetoed by the Bundesrat. Eventually *Mittelstand* groups came to the same realization. Thus the history of the DKP's *Mittelstand* policies in these years has been described as the 'most unhappy chapter in the history of the Conservative Party'.[54]

The tale of the *Kreuzzeitung* group's opposition to Bismarck between 1884 and 1890 is a rather sordid one, whose details need not concern us here. It is filled with rhetorical sophistry, court-room scandals, secret correspondence, backstairs intrigue, banishments from court and astonishing revelations in the Socialist press (some published only years later).[55] An overview is necessary, however, not only to explore further the limits of anti-liberalism under Bismarck but also to underscore the intensity of the campaign against Helldorff and the Kartell, which came to full bloom only after Bismarck's dismissal in March 1890.

In 1884 the National Liberals and Free Conservatives began to differentiate more often between the 'moderate' and 'extreme' wings of the Conservative Party. After Stöcker suffered personal scandal in 1885, the National Liberals proved extremely reluctant to support Ultra candidates in any Reichstag constituencies in the election campaign of February 1887. For Hammerstein this was the 'darkest stain' on the Kartell. Yet Hammerstein, feeling the weakness of his own position within the party, did not dare to attack the DKP–FKP–NLP electoral alliance as such. Instead he pointed out the dangers of subsequent Reichstag legislation based on Kartell considerations. By 1887 a note of resignation had crept into Hammerstein's editorials. As was to happen repeatedly over the next few years, this discouragement spread to other Conservative reformers in the countryside.

Not all clouds on the political horizon were dark. *Kreuzzeitung* prospects brightened when it became known even before Kaiser Wilhelm I died in 1888 that his son, Friedrich III, was terminally ill with cancer. Wilhelm II was therefore likely to ascend the throne within months. Stöcker and Waldersee, it was also known, appealed to two particular aspects of Wilhelm's character: his instinctive desire to be recognized as a social reformer and his militarism. On 28 November 1887 Wilhelm and his wife appeared at the famous 'Waldersee meeting', which brought together conservative friends of the Berlin City Mission. The meeting attracted considerable attention by virtue of a speech – immediately printed in the *Kreuzzeitung* – in which Wilhelm declared that 'the Christian-social idea must be stressed more than it has been heretofore'. Bismarck recognized that the *Kreuzzeitung* group's reputation and its position within the Conservative Party would be enhanced by this endorsement. Through inspired articles in the official and Kartell press, and in an exchange of letters with Wilhelm in December and January 1887–8, Bismarck persuaded the future Kaiser not to identify himself too closely with the Christian Socials or with any political party. He also sowed the seeds of doubt in Wilhelm's mind whether Stöcker could be both a court preacher and social reformist politician. But Bismarck at the same time angered Wilhelm with this heavy-handed pressure. Hammerstein's editorials, defending the independence of the future monarch against Germany's elder statesman, reinforced Wilhelm's belief that he would eventually have to break with the chancellor.

It was in the wake of the failure of the Waldersee meeting that Hammerstein made his appeal to the Centre Party for another 'Christian-social alliance'. The desperation of this call was not lost on the NLP leader, Bennigsen, who in January 1888 wrote to a friend: 'Unfortunately no peace is to be made with the *Kreuzzeitung* party, which now has in mind nothing but the most confused reaction in state and church affairs, and therefore tries to attach itself to the Ultramontanes [the Centre] *à tout prix*.'[56] Hammerstein's campaign against Bismarck and the Kartell was interrupted in early 1888 during the 99-day reign of Friedrich III. But as the Prussian Landtag elections of November 1888 approached, Hammerstein and Helldorff waged a bitter duel for control of the DKP executive and its press, as well as for the sympathy of the new Kaiser. Helldorff was also trying to win a seat in the Prussian Landtag, to replace Rauchhaupt as caucus leader there. There was no doubt whom Bismarck favoured.[57]

During the Landtag election campaign, Hammerstein realized that Bismarck had won Wilhelm completely for his Kartell. The Kaiser referred to the *Kreuzzeitung* group as 'half crazy and too obtuse', and he declared publicly, if with circumspection, that he rejected anti-Semitism.[58]

Hammerstein briefly changed his tactics to indirect intrigue, following Stöcker's advice as outlined in the subsequently notorious 'Funeral Pyre' letter of 14 August 1888.[59] When this strategy did not prevent the Kartell from registering gains in the Landtag elections, Hammerstein abandoned temperance once again.[60] The next year, still seeking to separate Wilhelm from Bismarck, Hammerstein devoted more attention to foreign policy. His attempt to play the 'Waldersee card', however, foundered. For despite his awareness that Wilhelm, in contrast to Bismarck, shared his anti-Russian sentiments, Waldersee was unwilling to align himself too closely with Hammerstein.[61] Both Hammerstein and Stöcker, meanwhile, were touched by minor scandals, necessitating the latter's promise in April 1889 that he would withdraw from politics 'for the time being'. By mid-1889, then, it appeared that the reputation of the *Kreuzzeitung* group, at least when viewed from high political circles in Berlin, had reached its nadir. In his memoirs Stratz contrasted the fortunes of Helldorff's group and those of Hammerstein's. On the one side stood Helldorff and his colleagues, absorbed in the world of the court, the Herrenhaus, and 'cabinet politics'. They basked in 'the warming rays of the imperial sun' and 'spoke softly'. On the other hand, those gathered around Hammerstein could only wait and plot in conspiratorial meetings:[62]

In the smoke-filled room of one of these *Kreuzzeitung* evenings there would be proposed a list of the new, highly reactionary cabinet, half in jest, half in earnest: Waldersee, Chancellor. Puttkamer, Minister of the Interior again. Stöcker, Culture and Education. Hammerstein – to general amusement – Finance.

NOTES

1 Gerlach, *Von rechts*, p. 103.
2 Wilmowsky, *Rückblickend*, p. 19; cf. the positive assessments from the Nazi era: BAK, NL Seeberg, 20, f. 3, Seeberg, 'Adolf Stöcker zum Gedächtnis', MS (1934); Dierks, *Altkonservativen*, pp. 170 f.; also Brakelmann, Greschat and Jochmann, *Protestantismus*, pp. 7 f.
3 The literature on Stöcker, Christian social reform, the Protestant trade unions and nineteenth-century anti-Semitism is of course enormous. The Stöcker Nachlaß in ZStA II was not made available for the present study.
4 Oertzen, *Stöcker*, p. 174. The CCC's 'Programm der Conservativen in Berlin', 7.4.81, and other details in Schön, *Berliner Bewegung*, pp. 105–9, 169–71 and *passim*.
5 Heffter, *Kreuzzeitungspartei*, p. 21.
6 The most notable in the 1880s and 1890s were Wilhelm Marr, Max Liebermann von Sonnenberg, Bernhard Förster, Ernst Henrici, Otto Böckel and Hermann Ahlwardt.
7 PAH debates, 22.11.80, cited in Engelmann, 'Entwicklung', p. 109; cf. Lucius, *Bismarck-Erinnerungen*, p. 217; Frank, *Stöcker*, pp. 109 ff.' Stern, *Gold and Iron*, pp. 389 f., 526–31.
8 Stern, *Gold and Iron*, p. 529, Bleichröder to Wilhelm I, 12.5.84.
9 See Leuß, *Hammerstein*, pp. 12–44, and, for the following, Heydebrand, 'Beiträge', p. 500.

10 Both Rauchhaupt in the PAH and Kleist-Retzow in the PHH moved in and out of sympathy with Hammerstein in the 1880s.

11 Cited in Heffter, *Kreuzzeitungspartei*, p. 33.

12 *Rkz.* 1608, f. 56.

13 Letter of 20.6.88 (original emphasis), cited in Walter Kaufmann's notes to Friedrich Nietzsche, *On the Genealogy of Morals. Ecce Homo* (New York, 1969), p. 297.

14 Gerlach's following observations in *Von rechts*, pp. 102–4.

15 Cf. Spitzemberg, *Tagebuch*, pp. 213, 232, 306, 386.

16 Minnigerode to Stöcker, 27.6.85, cited in Frank, *Stöcker*, p. 107; cf. Petersdorf, *Kleist-Retzow*, p. 493.

17 BAK, NL Bismarck, Bestand B, 117, Tiedemann to Herbert von Bismarck, 20/22.11.80.

18 BAK, NL Rottenburg, Rantzau to Rottenburg, 22.10.85; cf. Engels, *Role of Force*, p. 104.

19 Notes of 29.9.80 cited in Jöhlinger, *Bismarck*, p. 143.

20 Bleichröder to Wilhelm I, 18.6.80, and Bismarck to Tiedemann, 21.11.80 (original emphasis), cited in Stern, *Gold and Iron*, pp. 513, 516.

21 See Lucius, *Bismarck-Erinnerungen*, p. 443.

22 For this and the following, see Frank, *Stöcker*, p. 105; Stratz, *Schwert*, pp. 166, 168, 175; Gerlach, *Von rechts*, pp. 132 f.

23 Cited in *LeipZ*, 5.1.91.

24 'Hofprediger a.D.' (*außer Dienst=aller Deutschen*).

25 Mehring, *Stöcker*, pp. 100 f., and for the following.

26 Gerlach, *Erinnerungen*, pp. 79–84.

27 See mainly Schön, *Berliner Bewegung*, *passim*.

28 Greschat, 'Stoecker', p. 29; cf. Brakelmann, 'Stoecker', p. 135; Jochmann, 'Stoecker', p. 165.

29 See Pulzer, *Rise*, p. 99 n.

30 Frank, *Stöcker*, p. 77.

31 Jochmann, 'Stoecker', p. 156 f.; Frank, *Stöcker*, p. 76.

32 Frank, *Stöcker*, pp. 76 f., 108 f.; Stratz, *Schwert*, p. 38; Gerlach, *Von rechts*, p. 102; Mumm, *Gedanke*, pp. 20–5. Cf. Hamel, *Völkischer Verband*, pp. 32 f., 44 ff.; Jochmann, 'Stoecker', pp. 162–7; Oberwinder, *Sozialismus*, pp. iii f.

33 For the following, see Busch, *Stöckerbewegung*, especially pp. 126–41, and Hoener, 'Christlich-konservative Partei', *passim*.

34 BAK, Kl. Erw. 227 (Hüpeden), Hüpeden to Walter Frank, 2.9.28.

35 See materials in ZStA I, NL Naumann, 52, f. 16 ff.; Weber, *Anweisungen*; on relations with the DKP press, Gasteiger, *Arbeiterbewegung*, p. 185.

36 Gerlach, *Von rechts*, p. 131.

37 Speech of 20.1.85, cited in Anderson, *Background*, pp. 37 f.

38 See Stock, *Bestrebungen*, p. 105.

39 Cf. Droz, 'Préoccupations'.

40 See Tal, *Christians*, pp. 121–59.

41 See, for example, *KZ*, 22.8.78.

42 *Neue Evangelische Kirchenzeitung*, 1.7.76, cited in Frank, *Stöcker*, p. 32; cf. Leuß, *Hammerstein*, pp. 51–3.

43 Reck, *Laien-Gedanken* (1879); BAK, NL Bismarck, 117, Reck to Bismarck, 17.11.79, and materials in BAK, Kl. Erw. 455 (Reck), *passim*.

44 BAK, NL Fechenbach, 103, Durant to Fechenbach, 14.3.81; cf. ibid., 53, Hermann Lange to Fechenbach, 14.1.85.

45 Frank, *Stöcker*, pp. 158 ff.; Petersdorff, *Kleist-Retzow*, pp. 514 ff.; BAK, NL Rottenburg, 10, Stolberg to Rottenburg, 5.3.86, 14.4.86, 16.3.87, 29.4.87.

46 *KZ*, 1.3.83; Stöcker, *Christlich-Sozial*, p. 514; Leuß, *Hammerstein*, pp. 109, 118 f.; Heffter, *Kreuzzeitungspartei*, pp. 60 f.; Gerlach, *Erinnerungen*, pp. 81 f.; Lucius, *Bismarck-Erinnerungen*, pp. 185, 242; Anderson, *Windthorst*, pp. 307 f.; Fechenbach, *Fürst Bismarck*, p. 123; cf. Hannay, 'Gedanke', and Zeender, 'Concept'; for the following see *KZ*, 3.12.81, 20.1.88; and Heffter, *Kreuzzeitungspartei*, pp. 14, 54.

47 Exactly the same formulation appeared in Werner, *Sozialrevolution*, p. 8.

48 Bismarck to Wilhelm, 6.1.88, cited in Frank, *Stöcker*, p. 156; cf. Lucius, *Bismarck-Erinnerungen*, p. 333.

49 See the more detailed discussion in my 'Reformist Conservatism', pp. 96–103.
50 Cf. Born, Henning and Schick (eds.), *Quellensammlung*, pp. 11 ff.; Stock, *Bestrebungen*; Femerling, 'Stellung'; Blasius, 'Sozialpolitik'; Bock, 'Konservativen'; Richthofen, 'Stellung'.
51 Wagener, *Erlebtes*, p. 82; cf. Wagener, *Mängel*, p. 25, and Wagener, *Rodbertus' Nachlaß*, p. 41.
52 Cf. Blackbourn, '*Mittelstand*'; Angel-Volkov, 'Anti-modernism'; Volkov, *Antimodernism*; Lebovics, 'Agrarians'; Lebovics, 'Socialism'; Gellately, *Politics*.
53 See Volkov, *Antimodernism*, pp. 20, 232 ff.; Stock, *Bestrebungen*, p. 69; *KZ*, 27.2.84.
54 Stock, *Bestrebungen*, p. 59.
55 Cf. Heffter, *Kreuzzeitungspartei*; Leuß, *Hammerstein*; Frank, *Stöcker*; Waldersee, *Denkwürdigkeiten*, Vol. 1, pp. 352 ff.; further references in my 'Reformist Conservatism', ch. 4. Unfortunately, Nichols's splendid study, *Year of the Three Kaisers*, appeared too late to use for this chapter.
56 Oncken, *Bennigsen*, Vol. 2, p. 539.
57 Rauchhaupt to Hammerstein, 19.8.88, in Leuß, *Hammerstein*, p. 73.
58 Lucius, *Bismarck-Erinnerungen*, p. 465.
59 Printed in Frank, *Stöcker*, pp. 318 f. The *Scheiterhaufenbrief*, first published in 1895, suggested that Hammerstein erect a metaphorical circle of funeral pyres around Bismarck by sowing discord between him and Wilhelm and by directing public attention to issues on which they disagreed.
60 *KZ*, 14/18.12.88.
61 ZStA II, NL Waldersee, B I, 50 and B II, 5, especially Hammerstein to Waldersee, 8.2.89; cf. Canis, *Bismarck und Waldersee*.
62 Stratz, *Schwert*, pp. 174 f. The 'amusement' Stratz notes in the last line is retrospective; the 1895 Hammerstein scandal centred on his embezzlement of *Kreuzzeitung* funds.

5

The Party at Large:
Regional Organizations and the Conservative Press

Despite the extreme unevenness of Conservative Party development across Germany, the dynamic of the 1880s clearly lay more with the *Kreuzzeitung* faction than with the Helldorff group. The appeals of Hammerstein and Stöcker seemed to characterize all that was forward-looking in the young Conservative Party. Although the proselytizing zeal of *Kreuzzeitung*-group Conservatives sent them in many different directions, they all believed that the Conservative Party could achieve its Christian, social and 'popular' goals through the expansion of its regional organizations and its propaganda. This faith found its truest expression in the self-sacrifice and isolation which dissident Conservatives were willing to endure as long as Bismarck and Helldorff remained ascendant. Yet the organizational take-off that occurred in these years also offered an unprecedented opportunity to change the popular image of the Conservative Party.[1]

In January 1882, when he read newspaper reports about the Berlin meeting[2] between *Wahlverein* leaders and local delegates that had so few tangible results, a Bavarian aristocrat immediately scribbled down his indignant reactions.[3] Referring to 'the *high* and *wise* executive of the "German" Conservative Party', he wrote: '"Deeds" and not "phrases" are what is needed ... This meeting is in line with all that have come before it.' The man who penned these bitter lines of criticism was *Reichsfreiherr* Friedrich Karl von Fechenbach-Laudenbach. In a survey history of German Conservatism, Fechenbach would perhaps merit a footnote.[4] But this nobleman was a keen observer of party activities, both in Prussia and in the western German states, and he was intimately involved in the early shaping of west German Conservative *Vereine*. Moreover, in contrast to the *Wahlverein* of 1883, Fechenbach sought to take eminently practical steps in his attempt to reform Conservative Party institutions and policy. Fechenbach's belief that organizational and programmatic reform had to proceed hand in hand gained publicity at a time when the DKP's parliamentary leadership was newly ensconced in the Bismarckian camp and eager to remain there. Likewise, his disturbing scheme to unite Catholic and Protestant conservatives on the basis of social reform in an anti-liberal direction threatened to swing the balance of power within the DKP in the direction of Hammerstein and Stöcker. Fechenbach's effort, like theirs, illustrated why Helldorff could not dare to follow the lead of a radical organizer preaching the gospel of 'no compromise' with capitalism and the National Liberal Party.

Fechenbach began his efforts to found a 'Social Conservative Alliance' in 1880 by enlisting the aid of Stöcker, Hammerstein, Ungern-Sternberg, Perrot and his own brother-in-law, Thüngen-Roßbach. Stöcker and Hammerstein in particular warned Fechenbach that resistance from the majority of Prussian Conservative leaders and from the government would be substantial. Regarding one of the stronger anti-Semitic passages in Fechenbach's programme, Stöcker wrote that 'for propaganda purposes this point must be omitted; in principle it is correct, but at present impossible. For statesmen and ministers, the point cannot be implemented.' Hammerstein remarked that the Conservatives in northern Germany would have little sympathy for or understanding of the scope of the proposal. He wrote: 'The social question is still too unfamiliar to most; what they alone recognize is the smack of Social Democracy and there is no end to the frightening effect that has here.'[5] Although various Conservatives were attracted by the anti-liberal possibilities of this interconfessional alliance, they tended to see practical difficulties or Popish dangers at every turn. Yet Frege – who after 1883 sat on the DKP's executive committee and thus stood in some proximity to Helldorff – offered some particularly enlightening comments on the Conservatives' divided loyalties:

> We unfortunately have in our midst, due to the 'might before right' policies of the last twenty years, such a large number of pseudo-conservative creatures, so many fearful souls who want never to incur the displeasure of the government or the so-called liberal *Bürgertum*, that – between us – I think we cannot have doubts about how weak our cause still is . . . I believe, therefore, that . . . we must refrain from appearing before the masses with promises and slogans, whose sad impossibility of fulfilment is all too clear, at least to those of us in the Reichstag.

Eventually Fechenbach's Alliance met in Frankfurt on 10 November 1880. Despite the baron's devious ploys to attract leading Catholics to this assembly, the Centre Party leader, Ludwig Windthorst, had advised his followers not to attend. Conservative parliamentary leaders arranged a similar boycott, though with rather less success. About one hundred men could not be kept from discussions that held the portent of new directions for the Conservative Party, any proclamations from above notwithstanding. By the end of the meeting it had become clear to most of these

Conservatives that Fechenbach's project for a Conservative–Centre alliance could be forged only on the anvil of Ultramontanism.[6] Nevertheless, the reluctance expressed in some of the Conservatives' rejections indicated the persistent strength of reformist ambitions within the party. Indeed, an appreciation of the confessional suspicions that doomed Fechenbach's project only makes more persuasive the argument that it was the prospect of a new *form* of Conservative politics that many of his supporters valued most highly in his initiative. Stöcker, for example, looked towards 'a Christian-social-reformist *Volkspartei*'. The *Reichsbote* spoke of Fechenbach's 'untiring and self-sacrificing activity . . . aimed at making the Conservative Party a *Volkspartei* in the best sense of the word'.[7] Other Conservative newspapers, especially those edited by newcomers to Conservative affairs or representing non-Prussian Conservatives, expressed similar hopes, as did the Tax and Economic Reformers' *Deutsche Landes-Zeitung*.[8]

Despite the initial lack of leadership from the top party ranks, the establishment of Conservative newspapers in Berlin and in other parts of Germany proceeded after 1876. These foundings were taken in hand largely by men concerned with refining the party's popular appeal. Especially in western and central Germany, but by no means only there, a corps of entrepreneurs and editors emerged who tried to translate their reformist ambitions into practical terms. These men's self-confidence, their reputations, and their sense of collegiality rose quickly. This process was accelerated by the connections that many of them shared, either personally or through successive affiliation with a number of newspapers. (See Appendices 4 and 8.) By combining a regard for Berlin politics with a focus on local issues and activities, these editors performed a function of which the DKP *Wahlverein*'s publications were incapable. Inevitably, the quicker pace of political life in these areas made Conservative editors less than willing to subordinate their efforts to the direction, or neglect, of *Wahlverein* notables.

Probably nothing exemplifies better the diversity and strength of the reformist impulse within this new community of Conservative journalists than the career of Dietrich von Oertzen. One of thirteen children born to a Mecklenburg estate owner and judicial councillor, Oertzen grew up in the most important newspaper city in western Germany, Frankfurt am Main. After his schooling, Oertzen managed a small estate in Hanover from 1874 to 1877, but without any particular interest or success. He then began a journalistic tour of duty that spanned not only thirty years but all the tensions between older and newer styles of Conservatism. His outlook, he claimed later, was consistently 'Christian Conservative' in political matters and 'Christian Social' in economic matters. Because Oertzen worked closely with such a wide range of Conservative newspapers and

Vereine, his experiences run like a thread through the history of the Conservative press.[9]

The *Reichsbote* must be counted as the second most important Conservative newspaper sympathetic to the *Kreuzzeitung* group's cause. Heinrich Engel, the son of a pious Hessian peasant, had worked as a preacher in a number of districts in his homeland.[10] Selected by Nathusius-Ludom to head the new *Reichsbote* in 1873, Engel served in this post until his death in 1911. It was largely this sustained effort and Engel's good business sense that kept the newspaper in an uncommonly good financial situation (by Conservative standards) for most of its history. Oertzen – who was hired by Engel as foreign editor of the *Reichsbote* in the early 1880s – described Engel as 'gnarly, cantankerous, gruff and unobliging'. But Engel took his role as doyen of Conservative editors very seriously indeed. Despite his lack of formal education he showed an early talent in his lead editorials for grasping the essentials of an issue quickly, stating his own view clearly and gauging the reactions of his readership accurately. Engel's editorship of the *Reichsbote* consolidated it as the Conservatives' '*Pastorenblatt*'. However, Engel's pro- and anti-government stances through the years (like his pro- and anti-agrarian ones) defy simple categorization. He generally endorsed the anti-Semitic tone of other Conservative editors and agitators, and was perhaps more consistent than anyone else during the 1880s in linking the 'Jewish threat' to the liberal age of capitalist exploitation. Yet he was also among the most prominent critics of old-style politics, and he saw the futility of extreme reaction. Forced to define his allegiances within the DKP in the early 1890s, Engel personified the many dilemmas facing Conservative propagandists in an uncertain age.

The history of the *Konservative Monatsschrift* illustrates the breadth of Conservative journalism in the Second Reich, for this journal's appeal was nothing if not eclectic.[11] The *Monatsschrift*'s monthly reviews of political events were eventually supplemented by reviews on church affairs, social reform, economic matters, foreign relations and colonial issues. The *Monatsschrift* never claimed to be an official organ of the Conservative Party. Yet its commitment to 'modernizing' the party on the one hand, and its concern with older Christian principles on the other, illustrated its affinity with the *Kreuzzeitung* group. A generally anti-Kartell orientation was reflected in proposals for changes to the official Conservative programme, to the DKP's alignment with other parties and to the party's policy on the *Kulturkampf*.[12]

The *Deutsches Adelsblatt* provided one more rallying-point for the reformist ambitions of the *Kreuzzeitung* group. Founded in April 1883 by Baron Paul von Roëll, the *Adelsblatt*'s programme was provided in its subtitle: 'For the Interests of the German Nobility of Both Confessions'. It served as official news-sheet and popular journal for an obscure organization rarely mentioned in histories of German Conservatism, the German Society of Nobles.[13] This society was hardly a mass-based organization. At its founding it numbered only 174 members, and it grew slowly, numbering about 1,300 members in 1890 (of whom 800 were in arrears with their yearly dues).[14] Nor was the *Adelsblatt* among the more popular weeklies of the day. But the ties between the DAG and its journal on the one hand, and the Conservative Party and its press on the other, were very close. Like those between the *Konservative Monatsschrift* and the DKP, these links provided a means to inject less reactionary views into majority Conservative opinion. The *Adelsblatt*, often cited in the contemporary press as representing more 'enlightened' Conservative views, helped keep the idea of *noblesse oblige* alive as the party seemed to be moving in a more reactionary direction. More concretely, the personnel of the Society of Nobles included some Conservatives from the highest ranks of the party. For example, Schulenburg-Beetzendorf was chairman of the DAG from 1881 to 1903, when he was succeeded by Wilhelm von Wedel-Piesdorf, who combined this post with chairmanship of the Conservative Party in 1911–13. The DAG also counted among its leading members some of the most prominent chairmen of regional Conservative *Vereine*, including Durant (Silesia), Friedrich von der Leyen-Blömersheim (Rhine Province) and Heinrich von Friesen-Rötha (Kingdom of Saxony).[15]

Explicitly dedicated to an interconfessional alliance of conservatives, the *Adelsblatt* not surprisingly gave Fechenbach the most consistent support of any major Conservative journal.[16] Anti-Semitism was very pronounced,[17] while a high profile was also given to anti-Kartell sentiments, polemics against the *Kulturkampf*, calls to expand the Conservative press, reports from southern and western *Vereine* and advocacy of more sophisticated methods of political organization as a means to popularize the Conservative Party. These desiderata are by now all familiar features of the reformist campaign within the Conservative Party. The one area where the *Adelsblatt* far outpaced its fellow journals was in the determination with which it pursued its special calling: the awakening of Germany's nobility to its responsibility for the welfare of the lower classes.[18] On this basis the *Adelsblatt* repeatedly called on the DKP to transform itself into a true *Volkspartei*.

Other organizations and literary enterprises also contributed to Conservative propaganda. The Association for the Distribution of Conservative Journals, for instance, was allegedly founded in 1883 with money from Bismarck's famous Reptile Fund.[19] The Christian Book League, founded in 1880, and its sister organization, the Fatherland League (1894), distributed mainly religious and anti-Socialist brochures.[20] The congresses of the Inner Mission debated press affairs on a number of occasions, attempting to make the Christian Conservative press a 'pulpit' and a 'spiritual power among our people'.[21] The *Collection of Discourses for the*

German People and the series entitled *Contemporary Issues in Christian Life* also provided a wide selection of cheap, popular texts, bringing the writings of men such as Nathusius, Stöcker and Mühlhäußer to the people.[22] Finally, the Conservatives' many brochures, flyers, leaflets and handbooks focused the party's propaganda effort at election time.

Any picture of a thriving Conservative press in the 1880s must be tempered with an appreciation for the widespread mismanagement, apathy and resignation that also afflicted Conservative newspapers and their audience. Oertzen's reflections on his own career illustrate this very clearly. They also indicate, however, why the difficulties of the Conservative press cannot be summed up merely by documenting unimpressive circulation figures and repeated bankruptcies. The inability of the *Kreuzzeitung* group to rally the majority of Conservatives behind its press was the manifestation of a deeper inconsistency within the DKP and its attitude towards 'popularity'.[23]

Conservative editors often chafed under the neglect of the parliamentarians they sought to serve. Oertzen recalled that when he imagined he ought to introduce himself, as the editor of the *Konservative Monatsschrift*, to one of the DKP's leading deputies in Berlin, he realized after being denied a visit that his opinion was of no consequence to this man. DKP editors also complained that their party colleagues preferred to publish announcements and insert advertisements in the liberal or 'nonpartisan' newspapers, which reached a far greater audience. When such a newspaper was found in a Conservative household, embarrassed explanations often included reference to the thickness of the reading-matter and its uses for lighting fires and wrapping fish. (Much the same is said of the New York *Times* today.) After the turn of the century, the *Konservative Monatsschrift* editors tried to solicit short biographies of recently deceased party notables. But they found that such articles, together with the late Conservatives' private papers and correspondence, were often sold instead to left-liberal journals, even to those, Oertzen indignantly noted, edited by Jews.

Oertzen's last comment points to the close connection between Conservative journalists' lack of business acumen and their belief that Germany's large liberal newspapers represented one of the most dangerous sources of Jewish influence. Stöcker once remarked that the press was one of the commanding heights of popular opinion the Conservatives had surrendered to their opponents – by whom he meant primarily the Jews.[24] The perceived growth of Jewish influence in the German press was furthermore linked by Conservatives to the alleged Jewish–liberal foundations of capitalism itself. This facilitated the attempts of Conservative editors to explain in anti-Semitic terms their lack of cleverness in attracting advertisers or making their newspaper concerns efficient.[25] True to their Christian Conservative beliefs, they continued to speak of 'advertising swindles' and the ephemeral profits derived from supporting 'the good cause'. Just as Stratz tried to disparage modern literary forms by polemicizing against foreign trends and 'Ibsenism' in the *Kreuzzeitung*,[26] these Conservative entrepreneurs used larger moral categories to explain why Conservatives had little success in making their press profitable. The continued failure of Conservative enterprises further disheartened the party rank and file and substantiated the Jewish spectre, just as the desperate situation of agriculture or handicrafts attested to the nefarious influence of economic liberalism. In short, all these Conservatives were attacking enemies in the popular realm by invoking the arguments they regarded as most appropriate to their political position. That they could not resort to hyperbole and *Klatsch*, despite the obvious popularity of such styles, was determined by the larger ideology of Conservatism, which sought to defend, not challenge, authority.[27] Oertzen summed up this dilemma when he wrote that the Conservative editor could not strive for the 'momentary sensation'. Instead, in certain instances, he had to remain silent. This was perhaps the hardest test for those whose job it was to write. But therein lay 'the topsy-turvy world of Christianity, that we do not do as we *wish*, but rather as we *should*'.[28]

The informal, unstructured politics of notables survived longest in the eastern provinces of Prussia.[29] (See Appendix 4.) In provinces like West Prussia and Poznan obvious 'foreign' enemies (the Poles) provided a permanent rallying-point for the Right. Thus formal *German* Conservative *Vereine* – as distinct from informal 'national' *Vereine* – were not normally considered necessary before 1900. In other provinces, such as Brandenburg and Pomerania, the lack of political activism in the sparsely populated countryside allowed Conservative organizers a similar luxury. In east Elbia and western Germany alike, the establishment of a provincial Conservative newspaper, the founding of a formal DKP *Verein* and the holding of a first party congress often went hand in hand.[30] In a few cases, local party secretariats were established in the 1880s and 1890s. But party business was not formalized to this extent in most regional organizations until after the turn of the century. Where a local or regional Conservative newspaper existed at all, it was typically its editor who took in hand the business affairs of the party. It was he, too, who generally reported to the regional congresses on the state of the regional press and plans for its improvement. But this pattern was never established uniformly for Conservative *Vereine* across Germany. The frequent renaming or refounding of local *Vereine* illustrated how easy it was for Conservatives, especially in the east, to fall back into their political 'slumber' between elections. This contributed to the slow establishment of party offices, because for years on end there might be literally no party business to transact. In any case, local Conservative groups were quite happy to have no bureaucratic ties to the central party office when the time came to select their candidates. Only the need for wider support in the party's larger newspapers, for tapping financial resources outside the locality and for leadership of their caucus in parliament compelled these notables, in time, to acknowledge that a formal party existed at all.

For these reasons it is impossible to document the full history of organizational initiatives across Prussia, a state that itself stretched from East Prussia in the east to the Rhineland in the west. Moreover, since political traditions in these provinces were astonishingly diverse, it makes little sense merely to record the number of Conservative deputies from east-Elbian and west-Elbian territories of Prussia, or from Prussian and non-Prussian territories, and then to draw conclusions from these figures about the party's ability (or inability) to expand its geographic base of support. First, considering the number of Conservative deputies in the Prussian House of Deputies, one finds that in 1886 almost one-quarter (30 of 132) came from constituencies lying west of the Elbe. After the Reichstag elections of 1887, sixty-one Conservative deputies came from Prussian territories. But of these sixty-one, twelve came from areas west of the Elbe. This is not a large proportion in itself; but it was significant enough that Conservatives could not have been indifferent to the fate of their *Vereine* in these regions. Second, one cannot assume that Conservative deputies from east-Elbian Prussia – or the newspapers they supported – automatically sided with their more reactionary colleagues against the reformist Conservatives who came largely, but not exclusively, from western Germany. Third and most importantly, central and south-western Germany provided the terrain where new strategies for political mobilization were not only most necessary but most troubling. It was here that Conservatives were forced to recognize the insufficiency of a traditional political style and to reflect on the implications of a new one.

As the second largest state in the Reich, Bavaria might have offered the Conservative Party an important foothold in non-Prussian territories. Its population was, and remains to this day, deeply conservative. This conservatism, however, did not translate into votes for the DKP, for two principal reasons: the German Conservatives represented to Bavarian particularists all that was to be feared or loathed from Prussia; and the Conservatives were the defenders of Protestantism, and thus unlikely to generate a following in a state that was 71 per cent Catholic in 1880. None the less, although the DKP never became a powerful political force in Bavaria, one historian has referred to the 'steady advance of Conservatism' in the Protestant areas of Franconia. Another has referred to the region of Middle Franconia, where Conservatives scored their only successes, as the political proving-ground in the state and as the birthplace of Bavarian anti-Semitism.[31] As evidence for a significant opportunity for the Conservative Party in the early 1880s, the Prussian envoy in Munich, Count

Georg von Werthern, reported to Bismarck in March 1881 that the Bavarian liberals had 'discredited' themselves of late; he noted regretfully that there existed 'no real Conservative party' to prevent the disaffected people from joining the Catholic Centre.[32] Bismarck had always favoured the National Liberals as the party of 'national unity' in particularist Bavaria. Therefore, in 1881, he and Werthern wanted to import Conservatism in the form of a pro-Reich 'middle party'. To this end Count Hugo von Lerchenfeld, the Bavarian envoy in Berlin, reported in April 1881 that Stöcker should be prevented from travelling to Bavaria, since anti-Semitism had allegedly not yet invaded that land. However, the advance of the Conservative Party in Bavaria began with an event – the founding of a Bavarian Conservative *Wahlverein* in June 1881 – that clearly supported the cause of Bismarck's enemies within the DKP. Ten years later, despite many set-backs for these anti-Kartell Conservatives, much the same situation prevailed.

That the Bavarian Conservative organization established extremely close ties with Fechenbach's Social Conservative Alliance was illustrated by the correspondence between Fechenbach and the later secretary of the Bavarian Conservatives, Rudolf Meyer von Schauensee. In January 1881 Schauensee reported that discontent among Bavarian artisans had created favourable opportunities for Conservatives, if only the 'fear of reactionary' intentions among artisans, 'for which conservatives here bear much of the blame themselves', could be eliminated.[33] Dissatisfaction with August Luthardt and other Bavarian notables had been brewing for some time.[34] Schauensee had just attended a meeting of Conservative delegates in Stuttgart, where 'the lack of an organization and particularly a strong, energetic upper leadership was very evident'. The Nuremberg Conservative *Verein*, chaired by Schauensee, was not willing to nominate Luthardt as a candidate because of his lack of popular appeal. As Schauensee wrote, 'Nothing is served by us having a leader who will not or cannot put himself forward and does not even want to have the leadership in name; although I personally admire and esteem Herr *Regierungsrat* Luthardt, I cannot say I agree with the management of south German Conservatives behind closed doors.'[35]

In June 1881 this impatience with party life in Bavaria was reflected in the new *Wahlverein*'s founding proclamation.[36] Its appeal was directed squarely at artisans and farmers. Significantly, Luthardt was not included in the *Wahlverein*'s seventeen-member executive. This was a socially heterogeneous group which included, on the one hand, most other Bavarian representatives on the first Berlin *Wahlverein* executive and, on the other, a number of members of the Social Conservative Alliance, including Fechenbach, Schauensee, Thüngen-Roßbach and the later Bavarian party chairman, Count Reinhard von Rechteren-Limpurg. By spring 1882 the Bavarian Conservative organization had issued detailed instructions for the establishment of district party *Vereine*, and by the following summer leading Fechenbachians had been appointed to head most of the eight Bavarian district groups.[37] With the development of an organizational structure in their own land, some Bavarian Conservatives inherited Fechenbach's proselytizing fervour. In preparation for a general assembly of south German Conservatives in Würzburg in July 1882, Schauensee had taken up negotiations with his Baden and Württemberg colleagues. In June he reported confidentially to Fechenbach that he planned to propose at the July meeting that southern Conservatives unite more closely. His purpose was unmistakable: 'I believe that through a union of south German elements we are capable of exerting a highly salutary pressure in social-political questions on the north German Conservatives.' The direct link these reformers drew between organizational development and a revision of DKP social policy was also reflected in the proposals for resolutions to be discussed in Würzburg and in the text of the final communiqué. Fechenbach for instance proposed that the Conservatives formulate a positive 'action programme' of Christian social reform to win their independence from the government. He also suggested the establishment of an 'action committee' and a network of 'party agents' to undertake the day-to-day work of party propaganda, including the delivery of public speeches, the expansion of the press, even the dispatch of the committee's paperwork.

Little is known of the proceedings in Würzburg on 31 July 1882.[38] The Würzburg programme reflected the reformers' basic argument that it was the duty of the DKP to undertake social reform in defence of the productive estates and their struggle against 'mobile capital' and Manchesterism. However, the means thereto was now the establishment of artisans' and farmers' associations appealing directly to the material interests of these estates. 'Only thus can the Conservative effort be expected to win for itself the vigour of a people's movement', these reformers believed. By late 1882 Fechenbach was actually more interested in working with the leading German anti-Semites and expanding his Association for the Protection of Artisans than he was with the Conservative Party *per se*. The implicit break with the traditional foundation of Conservative *Vereine* announced at Würzburg began a drift from the DKP which eventually led Fechenbach and Schauensee over to the Centre Party. The subsequent renaissance of well-connected notables within the Bavarian Conservative Party further alienated these men, for it was paradigmatic of what they regarded as the DKP's more general decline under the influence of the Kartell.

In the period 1884–7 a divided response to the Kartell reduced the Bavarian *Wahlverein* to a confused collection of individuals and *Vereine*. The Conservatives' fortunes in Reichstag elections in Bavaria declined precipitously. This, however, never silenced the significant reformist voice of the Conservative press there.[39] By far the most important Conservative Party newspaper in Bavaria in the 1880s was the *Süddeutsche Landpost*, which frequently printed articles from the *Kreuzzeitung*, the *Konservative Monatsschrift* and the *Reichsbote*. By 1889 the *Landpost* was uncompromising in its support for the *Kreuzzeitung* group. In response to reports in Kartell newspapers suggesting that the extreme Conservatives should be amputated from the DKP, the *Landpost* replied that '*history will go in exactly the opposite direction*'. The Conservative Party, it predicted, would indeed split, but those who left would be the 'half-Conservative' advocates of a Bismarckian *Mittelpartei*. The Conservatives who remained would be 'small but – pure of any smack of liberalism'. Thus the Bavarian Conservatives' manifesto for the 1890 Reichstag elections declared that Conservatives could elect 'no liberal, not even a Kartell candidate'.[40] This was not the last time the Bavarian press took up arms against a 'high-and-mighty' Conservative leadership in Berlin.

The Conservatives' first efforts at organization in the Kingdom of Saxony occurred in the wake of the 1848 revolution, when they established a 'Constitutional *Verein*'.[41] By 1871 the Conservatives – including those who called themselves Free Conservatives – had gained 48.7 per cent of votes to the lower house of the Saxon Landtag, and held thirty-seven of seventy-nine seats. Even then, however, the Conservatives felt themselves called upon to ally with the National Liberals at election time, particularly in Dresden, the capital. This Conservative–National Liberal alliance took more concrete form when elements of both groups formed the German *Reichsverein* in Dresden in February 1874. But NLP–Conservative tensions erupted again in the 1877 Reichstag elections. This prompted the Conservatives to form their own Conservative *Landesverein* (state association) for the Kingdom of Saxony on 3 May 1878, although it did not lead them to make any other distinctions between Free Conservatives and German Conservatives.[42] Despite the clear dominance of Conservatism in municipal and state politics, the Conservative *Landesverein* allegedly included only 880 official members in 1882.[43]

In 1883 Friesen took over as chairman of the Saxon Conservatives. His principal colleagues were Ackermann and Ackermann's son-in-law, Paul Mehnert. Mehnert was director of the Saxon Agricultural Credit Association; he also headed the Conservative *Verein* in the city of Dresden after 1887, and later assumed leadership of all Saxon Conservatives. Ackermann's advocacy of artisans' demands produced more resonance in Saxony than in the nation as a whole; but by the end of the 1880s Saxon Conservatives faced the powerful Saxon wing of the Social Democratic Party and some of the most radical anti-Semites in Germany. To combat these enemies, Friesen and his colleagues generally endorsed Kartell politics. They did not, however, advocate a Bismarckian *Mittelpartei*, and both the *Kreuzzeitung* and *Reichsbote* took great satisfaction in citing Friesen's remarks against such a 'mishmash party' in 1888.[44] Nor did the Saxons willingly alienate Stöcker and other anti-Semites who appeared to support the general aims of the Conservative Party.

The social make-up of the Saxon Conservative Party as a whole is impossible to ascertain. However, a study of their forty-seven deputies in the 1887 Landtag reveals a rather different picture than that of Conservatism in east Elbia.[45] In Saxony, few contemporaries called the Conservatives 'Junkers'. Instead, they could be characterized as thoroughly establishment members of a society that had proceeded further down the road to industrialization and urbanization than east Elbia but which lacked the firmer liberal traditions of the south-west German states. Fourteen of the Conservatives' forty-seven deputies in 1887 were elected in urban constituencies. Overall, the ranks of the Conservative Landtag caucus were made up largely of government bureaucrats and other state employees (including school directors and railway engineers) together with estate owners. Most Conservatives in the latter category owned middle-sized holdings, but there were a number of prominent large estate owners as well. The balance of the caucus comprised former army officers, mayors, lawyers, functionaries in agricultural associations and a few factory owners and artisans.

The Conservative press in Saxony was more firmly established than in many other regions of Germany. In 1909 the *Kreuzzeitung* referred to the Saxons' 'agitational press' as exemplary for the party.[46] Of 244 newspapers appearing in the kingdom in 1914, 37 were Conservative; these had a combined circulation of about 205,000, or 13.3 per cent of the total.[47] A relatively large proportion of these newspapers served rural districts, and a remarkably high number of them had been founded long before 1876. None the less, the Saxons' efforts to establish an official party organ in Dresden illustrated the uncertain development of party organization in the 1880s. The most important conservative newspaper in Saxony was the *Dresdner Nachrichten*, whose circulation approached 40,000.[48] However, on the staff of the *Neue Reichszeitung* in Dresden, Ungern-Sternberg and Oertzen struggled to represent reformist Conservatism in competition with this more popular and respectable rival. For the *Dresdner Nachrichten* always offered an uneasy mix of Conservative, Free Conservative, National Liberal and 'official' views. This made it a workable Kartell newspaper, but highly dissatisfying for those Conservatives who wished to stress the independence of the DKP and its regional branches. Thus, when the *Neue Reichszeitung* eventually ceased publication in 1879, the *Sächsischer Volksfreund* was established to replace it. Soon, however, a conflict arose between the *Dresdner Nachrichten*, the *Sächsischer Volksfreund* and the semi-official *Leipziger Zeitung*.[49] This drew the attention of Bismarck and the Prussian envoy in Dresden, Count Carl Dönhoff.

Dönhoff reported that Friesen was an 'extreme Conservative, particularist and pugnacious'. In reply, Bismarck noted that in believing they could pursue their own course independent of the Saxon government, the 'hyper-conservative elements' in the Saxon party presented 'dangers for the development of not only Prussian but also Reich politics that could not be underestimated'. The chancellor therefore exerted pressure on Friesen to express more enthusiasm for the Kartell. The official disfavour into which the *Sächsischer Volksfreund* subsequently fell was fatal. It ceased publication in May 1884. A few years later a less controversial party news-sheet – eventually named *Das Vaterland* – was established; it served Saxon Conservatives throughout the rest of the Second Reich.

The liberal traditions which delayed the expansion of the Conservative Party into south-west Germany were alluded to by the Württemberg *Staats-Anzeiger* in 1857: 'The conservative man certainly wants no revolution, but he wants to have an outlook that is liberal and progressive, liberal-conservative, anything but reactionary.'[50] No true Conservative movement existed in Württemberg until 1876. In the previous decade the offshoot of the National Liberal Party, the German Party, had rallied all right-wing elements against the regional representative of the Progressives, the German People's Party.[51] When the DKP was founded nationally, however, Württemberg Conservatives responded. The *Süddeutsche Reichspost* was moved to Frankfurt and renamed the *Deutsche Reichspost* in 1876. There it served as the leading Conservative newspaper for Württemberg and Hesse.[52] The *Reichspost* launched a campaign against local National Liberals and Free Conservatives symptomatic of the larger reformist campaign against the national Kartell. This naturally alienated some members of the German Party, but it also drew over a number of men who were willing to follow the DKP programme. In the Württemberg Landtag elections of December 1876, these Conservatives attempted to elect one of their number in Stuttgart; but all they achieved was to force a run-off election between candidates of the SPD and the German Party. After similar disappointments in the Reichstag elections of July 1878, the Conservatives realized that they could not make their way in Württemberg in direct competition with the German Party. By 1882 the two organizations shared an office in Stuttgart, and in elections to the municipal council there, ten of twelve candidates advanced by the two parties appeared on both electoral lists.[53] By 1884 the DKP had established separate *Vereine* in only four cities in the state: Stuttgart, Heilbronn, Hall and Besigheim. This illustrated that conflicts between different shades of 'nationalists' were being avoided at the cost of further DKP organization.

The Conservative press in Württemberg presented a somewhat brighter picture.[54] The *Evangelisches Sonntagsblatt* and another Sunday journal enjoyed relatively high circulations, the former estimated at over 115,000.

The *Stuttgarter Neue Bürgerzeitung* was taken over by the Conservatives in 1877, but it survived less than eighteen months. This left the Conservatives without a party organ in Stuttgart until the *Deutsche Reichspost* was relocated there in October 1880.

In 1879 the *Reichspost* was edited by Perrot, who (like Engel) grafted an attack on Jewish capitalism on to Conservatism's larger, traditional political goals. This campaign alienated some Conservatives; Oertzen, for instance, regretted that Perrot became so consumed by this struggle. But these polemics surely had an effect on the Conservatives in Württemberg who relied on the *Reichspost* for their information and entertainment. The organization of the party itself in south-west Germany was tied up with the larger view of society and politics which Perrot and his successors painted in such anti-Semitic hues. When the Conservatives from Baden, Württemberg and Bavaria met in Ansbach in May 1880, the *Reichspost* highlighted their attempt to give their assembly the character of a 'people's meeting' by citing the attendance of 'all classes', even the 'most simple worker'. This search for mass appeal was linked to another kind of popularity which the speakers tried to win through their emphasis on Conservatism's anti-Semitic, Christian and social message. In the five main programmatic speeches at this conference, the Bavarian Conservative leader, Friedrich Pfaff, spoke on the 'Christian state'; Thüngen-Roßbach spoke on usury; Perrot spoke on the stock exchange; and two others spoke on artisans' demands and the party press.[55] Each of these speeches contained obvious references to the Jewish threat. Perhaps most important of all, the *Reichspost* kept the Conservatives' quest for popularity alive. In late 1880 it summed up its programme for injecting a new spirit into the Conservative Party:[56]

> If parliamentary parties, which are elected through the universal franchise by the entire people, want to succeed, they have no choice but to go among the people, to make themselves known to them ... Nothing is accomplished with a reserved, temporizing, supposedly clever attitude. The people do not want to see only wrinkled brows, they want to hear warm words that come from the heart ... We therefore call on the Conservative Party: Step lively! Get up to date! Trust in the people, and you will win trust from them!

Probably nowhere else does the struggle of the 'Conservative as outsider' become more clear than in the history of the Baden Conservative Party.[57] In the 1860s and 1870s liberals and Catholics vied for control of the state bureaucracy, thereby establishing the basic political and religious divisions which coloured Baden politics throughout the Second Reich.[58] The sole Protestant conservative elected in 1868 was Göler von Ravensburg, who already sat in the upper chamber of the Baden Landtag. Göler stepped

aside to let Prince Wilhelm of Baden, the grand duke's brother, take over
this seat in 1871. (Although Wilhelm joined the Free Conservative caucus
in the Reichstag, his sympathies were understood to lie with Baden
Conservatives in general.) When the DKP expanded nationally in 1876
Göler became first chairman of the Baden Conservative Party. He also
represented another Reichstag constituency for the Conservatives
between 1881 and 1887. Other regional Conservative leaders who helped
shape the character of the party in these years were Mühlhäußer, whose
lifelong interests included the Inner Mission, the Protestant press and
conservative theology;[59] Adolf Hermann Marschall von Bieberstein, who
later served as Foreign Secretary under Chancellor Leo von Caprivi;
Count Wilhelm von Douglas, owner of the estate of Gondelsheim and
Reichstag deputy after 1888; and Barons Emil and Otto von Stockhorn.
Emil von Stockhorn took over from Göler as regional party chairman in
1885.

The Baden Conservative Party's electoral propaganda from the early
1880s reflected the difficulties inherent in its position between the far more
influential National Liberals and the 'Catholic People's Party', as the
regional variant of the Centre Party was called. The Conservatives' official
campaign flyer in 1881 presented a programme that was remarkably
defensive; it claimed the Conservatives would be 'unswayed by attacks
from the opposition [or] by artificially reinforced prejudices', and that
they would not be a 'sticking shoe' in the constitutional state.[60] Like the
National Liberals, Göler and colleagues rejected any particularist sympathies entertained by the Catholics; but like the Centre, they advocated the
perpetuation of the protectionist economic system erected by their
national leaders in 1879. They also favoured protection for artisans and
measures to overcome the 'dominance of capital'. Between the late 1870s
and 1887 the Catholics supported Conservative candidacies in a number of
Baden constituencies, for both Reichstag and Landtag elections. After
1887, however, Theodor Wacker led the Baden Catholics towards a closer
alliance with the left-liberals, until the Grand Bloc changed these relationships once again in 1905. Meanwhile Göler, who had always tended
toward Free Conservative or governmental views, was rather unceremoni-
ously deprived of his chairmanship in 1885. This allowed the Stockhorns
and their successors to steer the Conservatives into more agrarian,
oppositional channels in the 1890s. Otto von Stockhorn's many years of
service as Baden correspondent for the *Kreuzzeitung* only added to the
influence of this less governmental wing.

The Baden Conservatives had virtually none of the institutional support
which their Prussian comrades received from local administrators, judicial
officials, or royal patrons. When one compares an account of political life
under the 'yoke' of liberalism which Göler published in the *Konservative
Monatsschrift* in 1883 with a personal memoir Otto von Stockhorn drafted

in 1916, one sees the persistent effects of the prejudice and intimidation to which Conservatives were subjected by members of the Baden establishment.[61] These recriminations included disciplinary measures and involuntary transfers for any Conservatives who happened to be state officials; requests from the Ministry of the Interior (citing the anti-Socialist laws!) for membership lists of veterans' associations founded under Conservative auspices; court proceedings (usually unsuccessful) against Conservative newspapers; and public defamation or personal insult when Conservatives acknowledged their ties to Catholic allies. In such instances Conservatives were labelled 'Jesuit dogs' and 'enemies of the Reich',[62] although Otto von Stockhorn on one occasion was also called 'an orthodox-pietist full-blooded Junker'. When Marschall ran for election in a constituency that had suffered disaster due to Rhine floods, the state commissar for the district let it be known that relief funds would be cut off for any towns that voted Conservative. And when Prince Wilhelm became a conservative candidate, the official press launched a swingeing attack on him and called his supporters 'traitors to the fatherland, Social Democrats and assassins'. Election day came, and officials helped organize great 'hurrahs' in every village that voted for the liberal candidate, while in those that cast a majority of their ballots for the brother of the grand duke this conservative statement was greeted with 'pfuis' and grunts. It is understandable, then, that Otto von Stockhorn's impression of the Baden bureaucracy was extremely negative. He referred to it as pedantic, ill-trained and undisciplined, especially in comparison with Prussian officialdom. He also wrote that the liberal spirit in Baden and the actions of these officials made it easy for them to win favour among the 'circle of notables [in] our little official towns'. These men made political decisions in an atmosphere of 'beer and tobacco' and were fundamentally indifferent to religious principle.

The Conservatives in Baden never succeeded in breaking down their image as haughty aristocrats in the 1880s.[63] Otto von Stockhorn once had to compose an electoral flyer denying that he had remarked that 'with me, humanity begins at the level of baron'. Stockhorn attempted to break the mould of this exclusivity by establishing farmers' associations (*Bauernvereine*) in a number of districts of Baden in the early 1880s. According to his own account he succeeded in founding six such organizations. However, he also discovered that a liberal official followed him on his rural rides and warned farmers against the Conservative nobleman who made bread more expensive and taxed other consumer goods. The efforts of independent anti-Semites in the state, building on enthusiasm for Stöcker in the early 1880s, produced equally insignificant results before 1890.[64]

Finally, the official Conservative press in Baden was anything but impressive. When the Prussian envoy in Karlsruhe, Carl von Eisendecher, reported to Bismarck in 1889 about political newspapers in the state,[65] he noted that the Conservative Party, 'weak and without influence' except in alliance with the other parties, had only the *Badische Landpost* in Karlsruhe, which 'from time to time' brought forth 'good, reasonable' articles.[66] The *Landpost*, however, also illustrated that it took second place to no Conservative newspaper in the vigour with which it pressed the campaign against the Jews. In February 1880 it declared:[67]

> The Jews have our *finances* in their hands, the Jews have our *newspapers* in their hands, the Jews have our *trade* in their hands, the Jews have our *farmers* – in their pockets. In a word, the Jews have won superiority in our whole political and social life. That is the situation. How are we once again to escape it? That is the question, that is the Jewish question.

The Conservatives exactly doubled their Reichstag representation between 1877 and 1887, from forty to eighty seats, while their share of the popular vote also rose dramatically. In the Prussian Landtag their seats rose from 41 in 1876 to 129 in 1888. Even in the Saxon House of Deputies, with eighty available seats, Conservatives increased the number in their caucus from thirty-seven in 1877 to forty-eight in 1889. The significance of these statistics, however, cannot be appreciated without considering two other factors: first, the relative success of other parties, especially the National Liberals and Free Conservatives; and second, the disparity between the Conservative share of the vote won in different regions of the Reich. These factors help explain why young DKP organizations in many areas were frustrated by Helldorff's Kartell policy in the Reichstag elections of 1884 and 1887. In the eastern provinces of Prussia and in the Kingdom of Saxony, these elections saw the Conservatives win an increasing number of seats in alliance with their Kartell partners. Not surprisingly, Conservatives in the east tended to extol the virtues of Bismarck's Kartell. Either they saw their vote increase significantly, as in East Prussia and Mecklenburg, or they found that a relatively constant share of the vote resulted in an increase in the number of deputies elected, as in the Kingdom of Saxony. On the other hand, Conservatives in Berlin and in a number of middle German and west German regions saw their own election fortunes decline after 1881, while those of the National Liberals and Free Conservatives rose swiftly. The areas of Thuringia, Middle Franconia (and Bavaria as a whole), Hesse, Württemberg, Hanover and Schleswig-Holstein illustrated this development most clearly. Of the thirty seats gained by the DKP between 1881 and 1887, all but three were in Prussia, Saxony and Mecklenburg. Any claim of a roughly equitable trade-off of Kartell constituencies across Germany offered western Conservatives little comfort, especially when they could point to increases of 30 and 50 per cent in the share of the vote won by the FKP and NLP respectively, while the Conservative share shrank. For reform-minded activists, electoral defeat made immeasurably more bitter the formula of organizational neglect and 'unprincipled' Bismarckian policies dispensed by Helldorff.

The failure of *Kreuzzeitung*-group leaders to win over the majority of Conservative parliamentarians for their anti-liberal policies and their anti-Bismarck intrigues disheartened provincial activists further. The majority of Conservatives believed, as Fechenbach's correspondents suggested, that the Conservative Party in the 1880s was still 'too young' and 'too weak' to mount determined anti-liberal or anti-Bismarck campaigns. Again and again, Conservative leaders claimed that rank-and-file members first had to overcome their fears, their shyness, and their lack of solidarity. These leaders therefore pursued practical politics acceptable to Bismarck and his other supporters. Conversely, dissidents found themselves stifled by the pressure to work with other anti-Socialist parties, unable to acknowledge the wider implications of their pro-Centre Christian position and afraid to jeopardize their personal careers should their radicalism overstep the bounds of political convention. Eventually even Conservative dissidents were compelled to recognize how strongly traditionalism lived on within party ranks. Hermann Lange, the editor of the Conservatives' *Kasseler Journal*, had already come to this conclusion when he wrote to Fechenbach in 1885. Intending only to excuse his own ambivalence and to warn Fechenbach that radical programme reform could not succeed in the Conservative Party, Lange summed up the situation for all would-be reformers of the DKP at the time:[68]

In old Prussia, the people, always casting their eyes upward, are not yet so far progressed that they can rally themselves around a party programme or be led in *opposition* to a Bismarck . . . We true Conservatives have only the choice, either withdraw completely from the political arena, in that we declare war on Bismarck, or we fall in with the man, for better or worse, and do as much good as possible.

NOTES

1 Certain arguments in this chapter were first worked out in my unpublished essay, 'Blue and Gold: Conservative Propagandists, the "Jewish International" and Regional Politics in Germany, 1871–1900'.

2 See above, Chapter 3.

3 Undated notes, Sg F, '1888' (original emphasis).

4 Cf. *NDB*, Vol. 5, pp. 36 f.; Schoeps, 'CDU'; Volkov, *Rise*, pp. 224–8; Anderson, *Windthorst*, pp. 252–9, 449–52; and Fechenbach's own writings. Unless otherwise noted, all the following correspondence is from the years 1880–2 and is found in BAK, NL F, 28, 38, 91, 123, 143, 70 and 76, and Sg F, '1888'; detailed references in my 'Reformist Conservatism', ch. 2.

5 Hammerstein was correct; one leading Conservative had disparaged the CSP with the words: 'We are all Christian, and "social" belongs before the state prosecutor!'

6   'Protocoll der social-politischen Versammlung zur Beratung des Programms von 30. Juli 1880 ... am 10. November 1880'; Schoeps, 'CDU'; Curtius, *Weg*; ZStA I, NL Wagener, 30, f. 32, 'Denkschrift in Sachen der social-conservativen Bestrebungen' (27.3.81); Wagener to Meyer, 26.1.81, in Meyer, *Hundert Jahre*, p. 301; and Stöcker, cited in Schoeps, 'CDU', p. 271.

7   *Rb*, 26.11.80; *SchlMbl*, 25.2.81, 4–9.11.81; *Deutsche Landes-Zeitung*, 7.12.80; further references in my 'Reformist Conservatism', p. 75.

8   For further critiques of Conservative politics in these years see the 'Letter from the West' in *KM*, 40 (2), 1883, pp. 124–8; Lagarde, *Programm für die konservative Partei Preußens* (1884); Vater, *Zur Organisation der konservativen Partei in Preußen* (1887); and *Konservative Presse* (1885), pp. 12–16, 25, 39–43; all discussed in my 'Reformist Conservatism', pp. 75–82.

9   See Oertzen, 'Erinnerungen'; Oertzen, *Erinnerungen*; Oertzen, *Von Wichern*.

10 Obituary in *Rb*, 6.9.11; Oertzen, *Erinnerungen*, pp. 182–8.

11 Cf. Martin von Nathusius, 'Zur Geschichte der Monatsschrift', *KM*, 38 (2), 1881, pp. 242–5; Ulrich von Hassell, '75 Jahre. Zur Geschichte der Konservativen Monatsschrift. 1843–1917', *KM*, 75 (1), October–November 1917, pp. 48–53, 130–8; U. von Hassell, 'Martin von Nathusius', *KM*, 63 (7), April 1906, pp. 665–8.

12 M. von Nathusius, 'Conservativ', *KM*, 37, 1880, pp. 1–15; Oertzen, 'Die gegenwärtigen Parteien', *KM*, 38, 1881, pp. 261–76; Oertzen, 'Wahlreform', *KM*, 39, 1882, pp. 134–7; M. von Nathusius, 'Culturkampf und Conservative', ibid., pp. 406–21; E.K., 'Ein conservatives Programm', ibid., pp. 81–9.

13 *DAB*, 24.2.84; Fricke and Rößling, 'Adelsgenossenschaft'.

14 Fricke and Rößling, 'Adelsgenossenschaft', p. 530; *DAB*, 19.10.90, 30.11.90.

15 *DAB*, 30.3.84, and other membership lists.

16 *DAB*, 3.8.84, 11.1.85, 8.3.85, 18.12.87, 8.1.88, 8.6.90.

17 *DAB*, 26.4.85–17.5.85, 'Semitismus und Adel'; *DAB*, 27.6.86–18.7.86.

18 *DAB*, 7.12.84, 18.10.85–1.11.85; cf. Uechtritz, *Adel*, pp. 11 ff.; *DAB*, 8/22.8.86.

19 See Fischer-Frauendienst, *Bismarcks Pressepolitik*, pp. 69 ff.; cf. 'Verein zur Verbreitung konservativer Zeitschriften', circular, printed in *BT*, 30.9.92.

20 Cf. the Vaterland-Verein's *Zeitfragen* (1896), esp. pp. 59 ff.; ZStA II, Rep. 77, CB S, 126, Vol. 1, including *Senfkorn* and *Mitteilungen des Christlichen Zeitschriftenvereins*; Saul, 'Staat', pp. 336 ff.

21 *NWVZ*, 8.9.77; cf. Mehnert, *Evangelische Presse*; Werner, *Protestantismus*; Grisshammer, *Konservative Politik*.

22 *Sammlung von Vorträgen für das deutsche Volk* and *Zeitfragen des christlichen Volkslebens*.

23 For the following see Oertzen, 'Conservative Presse', *KM*, 39, 1882, pp. 55–9; Oertzen, 'Erinnerungen'; Oertzen, *Erinnerungen*, especially pp. 68–126.

24 Speech to a rally in Stuttgart, 1.4.81, cited in Massing, *Rehearsal*, pp. 27 f.

25 For a different perspective see Stark, *Entrepreneurs*.

26 Stratz, *Schwert*, p. 213; cf. Huber, 'Konservative Presse' (1846), especially p. 229; Rieger, *Presse*, p. 113.

27 Cf. *Konservatives Handbuch* (1894), 'Presse', pp. 297–300; DKP *Ratgeber* [1903], p. 49.

28 Oertzen, *Erinnerungen*, p. 125 (original emphasis).

29 Cf. Nipperdey, *Organisation*, pp. 242 ff.

30 As in Silesia: *SchlMbl*, *Probenummer* (22.11.79), *Jubiläums-Nummer* (1.12.04), *Aufruf* (1.10.80) and comments at the first congress (22.10.80) in *SchlMbl*, 1.9.04; cf. Klawitter, *Zeitungen Schlesiens*; Pittius, 'Tagespresse Schlesiens'.

31 See Thränhardt, *Wahlen*, pp. 63–8, 90 f.; Fenske, *Konservatismus*, pp. 31–4; Möckl, *Prinzregentenzeit*, pp. 213, 532. Middle Franconia's population was 76 per cent Protestant in 1880.

32 PA AA Bonn, I A Bayern 50, Vol. 3, Werthern to Bismarck, 5.3.81.; for the following, ibid., Hugo von Lerchenfeld to ?, 5.4.81., and [Reich chancellery] to Wilhelm I, 6.4.81.

33 BAK, NL F, 52, Schauensee to Fechenbach, 12.1.81; the following correspondence is also from this file.

34 Biographies of the seven Conservative LT deputies are in *Almanach für den Bayerischen Landtag*, (1881), pp. 82–93. These men's occupations were: bookseller, manufacturer/ retailer, farmer/Landrat, architect/master-builder, weaving mill owner, tenant farmer/

mayor and government councillor (Luthardt). Unfortunately Luthardt's illuminating memoir, *Mein Werden und Wirken*, was unavailable when this chapter was drafted.

35 Schauensee to Fechenbach, 28.10.81.
36 Founded 13.6.81; *Aufruf* in Sg F, '1888'.
37 Ibid., Schauensee to Fechenbach, 3.10.81; 'Wahlverein der bayerischen Conservativen, Direktiven für die Herren Bezirks-Vorstände', 25.3.82; *Wahlverein* circular, 1.5.82; cf. NL F, 52, Schauensee to Fechenbach, 29.12.83; 'Statut des Wahlvereins der bayrischen Conservativen' (Ansbach, 1881); Schauensee to Fechenbach, 9.6.82, and documents in Sg F, '1888'.
38 BAK, Sg F, '1888', Schauensee to Fechenbach, 26.8.82; 'Beschlüsse der konservativen Versammlung in Würzburg', Sg F, XXII, folder '1880/82'; Fechenbach, *Fürst Bismarck*, pp. 192 ff.
39 *Publicistik der Gegenwart – Bayern*, pp. 227, 248 f., 295 f., 331.
40 *SddLp*, 4.5.89, 12.10.89 (original emphasis), 22.10.89, 14.11.89; 'Aufruf', 23.1.90; 'Wahlaufruf', 6.2.90.
41 Holldack, 'Geschichte', pp. 13 f., 42–5; for the following see Richter, *Geschichte*, pp. 6–17, 58–62.
42 The first clear sign of a DKP–FKP split in Saxony came in 1892; *Rb*, 27.4.92.
43 *NAZ*, 2.4.82, cited in Nipperdey, *Organisation*, p. 250.
44 *KZ*, 31.7.88; *Rb*, 31.7.88.
45 *Sächsischer Landtags-Almanach* (1887), pp. 63–81.
46 *KZ*, 1.8.09.
47 Burkhardt, 'Tagespresse Sachsens', pp. 38–49. The circulation of eight FKP newspapers was estimated at 80,000.
48 Cf. *Jubiläums-Beilage* to the *DresdN*, 1.10.06.
49 See reports in PA AA Bonn, I A Königreich Sachsen 50, Vol. 1, Dönhoff to Bismarck, 5.1.81, 12.2.82, 24.3.83, 25.2.84; [Bismarck] to Dönhoff, 7.4.83.
50 *Staats-Anzeiger für Württemberg*, 8/9.10.57, p. 2030.
51 For this and the following, *PrJbb*, 54 (1), 1884, pp. 85–91, 'Die Parteien in Württemberg'.
52 'An die Anhänger des deutsch-konservativen Programms in Süd- und Mittel-Deutschland', Frankfurt a.M., August 1877.
53 *DtRp*, 11.6.82.
54 Plieninger, 'Württembergische Presse', pp. 1–15, 55 ff. and *passim*; Groth, 'Presse Württembergs', p. 106.
55 Complete texts in *DtRp*, 21.5.80–4.6.80.
56 *DtRp*, 3.10.80.
57 At this point I can gratefully acknowledge the assistance and advice of Hans-Jürgen Kremer, who provided me with correspondence from the Stockhorn Nachlaß and other materials in the GLA Karlsruhe.
58 See Dreher, 'Anfänge'; Göler, 'Die liberale Ära in Baden', *KM*, 40, 1883, pp. 117–34; Gall, 'Problematik'.
59 See Schmidt, 'Mühlhäußer'; Ungern-Sternberg, 'Zum 20. Januar', *KM*, 38, 1881, pp. 62–7.
60 GLA Karlsruhe, NL Stockhorn, 69h/133, 'Wahlprogramm der deutsch-konservativen Partei Badens' (September 1881); cf. 'Wahl-Aufruf' (1878) and 'An die badischen Reichstagswähler' (1881).
61 For the following, see Göler, 'Die liberale Ära in Baden', *KM*, 40, 1883, esp. pp. 125 ff., and GLA Karlsruhe, NL Stockhorn, 69h/146, 'Der Konservatismus in Baden bis 1916' (draft) [1916].
62 Cf. *BadP*, 18.10.05, 'Konservativ', for a longer list of such epithets.
63 Cf. Längin, *Charakteristik*, p. 4; Gageur, *Reform*, pp. 17 f.
64 Jacoby, *Antisemitische Bewegung*, pp. 5–7.
65 PA AA Bonn, I A Baden 33, Vol. 2, Eisendecher to Bismarck, 13.7.89; H.-J. Kremer kindly provided me with a copy of this correspondence.
66 Cf. *Publicistik der Gegenwart – Baden*, pp. 63, 84.
67 *BadLp*, 24.2.80 (original emphasis).
68 BAK, Sg F, II, 327, Lange to Fechenbach, 1.11.85 (original emphasis).

PART II

Rebellion and Reaction, 1890–6

6

The Attack on the Politics of Notables

The development of a basic Conservative antipathy to the policies of the 'New Course' under Chancellor Caprivi was a necessary but not sufficient condition for the party revolt against Helldorff in 1892. In that year a campaign was launched for a thoroughgoing reform of the DKP's programme, organization and agitational style. The inclusion of anti-Semitism in the party's programme was the focus of this break with traditionalism. The Tivoli congress in December 1892 provided a vitally important victory for the anti-Semitic reformers who had been struggling for a hearing within the party since the 1870s. However, the rebels' assault on the prerogatives of the party leadership extended far beyond the Jewish question.[1]

A struggle for control of the Conservative press marked one of the most important areas of conflict between Helldorff and the *Kreuzzeitung* group around 1890. The fate of the *Wahlverein*'s first weekly newspaper, *Der Deutsche Patriot*, is uncertain, but it was hardly likely to impress reformist editors. The *Deutsche Patriot* published its first edition in early July 1881.[2] It was explicitly calculated to have popular appeal, as Helldorff reported to Bismarck; it declared itself the 'true friend of the people' and promised 'all classes' that better times were just around the corner. However, Helldorff does not appear to have sustained his newspaper beyond the election campaign; mainly for lack of money, the *Deutsche Patriot* died on the vine. Through the 1880s Helldorff relied instead on the party's official *Conservative Correspondenz*. Martin Griesemann, later editor of the *Norddeutsche Allgemeine Zeitung*, generally held in check his co-editor, Ungern-Sternberg, and distributed Helldorff's line to over two hundred more of less Conservative newspapers.[3] Helldorff also enjoyed access to the explicitly Bismarckian *Deutsches Tageblatt*, which gradually distanced itself from Stöcker's following in Berlin. By the end of the 1880s it was regarded as another leading Kartell newspaper.

In reaction, provincial Conservative organs became increasingly eager to assert their independence. Oertzen and other editors tried to express their dissatisfaction with the party leadership in periodic meetings with their Conservative colleagues. Some provincial Conservative leaders also began to reconsider the style of politics practised by Helldorff, and they tried to restructure the decision-making apparatus of the Conservative

Party. In March 1888 the *Neue Westfälische Volkszeitung*, now edited by Lange, contrasted Conservatives' 'political awareness' in the east and west of Germany, seeking to explain the reasons for a Conservative defeat in a recent by-election in Pomerania.[4] The lack of organization and discipline in local Conservative politics in the east came in for criticism, as did those governmental Conservatives whose lethargy had contributed to the defeat. In Minden-Ravensberg, the *Volkszeitung* claimed, a man knew why he was Conservative, but not in the east; there, 'the "respectable gentleman" have the election in hand; Conservative rallies have only a negative effect . . . But what happens when the influence of the "respectable gentlemen" breaks down due to unforeseen events? Then even the most secure constituency is lost in a trice.' When Helldorff noted later in the same year that no money flowed from the provinces to support the *Conservative Correspondenz*, the Conservatives in Minden-Ravensberg launched a campaign against Griesemann, demanding his removal. When the *Conservative Correspondenz* editorialized in July 1888 about the low level of Conservative activity in the province of Hanover, the DKP's *Hannoversche Post* offered a bitter rebuttal. Engel wrote in the *Reichsbote* in November 1888 that the Conservative Party in parliament needed more deputies from Saxony, Hesse and southern Germany to avoid 'onesidedness' and to win 'new strength and fresh blood'.[5]

Another internal party development helped compensate for *Kreuzzeitung*-group set-backs in the public sphere. In the executive meeting of the DKP *Wahlverein* on 31 January/1 February 1889, dissidents demanded that Helldorff's control of the Conservative Party be circumscribed by the establishment of a 'managing committee' to co-ordinate the party's parliamentary activity and shaping of policy. Of this new body's nine members, Helldorff wanted five – a majority – to be chosen from the DKP's Reichstag caucus. Hammerstein, however, appealed against this plan. He helped institute instead the 'Committee of Eleven', with four members from the Reichstag, three each from the Prussian Herrenhaus and House of Deputies and one from the Kingdom of Saxony. Thus the less governmental representatives in the Prussian Landtag denied the Reichstag caucus a dominating influence in the party's top decisionmaking body. Around the same time the Westphalian Ultra, Reck, introduced an executive motion to stop Griesemann from continuing his polemics against the *Kreuzzeitung*. When this proposal passed, the *Conservative Correspondenz* was effectively reduced to a parliamentary reporter.[6]

In the six months leading to the February 1890 Reichstag elections which wrecked the Kartell and precipitated Bismarck's fall from power, this lack of a coherent DKP leadership had important consequences on both the party and national levels. In a number of ways Hammerstein helped focus the dissatisfaction with Bismarck which was growing not only among various political groups but also in the mind of the young Kaiser.[7] These crises were deepened by three internal DKP developments: (1) the *Kreuzzeitung*-group revolt led by Puttkamer-Plauth, who insisted (despite Helldorff's frenzied attempts at compromise) on such an extreme new anti-Socialist bill in January 1890 that no agreement between the Kartell parties was possible; (2) the controversy over Hammerstein's Reichstag candidacy in Bielefeld, which further sharpened conflicts within the Kartell and between Wilhelm and Bismarck; and (3) new proposals for a Conservative–Centre alliance against the 'middle parties', which fuelled rumours surrounding the chancellor's planned course after the 20 February elections. Without these direct consequences of the struggle for leadership within the Conservative Party, Berlin politics in early 1890 might have taken a very different course.

During the 1890 Reichstag campaign reformist Conservatives chafed under the Kartell yoke. As dissent began to turn into open rebellion, *Kreuzzeitung*-group editors looked not only to Hammerstein and Engel for leadership but now also to the co-editors of the new Christian Social newspaper founded in late 1888, *Das Volk*. Thanks to a large donation from an anonymous patron, the CSP had finally established its own official organ under the guidance of Hellmut von Gerlach and Heinrich Oberwinder.[8] Resignations from Conservative *Vereine* and protests against the Kartell were given special attention in the *Volk*, the *Reichsbote* and the *Kreuzzeitung*. The *Neue Westfälische Volkszeitung* asserted that Westphalian Conservatives, defending Christian principles against the liberal onslaught, would 'never lay down their weapons'. Similar sentiments were expressed in Bavaria, Hanover, Silesia and East Prussia. There was talk in Mecklenburg of founding a new party which would secede, 'to the right', from the Conservative Party.[9]

Just as the Kartell was breaking down and as Conservative–Centre affinities were being publicly reviewed, the publication of the Kaiser's two proclamations (*Erlasse*) in favour of social reform in early February 1890 gave a strong impetus to the *Kreuzzeitung* group's claim for leadership in the Conservative Party.[10] Hammerstein and Stöcker cited their own past reform proposals as evidence that they best understood the Kaiser's thoughts. In their view, king and Conservatives together could bypass parliament, Bismarck and the Kartell, to inaugurate a new form of 'social royalism'.[11] Immediately after the Reichstag elections, Hammerstein pressed the anti-Kartell line. Stöcker used post-election circumstances as an excuse to re-enter public life, while the Berlin *Bürgervereine* sent addresses to the Kaiser expressing enthusiasm for his social policy. When Bismarck fell from power on 20 March 1890, the Christian Socials proclaimed 'the dawn of a new era'. In mid-April, Stöcker rejoiced that 'the world has become Christian Social overnight!'[12]

These developments widened the split in the Conservative Party. Helldorff, whose reputation had suffered even among party notables because he had not been privy to Bismarck's counsel on the Anti-Socialist Bill,[13] was put on the defensive by the Kaiser's proclamations. He repeatedly warned against too much enthusiasm or overdue haste in carrying out the Kaiser's plans on the workers' question, since they required 'cautious and sensible' consideration, not 'headlong advance with a few slogans and cheers'.[14] The *Kreuzzeitung* group, on the other hand, kept pressing ahead. Fechenbach's book on the Kaiser's proclamations was praised in the *Kreuzzeitung*, the *Volk* and the *Neue Westfälische Volkszeitung*, while Oberwinder observed that the *Volk*'s new popularity would help support 'a social-monarchical party organization that will astound Herr v. Helldorff and colleagues'.[15] In line with Oberwinder's boast, Christian Social initiatives in 1890 included the founding of the Protestant Social Congress on 28 April; the founding of a union of Protestant Workers' Associations under Ludwig Weber on 6 August; the founding of a 'Social Monarchical Union' on 22 November;[16] the founding of a weekly journal, the *Deutsche Post*, described as a 'Christian Conservative family newspaper';[17] and an attempt by Pastor Hermann Dietz of Bielefeld to establish a network of 'German *Volksvereine*' to advance social reform. The *Conservative Correspondenz* called on Conservatives to oppose these efforts, and this advice was followed by enough party members that most of these projects never got off the ground. However, the reformers were heartened that the Supreme Protestant Consistory seemed to look favourably upon such activity by Conservative pastors.[18]

Through much of 1890 there existed a kind of truce between Hammerstein and Helldorff. That few initiatives from either side sought to undermine the other's position indicated the new legitimacy won by the *Kreuzzeitung* group. Helldorff in any case could not have found it easy to transfer his allegiance from Bismarck to the Kaiser and Caprivi, even though he did so with immodest haste after Bismarck moved into opposition to the New Course. The Christian Socials suffered a set-back when the Kaiser decided in November 1890 that Stöcker's political activity was no longer compatible with his pastoral responsibilities and asked for his resignation as court preacher. In 1891, however, the Conservative Party's growing opposition to Caprivi offered more opportunities to criticize Helldorff's vacillating, governmental stance. Professor Theodor Schiemann, who at this time was in the midst of taking over from Ungern-Sternberg as the writer of weekly reviews on foreign policy for the *Kreuzzeitung*, documented the growth of this antagonism within the party in his diary.[19] Schiemann reported in December 1890 that the Conservatives felt no area of public affairs was immune from Caprivi's reforming ambitions. This had not only greatly increased their willingness to oppose the Kaiser and the government, but had also heightened their fears that German politics stood at a decisive turning-point. By February 1891 Helldorff was being attacked by Mirbach and others in the inner councils of the Conservative Party, and only Bismarck's careful refusal to put anything in writing stopped Hammerstein from making public his indirect intrigues with Friedrichsruh. This antagonism towards Helldorff increased when Caprivi introduced his Rural Government Bill (*Landgemeindeordnung*) in 1891.[20] Although at first all Conservatives could unite against the government's plan to reduce the local prerogatives of Junker estate owners in the eastern provinces of Prussia, by April 1891 oppositional elements in the DKP were protesting Helldorff's personal dominance in policy-making for the party.[21] The final passage of the bill in June was a defeat for the Conservative Ultras, and came about in part because Helldorff had been appointed to the Herrenhaus in 1890. There, as Kleist-Retzow reported, he had acted like a 'volunteer government commission'. Hammerstein successfully played down this defeat for his group, but Rauchhaupt told Helldorff he would no longer work with him, and he wrote to Hammerstein in October: 'Bismarck is right, we are heading for a catastrophe.'

One important reason why Hammerstein's defeat on the Rural Government Bill did not vault Helldorff back into the unchallenged leadership of the party was that, concurrent with this legislation, another press war was raging within the DKP. In March 1891 the *Kreuzzeitung* suddenly bought out Helldorff's *Deutsches Tageblatt* and immediately announced that it would cease publication; Conservative readers were urged to switch their subscriptions to the *Kreuzzeitung*. There was more than a hint of scandal associated with this transaction, and Hammerstein was not universally backed in his unexpected manoeuvre.[22] But after the announcement that the *Deutsches Tageblatt* would be discontinued, Schiemann wrote: 'It is now a fact that Helldorff is silenced and Hammerstein stands as the stronger one. I now have reason to assume that Caprivi will make the attempt to find a *modus vivendi* with him [Hammerstein], and that would mean a change in the position of the Conservative Party.'[23]

Helldorff's isolation became more apparent through 1891 as he came into conflict with Hammerstein and other party leaders over colonial policy, Conservative by-election campaigns and relations with Caprivi's administration in general. Speculation appeared in other parties' newspapers about whether the DKP would split, with governmental moderates moving to join the Free Conservative Party. Such talk was increased when the Conservatives could not agree on a united policy for or against Caprivi's first major trade treaty, with Austria-Hungary, which passed the Reichstag in December 1891.[24] Because grain prices at the time were still high due to two successive bad harvests, many Conservatives had no objection to the reduced agricultural tariffs included in the legislation. But when the *Conservative Correspondenz* published an article in favour of the treaty, *Kreuzzeitung* protests forced the editors to admit that this was not an official party statement; a majority of the DKP Reichstag caucus had, in fact, voted against the treaty. Hammerstein replied that this retraction was not sufficient, and demanded changes in the press committee that oversaw the *Correspondenz*.[25]

Unfortunately for Helldorff, the crisis which Rauchhaupt had predicted in late 1891 came very quickly on the heels of the Austrian trade treaty. A Prussian School Bill was introduced in the Landtag in late January 1892 by the Minister for Cultural and Ecclesiastical Affairs, Count Robert von Zedlitz-Trützschler.[26] With this bill Caprivi explicitly calculated he could win the united support of the Conservatives and the Centre. After years of struggle, Zedlitz's School Bill seemed to offer both Protestant and Catholic conservatives the opportunity to bring their religious viewpoint to bear on politics directly. *Kreuzzeitung*-group hyperbole, however, contributed to an impassioned liberal outburst against clerical reaction and neo-feudal anti-intellectualism. *Kulturkampf* polemics reappeared on both sides. In the end, because of the opposition of the 'middle parties', Wilhelm intervened and demanded that the bill be withdrawn. By spring 1892 both Caprivi and the *Kreuzzeitung* group had suffered a legislative defeat of major proportions.

The way in which the School Bill fell had far-reaching consequences for the leadership struggle within the Conservative Party. The Ultras were of course outraged that the government had deserted them. Kleist-Retzow called it the capitulation of the Crown in the face of atheistic democracy, a new 1848.[27] But Helldorff had warned the Kaiser, with whom he had remained in close touch, not to try to push through the School Bill without the support of the National Liberals.[28] This warning went far beyond the misgivings other moderate Conservatives had expressed privately about the bill. It was seized on by Hammerstein in order to attribute full responsibility for the bill's withdrawal to Helldorff. Referring to Helldorff's disruptive governmentalism in the anti-Socialist débâcle of January 1890, the Austrian trade treaty and the Rural Government Bill, Hammerstein suggested that the DKP chairman had finally lost touch with majority opinion within the Conservative Party. However, Helldorff must have thought he still had a majority of the party behind him. For in the edition of his *Konservatives Wochenblatt* published on 4 April he called for a 'clean break' between the warring factions in the DKP. At last the decisive battle for control of the Conservative Party had begun.

As well as being an indicator of *Kreuzzeitung*-group disillusionment with Helldorff's leadership, the revolt against Helldorff in April and May 1892 also represented the culmination of years of effort to revise the Conservative Party's style of leadership and its programme. Particularly after March

1890, the *Reichsbote* emphasized the need to keep life in the party *Vereine* active between elections, and devoted much attention to the founding of new *Vereine* in the provinces.[29] In mid-1891 Engel wrote that party life at the grass-roots level was being threatened from two sides: on the one hand, from renewed efforts to establish the Kartell in the form of an '*Ordnungspartei*'; and, on the other hand, from the increasingly radical anti-Semites, who were winning the allegiance of traditional Conservative voters in Saxony, Hesse and elsewhere.[30] The only way to meet this danger, Engel argued, was with a reform of the party's agitational apparatus and a revision of its social policy towards *Mittelstand* and workers' interests. Engel admitted that allies might be necessary against the Social Democratic threat, but that in order to pursue a positive social policy the DKP needed to become self-reliant and popular. The same note was registered in a book by Julius Werner, a pastor from Prussian Saxony who was just becoming interested in Conservative affairs in 1891. In *Social Revolution or Social Reform?*, Werner asked:[31]

> Where are the idealistic men who are ready to make sacrifices? They are found most infrequently among those men of property who may have enough money to devote to glittering displays or to elegant or fatuous passions, but who are stingy and tight-fisted in supporting ideal and truly state-supporting efforts ... With toasting patriots and mere Hurrah-calls one cannot pursue reform policies.

Soon another new note appeared in party speeches and newspaper articles from the provinces. At a party congress in late 1891 Silesian Conservatives resolved to expand their own programme to include a clause calling for 'legal measures in the struggle against overwhelming Judaism'. The *Volk* immediately took up this cry, and so did the *Kreuzzeitung*; both added sharp attacks on large estate owners who paid only lip-service to anti-Semitism. Then, on 9 December 1891, Friesen gave a two-hour speech on programme revision to a meeting of the Conservative *Verein* in Dresden.[32] Friesen's main proposals dealt with the Jewish question; he regarded the Jews as the 'guests' of Germany. But he also drew up a comprehensive proposal for revising the DKP's 1876 programme. Before the new year Hammerstein, too, had written on the subject of programme reform, and the *Konservative Monatsschrift* offered a sympathetic review of these efforts in its December 1891 issue.[33]

As the School Bill moved to the centre of the political stage in January 1892, attention was diverted from this campaign for programme reform. However, when Helldorff threw down the gauntlet to his critics on 4 April, he suddenly found that supporters of the School Bill, critics of the Kartell, anti-governmental figures, agrarians, local party activists and advocates of programme reform were virtually united in their refusal to brook any more obstruction from him. After his call for a clean break, events moved swiftly against Helldorff.[34] Within a week resolutions declaring a loss of faith in Helldorff's leadership had been issued by Conservative *Vereine* and newspapers in Hanover, Pomerania, Magdeburg, Bielefeld, Berlin and elsewhere. In the meantime, Kleist-Retzow had written to Helldorff on 6 April, reporting that the DKP's Herrenhaus caucus felt he should withdraw from its ranks; with many members absent, the caucus had voted for this resolution thirty-five to two. Helldorff's closest colleagues then began to abandon him, including Rauchhaupt, Levetzow and his formerly loyal supporter, Baron Otto von Manteuffel-Crossen. On 28 April the Conservatives' House of Deputies caucus passed a resolution calling for Helldorff's resignation from the Committee of Three by a vote of 95:1:1. Finally, one month later, the Committee of Eleven met, and the triumvirate Helldorff–Levetzow–Rauchhaupt was replaced by the group Manteuffel–Mirbach–Rauchhaupt. By early autumn Manteuffel had taken over formal chairmanship of the Conservative Party itself.

In any brief outline of the final defeat of Helldorff there is a danger that the influence of the *Kreuzzeitung* group and the magnitude of the power shift within the top echelons of the party will be exaggerated. It would be wrong to imagine that Helldorff was immediately or irrevocably stripped of influence among moderate Conservatives. Throughout 1892 Helldorff continued to attack his opponents in the *Konservatives Wochenblatt*. In one *Wochenblatt* issue he offered no fewer than five anti-*Kreuzzeitung* articles.[35] Helldorff's cause was aided when his close associate in the Reichstag, Kleist-Schmenzin, withdrew from the DKP's House of Deputies caucus in protest against its 'dishonourable' treatment of Helldorff. More importantly, governmental Conservatives continued to be well represented on the Committee of Eleven. Helldorff, Kleist-Schmenzin and Levetzow remained as Reichstag representatives. While Limburg, the loyal follower of Bismarck, was the strongest anti-government figure among the House of Deputies representatives, Baron Hermann von Erffa-Wernberg and Rauchhaupt were more moderate. Of the Herrenhaus representatives, Manteuffel was considered the most governmental, though contemporary observers offered contradictory views of him falling under the influence of both Helldorff and Hammerstein. Both Manteuffel and Mirbach were welcome guests at the Kaiser's court. The other Herrenhaus members were Count Georg von Schlieben-Sanditten, who later led the anti-Stöcker campaign in 1895–6, and Count Clemens von Klinkowström, who replaced Kleist-Retzow after his death in May 1892. Finally, Friesen, who had offered his own prescription for programme reform but who could not really be considered a *Kreuzzeitung* man, represented Saxon Conservatives.

Through April and May 1892 there was considerable uncertainty even within the new DKP executive as to the direction of Conservative policy on three central issues: the Kartell, anti-Semitism and programme reform. Individual Conservatives continued to publish programme proposals, while Hammerstein printed as a brochure a speech he had delivered over a decade before on the Jewish question. His aim was to illustrate that the *Kreuzzeitung* group had long regarded the now-popular anti-Semitic issue as its own.[36]

At this juncture Hermann Ahlwardt's 'Jewish rifle' scandal broke.[37] The scandal was used by Stöcker to push the Conservatives in the Landtag to make a statement on anti-Semitism, since a Conservative nobleman was implicated. The House of Deputies caucus subsequently voted overwhelmingly, though with many absentees, in favour of incorporating an anti-Semitic plank into the party programme. Through May, however, the scandal grew. On 29 May the Minister of War officially denied Ahlwardt's allegations about Jewish corruption in the armaments industry, and four days later Ahlwardt was in jail on a libel charge. These developments made many Conservatives, even in the Landtag, dubious of the political rewards to be gained from the anti-Semitic issue. Thus in the last week of May the Conservatives in the House of Deputies reversed themselves. With two-thirds of the caucus absent they approved a motion tabled by the leading agrarian, Count Hans von Kanitz-Podangen, to postpone a revision of the programme due to current uncertainties. In the meeting which saw Helldorff dropped from the Committee of Three, the Committee of Eleven opposed the call for programme reform and postponed a final decision until the Reichstag caucus was convened. The only concession the moderates offered the *Kreuzzeitung* group was the striking of a committee (on which the moderates held a majority) to draft a proposal for programme revisions. For even Helldorff was now willing to admit that some clauses of the 1876 programme were out of date.[38]

Faced with what they regarded as overdue caution in top party ranks, Stöcker and other *Kreuzzeitung* men called on provincial Conservative *Vereine* to escalate their agitation for programme revision. Since by this point it was considered an essential forum for discussion of such reform, they also demanded the convening of a general party congress. The reformers' argument was that the DKP's brush with scandal did not necessitate a turning-away from the anti-Semitic cause. A firm alliance with the radical anti-Semites was not the only way the party might profit from the popularity of the issue. They believed this to be especially true if a large and well-publicized party congress sanctioned an anti-Semitic programme for the DKP. Then the Conservative Party would be a step closer to being all things to all men.

Apparently in response to this call, the Saxon Conservatives met for a regional party congress on 13 June 1892. However, the vague anti-Semitic rhetoric employed by Friesen hardly satisfied the more determined advocates of party reform. Helldorff claimed (correctly) that Friesen in fact helped define the limits of Conservative co-operation with the extreme anti-Semites. Friesen's speech was supported by both Ackermann and Mehnert, but Saxon anti-Semites proclaimed their disappointment with the congress, and Engel of the *Reichsbote* followed suit. Echoing Werner's sentiments, he wrote:[39]

> To give generalized programme speeches, to reach general conclusions and then to honour the people later with toasts at dinner – that leads to nothing . . . The ways to reach the people are . . . the press, the people's meeting and the *Vereine* . . . The main thing is activity, work, action . . . Therefore one must allow freedom to prevail . . . When the executives work and take part in things personally . . . then the leadership occurs of its own accord; as soon as the executives set themselves up as party directors and leaders, however, and want to be respected as such, then the thing is ruined.

Helldorff's reaction to Engel's outcry was, as usual, uncompromising. He wrote: 'The result of the sort of "party work" which would emerge from the ideal picture drawn here by the *Reichsbote* is chaos [and] lack of discipline.'[40] A similar reception greeted the *Neue Westfälische Volks-zeitung*'s demand for a party congress whether or not the Reichstag caucus agreed. Helldorff replied: 'For us it is simply inconceivable how one can fail to see that any party possesses in its parliamentary representatives a continuing "party congress" perfectly suitable for expert opinions and resolutions.' Between Engel and Helldorff, the conflicting images of Conservative politics in 1892 could hardly have been more clearly set out.

In the late summer and autumn of 1892 the controversy about programme reform came to a head. The *Kreuzzeitung* editors sought to use their adherents' long-standing antagonism towards leading parliamentarians to ensure that the party congress also addressed questions of agitation and the party structure, or indeed took place at all. In this conflict Manteuffel, now directing the *Conservative Correspondenz*, gradually replaced Helldorff as the most influential advocate of a go-slow policy, although he was not acting alone. As the *Correspondenz* articles of early August indicated, the question of DKP organization was crucial for two main reasons. First, the moderates' argument that the Conservative Party already possessed an effective operational structure was used to suggest that parliamentarians in general did not have undue influence in the party's top decision-making committees. Second, the question of 'party democracy' was recognized to affect the format and mandate of the party congress itself.[41] Implicit in the leaders' argument was the proposition that the Conservative cause would benefit more from 'good discipline', 'party unity' and 'local initiative' than from dissent and negativism. The reformers were further chastised for pinning all their popular hopes for the party on the chimera of programme revision in an anti-Semitic direction. The Manteuffel group regarded reform as all the more odious because it involved association with some of the most demagogic opponents of the Wilhelmine establishment, the independent anti-Semites, and because it ensured the DKP's alienation from Kartell allies.

The traditionalists in the DKP succeeded with their delaying tactics largely because the elements of the *Kreuzzeitung* group found only an elusive unity in their expectations for the party congress. The *Kreuzzeitung* directed its main effort towards programme reform, while Lange's *Neue Westfälische Volkszeitung* seemed more eager to press for the widest possible interpretation of party affiliation in selecting delegates to the congress. Engel offered the most complete discussion of the issues connected with the party congress. In the *Reichsbote*'s lead article of 19 August, for example, he dealt with six main points. He argued (1) that programme revision was not a cure-all for DKP difficulties; (2) that the upcoming congress should establish both a 'general programme' and an 'action programme' to serve for each legislative period; (3) that the influence of parliamentarians in the DKP executive committees had to be reduced and that of regional *Vereine* increased; (4) that the congress must exclude members of the anti-Semitic German Social Party but not the Christian Socials; (5) that the Conservative press (except for the *Conservative Correspondenz*) must remain independent of the top party leadership; and (6) that the DKP must stop seeking protection and support from the government.[42] Meanwhile, the *Volk* called for younger, more practical leaders for Conservative *Vereine*. The *Konservative Monatsschrift* reintroduced the idea of a Conservative–Catholic alliance in its October issue. And Stöcker wrote that the DKP must become an 'independent *Volkspartei*'.[43] Once again, the confluence of reformist ideas about organization and policy is unmistakable here, as is the consistency of these appeals with others advanced by the *Kreuzzeitung* group and Fechenbach in the 1880s. In 1892 as before, permanent programme revision was to be both the cement of the reformers' victory over Helldorff's governmentalism and the foundation for a Conservative *Volkspartei* of the future.

A last-minute protest against the agitation of the *Kreuzzeitung* group was issued by the Kartell-oriented Conservative *Verein* in the Rhineland, under the leadership of Baron Gustav von Plettenberg-Mehrum. It declared it would send no delegates to the party congress – and thereby united the reformers in their denunciation of this move.[44] But finally Manteuffel could delay no longer. On 1 December he published the programme committee's draft and announced that the DKP general congress would be held in the Tivoli brewery in Berlin on 8 December. As the political press discussed this programme proposal in the first week of December, two main clauses of the draft were highlighted.[45] First, the reformers were not satisfied with the preamble, which reaffirmed the party's allegiance to the 1876 programme and stated that it merely wished 'in accordance with these tried and true principles, to take a stand . . . on the important tasks of the present'. In response to this effort by the programme committee to undercut the reformist movement, even the *Reichsbote* concluded that two programmes for the party were no longer possible. Second, the reformers, led by the *Volk*, objected to a clause in the proposal's first paragraph. This called for Christian authorities and Christian teachers for Germany, but also declared that the Conservatives 'condemn the excesses of anti-Semitism'. Gerlach and Oberwinder were concerned that the moderates were seeking once again to disavow the anti-Semitic premiss of the congress. They therefore issued a call for the deletion of this clause. For his part, Fechenbach was jubilant. Feeling that his struggle against opportunism in the DKP had finally been vindicated, he wrote: 'Now everything depends on this being carried out *in practice*.'[46]

These press observations and the final preparations for the Tivoli congress were made under the shadow of a Reichstag by-election in the Brandenburg district of Arnswalde-Friedberg. On the first ballot the anti-Semite Ahlwardt outpolled his left-liberal opponent, who finished slightly ahead of a Conservative candidate. As soon as it became known that a run-off ballot would be necessary, the local Conservatives supported Ahlwardt. In the second poll of 5 December, Ahlwardt won with an 8,000 vote majority.[47] Thus even greater importance was attached to the DKP congress just three days hence. Political observers held their breath waiting to see how the Conservatives would react to this latest surge of the anti-Semitic tide.

NOTES

1 The reorientation of agrarian politics between 1890 and 1893 has been deliberately excluded from this chapter.
2 BAK, NL Bismarck, Bestand A, 116, Helldorff to [Herbert] von Bismarck, n.d. [*c.* August 1881]; *Der Deutsche Patriot*, 1, 3.7.81.
3 BAK, Sg F, 328, Seckendorff to Fechenbach, 28.1.84.
4 *NWVZ*, 8.3.88.
5 *Rb*, 31.7.88, 16.11.88; *NWVZ*, 22.11.88.
6 Reck to Helldorff, 3.7.89, cited in Heffter, *Kreuzzeitungspartei*, p. 164; cf. *NWVZ*, 17.5.89.
7 See BAK, NL Bötticher, 48, Bismarck to Karl H. von Bötticher (copy), 23.12.89, and 36, protocol from the crown council meeting of 24.1.90; Eulenberg, *Korrespondenz*, Vol. 1, pp. 375–97; Helldorff, 'Fall'; Zechlin, *Staatsstreichpläne*; Frank, 'Vorgeschichte'; Röhl, 'Disintegration'; Seeber *et al.*, *Sturz*, especially pp. 330–86; further references in my 'Reformist Conservatism', p. 128.

8   On Oberwinder's background see Fricke, *Prätorianer*, pp. 223–7; Eley, *Reshaping*, pp. 96 n. and *passim*; and Oberwinder's writings.

9   *Vk*, 6.10.89; *Rb*, 9.10.89; *NWVZ*, 13.10.89; *KZ*, 9.1.90; *NWVZ*, 10.1.90; NAZ, 21.1.90, 15.2.90; *KnZ*, 14.2.90.

10 Cf. Rosenmund, *Erlasse*; Fechenbach, *Erlasse*; Nichols, *Germany*, pp. 12–26; *KZ*, 26.2.90.

11 Cf. Eisenhart, *Königtum*, pp. 23 ff.; Stöcker, *Sozialdemokratie und Sozialmonarchie*.

12 *KZ*, 26.2.90; *Vk*, 2/7.3.90; Heffter, *Kreuzzeitungspartei*, p. 213; Frank, *Stöcker*, pp. 212–16.

13 See Helldorff, 'Fall'; BAK, NL Delbrück, 7, including Helldorff to Hans Delbrück, 9.2.07 and 1.3.07; BAK, NL Bötticher, 48, *passim*.

14 Helldorff in the *CC*, cited in Fechenbach, *Erlasse*, pp. 64 f.

15 *NWVZ*, 22.6.90; *Vk*, 22.6.90; BAK, NL F, 122, Lange to Fechenbach, 21.4.90; Sg F, XVII (333), Oberwinder to Fechenbach, 21.6.90 and reply, 22.6.90.

16 Statutes and organizational plan in Stöcker, *Sozialdemokratie*, pp. 30–2.

17 BAK, NL Bismarck, Bestand A, 66, R. v. Mosch *et al.* to Bismarck, 14.12.90, with *Probenummer*.

18 Frank, *Stöcker*, pp. 216 f.; *NWVZ*, 24.6.90; *KWbl*, 21.6.90; *NAZ*, 21.6.90.

19 Following references from GStA Berlin (Dahlem), NL Schiemann, 155, diaries and correspondence.

20 See Nichols, *Germany*, pp. 88 ff.; Kröger, 'Konservativen', pp. 30 ff.

21 Hohenthal-Dölkau to the *KZ*, printed in 19.4.91; for the following, Petersdorff, *Kleist-Retzow*, pp. 523–8, and Rauchhaupt to Hammerstein, 7.10.91, in Leuß, *Hammerstein*, p. 103.

22 See Thiel, *Fusion*.

23 Diary entry of 21.3.91.

24 *Schultheß' Geschichtskalender* (1891), pp. 178 ff.

25 *Rb*, 15/18.12.91; cf. Schiemann to Hugo Jacobi, 23.12.91.

26 Full details in Nichols, *Germany*, pp. 160–91; Röhl, *Germany*, pp. 76–84.

27 Petersdorf, *Kleist-Retzow*, p. 531; cf. Perthes, *Partei*; *KWbl*, 14.5.92; *DAB*, 7.8.92; BAK, Kl. Erw. 455 (Reck), f. 40 ff., Reck to Caprivi (draft), 20.3.92; and materials in *Rkz*. 2215.

28 See BAK, NL Eulenburg, 17, p. 49, Helldorff to P. Eulenburg, 4.2.92.

29 Cf. *Rb*, 14.6.90, 'Konservative Organisation!'

30 *Rb*, 24.6.91, 'Eine Mahnung an die Konservativen'; cf. *Grenzboten*, 1891, 2, pp. 337–41; *Rb*, 10.4.91, 1.12.91.

31 Werner, *Sozialrevolution oder Sozialreform?*, pp. 8–15, 45–64.

32 *DresdN*, 11.12.91; Friesen, 'Gesichtspunkte für ein revidiertes konservativen Programm' (1891), in BAK, Sg F, XIX; cf. the Saxon Conservatives' *Konservativen im Kampfe gegen die Uebermacht des Judentums* (1892).

33 *KZ*, 7.1.92; cf. *KWbl*, 2.1.92; *NZ*, 5.1.92; *KVZ*, 7.1.92; *Vk*, 10.1.92.

34 *BT*, 7/8.4.92; Eulenburg, *Korrespondenz*, Vol. 2, pp. 824–7, Helldorff to P. Eulenburg, 24.3.92; *KVZ*, 8.4.92; *Rb*, 10/21.4.92, 1.6.92; *DtWbl*, 14.4.92; *KWbl*, 16.4.92, 21.5.92; *NAZ*, 12.4.92; *FsZ*, 12.4.92.

35 *KWbl*, 7.5.92.

36 *Rb*, 27.4.92; *KWbl*, 14.5.92, 11.6.92; *DAB*, 7.8.92, 6.11.92, 18.12.92; *KZ*, 18.9.92; *BT*, 11.8.92; BAK, Sg F, XX, 5, Durant, 'Entwurf für das Programm der deutschen Conservativen vom Jahre 1892' (May 1892); Hammerstein, *Judenfrage*.

37 Ahlwardt, *Judenflinten*; cf. Nathan, *Blutmord*; Levy, *Downfall*, p. 79.

38 *NAZ*, 28.5.92; *Rb*, 1.6.92; *KWbl*, 4.6.92.

39 *Rb*, 17.6.92.

40 *KWbl*, 18.6.92; cf. *KM*, 49, 1892, pp. 978–81.

41 *NAZ*, 3.8.92; *Rb*, 6/21.8.92, reviewing formulas for selecting delegates; Lange's comments below cited in *DAB*, 7.8.92.

42 Cf. *Rb*, 22.10.92; ZStA II, NL Tippel, 2, f. 161, Otto Tippel (editor of the *TR*) to Durant (draft), 9.8.92; Reck to Levetzow, 17.8.92, Rauchhaupt to Reck, 19.8.92, and reply, 23.8.92, in Hoener, 'Christlich-konservative Partei', pp. 85 ff.

43 See *Deutsche Reichszeitung*, 17.8.92; *NZ*, 15.8.92; *KWbl*, 7.11.92, 5.12.92; *BT*, 27.10.92; *Vk*, 4.11.92; *Rb*, 19.8.92, 22.10.92.

44 *KWbl*, 14.11.92; *Rb*, 11/17.11.92; *DAB*, 4.12.92.
45 *Wahlverein* draft (26.11.92) printed in *Rb*, 2.12.92; press review in *KWbl*, 7.12.92.
46 BAK, Sg F, XXI, 26, 7/3 (original emphasis).
47 GStA Berlin (Dahlem), Rep. 90, 306, 'Wahlprüfungskommission Bericht', 113 (February 1893), pp. 2, 9.

7

The Tivoli Congress and Conservative Demagogy

The Conservatives' Tivoli party congress in December 1892 was the first occasion on which an established party of the right officially accepted anti-Semitic doctrines into its programme. Hellmut von Gerlach wrote in 1904 that anti-Semitism 'made the greatest possible gain in prestige when it was included in the Conservative programme ... Now it became the legitimate possession of one of the greatest parties, of the party closest to the throne and holding the most important positions in the state. Anti-Semitism had moved up close to the border of social acceptability.'[1] Yet anti-Semitism was only one part of a broader strategy to make the Conservative Party popular. Conversely, anti-Semitic radicalism was only one among a number of reasons why critics labelled the reformers' strategy 'demagogic'. It is essential, therefore, to consider Tivoli not only in terms of its anti-Semitism but also as an important symbol of the breakdown of traditional politics in the Second Reich.

The *Kreuzzeitung* group was able to steer events at Tivoli in its direction for a number of reasons.[2] The sheer number in attendance – somewhere between 1,000 and 1,500 – meant that party notables were not well placed to deal with rowdy members of the German Social Party and other anti-Semites who entered the congress as 'party comrades' with only the most cursory examination of credentials. More importantly, the reformers made certain that the moderates around Manteuffel would not be able to exploit their differences, by agreeing on tactics the night before the congress. To avoid the appearance that the Berliners were dominating the congress, the two amendments to the draft programme – on the preamble and on the clause about 'anti-Semitic excesses' – would be proposed by Dr August Klasing. Klasing was a Bielefeld lawyer, staunch supporter of Stöcker and leader of the Conservatives in Minden-Ravensberg. Unity among the reformers, however, required 'the renunciation of all separate demands', as a Mecklenburg delegate later recalled. Thus at a stroke all organizational reform proposals advanced so vehemently earlier in the year by Hammerstein, Engel, Durant and others were dropped, in order to meet this obstructionist challenge.

From the moment the presiding officers of the Tivoli congress were selected the next day, with Manteuffel in the chair, it was clear that the

Kreuzzeitung-group reformers were not going to defer to the Conservative notables in attendance. The opening rounds of criticism were fired by the renowned anti-Semitic agitator and writer, Otto von Diest-Daber, and by an anti-Semitic haberdasher from Saxony, Eduard Ulrich-Chemnitz. Diest-Daber declared that the DKP 'must be respected from above (applause) as a party that can also offer opposition. (Bravo!)' Introducing himself as a 'man of the people', Ulrich then issued his famous call for the Conservative Party to become 'a little more demagogic'. Since this phrase was subsequently so often quoted out of context, Ulrich's critique of *Honoratioren* politics deserves to be cited in full:

> Gentlemen, it must be said today to our honourable leaders: the Conservative Party wishes to be a *Volkspartei*; it therefore does not want to see itself all the more insulted with talk of 'demagogy'. It is common practice today among the leading circles of the Conservative Party, that everything . . . which moves the people is very easily dismissed with the stock phrase 'demagogic'. (Quite right!) I must ask our honourable deputies to become a little more 'demagogic' – but not in the bad sense, rather in the good sense. (Bravo!) It is necessary that the leaders of our party become more accustomed to striking the tone of the people (*Volkston*).

According to plan, Klasing delivered the major speech for the reformers, ending with an appeal that the congress accept his amendments *en bloc*. Klasing addressed himself first to the preamble of the programme draft, arguing that this was an attempt to inject the disease of compromise at the very birth of the new programme. Quoting a *Kreuzzeitung* article, Klasing declared: 'Two programmes, one for the summer and one for the winter, we surely cannot have.' Klasing would have preferred to drop the preamble completely, but he proposed a revision instead; this presented the new programme as *the* Conservative programme, 'in accordance with the valid principles which are expressed in its programme of 1876'. The change in nuance was enough to win the approval of the assembly, and Klasing's revision was accepted overwhelmingly. As his second point, Klasing spoke on the paragraph condemning the excesses of the anti-Semites. Working with success to rouse the passions of his audience, he referred to the clause as another 'back door' whereby the moderate leaders would take the edge off the new programme. His most forceful point was that the DKP had the mission and the responsibility to become a *Volkspartei* and to lead the anti-Semitic movement. The anti-Semites in Germany, he declared, 'must be mollified . . . By necessity the abuses of anti-Semitism must disappear as soon as the leadership is a correct one.' As Klasing left the podium, the Tivoli brewery erupted into stormy and lengthy applause.

Now it was the moderates' turn. Manteuffel read aloud a declaration from Helldorff and twenty-one other members of the DKP's Reichstag caucus, who had refused to attend the congress. Among the leading names were Kleist-Schmenzin, Ackermann (Saxony), Douglas (Baden), Count August von Dönhoff-Friedrichstein (East Prussia) and Carl Bock (Minden). This declaration claimed that the Reichstag caucus had resolved 'without objection' to stand by the 1876 programme and to regard the new programme as nothing more than a statement of party policy on contemporary issues. Immediately following this declaration, a chamberlain from Saxony, Werner von Blumenthal, presented a courageous and well-reasoned speech countering Klasing's argument. He warned of the dangers presented by the demagogic or 'rowdy' anti-Semites: 'Between us and them there can be only a contest for popularity with the people . . . Surely no one among you thinks we can, with our demands, match or trump the anti-Semites?' During his speech, Blumenthal was shouted down many times. When he pointed out that one could not at the same time be a true Conservative and elect a man like Ahlwardt, the defeated DKP candidate in Arnswalde rose and declared, to thunderous applause, that even he had voted for Ahlwardt in the run-off election, adding: 'Better ten Ahlwardts than one left-liberal!'

Eventually Stöcker appeared on the podium and demanded that the debated clause be deleted from the new programme. A vote (by show of hands) was taken, and against only seven dissenting votes the clause fell. At this point in the congress the leaders around Manteuffel were at their most ineffective. The chair was incapable of providing a fair forum for Blumenthal and other moderates. Many Conservatives in attendance clearly opposed the abandonment of this cavil against the radical anti-Semites, but they did not dare to raise their hands, or voices, in protest.

As the debate on the anti-Semitic paragraph was drawing to a close, a third major conflict arose. At this juncture, the *Kreuzzeitung* group was unable to maintain the semblance of unity which had proven so successful in carrying the first two amendments. This was due to long-standing differences between Christian Socials and more reactionary reformers on the means for combating Social Democracy. During 1892 Hammerstein, Friesen, Durant and Reck had included in their proposals for programme revision various changes to the Reichtag's universal franchise.[3] Opposition to these reactionary plans arose from the editors of the *Reichsbote* and the *Volk*, who warned against any tampering with the franchise and who recognized the incompatibility of these anti-democratic ambitions with the effort to transform the DKP into a *Volkspartei*.[4] Perhaps in a conscious attempt to 'divide and rule', more probably due to a deep anti-Socialist impulse within their own ranks, the Manteuffel group had included as Point 14 of its draft programme a clause which stated: 'The adherents of Social Democracy and anarchism, whose unpatriotic efforts towards

93

revolution endanger wide circles of our populace, are to be designated by law as enemies of the political order and combated accordingly with the power of the state's authority.' This clause was all the more painful to the Christian Socials because Stöcker's social ideas received short shrift in the new programme. Stöcker, Gerlach, Hüpeden and other Christian Social leaders had always been suspicious of exceptional laws. They knew that if the anti-SPD resolution now passed unamended, they would have difficulty continuing their work in the Inner Mission, the Protestant workers' associations and other working-class institutions in which they saw their only real hope of winning the lower orders away from the SPD. Therefore, at this point Gerlach, Stöcker and Hans Leuß[5] approached Manteuffel in the chair. They threatened to 'raise the flag of rebellion' in the congress hall – and in public – if the party leadership did not strike Point 14 from the programme. Enraged, Manteuffel had little choice but to allow Gerlach and Stöcker to speak in favour of an amendment. They proposed a paragraph which read that only '*those* Social Democrats whose disloyalty and revolutionary activities threaten large circles of the populace are to be opposed as enemies of the political order'. The phrase about the use of repressive legislation and state force was dropped. When this amendment was finally passed, the party traditionalists could only look on in silence. They were joined in their discontent, however, by Hammerstein, who suddenly revealed how cynical he had become about the Conservatives' ability to win mass appeal among the workers. When Leuß asked him to lend his support to Gerlach and Stöcker, Hammerstein replied that the only way to deal with the Social Democrats was 'to provoke the workers and have them shot'. This extreme reactionary statement came to light only some years later.[6] But as Gerlach wrote in his memoirs, if he had been aware of it at the time he would have better understood the background to Hammerstein's political thought: 'He did not want a Conservative *Volkspartei* at all, but rather a Conservative anti-*Volkspartei*.'

After the anti-Socialist issue was settled, the assembly had little patience for later speakers. The resolutions on party organization (of which no mention was made in the official congress transcript) were treated as of very secondary importance. A Berlin *Bürgerverein* leader introduced and carried a motion which called for the greater representation of middle-class and peasant circles in the make-up of DKP executive committees and parliamentary caucuses. Mehnert carried a related motion which charged the present *Wahlverein* executive with the task of constituting 'a committee of about forty-eight members enjoying the trust of the party and representing all occupational groups'. Though no details were provided as to how the balance would fall, this new executive was to be 'chosen' in part from members of the parliamentary caucuses and in part from the 'party comrades' in the provinces. Finally, the usual 'Hail!' to the Kaiser closed the congress.

*

It is no moot point to ask exactly what Ulrich-Chemnitz meant when he called on the Conservatives to become 'demagogic in the good sense'. A clue to how contemporaries defined 'bad demagogy' is provided in accounts of anti-Semitic leaders and their agitation at this time. It was reported, for example, that Otto Böckel once told an audience in Gießen that the Rothschilds had bought up the world's supply of oil.[7] Gerlach provided perhaps the most revealing portrait of 'rabble-rousing' anti-Semitism when he described Ahlwardt's campaign in Arnswalde-Friedberg in November 1892:

> Accompanied by his secretary, he [Ahlwardt] made the rounds of the farms and asked every peasant how many acres of land and how many head of cattle he had. Then he would turn to his secretary, who flashed a gigantic notebook, and would dictate to him: 'Take it down! Gussow has 12 acres, 5 cows, 4 pigs. Should have 24 acres, 12 cows, 10 pigs.'

If this was the sort of agitation that could be expected of the Conservative Party after Tivoli, it is no surprise that members of the Wilhelmine establishment reacted violently to the events of December 1892.

In fact the wider significance of the inner-party crisis between 1890 and 1893 was evident in the way official government circles, including the Kaiser, closely monitored the struggle between Helldorff and Hammerstein.[8] In the wake of Tivoli, the men close to the Kaiser expressed exaggerated fears of a Conservative–Centre alliance, a radical realignment of the Conservatives' social policy, an integration of the DKP into the 'Bismarck Fronde' and new initiatives against the Jews. More importantly, these men also drew a direct connection between, on the one hand, the growth of dissent, insubordination and demagogy within the Conservative Party and, on the other, the larger threat to the stability of party alignments in Germany, to domestic peace and to the monarchy itself. The struggle for control of the Conservative Party, as Helldorff reported to Wilhelm's closest friend and adviser, Philipp Eulenburg, was now recognized to have 'long-lasting significance for the fate of the Reich and for the monarchy' as well. Helldorff did all he could to fuel these fears, writing immediately after Tivoli: 'We are faced with a frightful brutalization of public opinion.' He also argued that the anti-Semitic movement was 'the certain seed of Social Democracy' because radicals like Böckel and Ahlwardt had been inciting German peasants against large landowners and big business men. The Kaiser and his circle apparently agreed that the Conservatives' action at Tivoli was not conducive to the ideal of authority, either within the party or in the larger political realm. Friedrich von Holstein of the Foreign Office noted after the congress that 'the Conservative parliamentarians have the feeling that they have surrendered the

leadership to "the clubs". Many to whom I spoke are hanging their heads.'
Soon thereafter Eulenburg wrote to Wilhelm to suggest that he make a
decisive move; as Helldorff had already suggested, an unambiguous
statement of position by the Kaiser might 'bring the Conservative Party
back to order again'. Otherwise, Eulenburg wrote, 'the monarchical
principle' was in danger of being 'shaken to its foundations'.

The battle of 8 December 1892 was only one victory, however heralded,
in a war which was to last another three years. Contemporaries could
hardly have known that Tivoli represented the high tide, not just the first
wave, of *Kreuzzeitung*-group accomplishments. As applause or condemnation for the Tivoli reformers began to appear in statements by Conservative politicians, in the press of other parties and in the correspondence of leading reformers, it seemed that Conservative Party unity was,
as the jubilant *Kreuzzeitung* press announced, finally at hand.[9] But the
first backlash against Tivoli came as early as 12 December, when Caprivi
delivered a speech in the Reichstag criticizing the radical anti-Semites and
their supporters. In the same session the agrarian leaders Mirbach and
Frege both expressed a distinct lack of enthusiasm for 'rowdy' anti-
Semitism as well. Before the end of the month, Blumenthal had published a
declaration reinforcing his objection to the anti-Semitic clause in the new
programme. He was followed by individual supporters of Helldorff and
by Conservative *Vereine* in East Prussia, Saxony, Westphalia and even
Berlin. Ulrich-Chemnitz felt compelled to write to Caprivi explaining just
what he had meant by 'demagogic in the good sense'.[10]

To combat this backsliding and resurgent governmentalism in the party,
the *Kreuzzeitung* group tried to underscore the radical break with the past
the DKP had made on 8 December. As Stöcker told an appreciative
Bielefeld audience, Tivoli had been a Conservative congress 'not in black
tails and white gloves but in street clothes. This was the Conservative
Party in the era of general and equal suffrage.'[11] But it was the *Volk* which
took the lead in pressing the dual campaign against the Helldorff clique
and for the anti-Semitic Conservatives. Gerlach and Oberwinder warned
the twenty-three Reichstag dissenters in late December 1892 that they
stood little chance of re-election.[12] In early 1893 Max Liebermann von
Sonnenberg, the most conservative of the anti-Semitic leaders and chairman of the German Social Party, wrote to Manteuffel. He complained of
past DKP opposition to the anti-Semitic cause and warned him not to
allow the revival of such sentiments within the party.[13] Manteuffel's
reaction was registered later in his typically ambivalent observation that
'the Jewish question was not to be avoided unless we wanted to leave the
full wind of the movement to the demagogic anti-Semites; with it they
would have sailed right past us'.[14] The new DKP chairman realized that he
might suffer the same fate as his predecessor if he did not at least pay
lip-service to the rebels' demand for restitution against Helldorff.

Helldorff still had a number of arrows for the bow he used in his ongoing defence of traditional Conservatism. To discredit Hammerstein he claimed in his *Konservatives Wochenblatt* that the *Volk* had become the leading Conservative newspaper, knowing that such a prospect would outrage many moderates. He made sure that the columns of his *Wochenblatt* were open to any Conservative *Verein* or individual wishing to protest against the Tivoli congress or the new programme. He also printed articles from the *Conservative Correspondenz* and excerpts from parliamentary speeches which suggested that Conservative leaders were uncomfortable with the revision of the anti-Socialist Point 14. By March 1893 Helldorff had turned his attention to the proposed reform of the Conservative Party's executive.[15] Rather than seeking popularity by 'exploiting the momentary mood for momentary successes', and rather than calling on a large assembly to make 'decisions on political questions of the greatest gravity', he advocated the building of a party leadership with more traditional guarantees for 'capable performance and political judgement'. Any other plan would be 'far removed from the true Conservative view'. Helldorff also tried to win the remaining uncommitted Conservatives on to his side by drawing parallels between the challenge of the *Kreuzzeitung* group and the challenge presented by other demagogues who had changed parliamentary life in Germany. His conclusion – almost literally, for this article appeared in the penultimate issue of the *Konservatives Wochenblatt* – was that the DKP needed to co-operate with the other right-wing parties if this demagogic danger, within and without, were to be conquered.

In the six months between Tivoli and the Reichstag elections of June 1893, the *Kreuzzeitung* group began to lose ground on a number of fronts. The radical anti-Semites were neither convinced of the Conservatives' change of heart nor fearful of their competition. Many of them would have agreed with Böckel's contemptuous appraisal of the DKP's ability to compete for peasant and *Mittelstand* votes: 'A party of the nobility and great landowners is still a long way from being a *Volkspartei*, even though its programme is patched up with a piece of the Jewish question.'[16] These doubts were increased when Mirbach and other party notables warned of the affinity between Social Democratic and anti-Semitic ideas. Claiming to represent agrarian opinion within the party, Mirbach declared in March 1893: 'We are by no means blind to the good kernel within anti-Semitism . . . however, we regard it as a very difficult task to keep the anti-Semitic stream within the proper bounds.'[17] By the end of the month Ahlwardt had declared in a meeting of the German Anti-Semitic League that all Conservative seats in parliament were now 'free game'. The *Volk* suddenly realized that *any* Conservative could now be denounced by the radical anti-Semites as 'Helldorffian'.

In late May, Caprivi announced new Reichstag elections, in order to create a parliamentary majority willing to pass the large army increases he and the Kaiser desperately wanted. Now Hammerstein, too, concluded that the anti-Semites around Böckel and Ahlwardt – and even some members of the more moderate German Social Party – were not worthy of Conservative help.[18] The anti-Semitic radicals responded by escalating their campaign, blacked with the slogan: 'Against Junkers and Jews'. When election day came, Conservatives could not fail to see what a two-edged sword the anti-Semitic issue had become. In some cases, as with Hüpeden's campaign, Conservatives found anti-Semitic agitators either had prepared the ground for them or were willing to assist with emphatically anti-Semitic campaigns, as in certain constituencies in Saxony, Brandenburg, Silesia and Pomerania.[19] In seven cases, joint candidates received substantial help from anti-Semitic groups and then 'defected' to the Conservative caucus in the Reichstag after the election. Far more frequently, however, Conservatives found themselves directly opposing anti-Semitic candidates or abandoning the anti-Semitic appeal altogether.

Of sixteen seats won by the anti-Semites in June 1893, ten had been held formerly by Conservatives. This accelerated the alienation of the DKP from its 'allies'. Helldorff found a favourable hearing when he published a strong attack on Hammerstein's leadership in late July. He charged that the *Kreuzzeitung*'s disastrous flirtation with the anti-Semitic parties had led to Conservative decline at the polls.[20] Even Hammerstein could not neglect the new climate of opinion in the party. With the rapid rise of the agrarian movement, he was aware that the winds of change might sweep from influence any leader who relied solely on a radical anti-Semitic policy. He made it clear that Conservative Party support for the sixteen anti-Semitic deputies in the Reichstag would not be forthcoming on a regular basis. At the end of July 1893 Hammerstein wrote in the *Kreuzzeitung* that 'the development of the anti-Semitic movement has an unmistakable similarity to that of Social Democracy'. The die was cast. By December the Saxon Conservative leaders were condemning members of the German Reform Party in bitter terms. They decried their 'selfish ambition', their 'immoderate and impossible demands', their appeals to 'popular passions' and their predisposition for 'noise and scandal'.[21] This change in attitude prompted a prominent German Reformer to complain that the 'Conservatives treat us worse than the Jews.'[22] Stöcker, too, complained about renewed Conservative timidity, but he did not complain in the Reichstag; due partly to opposition from Böckel and Ahlwardt, the Christian Social leader had been defeated in June 1893 by a National Liberal. The insufficiency of anti-Semitism alone to preserve Stöcker's ascendancy – either in the DKP or in the larger anti-Semitic movement – could not have been made more clear.

NOTES

1 Gerlach, 'Vom deutschen Antisemitismus', *Patria!*, 1904, p. 154.
2 For the following, DKP, *Stenographischer Bericht über den allgemeinen konservativen Parteitag ... am 8. Dezember 1892*; *Rb*, 6.12.92, 12.1.93; *KWbl*, 7.1.93; *Vk*, 6.1.93; *KZ*, 6.4.94; *Die Zeit*, 9.12.96; Nipperdey, *Organisation*, p. 255.
3 *DAB*, 7.8.92; Friesen, *Conservativ! Ein Mahnruf*, discussed in *Rb*, 28.7.92; *KWbl*, 21.5.92; BAK, Kl. Erw. 455 (Reck), f. 50, Reck to Caprivi, 4.8.92 (draft); cf. Friesen, *Schwert, passim*.
4 *FkZ*, 18.8.92; *Rb*, 19.8.92; see also Chapter 12.
5 Hammerstein's biographer and, at that time, one of the leading members of the anti-Semitic German Social Party.
6 Gerlach, *Von rechts*, pp. 133 f; Frank, *Stöcker*, p. 234; Heffter, *Kreuzzeitungspartei*, p. 232; cf. Fechenbach, *Soll man*.
7 Pulzer, *Rise*, p. 112; for the following, Gerlach, *Von rechts*, pp. 113 f.
8 The best sources are BAK, NL Eulenburg, and Eulenburg, *Korrespondenz*, Vol. 2; full references in my 'Reformist Conservatism', pp. 169–74, and my 'Conservatives *contra* Chancellor', pp. 210–15.
9 Cf. Gerlach, *Von rechts*, p. 133; *DAB*, 11.12.92; *Vk*, 10.12.92; *DtRp*, 14.12.92; *SddLp*, 10/13/20/24.12.92.
10 *DAB*, 18/25.12.92; *KZ*, 1.1.93; *FkZ*, 20.12.92; *Vk*, 24.12.92; *BT*, 17/21.1.93; *NAZ*, 17.12.92; *KWbl*, 21.1.93; *Rkz*. 673, f. 93, Ulrich to Caprivi, 14.12.92; cf. *Rkz*. 680, f. 443, Tippel to Caprivi, 14.12.92, and *PrJbb*, 81 (January 1893), pp. 385–7.
11 Speech of 28.2.93; Frank, *Stöcker*, p. 233.
12 *Vk*, 10/24.12.92.
13 ZStA I, NL Liebermann von Sonnenberg, 2/16, Liebermann to Manteuffel, 25.1.93.
14 Speech of 13.5.93; Frank, *Stöcker*, p. 234; cf. Broszat, 'Bewegung', p. 84.
15 *KWbl*, 7/21.1.93, 27.3.93.
16 Cited in Levy, *Downfall*, pp. 83 f.
17 See *KZ*, 13.3.93; *KWbl*, 13.3.93; *SddLp*, 18.3.93.
18 *Vk*, 9.3.93; *KWbl*, 13.3.93; *Rb*, 12.3.93; *KZ*, 30.5.93; on the Army Bill and the election campaign cf. Nichols, *Germany*, pp. 192–264.
19 Campaign publicity materials in GStA Berlin (Dahlem), XII, *Hauptabteilung* IV, 171; cf. Tal, *Christians*, pp. 320 f; Levy, *Downfall*, p. 85; Frank, *Stöcker*, pp. 237–40.
20 *NAZ*, 27.7.93.
21 See Tal, *Christians*, pp. 134 f.
22 Cited in Levy, *Downfall*, p. 100; cf. DKP, *Konservatives Handbuch* (1894), 'Antisemitismus', pp. 12–23.

8

The Farmers' League and Agrarian Mobilization

The oppositional sentiments aired at Tivoli, together with growing unrest among peasants and Caprivi's determination to press for further reduction of tariffs, accelerated the alienation of the Conservatives from the government. It also increased their desperation to break new ground in popular political agitation. The result was the founding of the Farmers' League in February 1893. Within a few months this new organization had shown what it could achieve in the popular sphere, and over the following years it grew into one of the largest and most influential interest groups in the Second Reich. Nevertheless, most features of the Conservative–agrarian realignment of 1893 had already been proposed in the 1880s. These included the apparent break with traditional styles of politics, the search for new leaders, a willingness to oppose the government, anti-Semitic rhetoric, a commitment to more authoritarian ideals and the recruitment of new social groups.[1]

In September 1889 Johannes Miquel diagnosed a deep crisis in the German party system. He wrote that the present political parties had outlived themselves; as products of past relationships, they were no longer capable of meeting the challenges of agricultural and industrial depression. He predicted that future political crises would 'destroy these parties'.[2] Miquel's political insight had led to reorientations of his own National Liberal Party in previous 'moments of fission' in German politics. Most other German parties, too, had formed or re-formed themselves in the 1860s and late 1870s, and they were again undergoing major ideological or organizational upheavals in the period 1890–3.[3] A specific conflict between the NLP and its most important patrons in heavy industry had repercussions that extended to the Free Conservatives, German Conservatives and other nationalist groups. With their close contacts with Bismarck, now in embittered opposition in Friedrichsruh, Rhenish-Westphalian industrialists around Emil Kirdorf attempted to found a 'German Economic Party' in the winter of 1890–1. Helldorff's own battle within the DKP, however, made the links between heavy industry and the Conservative Party precarious at best. In April 1891 another anti-establishment group appeared on the scene: the General German League, later renamed the Pan-German League (Alldeutscher Verband, or ADV).[4]

Mirbach and some other Bismarckians in the Conservative Party hoped that the Pan-Germans might provide a rallying-cry to resurrect the Kartell, though now more or less in opposition. Other 'Frondeurs' decided that a new 'National Party' (*Nationalpartei*) was needed.[5] Among the leaders of the planned organization were men committed to founding a 'strong, popular party' in support of a 'strong, popular government'.[6] These reformers obviously considered the Conservatives' plans for programme reform to be insufficient for the resurrection of an influential party-political Right.[7] In the winter of 1892–3, when the Conservatives were in disarray, the National Party seemed to offer a brief hope for uniting the opposition to Caprivi. However, the Kaiser's disapproval and other indiscretions doomed the new enterprise before it got off the ground. In any case the National Party had been rightly described by one sceptical left-liberal as 'neither fish nor fowl'.[8]

The Farmers' League was not some kind of pre-ordained end-result to these conflicting campaigns seeking to redefine the right-wing parties. When Baron Conrad von Wangenheim-Klein-Spiegel issued his declaration of 28 January 1893, which eventually led to the founding of the BdL the next month (see below), he offered the prescription for another 'German Economic Party'.[9] However, it soon became apparent that the leading agrarians were interested not in an 'economic party' in the wider sense (which would balance industrial and agrarian interests) but in an explicit 'Agrarian Party' (*Agrarpartei*) which would take as its first priority the salvation of agriculture. Between February and July 1893 there was no certainty about exactly what sort of party or interest group might emerge from this confusion; it might have been an Economic, National, Agrarian, *Ordnungs-*, Bismarck, or Middle Party. There was even speculation that a new Young Conservative Party would be established.[10] The founding of the Farmers' League did not end this controversy. Later in the decade, tensions between the BdL and the Conservative Party prompted further conjecture about a possible conflict between interest groups and political parties; contemporaries wondered whether the agrarians would establish their own *Mittelstand* Party or Agrarian Party. Many more such combinations were discussed in the following years, before the German Fatherland Party appeared in 1917. However, even in the early 1890s the quasi-conspiratorial background to the National Party was only one feature of a wider questioning of party-political practices.

Anti-establishment resentment emanating from the agricultural community was another major destablizing factor in Conservative politics at this juncture. This resentment was the consequence of real economic grievances felt by German farmers on the one hand, and a more vague perception of exploitation by distant economic and political forces on the other. In the first category one can include a downturn in agricultural prices, foot-and-mouth outbreaks and shortages of fodder in the southern German states, Caprivi's trade treaties and the government's Army Bill, which threatened a tax increase. The second, more nebulous aspect of rural discontent exhibited itself in antagonism towards officials who were considered out of touch with the farmers' immediate concerns.[11] This antagonism spilled over to include the German Agricultural Council, the German Peasants' League and other agricultural associations.[12] The high proportion of farmers who preferred not to join them indicated the social cleavages that existed in the countryside.

It was precisely this swelling protest movement that anti-Semitic agitators like Böckel and Ahlwardt managed to exploit in central and western Germany. These 'peasant kings' illustrated that anti-Semitism could shake the established order; they also destroyed the idea that the Conservatives had a stranglehold on the votes of small farmers. The Conservatives made a weak attempt to reverse this trend at Tivoli. But it soon became clear that other groups like the peasants' leagues in Bavaria were achieving greater resonance with slogans like 'No aristocrats, no priests, no doctors and no professors, only peasants for the representation of peasant interests'.[13] In other works, Tivoli was a far from adequate response to the rural discontent that directed itself only in part against Jewish influence. One Free Conservative reported after Tivoli that he had never before witnessed the bitterness currently seething among peasants in his home province of Silesia; he predicted that the Conservatives would 'experience the consequences in the next election'.[14]

Viewed from this perspective, the events of February 1893 can be seen as a *reaction* to pressures from below, rather than a manipulative strategy carefully thought out to generate opposition to Caprivi.[15] To be sure, even before the *Kreuzzeitung* group had toppled Helldorff, Limburg had summed up the Conservatives' bitterness towards Caprivi's administration. At the time of the Austrian trade treaty debates, he published an article in the *Kreuzzeitung* which warned that traditional Conservative politics were no longer adequate in dealing with a government that treated Conservatives and German agriculture unjustly.[16] Limburg was subsequently dismissed from his diplomatic post by Caprivi and deprived of his pension, which further increased oppositional sentiments within the party. But Limburg's article was published fourteen months before the founding of the BdL. In the meantime other factors had become decisive, including the precipitous downward course of grain prices after good harvests in 1892, the *Kreuzzeitung*-group campaign against 'governmental' Conservatism, the disruption of traditional leadership in the DKP and the realization that peasant unrest needed to be contained. In fact from late 1890 onwards various agricultural bodies had been attempting to mobilize their members. The VdSWR resolved in February 1891 to establish committees and to hold rallies in protest against the lowering of grain tariffs; a year later Puttkamer-Plauth tried to found 'a new political party on agrarian principles'.[17] Clearly the Farmers' League did not appear out of thin air.

When Caprivi declared in his Reichstag speech of 12 December 1892 that anti-Semites, bimetallists and opponents of his Army Bill all shared similar unpatriotic, demagogic motives, the Conservative–government conflict escalated rapidly. On 21 December an obscure Silesian farmer named Alfred Ruprecht-Ransern issued a call for the agrarian community to make explicit its break with the government.[18] In line with other attempts to redraw party lines at this juncture, Ruprecht called for a 'single great agrarian party'. The activity and orientation of this new party would mark a dramatic break from the past:

> We must shout so that the whole nation hears it, we must shout so that it echoes in the parliaments and the ministries – we must shout so that it is heard even at the steps of the throne! . . . I am suggesting nothing more nor less than that we join the Social Democrats in a solid front against the government, to show them that we do not wish to be handled so badly in the future and to let them feel our power.

As other agrarians took up Ruprecht's call they quickly dismissed any literal interpretation of his threat to join the Social Democrats. They stressed instead his demand for the 'ruthless and uncamouflaged' pursuit of interest politics and for the organization of Conservative agitation independent of the government. A meeting of some 130 farmers elected an organizing committee of twenty-five leading agrarians on 4 February 1893. Then four previously established agrarian organizations held meetings in the capital at mid-month to assist at the birth of the Farmers' League; these were the German Peasants' League, the VdSWR, the Congress of German Farmers and the Association for International Bimetallism. Stöcker and other leading members of the *Kreuzzeitung* group were not drawn into the preparations for the founding assembly of the BdL. The provisional executive, together with its 'advisers', was markedly aristocratic.[19] None the less it reflected mixed political tendencies. It included Tax and Economic Reformers like Friedrich von Knebel-Döberitz, Frege and Thüngen-Roßbach; Conservative agrarian spokesmen like Mirbach, Limburg and Puttkamer-Plauth; newcomers like Ruprecht, Wangenheim and Dr Gustav Roesicke; and DKP leaders like Manteuffel, Erffa and the later Minister of Agriculture, Baron Ernst von Hammerstein-Loxten. This last group certainly was unnerved by the prospect of a complete break with the government. The fluidity of opinion on the advisability of an extreme anti-government orientation for the Farmers' League was also reflected in the negative initial observations about the BdL offered by men of such diverse political views as Hammerstein, Engel, Fechenbach, Helldorff and Bismarck.[20] Conversely, the BdL leaders may have been hedging their bets when they included governmental Conservatives like Douglas (Baden), Plettenberg-Mehrum (Rhine Province) and the later Minister of Agriculture, General Viktor von Podbielski (Brandenburg), as regional representatives in the new executive.[21]

The founding meetings of the Farmers' League on 18 February 1893 were carefully arranged by the provisional committee to preclude the unpredictable results which the Conservatives' party congress in the same hall had yielded two months earlier. These meetings were held one after the other because the 10,000 or so attendants[22] could not all be accommodated in the Berlin Tivoli brewery at once. Stöcker spoke at the rally, but his introduction of himself as a German farmer was greeted with general amusement. Otherwise the leaders declared their opposition to demagogy, neglected the issue of anti-Semitism and reaffirmed their monarchist principles. They even deflected calls from the floor for a toast to Bismarck, preferring to avoid such an obvious motion of no confidence in the government. In short, the focusing of attention on economic matters took precedence in February 1893 over any more radical shifts in Conservative allegiances. Priority was given to the battle against further tariff reductions, the organization of local BdL branches and an agrarian press, electoral campaigning for candidates committed to the League's programme and the reinforcement of a sense of solidarity between large landowners and peasants. Other programme points called for bimetallism, stock-exchange reform, stricter measures against breaking of contracts by agricultural labourers, representative agricultural chambers and protection against diseased livestock imports. For these tasks, none of the existing parties sufficed, whether pro- or anti-government. The first BdL chairman, Berthold von Ploetz-Döllingen, declared at the founding assembly that 'the flames of enthusiasm' which he had seen in farmers across Germany argued for a new organization 'free from any political party compulsion, free from any caucus politics!' Wangenheim agreed: 'If ever the adage holds true – that one cannot pour new wine into old bottles – it does so here.'

If there was some uncertainty at the outset about how radically the Conservatives might pursue their oppositional course, Caprivi's response to their agitation solidified the battle-fronts very quickly.[23] In Reichstag speeches of 15 and 17 February, in the midst of the 'agrarian week' in Berlin, Caprivi wondered aloud whether those who were pressing the 'sharpest attacks' against the government were perhaps trying to overthrow it.[24] He also proclaimed his allegiance to conservatism as 'the manifestation of an overall philosophy of life' but admitted that he was no agrarian: 'I own no plot of ground, no blade of straw, and have no idea how I could possibly become an agrarian.'

Caprivi did not succeed with his attempt to divide Conservatives and radical agrarians, for three main reasons. First, the Farmers' League leaders quickly proved their ability to mobilize a rural constituency, especially in areas west of the Elbe river (see below). Soon other agrarian interest groups such as the Congress of German Farmers and the German Peasants' League discontinued their activities, although the Association of Tax and Economic Reformers did not. Second, further trade treaty legislation reduced tariffs with Spain, Serbia and Romania in December 1893 and with Russia in March 1894. These developments forced Conservative estate owners and smaller farmers to continue to endorse the programme of the BdL, even if they did not agree with all aspects of its agitation. After the Reichstag elections of June 1893 the Farmers' League began to flex its parliamentary muscle. An 'Economic Union' (Wirtschaftliche Vereinigung, or WV) was formed on 14 July 1893 by about 150 Reichstag deputies from the right-wing parties.[25] Caprivi now had to contend with a solid phalanx of BdL-affiliated deputies determined to oppose further tariff reductions. Third and finally, the Kaiser's own doubts about Caprivi grew as the agrarian–Conservative camp displayed its resolute refusal to support a chancellor who took such pride in owning no land or 'blade of straw'.

As the agrarian–government conflict entered its decisive phase in the winter of 1893–4, Caprivi used every means at his disposal to undercut the opposition of the BdL. On 18 December 1893 he convinced his colleagues in the Prussian state ministry to issue a decree reminding government officials that disciplinary action could be initiated against them if they opposed the Crown and supported the League's agitation.[26] He also exploited the effort of some old-style Conservatives – including Stolberg, now provincial governor in East Prussia – to win economic concessions for their own provinces.[27] He encouraged them to report on BdL activities and prevent the spread of radical oppositional sentiments in the countryside.[28] However, the Conservatives and leaders of the Farmers' League were now on a course from which they could not back down. In November 1893 Hammerstein wrote in the *Kreuzzeitung* that 'We must rip up the trade treaties with Austria and Italy, if necessary with sword in hand!'[29] This sword was two-edged; as an official BdL statement declared, 'the person of the Reich Chancellor is dispensable, but German agriculture is not'.[30] In mid-December 1893 Caprivi succeeded with the passage of his trade treaty with Romania in the Reichstag. But this time the margin of victory was very slim indeed. On 20 December the *Kreuzzeitung* formally declared war on Caprivi, writing that an 'unbridgeable gulf' now existed between party and chancellor.

Over the next few months a period of unprecedented intrigue ensued, as the Conservatives, agrarians and anti-Caprivi forces within the government used every means available to sow discord between the chancellor and Wilhelm.[31] However, the Kaiser declared publicly that he stood by Caprivi, offering a number of notable remarks in favour of the Russian trade treaty. On one occasion Wilhelm noted that he had no desire to go to war with Russia 'because of a hundred stupid Junkers'. Later, after the treaty finally passed, he cabled one East Prussian Conservative who had broken ranks and voted for the treaty: 'Bravo! Well done like a nobleman!'

By January 1894 the alienation between party and state had never been so profound.[32] Thüngen-Roßbach came close enough to *lèse-majesté* that Caprivi launched legal proceedings against him and considered it against other Conservatives. But most Conservatives remained convinced of two things: first, that if they backed down on the Russian treaty they would lose the leadership of the agrarian movement to more radical demagogues; and second, that compromise would represent such a momentous defeat for the party that it might not survive the crisis intact. In January 1894 Schiemann wrote that 'a defection [to the government's side] would be the death of the party, whose legacy would then be taken up by Social Democrats and anti-Semites'. In February he wrote: 'A Conservative Party that lets its back be broken now is broken for ever. But what will then become of Prussia?'[33]

In the end Caprivi mustered enough votes for the passage of his Russian trade treaty legislation on 16 March 1894. On the decisive second reading (10 March) the Conservatives voted solidly against the treaty, with the exception of four 'nays' and seven deputies who absented themselves for the vote. Even the apparent success of the government's campaign, however, did not significantly increase Caprivi's standing with the Kaiser. Instead, Wilhelm and many other members of the political élite, for all their antipathy to radical agrarian interest politics, now saw the incompatibility of a 'conservative' state and a 'liberalizing' chancellor. As *Die Nation* put it, 'The Prussian *Kraut-Junker* ... has entrenched himself ... Coldbloodedly like a Cooperian Indian on the warpath, he will lie in wait for the opportunity when he can get rid of the hated Reich chancellor.'[34] In October 1894, having exhausted his political capital, Caprivi submitted his letter of resignation. A few days later Germany had its third chancellor, Prince Chlodwig zu Hohenlohe-Schillingsfürst. But the legacy of Caprivi's struggle against agrarian chauvinism persisted much longer. As Caprivi noted some months after his departure from office: 'When our Junker begins to make his convictions dependent upon his income, and when he makes it a condition of his royalism that the state should do the impossible for him ... one must ask oneself: Is it still worthwhile to sacrifice for this class?'[35]

Arising out of a period of unprecedented turbulence, the Farmers' League was designed to overcome the debilitating divisions within Conservatism that had rendered the DKP so helpless in the face of Caprivi's reforms in

1890–3. Its leaders therefore conceived of political organization and discipline in very different ways than did traditional Conservatives. As Wangenheim declared at the founding assembly, he imagined the BdL as an organization where delegates would be found in the smallest village of the land and where 'one need only push a button in Berlin' to have German agriculture speak out with a single voice at the right moment. Later apologists for the BdL claimed that when the 'button' was pushed the League's apparatus sprang into action: 'One knew from Memel to Kaiserslautern, from Kiel to Kattowitz, what the opinion of the League was – and one followed unconditionally.'[36] But who exactly were these 'new men' that the Conservatives seemed so desperately to need in 1893?

Berthold von Ploetz had already established his name in agrarian circles before 1893 as leader of the German Peasants' League.[37] This argued for his election as first chairman of the BdL in February 1893, as did the 40,000 marks and 40,000 members he brought with him. Although it was not until after Ploetz's death in July 1898 that he was hailed as an idol and 'founder of the movement' by other leaders of the League, Ploetz played a major role in establishing the BdL in its early years and in fostering links with prominent Conservatives. Gustav Roesicke was elected deputy chairman of the BdL on 18 February 1893. Probably the most energetic of the League's leaders and the most tactically gifted among them, Roesicke directed much attention to refining the BdL's political programme, securing its influence in the Conservative Party (to which he belonged) and co-ordinating League activity in the various parliaments of Germany. Less a natural agrarian than a 'manager of interests', Roesicke's style contrasted with that of his colleagues on the BdL directorate; he was more conservative than Diederich Hahn and more radical than Wangenheim.

The first director of the BdL was Dr Heinrich Suchsland. Suchsland's organizing talents were considerable, but his speaking abilities and radicalism fell far short of his successor's. Diederich Hahn became director of the BdL upon Suchsland's death in 1897. He proceeded over the next two decades to become the most renowned 'demagogue' in the organization and, according to some, in all of German politics. Heinrich Mann allegedly used the figure of Hahn in drawing the caricature of Diederich Hessling as a grasping 'man of straw' in his novel *Der Untertan*. Hahn incorporated in his person the variety of allegiances which the Conservatives, through the Farmers' League, hoped to win for their cause. He was a native of Hanover in northern Germany; he had been elected first chairman of the anti-Semitic Association of German Students in the 1880s; he was one of the most radical nationalists among the agrarians; and he even exceeded most Conservatives in his devotion to Bismarck. Hahn's appointment as BdL director was part of a reorganization which created a new three-man directorate. There Hahn became what some have called the prototype of a 'full-blooded' professional politician on the Right. However, Hahn was

not the most influential figure within the BdL directorate. That designation would arguably belong to Conrad von Wangenheim. Although
Wangenheim had been instrumental in the founding of the Farmers'
League, he did not join its leading executive committee until the reorganization of August 1898. After that time the directorate consisted of the two
chairmen (Roesicke and Wangenheim) and the director (Hahn). Wangenheim was always more aristocratic in bearing than his colleagues and more
in tune with traditional Conservatism, but his talent for compromise
greatly facilitated the effort of the BdL leadership to show a united front
outwardly. As his correspondence with Roesicke shows, the geographic
and organizational division of duties these two men worked out did not
significantly affect their ability (or their desire) to share responsibility for
the League's actions.

To this list of leaders must be added a much larger body of editors,
functionaries, *Verein* leaders and local adherents of the Farmers' League
who gave this new interest group its most immediate impact on political
affairs. Among these subordinates was Georg Oertel, the first editor of the
most important BdL-affiliated newspaper, the *Deutsche Tageszeitung*.
Together with Hahn, Oertel proved himself one of the most outspoken
defenders of the anti-Semitic, agrarian and authoritarian ethos which
infected the League. But even Oertel's roots lay largely in the Conservative camp, as he displayed in the argument of his book about 'Conservatism as a *Weltanschauung*'.[38] Other auxiliaries who supported the
League's activities in different ways were academic writers such as
Professor Gustav Ruhland,[39] and notable Conservative parliamentarians
such as Elard von Oldenburg-Januschau, who headed the BdL apparatus
in West Prussia.[40] Finally, the lesser functionaries who led the BdL
'machine' in Berlin and in the regions, together with the rank-and-file
farmer who looked to the League for benefits of an everyday nature,
provided the strict discipline and mass basis for the agrarian movement.

The scale of activity initiated by the BdL is the most indisputable aspect
of agrarian success in the 1890s. Compared to the official membership of
the DKP's *Wahlverein*, which was estimated at about 20,000, the BdL's
achievement in recruitment is astounding. Within four months of its
founding the League's membership stood at over 160,000. By 1900 it was
over 200,000, and in early 1914 it was roughly 330,000. Although the
number of local BdL *Vereine* east of the Elbe remained higher than in the
west, after 1896 the majority of the League's members were from western
Germany. This fact was loudly proclaimed by the (mainly) east-Elbian
leadership as indicative of the League's ability to represent smaller
landholders and *Mittelstand* groups. The BdL's vast membership was
organized into local, county, regional and provincial *Vereine*, with a
degree of bureaucratic rationality unprecedented in Conservative circles.
Between these levels and the directorate stood two executive committees,

composed of forty-two and fourteen members in 1893. There also quickly arose a body of officials and functionaries which grew from 65 in 1894 (with 10 alone in the press division) to 67 'upper' officials and 285 other functionaries in 1913. Counting League employees in publishing enterprises, another four hundred is added to this total. This band of officials helped rally the mass of German farmers who travelled to Berlin in February every year and who generally approved unquestioningly the resolutions put before them by the directorate.

With an annual budget larger than that of the Social Democratic Party, amounting to around one million marks in 1907, the BdL was divided into twenty divisions (*Abteilungen*) dealing with organization; finance; technical, co-operative and insurance programmes; publishing; the press; elections; parliament; and other affairs. Each of these divisions had by 1914 made major advances in refining the art of political influence. For example, the economic division was concerned with providing advisory, credit and other practical benefits which spoke directly to the material needs of the mass of League members. The parliamentary office prepared speeches and legislative proposals for BdL-pledged deputies. And the vast press archive, numbering over 4,500 volumes in 1916, had subject and personal indexes for easy use by parliamentarians and writers who needed to be (or appear to be) experts on increasingly technical economic topics.

In the 1907 Reichstag election campaign, the BdL fielded 116 travelling speakers; it also distributed 44,000 campaign brochures and three million leaflets. In 1911, leading up to the Reichstag elections of January 1912, it staged almost 10,000 electoral rallies.[41] But far from unpacking their campaign suitcases immediately after the polls closed – as Conservatives had always been wont to do – the BdL leaders recognized the importance of continuing the League's agitation and expanding its influence between elections. By 1910 the BdL had eleven mobile libraries, and a year later it was sponsoring more than one hundred political instruction courses with over 4,000 participants. Though it fell shy of the SPD's success in providing a full social community for its members, the BdL's range of agitational material, extending from calendars to songbooks, indicated that it went far beyond most political parties in appealing to many different facets of farmers' lives. The connection between such 'total' politics and the ability of the League to generate petitions with one to two and a half million signatures may be indirect and unclear, but it is impossible to deny.

Another significant point of contact between leaders and rank-and-file members was the collection of newspapers at the League's disposal. The weekly *Bund der Landwirte*, sent directly to members' homes, reached a reported circulation of 247,000 in 1912. The *Deutsche Tageszeitung* was nominally independent but almost always represented the BdL directorate's views. Soon after its founding on 1 September 1894 it had a circulation of about 40,000, which climbed to over 65,000 in the war years. These newspapers were typically much cheaper than the leading Conservative organs. Whereas the *Kreuzzeitung* cost 8.5 marks per quarter, the *Deutsche Tageszeitung* cost just 1.5 marks. Moreover, the BdL organs made inroads and sometimes replaced the older DKP newspapers among estate owners, officials and professional classes; they were by no means restricted to farming circles alone. A more precise differentiation between BdL and DKP readers is impossible. But the strength of the regional editions of the leading League newspapers – with circulations totalling over 120,000 in 1919 – attests to the significant breakthrough achieved by BdL propagandists.

With this leadership, structure and propaganda network, the Farmers' League quickly became a crucial ingredient among the factors affecting the success of legislation or the election of candidates to the Reichstag. Claiming to stand apart from, or 'above', party politics, the BdL supported candidates from other parties besides the Conservative Party. Indeed, in many western provinces it was the National Liberal Party which benefited most directly from League agitation. However, the long-term relationship between the BdL and the DKP was the closest. It is much more difficult to apprehend or quantify the new departures by the Farmers' League in the sphere of ideology. The BdL pushed the Conservative Party towards new conceptions of a *völkish*, authoritarian, expansionist state. League propagandists also played a large role in postponing the inevitable demise of an image of Germany as an agricultural idyll, free from the blight of urbanism and sustained by the independent virtues of the *Mittelstand* and the peasantry.[42] Finally, the BdL increased the capacity (though not always the inclination) of the Conservative Party leaders to exploit the opportunities for influence which Wilhelmine Germany's particular constitutional structure afforded such economic interest groups.[43] This provided a rudimentary pattern of legalism combined with anti-parliamentarism which, after much redrafting, was one of a number of possible blueprints for later dismantlers of the traditional political edifice in Germany. Nevertheless these new political priorities within agrarian Conservatism could not totally change the outlook of the old-style Conservatives around Manteuffel. Nor could they immediately silence the more socially conscious members of the *Kreuzzeitung* group. Each of these factions within the DKP continued for some years after 1893 to oppose a political philosophy which reduced Conservatism to the defence of a narrow economic interest.

NOTES

1   I have not burdened the following account with specific references to the fine points of an ongoing historiographical debate about the 'manipulation' or 'self-mobilization' of

the agrarian sector; see Blackbourn, 'Peasants'; Eley, 'Anti-Semitism'; Moeller, 'Introduction' to *Peasants*; Moeller, 'Peasants and Tariffs'; Hunt, ' "Egalitarianism" '; Farr, 'Populism'; Farr, ' "Tradition" '; Farr, 'Peasant Protest'; Stegmann, 'Between Economic Interests'; Puhle, *Interessenpolitik*; and other works by these authors listed in the Bibliography.

2 Speech of 22.9.89, cited in Stegmann, 'Between Economic Interests', p. 1.

3 Cf. Anderson, *Windthorst*, pp. 391 ff.; Zeender, *Center Party*, pp. 19 ff.; O'Donnell, 'National Liberalism'; Mundle, 'National Liberal Party'; White, *Splintered Party*; Knobel, *Hessische Rechtspartei*, pp. 234 ff. For discussion of a proposed 'Reich-Conservative Party', *KM*, 46, 1889, pp. 408 ff.

4 See below, Chapter 15.

5 Sources on the planned *Nationalpartei* are in PA AA Bonn, Deutschland 125, 9, 'Nationalpartei'; ZStA I, Alldeutscher Verband, 3; and BAK Koblenz, NL Bismarck, Bestand A, 69, 'Presse 1890–94'; the most revealing documents in the latter file are the thirteen-page draft *Aufruf* of the *Nationalpartei* with Bismarck's marginalia, n.d. (f. 795 ff.); Hugo Jacobi to Bismarck, 15.1.93, 3.3.93, 3.5.93, 7.7.93; Karl Egon Fürst zu Fürstenberg to Bismarck, 27.3.93; cf. Hank, *Kanzler*, p. 495; Stegmann, 'Between Economic Interests'.

6 *DtWbl*, 22.12.92, cited in Stegmann, 'Between Economic Interests', p. 19.

7 Cf. M. Harden, 'Ein konservatives Programm', *Die Zukunft*, 11, 10.12.92, pp. 481–91.

8 *VossZ*, 14.12.92.

9 'Aufruf der Deutschen Wirthschaftspartei' (n.d.), and Bismarck to Berthold von Ploetz, 24.5.93, in BAK, NL Bismarck, 29; cf. ZStA I, NL Roesicke, 23, f. 2 ff., Wangenheim to Roesicke, 6/12.4.93; *Rb*, 7.4.93; Stegmann, 'Between Economic Interests', pp. 26 ff.

10 Kröger, 'Konservativen', p. 48.

11 For this and following citations see Blackbourn, 'Peasants', p. 55 and *passim*.

12 Cf. Gottwald, 'Landwirtschaftsrat'; Hartwig, 'Deutscher Bauernbund'.

13 These arguments are exemplified in the brochure, *Halt – mehr rechts! Ein Wort zur Abwehr unwürdiger Fremdherrschaft* (1892); cf. Blackbourn, 'Peasants', especially p. 59.

14 Kardorff to Baron Carl F. von Stumm, 26.12.92, in Kardorff, *Kardorff*, pp. 275 f.

15 Cf. Eley, 'Anti-Semitism', p. 37.

16 *KZ*, 14.12.91.

17 Stegmann, 'Neokonservatismus', p. 202; *Rkz.* 673, f. 82, Ludwig Herrfurth to Caprivi, 12.2.92.

18 Ruprecht's article appeared in the *Landwirtschaftliche Tierzucht*, 21.12.92; Wangenheim's declaration appeared on 21.1.93; both are printed in Kiesenwetter, *Fünfundzwanzig Jahre*, pp. 335 ff.

19 Committee listed in Puhle, *Interessenpolitik*, p. 34.

20 See *KZ*, 1.2.93, 14.2.93, and (more positively) 19.2.93; *Rb*, 20.3.94, 23.6.94; Hank, *Kanzler*, pp. 496 ff.; BAK, NL F, '1890ziger Jahre', Mehnert to Fechenbach, 24.2.93; *KWbl*, 27.3.93.

21 Kiesenwetter, *Fünfundzwanzig Jahre*, pp. 28 f.; cf. 'Aufruf an die Landwirte von Baden, Hessen, Hessen-Cassel, Hessen-Nassau, Bayern, Württemberg und Elsaß-Lothringen', ibid., pp. 344–6.

22 Estimates ranged from 5,000 to 15,000; for the following see BdL, *Stenographischer Bericht über die konstituirende Versammlung des Bundes der Landwirte*, *passim*; cf. Puhle, *Interessenpolitik*, pp. 34 ff.; Fricke and Hartwig, 'Bund', pp. 244 ff.; Hartwig, 'Konzeptionen', pp. 91–5; Eley, 'Anti-Semitism', p. 39.

23 For greater detail in the following discussion see Nichols, *Germany*; Röhl, *Germany*; Weitowitz, *Deutsche Politik*.

24 *SBR*, 1892–3, Vol. 2, pp. 1114–16, 17.2.93.

25 *KdBdL*, 15.8.93. A more informal WV was organized in the PHH in early 1895.

26 GStA Berlin (Dahlem), Rep. 90, 306, minutes of St. Min. meeting of 18.12.93; text of Caprivi's *Erlaß* in Reichs- und Staatsanzeiger, 21.12.93; cf. *Rkz.* 418, f. 95, Caprivi to B. Eulenburg, 23.12.93; and Oehlmann, 'Studien', pp. 276 f.

27 Cf. Mirbach-Sorquitten, *Fortfall des Identitätsnachweises*; Schöller, *Staffeltarife*; Bauer, *Caprivi und die Konservativen*, p. 27.

28 Correspondence in *Rkz.* 416–18, *passim*; and BAK, NL Eulenburg, 25, especially pp. 432–4; further details in my 'Reformist Conservatism', pp. 238–42.
29 *KZ*, 24.11.93.
30 'Schafft Klarheit!' in Kiesenwetter, *Fünfundzwanzig Jahre*, p. 349.
31 Cf. GStA Berlin (Dahlem), NL Schiemann, 155, f. 123 ff.; Eulenburg, *Korrespondenz*, Vol. 2, p. 1029, P. Eulenburg to Caprivi, 24.2.93; BAK, NL Eulenburg, 28, pp. 151 f., P. Eulenburg to B. Eulenburg, 9.2.94, and p. 231, Holstein to P. Eulenburg, 12.3.94; also *BT*, 31.1.94.
32 See the *CC*, cited in *Schultheß' Geschichtskalender* (1894), p. 4; *Vk*, 25.2.94; Thüngen-Roßbach, *Thüngen contra Caprivi*, p. 4; BAK, Kl. Erw. 455 (Reck), f. 108, notes from a meeting with Miquel, 22.2.94.
33 GStA Berlin (Dahlem), NL Schiemann, 155, diary entries of 13.1.94 and 13.2.94.
34 Cited in Nichols, *Germany*, p. 267.
35 Caprivi to Max Schneidewin, 22.2.95, in Schneidewin, 'Briefe', p. 146.
36 Cited in David, 'Bund', p. 57.
37 Following details are taken mainly from Kiesenwetter, *Fünfundzwanzig Jahre*, pp. 30 f. and *passim*, supplemented by Puhle, *Interessenpolitik*, pp. 295–7; Lindig, 'Einfluß des Bundes'; David, 'Bund'; Fricke and Hartwig, 'Bund'; Wangenheim, *Wangenheim*; and other works on the BdL.
38 See Oertel, *Konservatismus als Weltanschauung* (1893), especially pp. 6–11, 49, 55–62; Needon, *Oertel*, especially pp. 21–38.
39 Cf. Pacyna, *Ruhland*; Kiesenwetter, *Fünfundzwanzig Jahre*, pp. 30 f.
40 Oldenburg-Januschau, *Erinnerungen*, especially p. 61.
41 See Puhle, *Interessenpolitik*, pp. 165, 325 f.; Fricke, 'Bund', p. 138.
42 Cf. Bergmann, *Agrarromantik*; Puhle, *Interessenpolitik*, pp. 83–110; Barkin, *Controversy*; Gagliardo, *Pariah*; Lees, 'Debates'.
43 See especially Puhle, *Interessenpolitik*, p. 261.

9

The Abandonment of Reformist Conservatism

As long as debate raged over Caprivi's trade treaties, Conservative and agrarian notables were more interested in exploiting opportunities for political mobilization through the Farmers' League than through Christian Socialism. When the Kaiser sought to 'rehabilitate' the DKP in September 1894, the increasingly leftist orientation of the Christian Socials became a liability the DKP could no longer tolerate. To be sure, Christian Social agitators were still cherished for their ability to deliver middle-class recruits to the Conservative cause. By early 1896, however, the CSP was regarded as an ally which offered fewer political rewards than the better-organized agrarians. When the Conservative leadership realized this, Stöcker became a symbol of Conservative popularity which was no longer indispensable.

Nevertheless, mobilization of support for Stöcker by members of the party at large in 1894–6 revealed the persistence of a strong 'social' component among regional Conservative organizations; it also revealed their members' desire for less exclusive decision-making within the party. Before Stöcker was forced to leave the Conservative Party he had inaugurated an embarrassingly public debate about the 'popular mission' of a Conservative *Volkspartei*. Although after 1896 such a *Volkspartei* was further than ever from realization, this debate illustrated how deeply hopes for a Christian Social variant of right-wing mobilization had struck root. Many contemporaries wondered aloud whether Conservatism without a Christian Social component was viable at all. The advent of the Farmers' League, at least in the view of contemporaries, had not provided the last word on Conservative popularity.

In the months after Tivoli the possibilities for strengthening the *Kreuzzeitung* group's influence within the DKP leadership were very limited. Hammerstein had little choice but to throw in his lot with the agrarians, although he did his best to outbid his competitors with the radicalism of his demands for agriculture. Both Hammerstein and Stöcker searched in vain for a non-agrarian issue capable of rallying their followers or maintaining their reforming zeal. Nothing seemed as urgent as the anti-Helldorff and programme reform campaigns of 1892. A formal restructuring of the top DKP leadership did not occur, and the establishment of barriers against *Kreuzzeitung*-group reformism proceeded apace. By April 1893 Durant was writing to Lange to complain that the resurgent old guard wanted to abandon Stöcker and 'a healthy social policy' as soon as possible.[1]

The amelioration of antagonism between moderate Conservatives and the government began immediately after passage of the Russian trade treaty. In May 1894 August Eulenburg wrote to his cousin Philipp that, although the Conservatives were still 'acting like the biggest fools under Hammerstein's leadership', there was 'undoubtedly a rehabilitation process in train, which one would only upset with forceful measures'.[2] This process of rehabilitation was especially problematic because from 1893 to 1895 there were so many different cross-currents flowing within the Conservative–agrarian community. The Helldorff–Hammerstein dichotomy which had arisen in the period 1890–2 no longer existed. Moderates were no longer *ipso facto* governmental. Agrarians might be either for or against old Kartell relationships. And *Kreuzzeitung*-group reformers regarded party policy differently depending on whether they followed Hammerstein, Stöcker or the leader of some regional group. All these Conservatives claimed they only wanted a fair hearing within the party. But the statements of official Conservative policy which emerged in these years were often little more than cacophonous.

In this fluid situation one issue gradually emerged which tended to polarize Conservatives into two distinct groups. This was the issue of social reform, and it divided the DKP into camps which advocated either an 'enlightened' or a repressive policy. The centrality of this issue was an almost necessary consequence of the trend in the Christian Social Party away from concentration on anti-Semitism towards a more radical stance in support of the social, economic and (eventually) political rights of workers. This issue was highlighted by the perceived revolutionary threat of European assassinations in the summer of 1894, and by the government's Anti-Revolution Bill drawn up later in the year to meet this threat. Also, by the summer of 1894 the Kaiser was well aware of the resurgent forces within the DKP which were pro-government, pro-Kartell and strongly against the continuation of social reform for the benefit of workers.[3] Wilhelm had finally come to the conclusion that he was doing more harm than good by maintaining the illusion of a 'social monarchy'. The persistence of BdL opposition to the government after the Russian treaty complicated matters, so that even in the late summer of 1894 the Kaiser struck the names of some leading agrarian Conservatives off the invitations to his dinner table during a trip to East Prussia. But Wilhelm was pursuing a two-pronged strategy. During the same visit to East Prussia, on 6 September 1894, he delivered a speech in Königsberg in which he called for a new campaign for 'religion, morality and order'. Not only was this speech welcome to Conservatives like Manteuffel who wanted to re-establish some measure of trust between the DKP and the Kaiser. It also held out to more reactionary Conservatives the hope for a new, repressive policy from the government. As Reck rendered the Conservatives' new battle-cry: 'Ma vie au Roi, Mon coeur aux Dames. L'honneur pour moi!'[4]

Reformist Conservatives reacted rather differently.[5] Hammerstein rejected the claim that the only chance to pass anti-Socialist legislation was to establish a broad Kartell. Engel sought to make the fight against revolution compatible with social reform, advising against any 'one-sided battle with police measures'. And Stöcker thought that any obvious attempt to abolish the universal franchise 'would put an irresistible torch for agitation into the hands of political and Social Democracy'. Gerlach and Oberwinder responded even more allergically. Faced with what they regarded as a call for a *Staatsstreich* or *coup d'état* from above, they launched a vigorous attack on such plans in the columns of the *Volk* throughout September 1894.[6] This protest played a crucial role in dissuading the government from a reactionary leap in the dark at this point. Caprivi remarked in a Prussian state ministry meeting of 12 October 1894 that he was 'dubious whether the Conservative Party in its entirety would be won for an anti-revolutionary bill'.

In 1893–4 the immediate post-Tivoli antagonism between the *Volk* and Helldorff was also evolving into a conflict between the Christian Social and Conservative parties themselves. A Christian Social manifesto in May 1893 announced that the CSP would offer independent candidates in the upcoming Reichstag elections. In the months ahead, however, signs of CSP decline multiplied. The Conservative Party leaders offered Stöcker no safe constituency in which to regain his parliamentary seat. In a June 1893 rally Stöcker found himself shouted down by Ahlwardt's rowdies, and a Berlin police report the next year observed that many of the CSP rank and file seemed to have crossed over to the other anti-Semitic groups.[7]

In the winter of 1893–4 Gerlach and Oberwinder grew increasingly impatient with DKP leaders who advocated only interest politics or repressive measures against the SPD. More and more often the *Volk* editors were called on to define their position between the Conservative Party and Friedrich Naumann, a Protestant pastor rapidly gaining influence on the left wing of the Christian Social Party.[8] This intermediate position became more difficult when Naumann declared in October 1893 that he wished to see a Christian Social Party which was 'not conservative'. To the applause of the National Liberal and Free Conservative press, Manteuffel and the *Conservative Correspondenz* disavowed the *Volk* as an official Conservative newspaper.[9] Naumannites also began to dominate the Protestant workers' associations under Ludwig Weber and the Protestant Social Congress led by Paul Göhre. By April 1894 Stöcker found

115

himself resisting demands for a revision of the CSP programme, for the organization of rural labourers and for a sharper distinction between the DKP and CSP. Soon a flood of brochures appeared on the general theme of 'revolution or reform'; these suggested that the path of Naumann's social reformers was diverging from the mainstream of Conservative thought. Although an anti-Socialist impulse could be found in both groups, the Naumannites tended to argue that progressive social reform was the best way to insulate the lower orders against revolutionary agitation. Most Conservatives, on the other hand, agreed with Baron Carl Ferdinand von Stumm, the Free Conservative deputy and Saarland industrialist.[10] As Hüpeden later recalled:

> The Conservative deputies instinctively stood more or less behind Baron von Stumm on the workers' issue. In any case they were never faced with the question: do you want to solve the social question through reform or 'sheer force'? They wanted both: first to fight the Social Democrats decisively and break their influence, and then to support moderate reforms.[11]

When Stöcker spoke out against Stumm in the Prussian Landtag in March 1895 he was greeted with icy silence from the Conservative benches. The final stages of the Anti-Revolution Bill debates in early 1895 further convinced many Conservatives that the Christian Socials were too intent on preserving the universal franchise.[12]

When the conflict between Naumann and the Conservatives broke out in full form in late April 1895, Stöcker, Engel and others did their best to argue that there existed no sharp distinction between CSP and DKP policy.[13] The editors of the *Konservative Monatsschrift*, Oertzen and Martin von Nathusius, concluded that the CSP's best tactic was to '*win over* the Conservatives rather than separate from them'. But soon the atmosphere was further poisoned by two conflicts in Pomerania.[14] When a pastor told a Conservative *Verein* meeting in Greifenberg that more must be done for labourers on the estate of a local notable, he was shouted down and eventually transferred to another parish. The affair drew attention to the willingness of the more politicized clergy, even in east-Elbian Prussia, to speak out against the oppression of rural workers and to demand the extension of social reform to the countryside. These worries were compounded by a Conservative defeat in a by-election for the Pomeranian district of Kolberg-Köslin. Here an aged Conservative deputy, representing what had traditionally been one of the Conservatives' safest seats, had been defeated largely because of his extreme complacency during the election campaign. The *Volk* took this occasion to deliver a broadside attack on the liabilities of *Honoratioren* politics in general. It reviled the defeated Conservative as an opponent of the Tivoli programme, and it concluded that what was needed above all in such areas was 'a little more popular Christian Social spirit!'

Just at this juncture, the Hammerstein scandal broke.[15] The charges eventually laid involved the misuse of *Kreuzzeitung* pension funds and Hammerstein's secret deal with suppliers of newsprint at vastly inflated prices. By April 1896, when he was sentenced to three years in prison, Hammerstein was a broken man both politically and morally. More importantly, the Hammerstein affair tarnished the image of the Conservative Party in a number of ways. The new editor of the *Kreuzzeitung*, Kropatschek, was unable to copy his predecessor's vibrant style. Soon the leading Conservative newspaper was suffering from a series of satirical attacks against it in the humorous journals of the day. More significant was the escalation of the affair into an attack on Stöcker and the Christian Social–*Kreuzzeitung* group.[16] By late October the real issue at hand had been revealed when the *Conservative Correspondenz* declared an official break with Naumann's wing of the CSP.[17]

The significance of this rapidly deepening crisis – and *sense* of crisis – within the Conservative Party was revealed in the failure of attempts to revive the image of the DKP as a *Volkspartei* after Tivoli. Heinrich Engel and others continued to report on reformism within the DKP.[18] Nevertheless, DKP leaders proceeded very slowly with the minimal organizational changes which had been promised in December 1892. At a *Wahlverein* executive meeting of 20 March 1893 a committee was established to prepare the way for a reorganization of the Committee of Fifty; its members were Manteuffel, Limburg and Mehnert. Almost a year later, on 17 February 1894, the new plan for the Committee of Fifty was presented to, and approved by, the *Wahlverein* executive. According to this scheme the new party executive was to consist of fifty-three members, of whom twenty-nine would be chosen by party *Vereine* at large and twenty-four would be selected from the party's parliamentary caucuses. As the *Conservative Correspondenz* stated, it was expected that the various occupational classes would be represented in the group of regional delegates.[19]

Unaware at this point how many months would pass before the new Committee of Fifty was constituted, Engel expressed reserved agreement with the plan on one point and strong disagreement with it on another. He agreed with the decision not to place Conservative editors on the new executive. The real disappointment for Engel was the balance that had been struck between parliamentary and regional delegates. For as he rightly pointed out, the 24:29 ratio would not be reflected in the attendance of delegates at any given executive meeting. Due to the difficulties of travel and other commitments, there was a likelihood that perhaps only one-third of the provincial delegates would be able to attend each executive meeting in Berlin. In Engel's view the protest launched at Tivoli against parliamentarians and their dominance had come to nought. The relationship between party and people, to which the Tivoli congress had tried to give expression, remained as tenuous as before.

Engel could hardly have been heartened when, in the first week of April 1895, the new DKP executive organs were finally established, more than two years after Tivoli. In the Committee of Three, Manteuffel, Limburg, and Mirbach retained their position. In the Committee of Eleven, the reformers were represented by Durant, Klasing and Stöcker. As later events were to prove, however, they still faced strong opposition from governmental moderates and agrarians. On the Committee of Fifty itself, the few unfamiliar names selected by provincial *Vereine* lacked the social background, independence, or experience to allow them to match the influence of the leading parliamentary representatives. Klasing represented Westphalia, and Stöcker was a Brandenburg appointee, but otherwise most regional delegates were either nonentities or closely tied to the traditional leadership. Bavaria remained without representation altogether. Moreover, the 'organizational committee' that was established at the 3 April 1895 meeting of the executive, charged with overseeing the expansion of the DKP's apparatus in the provinces, included almost no men who were not also Committee of Fifty delegates. Hence, this potentially influential committee was infused with neither new blood nor new ideas. There is no evidence that it contributed in any way to the development of the party's organization after it was constituted.

If Engel and provincial party activists had reason to be pessimistic about the sincerity of the Berlin leadership's commitment to organizational reform, Conrad von Massow might be counted among the few remaining party men who believed that a thoroughgoing reform of the DKP was still worth striving for. The son of Friedrich Wilhelm IV's Minister of the Royal House, Massow had spent fourteen years as a Prussian *Landrat*. After 1897 he wrote the monthly reviews on social policy for the *Konservative Monatsschrift*. Massow's standing among Conservatives derived largely from his activity in 1894–5, when he published two major works on Conservative politics.[20] The first of these books offered the thesis that only substantial social reform, not repression, could stem the tide of Social Democracy; the second book was more directly concerned with the practicalities of party life.

On the one hand, Massow argued that Conservative deputies should be obliged to account for their actions in parliament. Such an obligation, he felt, would generate among parliamentarians a greater sense of responsibility, not only to their voters or their caucus colleagues but to the party as a whole. Thus Massow sought to introduce the concept of a Conservative caucus which answered to the party at large, and which was conceived not as a party leadership élite but rather as an *extension* and a *tool* of the greater

Conservative community. On the other hand, Massow also sought to probe further into the reasons for inadequate Conservative leadership. He believed that present DKP leaders were incapable of implementing reform because most of them had not learned politics 'from the bottom up'. *Honoratiorenpolitik* was to blame. To illustrate his argument, Massow contrasted Conservative leaders with their Social Democratic counterparts, asking why the latter had achieved such success. He answered his own question:

> Because they have been brought up in political life, because behind them stands a party in which there is a pulse of real political life. Whether they disagree among themselves, whether they do battle at their party congresses, is all much less important than that they communicate with their voters, and that these voters are organized into an active party at large.

Although the Social Democrats attacked bourgeois capitalists at their meetings, they also tackled the hard questions of organization, tactics and finances. These were lessons the Conservatives had yet to learn. As Massow wrote, 'Occasionally mustered militia can achieve nothing against regularly drilled troops.' If the military analogy did not prick Conservative pride, the author might have thought, nothing would.

Critiques like these, arguing for greater decision-making input from the party at large, had their origin in the diversity of Conservative movements across Germany. Many CSP and DKP activists in the provinces believed that their autocratic party leadership in Berlin was so out of touch with regional circumstances that only a declaration of faith in Stöcker by the Committee of Eleven would resurrect Conservatism as a popular movement. Such a declaration would also reaffirm the loyalty of these rank-and-file party members to the Conservative cause. Yet just as these regional spokesmen had achieved very uneven success in establishing permanent party machinery at the local level since the 1870s, they also offered widely divergent solutions to the growing DKP–CSP conflict.

There is scant evidence in the eastern provinces of Prussia of any sort of reforming organizational activity that might have accrued to the fund of sympathy for Stöcker in 1895–6. The Christian Social line was very weakly represented in the Conservative newspapers in east Elbia. The founding of a Christian Social Union for Silesia in December 1895 alienated many Conservatives, since it seemed to signal the implementation of long-standing calls for CSP organizational independence. Only the efforts of Gustav Malkewitz, editor of the *Pommersche Reichspost*, made Pomerania something of an oasis in the wasteland of reactionary east

Elbia. By October 1895 Malkewitz was warning the DKP's Berlin leaders that they dare not 'underestimate or test the strength of Stöcker's following'.[21]

In Berlin the interpenetration of Christian Social and Conservative sympathies in the *Bürgervereine* eventually produced a new organization and a new determination to resist Conservative backsliding after Tivoli. In October 1894 some twenty *Bürgervereine* responded immediately when Gerlach and Oberwinder called for support against the government's reactionary plans, and early the next year the '*Wahlverein* of German Conservatives in Berlin' was established. Since the Berliners had chosen Stöcker as their representative on the Committee of Eleven, they threw their full support behind him in the autumn of 1895.[22]

In middle and western Germany support for the Christian Socials was uneven and often ambivalent. Pockets of CSP influence remained in both Hesse and Hesse-Nassau, but reformers like Hüpeden in Kassel and Werner in Frankfurt were fighting a losing battle against anti-Semites, Naumannites and Kartell-oriented Conservatives. Hanoverian politics were in turmoil in the early 1890s. By 1893 the editor of the Conservatives' *Hannoversche Post* had had to recognize the failure of his attempt to steer a Christian Social course in the face of German Social and National Liberal antagonism. There was arguably no area in Germany where Conservative–Christian Social factionalism was more pronounced than in the Minden-Ravensberg district of Westphalia. Klasing, Lange, Reck and other reformers faced strong challenges from radical anti-Semites and followers of the Farmers' League. After bitter antagonism arose among these groups over candidacies for both the Landtag and Reichstag elections of 1893, the leftist Christian Socials in the district began to establish independent CSP *Vereine*. They thereby antagonized old-line Conservatives further and opened the way for left-liberal victories at the polls.

Developments in the organization of the Conservative Party in the Rhineland illustrated the confluence of programmatic and organizational initiatives after Tivoli. In 1893 a specifically *German* Conservative organization in the province was established with the help of Klasing. When the new *Verein*'s first congress was held in Mühlheim in October 1893, it chose Dr Georg Burckhardt, a chemist, as its main speaker. In his speech Burckhardt criticized the former chairman, Plettenberg, and his colleagues for their social haughtiness and lack of organizational zeal. He charged that they had accepted unity with other Kartell partners only on NLP or FKP terms. Burckhardt also addressed the need for west German Conservatives to win the allegiance of both industrialists and workers. He concluded: 'The Conservative *Volkspartei* is the cliff upon which the sea of revolution will crash. It is our task to assist in its creation.' In the years ahead, however, Burckhardt found that divided loyalties among Christian Social Conservatives in his region greatly complicated his task as leader.

These conflicts permitted Free Conservative notables to re-establish themselves within the Rhineland organization.[23]

The Christian Socials probably drew their most consistent support from regional Conservative organizations in south-western Germany, though this statement must be qualified. In Württemberg much of the strength of Conservatism in the mid-1890s derived from the agrarian movement and the agitational successes of Farmers' League functionaries. Yet even Adam Röder, the *Badische Landpost* editor who published a polemical series of articles against the *Volk* in the summer of 1895, recognized the south German appeal of a 'healthy' brand of Christian Socialism. In the *Landpost* he wrote: 'Christian Social in Stöcker's sense is considered to be the same as decisively Christian Conservative, and in this sense we ... have always been emphatically "Christian Social".' In Württemberg, Stöcker and the *Volk* received substantial support from the *Deutsche Reichspost*.

Agrarian and anti-Semitic radicals were also potential rivals to Christian Socials in Bavaria. But by mid-1894 the Bavarian Conservatives were in a bitter duel with Manteuffel over his cricisism of the *Volk*. This campaign was led by the publisher and sometime editor of the *Süddeutsche Landpost*, Carl Friedrich Gebert, who wrote to Fechenbach after the latter had tried to intervene and moderate Bavarian dissent.[24] Gebert advised Fechenbach – and through him, Manteuffel – that the DKP leadership would have to reckon with a defection of south German Conservatives if its campaign against the CSP continued:

> We in Bavaria, who are happy that Helldorffianism has been eliminated, have become very mistrustful, in that from northern Germany absolutely nothing in the way of assistance with agitation, etc., has occurred. We Bavarian Conservatives have been thrown upon ourselves and have *no* obligation *whatsoever* to be silent party to the errors of the Berlin party leadership ...
>
> [We want] to warn the German Conservative leadership ... not to precipitate any division in the Conservative Party ... through its declarations, which are rather too much handed down from above.

It was because of editorials like this that Naumann believed he could draw Conservatives south of the Main on to his side, that is, away from the DKP and Stöcker altogether. In early November 1895 he wrote to Fechenbach, revealing just how fragile party unity was at this juncture: 'South German Conservatives are connected to the leaders of the party by only loose ties ... [They] are at root national-Christian-social. Of these many will probably support our beloved *Volk*.'[25] Naumann concluded his letter to Fechenbach by comparing their lonely struggles to inject a new spirit into Conservatism: 'It is remarkable how many questions lay fifteen years ago just as they do now.'

*

Among Conservatives in late 1895 there was little agreement about the character or significance of the internal party struggle. The only common sentiment was the fear that the liberal parties might watch the DKP destroy itself from within. Some contemporaries observed that the DKP was still struggling to come up with an answer to the question Röder had posed in the title of his articles in mid-1895: 'What is the significance of Socialism for the Conservative Party?' The ambiguity of the DKP's response was typified by the *Deutsches Adelsblatt*'s contradictory call for 'a little more popular, Christian Social spirit' in the DKP and for a revision of the universal franchise: 'Never reach into a wasps' nest, but if you do, grasp firmly!'[26]

The battle-fronts were hardened when the leaders of the Pomeranian Conservative *Verein* unexpectedly backed the reformist Protestant pastors in the province.[27] They issued a brochure, *For our Rural Workers*, which argued that Conservatives were no longer correct to regard rural workers as 'politically not of age'.[28] Around the same time the Conservative *Verein* in Elberfeld (Rhineland) demanded that the Berlin DKP leadership call another general party congress.[29] Eager to dispel the notion that the Conservative Party was 'only an agrarian party of nobles', the Elberfelders asked 'whether the founding of an independent Conservative *Volkspartei* might not be more appropriate to the interests of the Conservative cause'. By January 1896 Engel feared the worst. He wrote that the DKP would be blind to believe, 'in the age of the universal franchise and the widest publicity', that it could be an 'agrarian party of Junkers'. However, on 21 January, Limburg publicly called on the government to treat the social question as a pure question of power (*glatte Machtfrage*).

Thus, when the Stöcker crisis climaxed in a meeting of the Committee of Eleven on 1 February 1896, few men in either the CSP or the DKP could prevaricate any longer on the issue of social reform.[30] No longer were the lines blurred between Christian Social reformism and reactionary Conservatism.[31] The Committee of Eleven had debated Stöcker's relationship to the *Volk* on 2 December and 16 January. The campaign against Stöcker was led by the Herrenhaus notable, Schlieben-Sanditten, together with the later president of the House of Deputies, Jordan von Kröcher, and Manteuffel. Klasing and Durant rallied (though rather ineptly) to Stöcker's defence. By the meeting of 1 February, Stöcker was aware that some manoeuvring on his part was required to reap the greatest possible benefit from his impending break with the DKP. To this end Stöcker prepared a 'social motion' for the meeting's agenda, which was never discussed but which Stöcker subsequently published to illustrate his commitment to social reform.[32] Stöcker reinforced the effect of this 'non-declaration' with his own explanation of his withdrawal from the DKP, which he presented to his CSP followers at a Berlin rally on

8 February.[33] Here, too, Stöcker did his utmost to draw a clear line between 'his' Christian Social followers and the Naumannites, but the net effect suggested how reluctantly he had abandoned the Conservatives. Similar agonies suffered by the Conservative Party leadership – trying to prevent what eventually occurred, the full secession of the CSP from the DKP – illustrated how they, like Stöcker, feared the consequences of this necessary but unpopular act. In the contest to establish or break down the fiction of a continuing Conservative commitment to 'popular' politics, the DKP leaders knew immediately that they were going to have a very difficult time convincing rank-and-file reformers that the break with the Christian Socials had been merely a conflict over Stöcker's relationship to the *Volk*.

Reactions to the events of 1 February varied considerably, but most observers recognized the central issues involved: social policy and Kartell politics. The *Deutsche Zeitung* was typical of the Kartell press when it headed its article on Stöcker: 'Enough Social-Political Legislation for Now!'[34] The Free Conservatives left no doubt about where they thought the 'cleansing act' of Stöcker's dismissal would lead, while the National Liberals hoped that the abandonment of Stöcker would lead to the expulsion of other 'demagogues'; they named Ploetz as the next man to go. By contrast, the left-liberals spoke of the Conservatives' surrender to Stumm and of their new-found acceptability at court (*Hoffähigkeit*).

There were diverse reactions in the Conservative camp as well. The *Reichsbote* came down on the side of the Committee of Eleven, but Engel's overall response in the aftermath of the crisis was characteristically ambivalent. Although he wrote that the time had come for Stöcker to devote himself exclusively to the Inner Mission, he also opened the columns of the *Reichsbote* to Stöcker's supporters.[35] The *Kreuzzeitung* under Kropatschek was more firmly on the side of the party leadership; few observers failed to note the magnitude of the shift in *Kreuzzeitung* sympathies since the departure of Hammerstein. In provincial *Vereine*, however, and in the smaller Conservative journals that spoke for them, dissatisfaction with the party leaders reached a new peak in February and March 1896. The editors of the *Deutsches Adelsblatt* summed up the five main arguments used in this campaign.[36] They were convinced, first, that the Committee of Eleven had resolved to 'expel' Stöcker by demanding of him humiliating concessions. Second, they were outraged that many Conservatives were now choosing to ignore the decision of the Tivoli congress to renounce the use of forceful measures against Social Democracy. Third, they believed that the expulsion of Stöcker was going to force the right wing of the Christian Social Party towards a reconciliation and then an alliance with Naumann. Fourth, the abandonment of Stöcker was criticized as a *conditio sine qua non* and a cynical last step on the way to making the DKP once more worthy of being a Kartell partner. Lastly, they believed that the move against Stöcker was the final battle in a war against 'social conservatism' which stretched back to the time of Fechenbach's Social Conservative Alliance in 1881. Thus the *Adelsblatt* pledged to keep alive the 'social aristocratic idea'.

A meeting of Thuringian Conservatives in mid-February displayed, on the one hand, how the *Adelsblatt*'s arguments were seconded by regional Conservative spokesmen and, on the other, how circumstances conspired to convince many socially conscious party men that they would be left without influence if they, like Stöcker, decided to withdraw from the Conservative Party. Pastor von Gerlach-Ziegenrück declared in Erfurt that the diversity of interests within the DKP, which had been the party's great strength since 1892, was now to be abandoned. Gerlach proposed a strongly worded resolution against the Committee of Eleven. It quickly became apparent, however, that the resolution was too radical for the assembly. The CSP deputy Gustav Jacobskötter and others argued for a much milder text. Eventually a resolution was agreed upon, regretting Stöcker's withdrawal from the DKP but stating that the formation of an independent Christian Social Party was disadvantageous to the Conservative cause.

In Berlin, Pomerania, Hanover, Westphalia, the Rhineland and elsewhere, similar pressures for and against the Berlin party leadership were expressed. Although generally the same conclusions were reached about the need to remain in the Conservative Party, the bitterness generated reached unprecedented levels.[37] Members of one west-German *Verein* cheered a local pastor who told them that the Conservative Party faced the same fate that Germany might have suffered if Moltke had been removed from the Prussian General Staff before the Franco-Prussian war. Malke-witz called in the *Pommersche Reichspost* for all pro-Stöcker Conservatives to raise 'the sharpest protests' against the DKP leadership, while the *Badische Landpost* predicted that the DKP would be devastated by the crisis.[38] Bavarians, least surprisingly of all, agreed fully with this scenario. 'What shall we do in Bavaria?' cried the editors of the *Süddeutsche Landpost*. 'If the Conservative Party continues on the path it has taken, we will have to answer whether we are a conservative court party or a conservative *Volkspartei*.'[39] The future of German Conservatism had never been more clouded.

At a Christian Social rally on 26 February an independent CSP was founded under Stöcker's leadership. Before the end of 1896, however, it seemed that Naumann had drawn most remaining Christian Social reformist enthusiasm – together with Gerlach and Oberwinder – on to his side.[40]

As we look back on the events of 1893–6, two questions seem especially pressing. Why did the threatened rebellion against the Conservative Party leadership fail to materialize? And why did the protests of rank-and-file party activists in the provinces, supported by a significant section of the Conservative press, fail to halt the DKP leadership on its path towards *Machtpolitik*? Any answer to these queries must emphasize Wilhelm's growing distrust of social reform. This distrust played a decisive role in convincing the Conservative leaders that a swing to the right – necessitating a break with the CSP – was under way in German politics. Stumm's battle against Naumann, too, was an early development in the chain of events which led to more harmonious relations between Conservatives and former Kartell partners. The 'amputation' of Conservatism's social conscience opened the way for renewed ties between agriculture and heavy industry. It also facilitated the offering of government concessions to large estate owners, a strategy designed to undercut the propaganda of the Farmers' League. Perhaps it even set the stage for the introduction of the Kaiser's own idea of *Weltpolitik* (world policy), announced in a speech by Wilhelm on 18 January 1896.[41] Wilhelm's own perception of the situation in 1896 was as revealing as anyone's. When Stöcker withdrew from the DKP, Wilhelm offered the ironic comment that 'Stöcker has ended just as I predicted years ago. Political pastors are an impossibility. One who is Christian is also "social".' He then added: 'Christian Social is an absurdity (*Unsinn*) and leads to self-presumption and impatience.'[42]

Hellmut von Gerlach identified a much deeper reason why Stöcker failed to survive politically. In doing so he also provided a comment on the larger tensions confronting Conservatives in the *Kaiserreich*:[43]

[Stöcker] always cast his eyes upwards . . . He wanted to win the masses but on no condition lose the good will of the court and the aristocracy . . . Whenever it was a matter of 'either-or', he sought a 'not only but also'. That was his downfall . . . When he was faced with the decision: Above or below? For the lords or for the servants? – then he evaded the issue. He tried to reconcile the irreconcilable, until in the end almost no one trusted him any longer.

As Stöcker's hope for a social monarchy became more distant than ever in the changed circumstances of 1896, he found that effective co-operation between such different political forces as the Christian Social and Conservative parties was impossible.

In the end, the suddenness and completeness with which Conservative *Vereine* abandoned the Christian Social appeal remains baffling. To the mystery of Engel's sudden support for the Committee of Eleven can be added any number of other developments still shrouded in obscurity. One thing alone is clear; on a broad scale, in meeting after meeting in town halls across Germany, the vast majority of Conservatives decided that their interests could best be served by remaining loyal to the Conservative Party.[44]

This fact provides an important comment on the DKP's continuing ability to command respect as the party most representative of 'conservative' views in the *Kaiserreich*. Even though the specific policies it endorsed had alienated a large body of opinion within the Conservative community, the DKP had survived intact, and survival itself was a significant victory in the uncertain political atmosphere of the mid-1890s. This was not to be the last occasion on which a rebellion from the lower ranks threatened the authority of party leaders. But it may well have been the moment when those leaders first recognized that to display the full scope of the party's reactionary tendencies was not necessarily to commit political suicide. This was an unfortunate lesson for Conservative leaders to have learned, because it highlighted the DKP's affinities with other anti-democratic groups gaining strength in these years. But it reaffirmed many party members in their view that they had, in fact, chosen correctly in 1896. Now less interested in being all things to all men, the Conservatives could exploit their still considerable political strengths in other areas. This allowed them to focus their energies and to defend their economic interests during the quieter years ahead more successfully than if they had still been wracked with internal dissent on social policy. Only with the coming of new crises in 1909 would circumstances force Conservatives to rededicate themselves to their 'popular mission'. By then, the strategies for popular appeal and political mobilization that proved most successful had little to do with Christian Social reform.

NOTES

1 Frank, *Stöcker*, p. 239; Heffer, *Kreuzzeitungspartei*, p. 233.
2 Eulenburg, *Korrespondenz*, Vol. 2, p. 1313, letter of 28.5.94.
3 *KZ*, 19.5.94; Eulenburg, *Korrespondenz*, Vol. 2, pp. 1233 ff., Helldorf to P. Eulenburg, 1.3.94.
4 BAK, Kl. Erw. 455 (Reck), f. 83–100, including Reck to B. Eulenburg, 4.10.94 (draft); Reck to Wilhelm, 15.9.94 (draft).
5 *NWVZ*, 9.9.94; *Rb*, 8/12.9.94; *KM*, 51, 1894, pp. 1079 ff., 1233–8.
6 For this and the following see BAK, Kl. Erw. 455 (Reck), f. 80, 98, Engel to Reck, 12.9.94, and B. Eulenburg to Reck, 20.9.94; Schmitz, 'Bewegung', *passim*; Massing, *Rehearsal*, pp. 116 f; Gerlach, *Von rechts*, pp. 134 ff.; Gerlach, *Erinnerungen*, pp. 85 ff.; Oberwinder, 'Was ist konservativ und staatserhaltend', in *DtWbl*, 4.3.99, pp. 343 ff.; and other works on the *Kreuzzeitung* group.
7 ZStA II, Rep. 77, CB S, 165, I and II; CB P, 42.
8 Cf. Heuss, *Naumann*; Fout, 'Protestant Christian Socialism', Pt III; Fricke, 'Nationalsozialer Verein'.
9 *NAZ*, 8.3.94; *KnZ*, 2.10.93; *Vk*, 4.1.94, 4.3.94; cf. Oertzen, *Konservativ oder christlichsozial?*.
10 This conflict is reviewed in BAK, NL Harden, 77, f. 3, Naumann to Harden, 31.10.95; cf. Blumenthal, *Wer geht mit?*; and reviews of works on the social question in *KM*, 50, 1893, pp. 112 f., 578 f., and 52, 1895, pp. 423 ff.
11 BAK, Kl. Erw. 227 (Hüpeden), Hüpeden to Frank, 2.9.28.
12 *Rb*, 25.1.95, 23.3.95; *Vk*, 20.1.95, 3.3.95; Frank, *Stöcker*, p. 250; *KZ*, 22.3.95; *DAB*, 14.4.95.

13 See *Vk*, 2/4/8/11/15/17.5.95; *Rb*, 5.5.95; *KM*, 52, June 1895, pp. 645–8 (original emphasis); ZStA I, NL Naumann, 132, f. 8, Stöcker to Naumann, 8.6.95; Naumann to Stöcker, 22.6.95, and Liebermann von Sonnenberg to Stöcker, 8.4.95, in Eckert, 'Wandlungen', pp. 328 ff.

14 *KVZ*, 9.6.95; *NAZ*, 3.7.95; *DAB*, 7.7.95.

15 Besides the standard works on the *Kreuzzeitung* group, see Hall, *Scandal*, pp. 149–54; *Die Nation*, 18, 1.2.96; on stolen letters, BAK, Sg F, XXXVI, Gerlach to Fechenbach, 7.10.95, and ZStA I, NL Waldersee, B, I, 50, f. 4, Stöcker to Waldersee, 12.10.95.

16 The 'Funeral Pyre' letter of 1888 (see above, Chapter 4) was published in *Vw*, 5.9.95.

17 Cf. BAK, NL Harden, 77, f. 3, Naumann to Harden, 31.10.95.

18 For example, *Rb*, 26.7.93, 9.8.93.

19 For the following see the *CC* articles in *Rb*, 21.2. 94, 7.4.95.

20 Massow, *Reform oder Revolution!* and *Die Reform unseres politischen Parteilebens*; cf. BAK, NL Harden, 71, Massow to Harden, 10.11.94, 17.4.97.

21 *KVZ*, 7.10.95.

22 *Vk*, 7.1.94; *Rb*, 9.1.94, 21.9.95; *BT*, 7.1.94; *KZ*, 3.3.94; *KVZ*, 7.10.95.

23 Cf. Burckhardt to Stöcker, 3.9.95, and other correspondence in Fricke, 'Christlich-soziale Partei' (*Lexikon*), pp. 445 ff.

24 See the Fechenbach–Gebert–Manteuffel correspondence in BAK, Sg F, XXXIV.

25 BAK, Nl F, 43, Naumann to Fechenbach, 10/28.11.95.

26 See *KZ*, 25.11.95; *DAB*, 29.9.95; *KVZ*, 7.10.95; *Rb*, 20.8.95.

27 *Zukunft*, 6, 1895, pp. 249–56; *KVZ*, 25.10.95; *Rb*, 9.11.95; *Vk*, 16.11.95.

28 *Für unsere Landarbeiter*; works by the 'maligned pastors' are found in ZStA II, Rep. 77, CB S, 97, I; cf. *Sozialreform*, 2.11.95, pp. 545–9; *Rb*, 30.10.95; *DTZ*, 29.10 95, 16.11.95; *Vk*, 16.11.95.

29 *Rb*, 15.11.95.

30 Official DKP version in Krause, *Austritt*; CSP version in Kynades, *Herkules*; cf. Röder, *Austritt*.

31 Cf. ZStA I, NL Naumann, 132, f. 8, Stöcker to Naumann, 8.6.95.

32 Krause, *Austritt*, pp. 18 f.

33 See *Vk*, 8.2.96; Massing, *Rehearsal*, pp. 123 f.

34 *DAB*, 9.2.96; Oertzen, *Stöcker*, Vol. 2, p. 386; Frank, *Stöcker*, p. 272.

35 *Rb*, 21.2.96.

36 *DAB*, 9.2.96; cf. *Vk*, 30.1.96, and Kynades, *Herkules*, pp. 9 f.

37 For the following, see *Vk*, 2.2.96, 4/15.3.96; *Rb*, 1.4.96; *Deutsche Reichszeitung*, 7.2.96, 28.3.96; *KZ*, 11.4.96; on the particularly volatile situation in Westphalia, see BAK, NL F, 'Interna 1896', Lange to Fechenbach, 9.4.96; *NWVZ*, 10.3.96; *Rb*, 26.2.96, 8.10.96; Stöcker to Klasing, 14.2.96, in Hoener, 'Christlich-konservative Partei', p. 101; further references in my 'Reformist Conservatism', pp. 228–31.

38 *DtRp*, 2.1.96, 5/6/10.2.96, 6.3.96, 30.9.96.

39 *SddLp*, 4.2.96, 31.3.96; cf. *KM*, 53, 1896, 'Die Krisis in der konservativen Partei', pp. 299–305; BAK, NL Seeberg, 112, Martin von Nathusius to Seeberg, 2.2.96, 19.11.96.

40 Stöcker to Max Braun, 29.8.96, in Oertzen, *Stöcker*, Vol. 2, p. 397; on the later history of the CSP cf. the literature review in Fricke, 'Christlichsoziale Partei'; also Levy, *Downfall*, pp. 246–55.

41 Cf. Stegmann, 'Wirtschaft', pp. 170 ff.; Wilhelm's speech in Wippermann, *Geschichts-kalender* (1896), Vol. 1, pp. 37–45.

42 Telegram from Wilhelm to Stumm, 28.2.96, printed in *Die Post*, 15.5.96; cf. *PrJbb*, 84, 15.5.96.

43 Gerlach, *Von rechts*, pp. 104–7.

44 Cf. the copious reports in Wippermann, *Geschichtskalender* (1896), Vol. 1, pp. 230–68.

PART III

Agrarian Radicalism and the Conservative Response, 1896–1909

10

Conservatives, the Farmers' League and His Majesty's Government

The dilemmas inherent in the Conservative Party's intermediate position between radical agrarianism and moderate governmentalism reflected the party's failure to choose decisively between the politics of mass mobilization and the politics of élite influence.[1] However, to say that the DKP's role between 1896 and 1909 was 'quasi-oppositional' is not sufficient. Did the party 'hover' between the extremes of governmentalism and opposition, or did it 'oscillate' between these two courses?[2] From the one argument we might suppose that the Conservative Party's survival up to 1918 was due to its successful tightrope act between the agrarian and government camps. From the other we might surmise that the DKP was essentially a destabilizing force in Wilhelmine politics and that its erratic course presupposed a disastrous end. Neither view is entirely correct. A new perspective is required to depict the full complexity of the three-way relationship between radical agrarians, Conservatives and Wilhelm's government.

Soon after passage of the Russian trade treaty in March 1894 it became clear that the BdL leaders would continue to oppose the government on three major agrarian issues. They developed a programme of 'large demands' (*große Mittel*) which they believed would save German agriculture. These were: (1) the establishment of a state monopoly in grain imports, guaranteeing a minimum price to domestic producers (the so-called 'Kanitz proposal'); (2) the introduction of bimetallism; and (3) stock- and commodity-exchange legislation to limit trading in grain futures. Kanitz introduced his revolutionary proposal in the Reichstag less than one month after the DKP's defeat on the Russian treaty.[3] However, Caprivi and speakers from all but the two conservative parties dismissed it out of hand. They claimed that it benefited only large landowners and that it was based on the dangerous premiss of 'state socialism'. Faced with a vote of 219 to 97 against the third Kanitz proposal in January 1896, the Conservatives were finally forced to abandon the first of their three 'large demands' once and for all. They did no better with their second demand, the introduction of bimetallism. Only the third demand achieved any real resonance. The agrarians claimed that a reform of commodity-exchange regulations would protect German investors from unscrupulous speculators (whom the BdL usually characterized as Jewish). The League induced the government to introduce legislation meeting many (though not all) of its demands; on 22 June 1896 an Exchanges Act was passed by the Reichstag. It quickly became apparent, however, that the government was not interested in enforcing the new regulations rigorously. Critics such as Max Weber immediately began to argue for another revision, and a new Exchanges Act in 1908 largely reversed the 1896 legislation.[4]

In contrast to the determined opposition of the radical agrarians, Engel wrote in March 1894 that dissatisfaction among farmers and artisans had to be channelled back within proper limits. 'Opposition in principle', he declared, was a dangerous new feature of agrarian radicalism that did the work of democrats, anti-Semites and Socialists.[5] After the first Kanitz proposal was defeated in 1894, Conservatives began to wonder whether agrarian ambitions threatened their party itself, and this concern persisted.[6] The *Conservative Correspondenz* declared that it was not the task of the Conservative Party to help with the organizational work of the Farmers' League, and noted that in the last election the League had supported some opponents of the DKP. A year later the *Correspondenz* and the *Reichsbote* were still arguing that 'one cannot guard and preserve the independence of a *political* party too jealously'. But the agrarians were committed to radicalism. At one point the *Korrespondenz des Bundes der Landwirte* claimed that the German farmer was 'now inclined . . . to see the Kaiser as his political enemy'. Later the *Deutsche Tageszeitung* vented the BdL leaders' frustration with governmental Conservatives: 'When the *individual* wants to do something in the Reichstag, the *caucus* intrudes, fearful that . . . he could embarrass it or disturb it too much from its inactivity.'[7]

On the eve of a general party congress in early 1898, Edmund Klapper published a startling article in his new journal, the *Deutsche Agrarzeitung*. Entitled 'League or Manteuffel?',[8] it presented the DKP with the spectre of the Farmers' League reconstituting itself as a parliamentary party, as Klapper claimed it had originally intended. Klapper also charged that Manteuffel had 'gone with his following of courtiers over to the side of the government'. At their party congress a fortnight later, the Conservatives and agrarians succeeded in donning a mask of unity.[9] Yet it was clear that only a fragile compromise could be worked out between Ploetz and Manteuffel, with the former probably conceding less. Stretch as they might, Conservatives and radical agrarians could not bridge the gulf between their two conceptions of 'party politics'. Instead, they declared loudly that they had done so.

This brief chronicle of BdL–DKP antagonism in the 1890s indicates that some well-placed Conservatives felt their first allegiance was to the DKP, not to its agrarian interest group. To be sure, they defended their right to represent the interests of agriculture in parliament, in the press and at the

Kaiser's court. They also recognized that the government had good reason to retain the allegiance of Germany's leading élite in the rural east. But they knew that on certain key issues they could press the government only so far and no further. They were not interested in the prospect of more banishments from court. They were not interested in providing the government with a reason to rely on Reichstag majorities that excluded the Conservative Party. They were not interested in dissolving the Conservative *Vereine* in the provinces and leaving the tasks of agitation entirely to the Farmers' League. And least of all were they interested in jeopardizing a basic community of interest between the government and the DKP; both could agree on the need to resist democratization, to combat Social Democracy and to pursue a strong foreign policy.

Even these governmental Conservatives wished to see their party win popular appeal. But for them the distinction between the party and the interest group remained important. They opposed the new radicalism of the agrarian movement – at least once Caprivi had been toppled – because they believed that chauvinistic interest politics and radical anti-government propaganda were driving away some important groups from the Conservative Party. For them, the Conservative Party as such, not the Farmers' League, was to be the mainspring of an anti-Socialist crusade. These men were also unwilling to concede the principle of the imperative mandate, as was shown by the East Prussian nobleman's defection on the Russian trade treaty vote. Instead they believed they could strengthen the DKP's influence by setting limits to the BdL's extremism, not giving it free rein. By defending the organizational independence of their party and by preserving their right to determine official Conservative policy, these men claimed that the DKP, not the BdL, was responsible for attracting the broadest possible range of electoral support, for winning tactical advantages in parliament by compromising where necessary and for providing the fullest defence of the established order. In a number of ways, then, Conservatives refused to compromise on fundamental Conservative principles with which many believed the BdL leaders had broken long ago.

Governmental Conservatives wielded an especially problematic influence in top DKP ranks because it was difficult to determine exactly which Conservatives could be counted upon to support the government at what times, with what motives and with what success. Leaders like Manteuffel, Limburg, Kröcher, Stolberg, Mehnert and Klinkowström come to mind as the most prominent members of this group. But it would be entirely wrong to imagine that they pursued a consistently governmental course opposed to agrarian interests. Relative to other alliances and party groupings in the *Kaiserreich*, the Conservative-agrarian community remained a surprisingly cohesive force, winning major concessions from the government on many economic and political reforms which threatened their joint interests.

Nevertheless, factionalism within the Conservative–agrarian camp profoundly affected government policy on a number of crucial issues between 1896 and 1909. German chancellors and ministers often conspired to widen differences of opinion on the Right. Their drafting of legislation and their conduct of bills through parliament, their determination to root out excessive agrarian sympathies in the Prussian bureaucracy, their propaganda campaigns in the press and their arguments in Crown councils, even their readiness to dissolve parliament and call elections against the Farmers' League – all these policies endorsed by German chancellors after 1896 suggest how seriously the strategy of 'divide and rule' was pursued. Knowing that they could not bow to radical agrarian demands without disrupting the expansion of German industrial power and antagonizing the Left, both Hohenlohe and his successor, Bernhard von Bülow, acted upon the opportunities they found to draw the Conservative Party to their side. They often succeeded on issues which did not directly affect Conservative pocketbooks. They tended to fail when Conservatives were persuaded by their radical auxiliaries that the survival or demise of German agriculture was at stake. Even so, the government followed a surprisingly consistent policy. It repeatedly sought to separate the 'true' and the 'demagogic' spirits within Conservatism, hoping to isolate the agrarians in opposition. In this hope the government was repeatedly frustrated. For ministers and Conservatives alike there was no easy resolution to the paradox of 'loyal opposition'. The political sympathies espoused on all sides were too complex and too volatile to permit a stabilization of battle-fronts. But in believing that the Conservative Party had a vital role to play between the government and the Farmers' League, the moderate Conservatives were not mistaken.

In 1899 a bill was introduced into the Prussian Landtag which proposed the building of a long canal to link the Rhine in the west of Germany, the Ems and Weser rivers in middle Germany and the Elbe in east-central Germany.[10] Although primarily meant to help industry, the government believed that the *Mittelland* Canal Bill would contribute to the reconciliation of industrial and agricultural interests. It argued that the canal would stimulate industry and yet decentralize it, that farmers along the banks of the canal would benefit from improved irrigation and drainage facilities and that the Kaiser was determined to see the project win legislative approval.

Despite these arguments the agrarians immediately launched a number of objections to the bill.[11] The anti-capitalist, anti-industrial animus behind their position was evident from the outset. The Farmers' League claimed, first, that the canal would open the floodgates to foreign grain imports, which could then be distributed more cheaply in Berlin and throughout the nation. It claimed, second, that better transportation would aggravate the 'flight from the land' which was reducing the work-force of agricultural labourers in east Elbia. Finally, it argued that the finances of the Prussian state would be gravely jeopardized by construction of the canal, since income from state-owned railways would be reduced. All these points were included in the BdL's counter-proposals without, however, giving them inner consistency. In fact the variety of compensations demanded by different regional spokesmen contributed substantially to the impression that the Conservatives were disunited. The government quite understandably believed that individual deputies would be willing to vote for the canal if local objections were met.

Disunity in the agrarian-Conservative camp eventually induced thirty-nine DKP deputies to break ranks and vote for the final (much reduced) version of the canal project in February 1905. Both partners had maintained a relatively united front in the months before the Canal Bill suffered a preliminary defeat in the House of Deputies on 19 August 1899. However, eight Conservatives voted for the bill and another eight withheld their votes or remained absent. Both Röder and Engel advised Conservatives to make a 'royal sacrifice' and submit to the will of their king.[12] It subsequently became known that Rhineland and Berlin Conservatives had expressed similar sentiments. Such defections had already compelled the *Korrespondenz des Bundes der Landwirte* to warn the DKP that its aim to be a 'popular party' demanded that it not 'degrade itself as a tool of the government'.[13] The same bitterness greeted more serious defections to the government side when later versions of the bill were debated in 1901 and when final passage was won.[14] For example, Franz von Bodelschwingh-Schwarzenhasel, a BdL activist and radical anti-Semite from Hesse, spoke out against those Conservatives who accepted agrarian organizational and agitational help at election time and then abandoned its platform when faced with the possibility of opposition to the government. In a letter to the Conservative Party's Committee of Eleven, Bodelschwingh claimed that DKP deputies were voting for the government's bill only due to 'ignorance and weakness of character'. Despite such admonishments from radical agrarians, many moderate Conservatives feared the prospect of a 'liberal era' if the Conservatives were totally excluded from the Canal Bill majority. Typical was the view of Pastor Möller-Gütersloh, the leader of Westphalian Conservatives: 'We cannot agitate against the canal with democratic means, as the League under Hahn and colleagues is doing . . . We have certainly had to accept worse things than the canal.' Helpless to prevent final passage of the bill, the radical agrarians could only denounce such arguments – and the Conservatives who used them – as 'weak', 'feeble' and 'traitorous'.[15] In March 1905 the BdL press in effect offered local members an open invitation to drop pro-canal Conservatives as future candidates.

These differences between the Farmers' League and the Conservative

Party were over both tactical and substantive issues. But the canal crisis, especially in August 1899, represented the occasion on which the government most seriously considered abandoning the agrarians as an essential prop of the political status quo. These two aspects of the canal issue – BdL–DKP conflict and agrarian–government conflict – were intimately connected. Very different tactics were used by Hohenlohe in 1899 and by Bülow in 1905, depending on how each gauged the significance of BdL–DKP dissension. On the first occasion, when 'demagogic agrarianism' was perceived to be closely allied with traditional Conservatism, the government feared to act. On the second occasion, the government could bring its campaign to a successful conclusion precisely because it had achieved a separation of these spirits. That the more Draconian steps against the Conservatives were undercut from the beginning or abandoned altogether does not detract from the significance of the fact that such ideas were entertained seriously. Indeed, the inability of the Kaiser and his government to reconcile paradoxical views of the DKP's role in the political system of the *Kaiserreich* becomes all the clearer when such 'non-events' are reviewed.

In the early summer of 1899 Hohenlohe wrote to Philipp Eulenburg: 'If the Canal Bill is defeated we must have a [Landtag] dissolution, and the Prussian state will be moved on to rails further left. That does not frighten me; but it is always a step in the dark, and if it can be avoided, all the better.'[16] On 20 August, in the first of a series of state ministry and Crown council meetings over the next four days, Hohenlohe believed a dissolution was necessary to preserve the 'authority of the Crown and the government'. The DKP now regarded the canal issue as 'a question of power', the chancellor told his ministers:

> there exists the danger that the Farmers' League, including the Conservative Party, would force many officials more and more into its following and gradually, in common with the anti-Semites, reach for means against the government as pernicious as those used by Social Democracy.

Finance Minister Miquel, however, suggested that new elections were unwise. For in an election campaign the government would have to offer the slogan, 'Here the Crown, there the Farmers' League.' If the elections should fall to the latter ('which', Miquel noted, 'is not entirely impossible') the situation would become even more critical for the Kaiser.

At the opening of the Crown council with Wilhelm on 23 August, Hohenlohe dismissed Miquel's arguments and did his utmost to make the Kaiser move against the Conservatives. But Wilhelm in the end feared to launch such a campaign. Instead he merely adjourned the Landtag and had the offending Prussian officials dismissed from their posts. To make the

DKP 'feel his rage', Wilhelm thought that shutting their leaders from his court would suffice. This decision to dismiss the so-called 'canal rebels' – eighteen *Landräte* and two district governors – was highly controversial in its own right.[17] But Wilhelm saw few problems on the horizon when he deputized Bülow by telegram to 'let your press hounds loose and . . . crush the party'. Since he believed that the opposition to 'his' canal reflected 'crass stupidity' paired with 'malicious intent', Wilhelm sought to match his blustering against the Conservatives with practical measures against the Farmers' League. Prussian officials were forbidden from belonging to or supporting the BdL. The Kaiser's rhetoric, however, did not translate well into practice, as the provincial administrators charged with implementing his policy informed their superiors in Berlin.[18]

It was precisely this failure on the part of the government to divorce the BdL from the DKP in 1899 that inclined many government figures to draw back from a further heightening of tension.[19] Wilhelm himself had second thoughts. After two of his leading court figures lay down their posts in sympathy with the dismissed Conservative officials, Wilhelm complained to Bülow: 'The great men of my court are leaving me.' Bülow subsequently began the quiet job of reinstating a number of *Landräte* to their posts. Hohenlohe most clearly displayed the extreme ambivalence in government circles. For despite his earlier arguments, Hohenlohe could conceive of neither a full alliance nor a full break with the Conservatives:

To have a dissolution without detaching the officials from the Farmers' League would not have much use. Above all, the administration must be purged. Still, I regret we have not had a dissolution. I am sure the Conservatives would have suffered a healthy defeat. *But of course how would H.M.* [Wilhelm] *work with a liberal ministry?*

When thirty-nine Conservatives voted for the final Canal Bill on 8 February 1905, neither the agrarian nor the government side could legitimately claim a clear-cut victory. Beforehand the *Kreuzzeitung* had tried to explain away the partial Conservative defection. It claimed that Bülow succeeded only because the government had avoided many former mistakes and had not made the canal a *political* issue.[20] However, the government *did* regard the outcome of the *Mittelland* Canal Bill as a highly 'political' victory over the radical agrarians. This was made clear by one of Bülow's leading advisers shortly before the vote, when he wrote that

the whole *Conservative* press . . . has taken a stand against [agrarian] agitation. . . . If a majority can be won for the Rhine–Hanover Canal, that is at the same time a desirable strengthening of those Conservative circles who object to the demagogic intrigues of the BdL. The safe passage of the Canal Bill will therefore be at the same time an auspicious success for the whole of domestic politics in Prussia.

Unquestionably the most decisive agrarian issue which drew the attention of Conservatives in the period between 1896 and 1909 was the revision of the Caprivi trade treaties, which was debated intensely from 1897 to 1902.[21] During the twelve-year term of the treaties, disillusionment in Conservative circles mounted. Grain prices remained lower than the average for the 1870s and 1880s. Estate indebtedness grew to more distressing proportions, as did the flight from the land. In 1895, however, the Kaiser had instructed Hohenlohe to make whatever concessions were possible to agriculture, since Conservative votes were necessary to permit passage of some of Wilhelm's favourite projects. These included a Courts Martial Bill (1898), a Prison Bill (*Zuchthausvorlage*, 1899) and two Navy Bills (1898 and 1900). This general intention was also reflected in various ministerial shuffles which gave the Prussian state ministry a more conservative complexion.

As revision of Caprivi's tariffs became more immediate the government established an advisory Economic Committee (*Wirtschaftlicher Ausschuß*) in 1897. The willingness of the government to appoint men like Wangenheim to this committee illustrated how eager it was to anticipate and redress the complaints of agriculture. This did not mean, however, that either heavy industry or the government endorsed extreme BdL demands or wanted commercial interests excluded entirely. When Hahn tried to stake the BdL's claim to leadership in a new *Sammlung* or 'rallying together' of economic forces in 1897–8 his proposals met with passionate resistance from representatives of heavy industry, from leading Conservatives and even from Roesicke himself. Partly due to Hahn's radicalism the Reichstag election campaign of 1898 saw Conservatives and National Liberals far from united.[22] There was also considerable disunity on the government's side over tariffs.[23]

The precise level at which grain duties would be set dominated debates on the tariff legislation.[24] In 1899 the German Agricultural Council called for a duty on rye and wheat of at least 6 marks per 100 kilograms; other agricultural bodies subsequently proposed duties on these and other grains ranging from 6 to 8 marks. When the Economic Committee presented its proposals in October 1900, most agrarians could have been happy with its recommendation that the minimum duties for all four grains (wheat, rye, oats and barley) be set at 6 marks. At 1900 trading prices, this duty represented a tariff of 43 per cent on rye and 40 on wheat.[25] Over the next two years conflict raged over the new tariffs. The various proposals are summarized in Table 10.1 (opposite).

The political significance of the legislation was considerably increased by the parliamentary stalemate that ensued through much of 1902. This

Table 10.1 *Proposals for Agricultural Tariffs, 1901–2 (marks/100 kg)*

Proposal	Rye	Wheat	Barley	Oats
Previous (Caprivi) tariff	3.5	3.5	2.0	2.8
Economic Committee (Oct. 1900)	6.0	6.0	6.0	6.0
Government bill (June/Dec. 1901)	5.0	5.5	3.0	5.0
Reichstag commission (Oct. 1902)	5.5	6.0	5.5	5.5
Wangenheim (Oct. 1902)	7.5	7.5	7.5	7.5
Kardorff (Nov. 1902)	5.0	5.5	4.0/1.3	5.0
Final bill (14 Dec. 1902)	5.0	5.5	4.0/1.3	5.0

allowed tensions to rise, interest-group recriminations to become more distressing and Social Democrats to press their obstructionist tactics. When the second reading began in October 1902, speculation arose whether the government would dissolve the Reichstag and call for elections against the radical agrarians who refused to compromise. But Conservatives at that point grew desperate in the face of the SPD threat; they feared that the tariff increases would fail to win passage at all. At length, in November a way around the impasse was offered by Kardorff of the FKP, who was a member of the BdL but opposed its extreme demands. The so-called 'Kardorff proposal' restored the government's minimum grain duties, although it split the tariffs for barley between that used for human and for livestock consumption. Although the Farmers' League rejected this proposal, Conservative editors and parliamentarians now argued that larger political considerations required compromise. Kardorff's proposal was finally accepted, and the third reading of the tariff bill passed by a vote of 202 to 100 at four o'clock in the morning of 13–14 December 1902, after an eight-hour obstructionist speech by an SPD deputy.[26] Thirty of forty-three Conservatives who voted on 14 December supported the final tariff agreement.

Historians continue to debate whether the agrarians achieved their demands with the tariff increase of December 1902. On the one hand the moderate Conservatives could be satisfied with the considerable increase in duties included in the bill, especially in the face of Socialist obstruction.[27] On the other hand it is not difficult to see why the radical agrarians refused to compromise. They could safely vote against the bill on 14 December, knowing it would pass in any case, and then continue to call themselves good agrarians in the next elections. Yet neither of these explanations adequately accounts for the willingness of the BdL directorate to contemplate a final break with the DKP, a gamble that might well have brought disaster to the Farmers' League. But that is exactly the course the BdL pursued immediately after passage of the Kardorff proposal. When the BdL issued a call severing all ties with Reichstag deputies,

Conservative or otherwise, who had voted for the final tariff bill, they were not debating a mark here or there; even their insistence on questions of principle was unconvincing. What the BdL was inaugurating was nothing less than a *Machtprobe* or bid for power to decide which group would determine Conservative policy.[28] The result of this conflict between the BdL and DKP was itself ambiguous. Nevertheless, the estrangement between radical agrarians and moderate Conservatives in early 1903 highlighted a fundamental divergence of outlook between the two groups that had larger implications for the future of the Conservative Party.[29]

The DKP was divided in its response to the BdL's disavowal of all Conservatives who supported the Kardorff proposal. Manteuffel, Kröcher and others demanded the expulsion of Wangenheim, Roesicke, Hahn and Oertel from the party caucus. Heydebrand and the new DKP caucus leader in the Reichstag, Oskar von Normann, sided with the BdL.[30] When Wangenheim declared in a speech in Königsberg that the 'middle parties' (and especially the Free Conservative Party) had to be destroyed, Kardorff resigned from the Farmers' League on 24 December. If Kardorff's published correspondence is to be believed, Kanitz, Stolberg and Count Hans von Schwerin-Löwitz stood firmly behind him. As Stolberg wrote on 28 December: 'We Germans certainly have an uncommon lack of cleverness in political life. – Finally the state-supporting parties have pulled themselves together and knocked the Social Democrats on the head, and as soon as the goal is won, the Farmers' League falls on us from behind.'[31] Around the same time, some of the Conservatives' wealthiest patrons resigned from the BdL in sympathy with Kardorff.

A strategy of *public* reconciliation was inaugurated almost immediately. Even so, two of the most prominent actors in this drama revealed the depth of the antagonism between the Conservatives and the Farmers' League. Mirbach had already written to Bülow in December 1900 indicating his doubts about agrarian radicalism, and his view remained the same two years later. A 'decentralization of the Farmers' League', he felt, was necessary 'to break the influence' of Hahn and Roesicke. For in the face of a concerted Socialist threat a viable *Sammlung* of pro-government parties required the unity of German agriculture. For this reason Mirbach believed the DKP had to assert its authority over the BdL. The obverse of Mirbach's position was illustrated by Wangenheim just two days after the final tariff bill passed. Referring to the 'small clique' in the Conservative caucus 'which furiously hates the League and me', Wangenheim wrote that the crisis had shown 'what irreconcilable differences exist here between us and those who go another direction only out of weakness (*Schlappheit*) [and] side or private interests'.[32] Wangenheim listed 'nine or ten gentlemen' who would probably have withdrawn with him from the Conservative caucus, including Oertel, Oldenburg and the Württemberg

BdL functionary, Friedrich Schrempf. If a later break between the Conservatives and the Farmers' League occurred, Wangenheim predicted 'we would have a group of from twenty-five to thirty men, who would provide the starting-point for a new party'. Wangenheim's second estimate indicated the narrowness of this contest for the soul of the Conservative Party; twenty-five to thirty defections from the DKP to the BdL would have cut the Conservatives' Reichstag caucus exactly in half. But by Wangenheim's first estimate the Conservatives could easily have survived the proposed expulsions.

During the first six months of 1903 it seemed that Conservative–League differences erupted at every turn, despite frenzied attempts to downplay their significance. Mirbach, Kanitz and other moderate Conservatives – men whose agrarian credentials could not be disputed – continued to preach the 'politics of the attainable'. Yet the League's newspapers pressed the point about which group included the more principled defenders of German agriculture. The effort to leave mutual recrimination behind became more urgent during the Reichstag election campaign in the spring of 1903. Since so many Conservatives had disavowed their pledges to the BdL, the League nominated fifty-five independent candidates. The possibility that the BdL and DKP might go their separate ways was considered very real by the Bavarian envoy in Berlin and many others in top government circles.[33] In the Reichstag elections, however, only four of the BdL's fifty-five non-party candidates won election, and a number of leading League officials (Hahn, Oertel and Wangenheim) lost their seats. Subsequently, DKP and BdL leaders redoubled their efforts at reconciliation. An agreement was worked out for the Prussian Landtag elections of November 1903, and the benefits were quick to see; the majority of BdL-affiliated Conservative candidates were elected. When Heydebrand replaced Limburg as chairman of the DKP's Prussian House of Deputies caucus in 1905, Wangenheim wrote that Heydebrand was 'the only one who would lead the cause energetically and along agrarian lines'. All other possible candidates were 'devoutly governmental'.[34] From that point on, Heydebrand, Normann, Wangenheim and Roesicke worked together to avoid another such bitter conflict between the BdL and DKP.[35] After 1905 the working-out of DKP–BdL differences was undertaken with more give and take on both sides and was conducted as far as possible behind closed doors. It would be wrong, however, to imagine that fears of a Conservative defection to the government's side did not unnerve and enrage the radical agrarians in future crises. During the *Mittelland* canal debates Wangenheim revealed the essential dilemma that continued to confront the Conservatives:[36]

Success very doubtful, all the well-known people will likely defect in the end . . . In my opinion that will be the end of the Conservative Party; it only wants to fawn upwards, but from there it is trodden underfoot and has meanwhile lost its footing among the people, and will be superseded by the wild anti-Semites and comrades. *Quos deus perdere vult, dementat pius! –* [sic][37]

In the 'Hottentot elections' of January 1907 the right-wing parties and nationalist pressure groups waged a highly successful Reichstag campaign against the Social Democrats and Centre Party. The pro-government majority these elections yielded was known as the 'Bülow Bloc'. It extended from the Conservatives to the left-liberals and corresponded closely to Bülow's hopes for a 'pairing' of progressive and conservative forces in the empire. However, prospects for the successful resolution of a much-needed Reich finance reform were already murky when the government introduced its legislation into the Reichstag in November 1908. By then liberal ambitions for a reform of the Prussian three-class franchise, together with the disruption of the '*Daily Telegraph* affair', had put the Conservatives in an extremely antagonistic mood. (See Chapter 11.) The publication of the proposed tax reform drawn up by the State Secretary of the Treasury, Reinhold von Sydow, focused the Conservatives' long-standing opposition to a Reich tax on inherited wealth.[38]

When Sydow introduced his bill on 19 November 1908, the Conservative reaction was severe and uncompromising.[39] Having already labelled an inheritance tax 'the first step towards communism', the DKP's main spokesman during the finance reform, Baron Karl von Richthofen-Damsdorf, listed all the Conservative objections to the bill: it shook the integrity of the family (especially in the countryside) as a social institution; it imposed a harsh and unnecessary tax on wives and children at their moment of greatest grief; it burdened property far more than mobile capital; and it sought to infringe on the fiscal sovereignty of the individual federal states.[40] Over the next six months resolutions against an estate tax were issued by local BdL and Conservative *Vereine*, by the bulk of the agrarian press and by the German Agricultural Council and the Tax and Economic Reformers. Eventually on 24 March 1909 the Conservatives' Reichstag chairman effectively ended hopes for a Bloc compromise. Normann announced in the Reichstag that the Conservatives would carry out the finance reform only with a majority that accepted 400 million marks in consumer-goods taxes, rejected an inheritance or estate tax, preserved the traditional division of taxes in the empire and raised the last 100 million marks through contributions (*Matrikularbeiträge*) from the individual states.[41] When the Left walked out of committee meetings in late May 1909 the way was opened for the DKP and the Centre to develop alternative taxes which provided the required 500 million marks (partly through an imperial capital gains tax) but did not contain the hated estate tax.

The government's legislation was finally defeated by a vote of 194 to 186 on 24 June 1909.[42] Aware of having lost the confidence of his king during the *Daily Telegraph* affair and recognizing the larger failure of his Bloc policy, Bülow had already offered his resignation. He was requested by Wilhelm to remain in office until a final passage of the Conservative–Centre package was completed, which occurred on 10 July. A few days later Theobald von Bethmann Hollweg became chancellor. The Conservatives had registered their most significant economic victory over the government in the history of the Second Reich. In so doing, however, they had undermined their own anti-parliamentary principles by forcing a German chancellor to bow to the wishes of a Reichstag majority.

Even before the finance reform entered its decisive phase, the strains of the Bülow Bloc had brought out older tensions between moderate Conservatives and radical agrarians. To prevent a break, the BdL leaders and Normann had established their so-called 'Kolberg programme' in the late summer of 1908; this set out their common strategy to defeat Bülow's finance reform.[43] Yet as the finance reform crisis became acute in early 1909, dissent from the BdL grew within Conservative ranks. Baron Georg von Stössel, chairman of the local FKP–DKP *Verein* in Potsdam and later a Pan-German leader, sponsored a strong declaration which stated that Normann's refusal to break with the extreme agrarians had produced the danger of 'strong resentment' and 'great alienation' among urban Conservatives; in the future the DKP's Reichstag caucus might be neither 'loyally followed' nor considered 'nationally reliable'.[44] Stössel's argument did not undermine the Kolberg strategy; but its essentials appeared repeatedly in other anti-agrarian statements issued by various Conservative *Vereine* in the spring of 1909. These statements laid emphasis on the need for landowners to make the 'national sacrifice' of 500 million marks in new taxes; on the fear of popular and royal disapproval if Bülow were ousted; on the prospect of losing Conservative voters in the cities and among the *Mittelstand*; and on the wish to support a kind of 'noble Conservatism' standing above callous interest politics.

When Bülow's attacks on the agrarians in early 1909 led Oldenburg to counter with even more extreme polemics against the chancellor, many Conservatives felt caught in the middle. The Conservative chairman in West Prussia attempted to explain this situation to the former Conservative deputy who was now chief of Bülow's Reich chancellory, Friedrich Wilhelm von Loebell:[45] '[Oldenburg's] impulsive manner is . . . his *strength*, and one must bear with him if he sometimes lays it on too thick . . . In the committees and in the parliamentary caucuses, the "attainable" is separated from what is "sought after".' This letter and other Conservative statements like it created the impression in the chancellory that Conservatives were merely using BdL demagogy to win concessions from the government, and that they did not endorse the full agrarian programme. Certainly the BdL's leaders interpreted Conservative ambivalence in this light. In November 1908 Roesnicke warned Wangenheim that Bülow, an 'opportunistic politician' *par excellence*, would not miss the chance to exploit an anti-BdL backlash among governmental Conservatives if Oldenburg were given free rein to attack the chancellor: 'To precipitate this conflict would alienate a large number of Conservative caucus members.'[46] In April 1909 Roesicke's and Wangenheim's correspondence still noted that 'things are critically shaky on the Right' due to the Conservatives' 'lack of insight, resoluteness and reliability'. The characteristic feature of the Conservatives' reaction to the finance reform crisis, they felt, was 'the defection of all the weak ones'. League functionaries in the provinces expressed similar worries.

Bülow's efforts to prompt defections from the DKP in 1908–9 were in a way nothing more than a series of measures to keep from his own mind, and from Wilhelm's, the consequences if he should fail. On reports from Loebell and others warning him in the autumn of 1908 that the DKP would never accept an inheritance tax, Bülow wrote impulsively in the margin, 'Then the whole reform will fail', and carried on with his campaign to win public opinion and renegade Conservatives for his plans.[47] Among Bülow's successes were the German *Mittelstand* congress of 13 April 1909, at which the Conservative *Mittelstand* leader, Carl Rahardt, called for an end to agrarian opposition; the resolution of 6 April 1909 from the executive committee of the Conservative *Vereine* in the Kingdom of Saxony, recommending acceptance of the inheritance tax if necessary; and the *Reichsbote*'s consistent advocacy of a flexible and generous Conservative policy.

That a number of Conservatives desired the 'carrot' of government attention to their views is shown by their correspondence with the Reich chancellory. These sympathetic letters included Conservatives' own tax schemes, suggestions to help Bülow gauge the mood of the party and condemnations of the party leadership's short-sightedness. Bülow's reaction to such appeals was by no means passive. As one chancellory official wrote to a DKP dissenter in June 1909:[48] 'Could you not somehow state your opinion in the *Kreuzzeitung* or, if this refuses to accept, in the *Reichsbote*? It is still not impossible that your voice will elicit an echo.' More subtle intrigues were required to recruit the Saxon Conservative leader, Mehnert, for the government's finance reform. But shortly after the Saxon Conservatives' pro-inheritance-tax resolution was published, the Centre Party's press suggested the possibility that the backbone of Conservative opposition could be broken. Around the same time Loebell reported that a 'not inconsiderable majority' of DKP deputies were now in favour of an inheritance tax.[49]

We know that in the crucial vote of 24 June 1909 the backbone of Conservative resistance was *not* broken. Only six DKP deputies voted against the party majority, that is, for the government's tax. But once again, two other consequences of the finance-reform conflict seem equally significant. One was that Bülow staked his entire career on what turned out to be an exercise in self-deception. Clearly that self-deception was supported by conflicting signals emanating from the Conservative-agrarian camp. Secondly, Bülow's uncharacteristic inability to manoeuvre out of the crisis revealed a fatalistic attitude that the Conservatives were beyond reach.[50] Bülow's most revealing comments in this regard were included in his marginalia to memoranda from Loebell in April 1909.[51] Significantly, Bülow headed his musings about the possible defeat of his finance reform with two questions: 'What will the Conservatives achieve?' and 'What will the agrarians achieve?' To the latter question, Bülow replied that the agrarians would be labelled 'base egoists'. Bülow painted the DKP's prospects even more darkly:

> Confusion, bitterness, [and] depression among wide circles of Conservatives, especially in middle Germany, in the cities, among officials, lower-middle classes, etc. . . . real (not imaginary) compensations to the liberal-democratic idea in Prussia, in order to defend the party against the odium of a 'reactionary' rule by Junkers and priests. The Conservative Party will experience a set-back similar to [the one] in the '70s.

In June 1909, then, the Conservatives seemed to have chosen a political course which repudiated their ties with the Kaiser and his government; instead, they had chosen to appeal to radical oppositional sentiments among 'the people'. This turning-point in Conservative Party history was recognized at the time (and subsequently) as having major implications for the fate of the Reich.[52] It was acknowledged even by Heydebrand, who claimed in the Reichstag that the DKP's refusal to bow to the government's wishes had preserved the party's reputation with the people: '[Our] good conscience will maintain us when we go before the country and the voters to justify what we aimed for and what we have done.'[53] Little was Heydebrand to know that he would be continuing this campaign of self-justification five years later.

NOTES

1 Parts of this chapter first appeared in another form in the *Canadian Journal of History*: 'Conservatives *contra* Chancellor'; for fuller references throughout see my 'Reformist Conservatism', ch. 8.

2 Cf. Puhle, *Interessenpolitik*, pp. 204, 212; Stegmann, Wendt and Witt (eds.), *Deutscher Konservatismus*, p. vii.

3 Texts of the three proposals (7.4.94, 13.5.95, 4.12.95) in *SBR*, Vol. 137, p. 1414; vol. 142, pp. 938 f.; vol. 151, p. 91; cf. Kanitz, *Handelsverträge*; DKP, *Konservatives Handbuch* (1898), pp. 234 ff.; Puhle, *Interessenpolitik*, pp. 230 ff.; Fricke and Hartwig, 'Bund', pp. 246 ff.

4 Wippermann, *Geschichtskalender* (1896), Vol. 1, pp. 112–5, and (1897), Vol. 1, pp. 225, 363 ff.; DKP, *Konservatives Handbuch* (1898), pp. 529 ff.; Mommsen, *Weber*, pp. 73–6.

5 *Rb*, 20.3.94; cf. BAK, Kl. Erw. 455 (Reck), f. 80, Engel to Reck, 12.9.94.

6 Warnings by the *Rb*, *NWVZ* and *BadLp* cited in KVZ, 22.4.94; NAZ, 18.4.94; *Vk*, 3.3.95; *Rb*, 30.2.94.

7 *Rb*, 23.6.94, 23.8.95, 6/8.10.95; FkZ, 13.7.94; BNN, 9.7.95; DTZ, 9.7.95, 23.1.96; *Ger*, 25.10.96; *KVZ*, 27.11.96, 24.12.96 (original emphases).

8 *DtAgarZ*, 9/16.1.98; *CC*, 21/26.1.98.

9 Official protocol in *CC*, 4–12.2.98.

10 For the following see the DKP's 'Rechenschaftsbericht' in *CC*, 14–21.9.99; Eynern, *Kanalkämpfe*; Bialke, 'Kanalvorlage'; Horn, *Kampf*; Neumann, 'Innenpolitik'.

11 *CC*, 19.4.99, 3/16.5.99, 15/19/22/26.6.99, 17.8.99.

12 See *CC*, 17/21/31.8.99.

13 Puhle, *Interessenpolitik*, p. 222; *CC*, 18.9.99.

14 Correspondence between Reck, Bodelschwingh, Möller-Gütersloh and others, in BAK, Kl. Erw. 455 (Reck), f. 115–62.

15 Cf. ZStA I, NL Wangenheim, 1, f. 12, Roesicke to Wangenheim, 28.2.05.

16 BAK, NL Eulenburg, 54, p. 150 b, letter of 2.7.99. For the following see *Rkz*. 2003, f. 40 ff.; BAK NL C. Hohenlohe, 1612, *passim*; and ZStA II, 2.2.1., 29165, especially f. 162 ff., notes (22.8.99) on prospects for an election campaign against the Conservatives.

17 Cf. Horn, *Kampf*, pp. 139 f.; Rejewski, *Pflicht*.

18 Cf. GStA Berlin (Dahlem), Rep. 180, 13317, f. 1 ff.; *Rkz*. 1081, f. 3 ff.

19 See, for example, BAK, NL Eulenburg, 54, pp. 204 ff., P. Eulenburg to Bülow, 29.9.99, and 57, pp. 23 ff., 85 ff., P. Eulenburg to Bülow, 1.3.01 and 4.6.01; for the following, ZStA II, Rep. 53 E III, 4, f. 5–15; Bülow, *Denkwürdigkeiten*, Vol. 1, pp. 297 f.; BAK, NL C. Hohenlohe, 1612, f. 249 ff., C. zu Hohenlohe to Alexander zu Hohenlohe, 25.8.99 (emphasis added).

20 *KZ*, 21.12.04; for the following, *Rkz*. 2006, f. 98 ff., internal memorandum of 19.1.05 (original emphasis), possibly written by Loebell.

21 For background information and further references on the tariff issue, the *Sammlung*, and the so-called 'Kehr thesis', see Schöne, 'Verflechtung'; Bleyberg, 'Government'; Bonham, 'Modernizers', ch. 5; Stegmann, 'Wirtschaft'; Stegmann, *Erben*; Eley, 'Sammlungspolitik'; Puhle, *Interessenpolitik*, pp. 222–5, 238–40; Kehr, *Schlachtflottenbau*.

22 *CC*, 22.7.97, 16/20.9.97; Roesicke to Ploetz, 13.5.97, cited in Fricke and Hartwig, 'Bund', p. 250; Eley, 'Sammlungspolitik', pp. 49 ff.

23 Bonham, 'Modernizers', pp. 224 ff.

24 *SBR*, Vol. 182, pp. 2883 ff.; Vol. 185, pp. 5681 ff.; Vol. 186, pp. 7143 ff., for first reading (2–12.12.01), second reading (16.10.02–11.12.02) and third reading (13–14.12.02).

25 Hohorst, Kocka and Ritter (eds.), *Sozialgeschichtliches Arbeitsbuch*, Vol. 2, p. 123.

26 *SBR*, Vol. 186, p. 7232; *DTZ*, 15.12.02.

27 Conservative fears are starkly illustrated in BAK, Kl. Erw. 455 (Reck), f. 22, Reck to Bülow (draft), 8.12.02.

28 Cf. Puhle, *Interessenpolitik*, p. 223.

29 For the following see Kardorff, *Kardorff*, pp. 354 ff.; ZStA I, RLB/BdL press archive, 6516 ff., 'Handelsvertragspolitik', with over 500 pages of press clippings on this conflict; Limburg-Stirum, *Konservative Politik*, pp. 43 ff.; Schöne, 'Verflechtung', pp. 60 ff.; Bleyberg, 'Government', p. 408; Puhle, *Interessenpolitik*, pp. 223–5; Fricke and Hartwig, 'Bund', pp. 253 f.

30 On Normann's motives cf. BAK, NL Bülow, 107, f. 65, notes of 22.11.02.

31 Kardorff, *Kardorff*, p. 354 f.; cf. *KdBdL*, 17.12.02; *DtAgrarKorr*, 21.12.02.

32 *Rkz*. 316, f. 61 ff., Mirbach to Bülow, 17.12.00; reply, 26.12.00; BAK, NL Bülow, 105, f. 1, Mirbach to Bülow, 14.12.02; Wangenheim to his wife, 16.12.02, in Wangenheim, *Wangenheim*, pp. 76 f.

35 Lerchenfeld cited in Born and Rassow (eds.), *Akten*, pp. 137 f., 145 f.

34 ZStA I, NL Wangenheim, 1, f. 74, Wangenheim to Roesicke, 8.7.05.

35 Puhle, *Interessenpolitik*, pp. 224 f.; Stegmann, *Erben*, pp. 140–3.

36 Letter to his wife, 21.1.04, in Wangenheim, *Wangenheim*, pp. 77 f.

37 The last word should be 'prius'; 'Whom God would ruin, he first deprives of reason.'

38 On the finance reform see Witt, *Finanzpolitik*; Hartmann, 'Innenpolitik'; Bonham, 'Modernizers', ch. 6; on DKP policy specifically, Vogel, 'Konservativen'.

39 First reading of the finance reform (19–28.11.08 and 16–19.6.09) in *SBR*, Vol. 233, pp. 39 ff. and Vol. 237, pp. 8585 ff.; second reading (19.6.09–8.7.09), ibid., pp. 8692 ff.; third reading (9–10.7.09), ibid., pp. 9278 ff.

40 Cf. Vogel, 'Konservativen', pp. 243 ff.

41 *KZ*, 25.3.09.

42 For Richthofen's final speech and the roll-call vote, *SBR*, Vol. 237, pp. 8803 ff., 8826 ff.

43 ZStA I, NL Wangenheim, 3, f. 57 and 77, Wangenheim to Roesicke, 6.8.08 and meeting protocol, 2.9.08.

44 *KZ*, 25.3.09.

45 *Rkz.* 1391/5, f. 164f., Count Georg zu Dohna-Finckenstein to Loebell, 3.2.09 (original emphasis); cf. *KZ*, 28.3.09.

46 For this and the following, ZStA I, NL Wangenheim, 3, f. 87 f., Roesicke to Wangenheim, [14].11.08; ibid., 3, f. 102 f., and 4, f. 20–30, Heydebrand–Roesicke–Wangenheim correspondence from April 1909; ZStA I, NL Roesicke, 34, f. 267, 272, Ernst August Endell (BdL chairman in Poznan) to Roesicke, 3/19.4.09.

47 *Rkz.* 208, f. 21, marginalia to Loebell's notes of 8.9.08; cf. materials in GStA Berlin (Dahlem), Rep. 90, 1345, and *Rkz.* 209–13, *passim*.

48 *Rkz.* 213, Arnold Wahnschaffe to Dr Andrae (Kiel), 1.6.09; cf. correspondence with Mehnert, f. 89–119.

49 *KVZ*, 7.4.09, cited in Witt, *Finanzpolitik*, p. 278; ZStA II, 2.2.1., 27281, Vol. 3, f. 112, Loebell to Rudolf von Valentini, 28.4.09.

50 Cf. Loebell's reference to a Conservative–government 'test of power' (*Kraftprobe*) in the draft of a letter to Dohna-Finckenstein, 29.6.09; *Rkz.* 213, f. 266 f. Wilhelm referred to the 'so-called loyal Conservatives' in marginalia to press clippings in BAK, NL Bülow, 35.

51 Marginalia (8.4.09) to Loebell notes of 6.4.09, cited in Witt, *Finanzpolitik*, p. 275 f.

52 Cf. Eulenburg, *Korrespondenz*, Vol. 3, pp. 2259 ff., Johannes Haller to P. Eulenburg, 30.3.19.

53 *SBR*, Vol. 237, pp. 9322 ff., 10.7.09.

11

Nationalism, Monarchism and Anti-Socialism

After the mid-1890s the Conservatives found themselves forced to change a number of their fundamental attitudes regarding German nationalism, the role of the monarchy and the battle against Social Democracy. On one level the Conservatives' nationalist credentials were unimpeachable. Yet Conservatives gave only reluctant support to *Weltpolitik*; they preferred the Prussian army over the imperial navy; and they opposed the expropriation of Polish estates in the east. All these policies brought the Conservatives into conflict with others on the Right who were trying to define nationalism in their own terms.[1] The party's conception of monarchism also became highly problematic. How to be 'more royalist than the king' vexed Heydebrand and Normann after 1900 just as it had Hammerstein and Stöcker in the 1880s. At the same time, the growing Socialist threat forced Conservatives to reconsider their ideals and tactics on many other fronts.

Because of their many differences with the government on agrarian issues the Conservatives traditionally supported the foreign policy of German chancellors. Although there are many exceptions to this rule, the Conservatives' acclamatory role was a deliberate one.[2] This was revealed in the advice given by Count Kuno von Westarp to a *Kreuzzeitung* writer, Franz Sontag, who during the war was a leading Pan-German publicist. Sontag was advised that he 'should not be too severe on foreign policy' because the Conservatives already had 'so many differences with the government on domestic policy' that they were 'forced to hold back' in speaking out on foreign affairs. After the war Sontag was convinced that this pro-government attitude was one of the Conservatives' worst 'sins' against the radical nationalists' programme.

The DKP's anti-parliamentarism and its reverence for the authority of the state compelled the party to continue this tradition of restraint until the early years of Bethmann Hollweg's chancellorship.[3] Conservatives also felt that a parliamentary deputy was not privy to sufficient official information to officer criticism of the government's position or to advance alternative proposals on his party's behalf. A Polish deputy once spoke disparagingly of the Conservatives' lame efforts to restate a few essential points made previously in a foreign policy statement by Bülow; afterwards they 'returned home as confused as they were satisfied'. Although Heydebrand abandoned this policy of restraint with increasing frequency after 1909, it always contributed to the Conservatives' inability to match the radicalism of Pan-German speeches in either tone or substance.

Many areas of foreign policy directly affected the material interests of the Conservatives; yet other issues promised little reward. A German navy and German colonies were two such issues. Because other economic sectors like heavy industry or Hanseatic commerce were the principal beneficiaries of overseas expansion and shipbuilding, the Conservatives never generated any real enthusiasm for these campaigns. Even in the 1860s Ludwig von Gerlach had argued against naval construction on the grounds that the fleet was an idea – if not yet a reality – 'in which democracy has built itself a warm nest'.[4] The Conservatives continued to fear that a German navy, in contrast to the Prussian army, would be open to 'dangerous' democratic influences. Not only would the Reichstag have considerable control over an imperial navy, thereby increasing the impact of non-Prussian views on foreign policy. A navy would also be manned largely by bourgeois officer candidates, thus rendering it less reliable than the Prussian officer corps. The same anti-industrial arguments opposing the *Mittelland* canal were also used against fleet construction; fears about the swelling migration of rural labourers figured prominently in both campaigns. Finally, a navy would be of little use against either the Socialist threat at home or the seedbed of revolution abroad, France. Thus, at the BdL's general assembly in February 1900, a resolution was passed advocating a return to 'Bismarckian policy'. It did not require Herbert von Bismarck's later comment in the Reichstag to recognize the ambivalent Conservative response to *Weltpolitik*: 'A place in the sun is certainly desirable; but there are places, and there can be temperatures, where the sun burns too brightly and where one can thankfully go about one's affairs in the shade.'[5]

If Conservatives were opposed to *Weltpolitik* and the navy in principle, they proved willing to support them for tactical reasons. In the colonial debates of 1884–5 they demanded the raising of grain tariffs as compensation for their support of Bismarck's overseas expansion. In 1894, when the fate of the Kanitz proposal was still undecided, the slogan launched by the agrarians was: 'No Kanitz, no ships.' And in 1905 one Conservative conspicuously used a parliamentary debate on naval increases to issue another call for repressive government measures against the Social Democrats.[6] In each of these campaigns there arose disagreements between the Conservative Party and the Farmers' League over naval policy. The radical agrarians and governmental Conservatives parted ways under circumstances and with motives very similar to those examined in Chapter 10. Both tended to react unenthusiastically to the announcement of new naval building plans. But the Conservatives consistently took the lead in arguing that, in the end, a national sacrifice was necessary.[7] Much has been made of the fact that just four days after the Centre and the Conservatives signalled they were going to permit final passage of the second Navy Bill in late April 1900, the government announced its support for the protection of agriculture and its intention to raise agricultural tariffs. But the real significance of Conservative support for the two Navy Bills lay elsewhere. On the one hand the Conservative Party recognized that the winning of a reputation for national reliability, when it demanded the abandonment of only secondary economic goals, argued for a temporary departure from interest politics. On the other hand the BdL learned within what limits it could pursue its opposition to the government. On the naval question the Farmers' League pushed those limits to the extreme, while the DKP was more faint-hearted. But this allowed the Conservative Party to reap greater political rewards for its national sacrifice than did the League, exactly as in December 1902 when it accepted the Kardorff compromise on tariffs. On both occasions the party chose to define its nationalist commitment in its own way.

In the government's programme of repression against Polish nationals in the eastern provinces of Prussia, the Conservatives also followed willingly. The DKP's endorsement of national goals was relatively un-problematic when Bismarck took hesitant, limited steps in 1886 to establish a Royal Settlement Commission to buy up Polish estates for resale to German farmers. The Conservatives also whole-heartedly sup-ported Bülow when he embarked on campaigns to limit the cultural, linguistic and political independence of the Poles; they applauded the so-called 'muzzle paragraph' which was included in the Association Bill of 1908. Such repressive measures against the Poles were politically valuable but materially inexpensive to the Conservatives. However, when the government's Polish policy threatened to set a dangerous precedent by expropriating Junker estates in the east or disrupting the supply of cheap Polish labour, the Conservative response was less straightforward.[8]

Some have seen the DKP's Polish policy as further evidence of a new racialist or 'revolutionary' strain within Conservatism. The Farmers' League, in this view, overwhelmed more traditional viewpoints within the Conservative Party and led it to endorse a policy of confiscating large estates in the east.[9] Closer examination reveals that a large proportion of Conservative landowners did not conceive of the 'war' in the east in racialist terms at all. The DKP and the government (especially under Bethmann Hollweg) shared a traditional, limited, 'Bismarckian' concep-tion of the Polish question which stood in clear opposition to more radical solutions endorsed by a small minority of BdL members and by the Society for the Eastern Marches (Deutscher Ostmarkenverein, or DOV).[10] When these nationalist groups rallied support for an Expropriation Bill in the Prussian House of Deputies in 1907–8 and then pressed for its implementation in 1911–12, the Conservatives showed how success-fully they could resist such a dangerous attack on the sanctity of private property. Heydebrand used the threat of a revolt by forty or fifty Conservatives in the Landtag to win many economic concessions and political privileges for the eastern Junkers, even while paying lip-service to the nationalists' campaign.

Exactly the same response was provided on the issue of Polish labour-ers. On the one hand the Conservatives continually pressed the govern-ment to keep open the borders to seasonal workers from eastern Europe, because this kept wages low.[11] On the other hand the Conservatives did their best to add their voices to those denouncing the growing Polish influence in Poznan and West Prussia. In the end, through the many compromises made between them, the Conservatives and the government together 'legitimized nationalist radicalism in *conservative* terms', as one historian has put it, rather than vice versa.[12] The Conservatives clearly recognized the 'democratic' and 'socialistic' tendencies of the radical nationalists; Wangenheim noted that 'the words "inner colonization" have become slogans for all the democrats and their press'.[13] Moreover, since the Conservatives were in no doubt about whether to permit confiscation of their estates or whether to employ cheap Polish labour, their response to a conflict between *Interessen-* and *Nationalpolitik* was a very traditional one. As Schwerin remarked in February 1910, 'the whole success of inner colonization depends, in the last analysis, on the fact that we get profitable prices for our agricultural produce.'[14]

This combination of indifference to nationalist appeals and reliance on traditional modes of influence in the countryside was to change after the finance reform of 1909. It then became much more difficult for the party to defend its political and ideological territory from either the Socialist Left or the nationalist Right. New nationalist campaigns, centred in geographic areas or social strata where the Conservatives commanded a weak follow-ing, made it virtually impossible for the DKP to resist the appeal of radical slogans.[15] But that change in political style did not happen overnight or uniformly in all parts of Germany. In the Prussian east, even after 1909, Conservative landowners preferred to see the Germanization of the Eastern Marches grind to a halt rather than make common cause with groups that differed from them so clearly in their social status, economic interests and nationalist ambitions.[16]

At least since Frederick the Great a tension had existed between Prussian aristocrats and the monarchy. After 1888, when Germans were ruled by a Kaiser known as Wilhelm the Sudden, this relationship became more difficult still. Even before the *Kreuzzeitung* group and the Farmers' League made explicit their criticisms of monarchical absolutism, it had been said of the Junkers that they paid absolute allegiance to the king 'as long as he does our bidding'.[17] But the Conservatives rarely acknowledged any ambiguity in their monarchist ideals. On almost every conceivable occasion (and some inconceivable ones) the party reaffirmed its motto: 'With God for King and Fatherland.' For the DKP, a defence of monarchical institutions was anything but a rhetorical centrepiece; it was the foundation of its whole political creed. A new and more critical attitude towards the monarchy, therefore, held the danger of undermining larger Conservative allegiances.

In 1903, when Bülow's inept defence of Wilhelm first made the Kaiser's 'personal rule' a topic of intense parliamentary discussion, Normann joined the other right-wing party leaders in an unsuccessful attempt to have Bülow warn the Kaiser of the consequences of his royal utterances.[18] The DKP's *Ratgeber* of 1903 caught this mood, expressing the Conservatives' desire for a monarchy free of 'absolutist arbitrariness', still directed by the grace of God but now attuned to the more worldly struggle against Social Democracy, anarchism, parliamentarization and a demagogic press.[19] In October 1908, when Wilhelm's notorious 'interview' on Anglo–German relations was published in the British *Daily Telegraph*, the German press in its entirety could not fail to see the liabilities of relying on the monarch to direct foreign policy.[20] It seemed the Kaiser was indeed, as Bismarck once described him, like a balloon: 'If you do not hold fast to the string, you never know where he will be off to.'[21]

The Conservatives, before they realized the scope of the parliamentary crisis the *Daily Telegraph* interview would evoke, sought to add their voice to those counselling greater restraint on Wilhelm's part.[22] Heinrich Engel advised the Kaiser to abandon his 'personal, impulsive and emotional politics of the moment' and to agree to 'more restrained comments in all political matters'. Germans were even more astounded to read a resolution from the DKP's Committee of Eleven, dated 5 November. This declaration was intended in the first instance to discourage further discussion of the affair. But it also called for more circumspection on Wilhelm's part, since his statements had 'not infrequently contributed to placing our foreign policy in a difficult situation'. It might appear that this was merely a parliamentary 'hiccup' that was immediately quelled by the cold dose of royalism provided by Oldenburg's subsequent declaration of allegiance to the Kaiser. Certainly Oldenburg's speech of 11 November was one of the most celebrated in a long line of parliamentary outbursts by a man who, it has been said, would have been more at home in West Texas than in West Prussia.[23] When Bülow sat silent on the second day of debate, an outraged Oldenburg rose and declared to the leftist deputies in the Reichstag:[24] 'For you the Kaiser is an institution, for us he is a person, and we will personally serve His Majesty the Kaiser, without fear but, to our last breath, with the old loyalty that we have never denied him.' Even Oldenburg's position, however, was not unambiguous, for he admitted in his memoirs that he had formerly warned his friend, Loebell, about the Kaiser's indiscretions. Oldenburg later suggested that the Kaiser should either 'rule within the constitution' or 'abdicate'.[25]

Statements by other leading Conservatives further dispel any notion that the party's declaration of 5 November was not meant in earnest.[26] But most revealing of all was the Kaiser's unsuccessful effort to have the Conservatives withdraw their declaration. Negotiations between the DKP leadership and the chief of the Kaiser's civil cabinet, Rudolf von Valentini, collapsed in March 1909 without result. Thirteen months later the Committee of Eleven issued an 'explanation' of the original statement; but this once again refused to disavow the call for restraint on the part of the Kaiser. In Bethmann Hollweg's view this statement was not sufficiently apologetic to be acceptable to the Kaiser. When members of the Committee of Eleven indicated their willingness to meet with Wilhelm to discuss the matter personally, they were rebuffed.

In their subsequent writings on the *Daily Telegraph* affair DKP spokesmen did their utmost to deny that the party had joined in the Reichstag's condemnation of Wilhelm's personal rule. They also denied that their role in precipitating Bülow's departure had undermined the Kaiser's exclusive right to appoint and dismiss his leading ministers as he wished.[27] In the end, however, through their actions in the extended crisis of 1908–9, the Conservatives *had* accelerated those trends they feared most: an increase in the effective power of the Reichstag and a diminution of monarchical authority. After 1909 the Kaiser slowly retreated in his public posture and in his influence over legislation. His chancellors, facing an increasingly democratic and determined Reichstag, were not allowed the same luxury.

It is impossible (and in any case unwise) to isolate the anti-Socialist strategy of one particular party from the larger web of offensive and defensive strategies undertaken by the Wilhelmine establishment. These strategies included state repression and indoctrination; the manipulation of electoral systems and practices; anti-Socialist alliances among the right-wing parties; and the 'stop and go' nature of social reform. To these must be added *Mittelstand* politics, as pursued by the parties and the state, which sought to insulate the middle classes against Socialist doctrine and economic 'proletarianization'.[28] At the BdL's first general assembly in 1894, Wangenheim stressed that the Farmers' League wanted to preserve not only agriculture but the whole *Mittelstand*, including 'the farmer, the artisan and the merchant, whose character signifies the most stable element within the disruptive tendencies of the present age'.[29] In the mid-1890s the Conservatives and the Farmers' League directed their special attention to the traditional artisan demand for obligatory guilds; their most important success here was the Artisans Bill of 26 July 1897. They also sought to limit the impact of other new features of economic life which threatened the material interests of the little man. These included consumers' co-operatives, chain department stores and artificial products such as margarine and saccharine. Finally, they attempted to recruit members of new social groups whose numbers were growing due to increased specialization in industry, a swelling government bureaucracy and an expanding service sector. This was the so-called 'new *Mittelstand*', comprised mainly of white-collar workers. The BdL and the DKP were not as intent on mobilizing the new *Mittelstand* as they were on protecting artisans, shopkeepers and small farmers, in part because members of the former group represented the dynamic industrial face of modern Germany which the Conservatives opposed. Also, the arguments and economic solutions proposed by the Conservatives in their *Mittelstandspolitik* were often contradictory; the little man could as often be a producer as a consumer. Nevertheless, the force of the Farmers' League's organic social ideal and the breadth of its propaganda gave new significance to the older anti-capitalist arguments of the Conservatives. By 1909 at the latest, *Mittelstandspolitik* was a major ingredient in the Conservatives' programme and an important part of their overall anti-Socialist strategy.

At different times during the history of the Second Reich different features of this anti-Socialist campaign were emphasized or revised, depending on the ability of the parties to co-operate among themselves or with the government. Broadly speaking, five main phases to Conservative anti-Socialist policy can be identified. In the first phase, between 1878 and 1890, Bismarck's anti-Socialist laws allowed the party to defer to state authorities in the struggle against the SPD. When those laws lapsed in 1890, the second phase began. This period was characterized by a two-front war for the Conservatives: on the one hand, a war in the rural east to resist the SPD's effort to win peasants and rural labourers (see below); on the other hand, the struggle within the DKP itself to define the limits of Conservative social reform. This phase ended when the SPD effectively abandoned its peasant policy at the Breslau meeting of late 1895 and when the Christian Socials and Conservatives parted ways in early 1896.

The third phase, considerably overlapping the second, found the Conservatives advocating a new, harsher anti-Socialist strategy in parliament. The abandonment of Stöcker opened the way for a revision of the Tivoli programme at the DKP delegates' congress in November 1896, which signalled this shift in Conservative policy.[30] After the striking of the explicit anti-Socialist passage at Tivoli, it was startling to see the openness with which the Conservatives now called for exceptional legislation against Social Democracy. Extending from about 1894 to 1903, this struggle for repressive legislation and for a halt to social reform resulted in something of a stand-off. All too often the Conservatives found that pro-reform ministers in government and left-wing parties in the Reichstag were capable of blocking any extreme measures. However haltingly, the cause of social reform continued to advance, and so did the acceptance of Social Democracy as a bona fide party with certain parliamentary privileges. This prompted Conservatives to speak more stridently than ever about the political divide between the Social Democrats and all other parties.

The fourth phase, extending to the outbreak of war, began when the Conservatives were forced to confront the implications of the SPD's dramatic gains in the 1903 Reichstag and Prussian Landtag elections (the latter had been contested by the Socialists for the first time). This was perhaps the most decisive shift in Conservative policy, and was recognized by a number of observers at the time.[31] The Conservatives' new determination to find common ground with other groups on the basis of an anti-Socialist campaign was reflected, first, in an exchange of letters between Stolberg and Bülow and, second, in the participation of leading Conservatives in the Imperial League against Social Democracy (Reichsverband gegen die Sozialdemokratie, or RvgSD).

Stolberg wrote to Bülow in late December 1903 to claim that it was the government's responsibility to show the right-wing parties the 'scope of the danger', to give them the 'nerve' to proceed and to assure the parties that they had the support of the government 'under all circumstances'.[32] This was the quintessential Conservative response to Social Democracy: to isolate the threat, to focus the attention of other parties on it and to demand the assistance of the state. However, the assurance that his government would support the parties 'under all circumstances' was exactly what Bülow could *not* provide the Conservatives. Bülow's reply in early January 1904 suggested instead that the government would have to continue to stand above the parties, and indeed that it would resist the most extreme demands of the Conservatives for armed conflict with the Socialists. Because the Conservatives and radical agrarians at this point were still disunited over the canal issue, Bülow's willingness to use the SPD threat as a political lever also became clear. Only if the Conservatives abandoned what Bülow referred to as their attempted 'degradation' of the Crown in the canal conflict would the state assist in the anti-Socialist campaign. Thus the Conservatives were forced to recognize the larger implications of their estrangement from the government and from other forces on the Right. That estrangement threatened the DKP's anti-Socialist strategy fundamentally. Even the arch-reactionary Reck began to ponder how anti-Socialist solidarity was possible as long as the DKP diverged from its right-wing partners on economic issues. He summed up this dilemma in the title of an article he tried (unsuccessfully) to publish in the *Kreuzzeitung* in January 1905; 'The *Mittelland* Canal in the Light of the Flames of St Petersburg, or: One Cannot Serve God and Mammon'.[33]

In the fifth and final phase, the domestic truce (*Burgfriede*) proclaimed at the outbreak of the First World War compelled the DKP to suppress its most vociferous attacks on the SPD. Within only a few months, however, the Conservatives began to resurrect earlier warnings about the Socialist threat. Anti-Socialism played a large role in determining the Conservatives' negative response to virtually all significant political reforms during the war.

One campaign which transcended all these phases was the effort to counter the Socialists' invasion of the countryside in east Elbia. This campaign, to use the military analogy so often employed by Conservatives, was only one of the more interesting battles within the larger war against revolution. It was, however, a campaign where both tactics and grand strategy were decisive; its outcome was determined as much by foot-soldiers as by generals.

Only twelve days after the anti-Socialist laws lapsed in October 1890, the Social Democratic party held its annual congress in Halle.[34] Because of the new possibilities for agitation and organization, and because the Reichstag elections of February 1890 had shown the potential for winning SPD votes in former Conservative preserves like Mecklenburg, Pomerania and East Prussia, it was decided in Halle that the time had come to devote special attention to the winning of peasants and rural labourers. During the winter of 1890–1 the SPD attempted to establish a party newspaper for rural workers. Other propaganda was soon being distributed in territories where people had only heard of, but never seen, Social Democratic agitators.

It became common to see troupes of SPD workers using their Sundays to travel out into the countryside, on foot or on bicycles, to distribute party literature. These Socialists, it is true, did not for the most part reach the completely isolated villages and estates in the east; instead they concentrated on rural districts lying near towns and cities, which could be visited in a single day. Usually the reception they received was anything but warm. In many areas they were treated as freaks – strange in costume, stranger in manners, strangest of all in the Marxist theory they attempted to introduce to a populace as aloof as it was illiterate. Virtually all public meeting-places were denied these agitators, and they often found attempts to stage open-air meetings broken up by gendarmes, officials, veterans' groups, even pastors and peasants. Beatings were not uncommon, nor was the practice of setting dogs upon the unwelcome visitors. In one famous incident in an outlying district near Bielefeld, the Socialists attempted to state their political programme on one side of a fence while a Conservative pastor led a local choral group in uncommonly robust song on the other. Eventually this demonstration degenerated into a brawl. The trampled fence between the two political domains symbolized the terrain on which many further battles were fought.

When it became apparent that the Socialist 'invasion' of the countryside was meeting considerable opposition, SPD leaders were forced to confront the larger implications of their effort to win over rural labourers and peasants. The result was an intra-party controversy which widened the split between revisionist and orthodox Social Democrats. Revisionists within the party argued that the peasant had to be offered something tangible from Socialist doctrine, but August Bebel insisted that he had no intention of feeding the 'fanatical private-property instinct of the peasant'.[35] At the SPD's Breslau congress of 1895, Bebel's view triumphed, signalling the end of determined Socialist agitation among peasants until the late 1920s.

The search for success among rural labourers was another matter. Here the Farmers' League found that its support for producers over consumers did not necessarily evoke a positive response, while the SPD was able to point out obvious inequalities of social, economic and political status to these workers.[36] The SPD none the less encountered many of the same difficulties with its agitation among rural labourers as with its appeal to peasants. These were compounded by other handicaps specific to agitation among the least affluent and most dependent social group in the countryside.

The limited success of the SPD in the countryside was also due to the counter-offensive launched in mid-1890 by the Conservatives and other anti-Socialist groups. Among the most frequently used arguments were warnings to small farmers that their harvests would rot in the fields as the result of a rural labourers' strike; that the 'right of association' was equivalent to the 'right to strike'; and that the flight from the land resulted not from better wages in the cities but rather from the 'pleasures and indulgences' found there.[37] However, there were some arguments that the DKP was very reluctant to use in this war. For even though landowners recognized that new efforts to insulate the countryside were necessary in the changed circumstances of the 1890s, they also feared the implications of bringing the political struggle within the horizons of the common man. The *Conservative Correspondenz* declared in August 1890 that the 'whole political conception of the common man' would be shaken if he saw that revolutionaries were being joined in debate or if their 'poison' were allowed to spread through word of mouth rather than being eradicated by decisive counter-attacks.[38] The last thing the Conservatives wanted was to prompt reflection among workers about the length of their working day, their housing conditions, or their wages. The rural population had to be armed for the onslaught, but not with sophisticated political arguments: 'When the enemy comes we want to serve him with fist and flail, according to the good old German custom!' It was this reaction to the SPD threat which the Christian Socials could not sanction.

By the mid-1890s the Conservatives seemed to be winning the battle in the countryside. The SPD restricted its agitation more and more to the short period of election campaigns, at least in the isolated districts. Rather than loudly proclaiming its victories when it managed to recruit workers in rural villages, it recognized that secret infiltration tended to avoid reprisals. Many other aspects of Conservative domination in rural areas remained in place. Due to difficulties of transportation and communication which persisted after the turn of the century, Socialist agitators were in a poor position to inspect official electoral lists. They also found it difficult to print electoral ballots, to use the post for the distribution of these ballots, or to travel out from the cities on election days to oversee the conduct of polling. For these reasons the stagnation of SPD votes in rural areas was very marked.[39] In communities with fewer that 2,000 inhabitants, the SPD's share of the popular vote in the Reichstag elections of 1912 was only 19 per cent; its share of the overall vote in the same year was 34.8 per cent. This relative weakness of the SPD in rural areas was most pronounced east of the Elbe.

Although the Conservatives thus had cause for hope that they would continue to prevail in their traditional domains, a much more concerted response was required when the Social Democrats first established a union encompassing rural labourers. In 1912 Wangenheim, Roesicke and a number of Conservatives participated in a series of meetings with government ministers, representatives of heavy industry and prominent figures from several nationalist pressure groups, in order to work out a more effective response to this latest SPD threat.[40] When these men discussed a plan to seize the initiative by organizing rural workers under the Conservative flag, the overriding question was: Is it too late? No unitary answer emerged from these and other pre-war conferences. But Oldenburg's gloomy predictions were perhaps truer than he realized: 'If we call into existence an organization of rural workers we do not know what direction it will take ...We have no legislative means to prevent the invasion of the Social Democrats into the countryside, as unfortunate as that may be, and I take the pessimistic viewpoint that we will achieve absolutely nothing with palliatives.' That few 'palliatives' were offered to the rural populace ensured that the full potential for social, economic and political conflict would be released under the impact of war and revolution. Whereas the socialist German Agricultural Workers' Association numbered only about 22,000 members in 1914, by the end of 1919 it comprised over 624,000 members.[41] The suddenness of this reversal would have astounded even the crusty Oldenburg.

NOTES

1 See also Chapter 15.
2 See Helldorff's RT speech, 19.2.78, cited in Albers, *Reichstag*, p. 38; BAK, NL 'Junius Alter', 6, 'Kampfjahre der Vorkriegszeit', p. 19, and 14, 'Die Sünden der alten Konservativen'.
3 See Westarp, *Konservative Politik*, Vol. 1, pp. 151–4; and speech by Kanitz, *SBR*, Vol. 260, p. 2133, 15.3.10.
4 Cited in Schüddekopf, *Innenpolitik*, p. 100.
5 Cited in Lindig, 'Einfluß des Bundes', pp. 206 f.
6 Berghahn, *Germany*, p. 57.
7 Cf. Kehr, *Schlachtflottenbau, passim*; *CC*, 8.12.97; Oertel's RT speech, *SBR*, Vol. 171, pp. 6022 ff., 12.6.00; DKP, *Konservatives Handbuch*, (1898), pp. 344–55, 'Marine-fragen', and the DKP's *Ratgeber* [1903], pp. 34 ff., 'Flotte'.
8 Cf. Land, 'Konservativen'; Hagen, 'Impact'; Hagen, *Germans*; Saul, 'Struktur Ost-elbiens'; Nichtweiß, *Saisonarbeiter*; and various studies by Bade.
9 Puhle, *Interessenpolitik*, pp. 255–61 – Puhle seems to disprove his own thesis by citing Heydebrand on p. 260; Hagen, *Germans*, p. 282 f., provides a more convincing account; cf. Booms, *Deutschkonservative Partei*, pp. 114–20.
10 Cf. Galos, Gentzen and Jacobczyk, *Hakatisten*; Tims, *Germanizing*; Hagen, *Germans*; Eley, *Reshaping*, pp. 58–68.
11 Nichtweiß, *Saisonarbeiter, passim*; VdSWR resolutions in Stephan, *25jährige Tätigkeit*, pp. 153 f.
12 Hagen, *Germans*, p. 287 (emphasis added).
13 Cited in Land, 'Konservativen', p. 72.
14 Cited in Peck, *Radicals*, pp. 62 f.
15 See materials in ZStA II, NL Kapp, C VIII, 1; C II, 10, 23, 25; Wolfgang Kapp pushed the Conservatives towards a more nationalist stance on inner colonization and the importation of seasonal workers, but before the war he met with very uneven success.
16 See especially Hagen, *Germans*, p. 284.
17 'Der König absolut, wenn er unseren Willen tut.'
18 Neumann, 'Innenpolitik', pp. 107–15; Westarp, *Konservative Politik*, Vol. 1, p. 40.
19 DKP *Ratgeber* [1903], pp. 44–9.
20 On the DKP's reaction specifically, the most useful accounts are Vogel, 'Konservativen', pp. 293–333; Hartmann, 'Innenpolitik', pp. 121 ff.; Cole, '*Daily Telegraph*'; Schlegel-milch, 'Stellung'; Westarp, *Konservative Politik*, Vol. 1, pp. 37–50, Westarp, 'Konserva-tive Partei'.
21 Cited in Kennedy, *Rise*, p. 405.
22 *Rb*, 3/12.11.08; *KZ*, 4/7/8/9/15.11.08; *DTZ*, 7/8/9.11.08.
23 Suval, *Electoral Politics*, p. 185.
24 *SBR*, Vol. 233, pp. 5436 f.
25 Oldenburg, *Erinnerungen*, pp. 58, 95–101.
26 *SBR*, Vol. 233, p. 5394, Heydebrand speech of 10.11.08; Heydebrand, 'Beiträge', pp. 574 f.; BAK, Kl. Erw. 455 (Reck), f. 28, Lange to Reck, 20.11.08; cf. *PrJbb*, 134, December 1908, p. 573; Westarp, *Konservative Politik*, Vol. 1, pp. 41 ff.
27 See mainly Westarp, 'Konservative Partei'. The Conservatives were not entirely successful in concealing this double game from Wilhelm; see BAK, Kl. Erw. 341 (Valentini), 1, 3, f. 15; Cole, '*Daily Telegraph*', pp. 264 ff.
28 On DKP *Mittelstandspolitik* see mainly Kaufhold, *Fürsorge*, which includes program-matic declarations, legislative reviews and sections on each major *Mittelstand* group; DKP, *Die politischen Parteien und das Handwerk* [1909]; DKP, *Konservatives Hand-buch* (1911), pp. 270 ff.; ZStA I, RLB/BdL press archive, files 2306, 5602, 6471, 6475, 9022.
29 Cited in Fricke and Hartwig, 'Bund', p. 249.
30 Congress resolutions (19/20.11.96) in Salomon, *Parteiprogramme*, Vol. 2, pp. 97–100; cf. DKP, *Konservatives Handbuch* (1898), pp. 418–37, 'Sozialdemokratie', and Kro-patschek's anti-Socialist polemic at the 1898 Dresden congress, in *CC*, 9.2.98.
31 Waldersee, diary entry of 1.7.03, cited in Hartwig, 'Konservative Partei', p. 298; cf. Fricke and Hartwig, 'Bund', p. 255.

32 BAK, NL Bülow, 107, f. 97 ff., Stolberg to Bülow, 27.12.03, and *Rkz.* 1391/5, f. 41 ff., Bülow to Stolberg, 7.1.04; cf. Eley, *Reshaping*, p. 228; Hartwig, 'Konservative Partei', p. 299.
33 BAK, Kl. Erw. 455 (Reck), f. 141 ff.
34 For the following see mainly Hussain and Tribe, *Marxism*, especially pp. 72 ff.; Lehmann, *Agrarfrage*; Maehl, 'Agrarian Policy'; Hübner and Kathe (eds.), *Lage*, pp. 229 ff.; Hübner, 'Ostpreußische Landarbeiter', pp. 561 ff.; Schaff, *Kampf*, pp. 269 ff.; Saul's 'Kampf', 'Struktur Ostelbiens' and 'Staat'.
35 Cited in Maehl, 'Agrarian Policy', p. 152.
36 Cf. Franz Rehbein, *Leben eines Landarbeiters* (1911), excerpted in Steitz (ed.), *Quellen*, pp. 400–8.
37 For the following see *DAB*, 28.9.90, 12.10.90; DKP, *Konservatives Handbuch* (1911), pp. 220–5, 'Landarbeiterfrage'; and works cited above.
38 Saul, 'Kampf', p. 177.
39 Cf. Lehmann, *Agrarfrage*, p. 261.
40 Protocols printed in Hübner and Kathe (eds.), *Lage*, pp. 409 ff.; cf. Gottwald, 'Reichsverband ländlicher Arbeitnehmer'.
41 Saul, 'Kampf', p. 167.

12

Electoral Franchises, Caucus Life and the Evolving Party Leadership

The Conservatives would have liked to do away with parties, programmes and polls altogether. Because they could not, there always existed a conflict between the party's basic anti-parliamentarism and its need to participate in a parliamentary forum where it never exercised true hegemony. We turn now to consider how the Conservatives sought to preserve or reinstate advantageous electoral franchises; how the social make-up of their national and state caucuses changed (or did not change) over time; and how the party leaders expanded their authority. By looking at how Conservatives reacted to the problem of pursuing politics in a hostile world we can better understand how they defined themselves as 'parliamentarians against parliament'.[1]

After 1871 the circumscribed role of Prussia within the empire continued to affront Conservative sensibilities, as did liberal ideals which had been incorporated into the constitution. But voices calling for the retreat of Prussia from the empire or for a drastic revision of the constitution were far more muted by 1900 than those calling for a revision of the universal franchise[2] and a more limited role for parliament. Even here Conservatives found that it was easier to criticize the 'creeping parliamentarization' of the Reich than to launch a frontal attack on the universal franchise. They repeatedly stated that while no move away from the idea of 'one man one vote' was imminent, they hoped that public opinion would soon be in favour of a break with this principle. In their private correspondence, however, they revealed their reactionary ambitions with much more candour.[3]

Conservatives advanced two main theoretical points against the Reichstag suffrage. They objected to it, first, because it was an 'individualistic' franchise which neglected the 'organic' organization of social estates and occupations. Second, it gave the principle of 'majority' precedence over the principle of 'authority', and thereby ignored the natural inequality of men. Both of these objections were as vehemently advanced by Conservatives in the twentieth century as when Bismarck first introduced the universal franchise into the North German Confederation in 1867. At that time, Adolf von Thadden-Trieglaff put it this way: 'I cannot recognize a basic principle according to which there is one elector for approximately 10,000 pounds of human flesh (including human bones), and perhaps 40,000 hundred-weight of these substances furnish a member of parliament.' In 1903 Conservatives still spoke of the 'animalistic principle' behind a suffrage which equated educated and uneducated Germans, those with property and those without, those flushed with youth and those with the wisdom of old age.[4]

There were particular features of Reichstag elections which the Conservatives had no inclination to change. They defended the increasingly disproportionate size of constituencies and practices of intimidation in the countryside against almost all efforts at reform. Positive 'remedies' for the universal franchise were none the less advanced by the Conservatives, most notably after Socialist breakthroughs in the Reichstag elections of 1890, 1903 and 1912. The Conservatives' suggestion to extend the length of legislative periods from three to five years had been implemented in 1888, but the party was not satisfied. Subsequent suggestions concerned the inauguration of mandatory voting; plural voting (giving extra votes to married men, men over 35 years of age, or those who had served in the army);[5] and the creation of an upper chamber (*Reichsoberhaus*) for the Reichstag. The last proposal was advanced so often by the Conservatives that the Reich chancellory had to set up a separate file in 1906 to include press reports covering these suggestions. After 1908 the Conservatives regarded the creation of such an upper house as an essential compensation for any adjustment of the Prussian three-class franchise. Other proposed amendments to the Reichstag franchise filled two further files in the chancellory, and newspaper clippings on the subject were collected in four thick volumes in the BdL's press archive.[6]

The most persistent demand for revision of the universal franchise was one which had been taken up by Stöcker and the *Kreuzzeitung* group in the 1880s: the replacement of a Reichstag elected by universal suffrage by a parliament elected and organized according to social estates (*Stände*). Concrete plans for such a parliament, even among Conservatives, varied enormously. One proposal by Oertzen in 1906 was typically mechanistic. Of four hundred Reichstag seats, one hundred were to be assigned to each of agriculture (half to large estate owners, half to peasants), industry (half to large industry, half to artisans), workers (half to rural workers, half to those in industry) and the professions (teachers, doctors, lawyers, officials, retired officers, the universities and the churches). Such an arrangement, Oertzen believed, would prevent the 'dictatorship of the proletariat'.[7]

The preference that would be given to the educated and propertied classes in these various schemes is obvious. The main social groups which the Conservatives claimed to represent or hoped to draw on to their side were given essential political advantages. It is also apparent that the increasing displacement of political questions by economic ones, and the concomitant growth of interest groups generally, were reflected in these calls for representation according to *Stände*. The Conservatives were certainly not the only ones who attempted to attract a new constituency with such appeals. The SPD's victory in the 1903 Reichstag elections increased calls for a *ständisch* franchise not only from Conservatives but also from employers' associations, army generals, *Mittelstand* groups and other right-wing organizations.[8] Nevertheless, it was usually the Conservatives who led the anti-democratic crowd, so much so that eventually they become isolated in the vanguard. For at each critical turning-point the other parties and interests retreated from a full-scale battle over the franchise. Many of them feared delivering the mass of voters over to the DKP almost as much as they feared the prospect of greater Socialist victories. In the end the universal Reichstag franchise was never overturned. The Conservatives were left to grumble on about the decline of parliament and the deliverance of political power to the masses. The realistic possibility of successful, decisive action against the universal franchise was one privilege which Bismarck, and all his successors, forever denied the DKP.

If Social Democrats had good reason to warn voters about the reactionary intentions of the Conservatives regarding the Reichstag franchise, the Conservatives gave away nothing to their opponents in their own defence of the Prussian three-class franchise. As Manteuffel declared at the Conservative delegates' congress in December 1907, any minister who proposed the Reichstag franchise for the Prussian Landtag would have to be charged with treason.[9] Dissatisfaction with the obvious discrepancies between the results of Reichstag and Prussian Landtag elections had accelerated after 1900 when the left-liberals began to make clear their intention to support the Social Democrats in demanding franchise reform.[10] Although he was not yet chancellor, Bethmann Hollweg's comments from 1906 illustrated that his thinking already diverged significantly from that of the Conservatives:[11] 'Our Prussian franchise is impossible to preserve in the long run . . . Its Conservative majority is so banal in spirit and so complacent in its feeling of inviolable power that it must be humiliating to any progressively minded man; we *must* find a new basis.' By early 1908 the left-liberal parties, now secure in the Bülow Bloc, demanded a comprehensive reform. At the same time the SPD had gone over to the tactic of organizing street demonstrations against the Prussian system.

To quell this rising tide Bülow had included in the Kaiser's throne speech of October 1908 a passage which promised that the Prussian suffrage would be modernized according to the principles of its own 'organic development'. The government signalled that it would introduce legislation designed to reward those whose social standing argued for greater political privilege, by means of plural voting. The eventual result was a government bill, introduced into the Prussian House of Deputies on 10 February 1910, which sought to appease both the Left and the Right without destroying the essential anti-democratic character of the Prussian franchise. In his calculations, Bethmann rightly supposed that the Conservatives could not afford another anti-popular campaign like the finance reform struggle of 1909, which had also involved an obvious defence of entrenched privilege. His aim was therefore 'to help the Conservatives make good the errors they had committed' and, as he later put it, to help them 'regain touch with the mood of the people'.[12]

Unfortunately Bethmann's modest franchise reform bill pleased no one.[13] Most loudly criticized for what it did *not* offer – the elimination of three-class voting – the government's proposal won only faint praise for its positive reforms. In the course of debate, moreover, the Conservatives and the Centre turned the government's bill on its head.[14] Instead of introducing direct voting, as the government intended, the bill emerged from committee debates that were dominated by the DKP and Centre in a form that resurrected indirect voting; and instead of preserving public voting, the committee insisted on the introduction of the secret ballot. Observers were astounded, for the Conservatives seemed to be voluntarily abandoning the public balloting that had so long preserved their political ascendency in the rural east.[15] However, the Conservative leaders had come to the conclusion that the secret Landtag franchise could be a benefit to them.[16] For it had recently become apparent that the Conservatives' intimidation of voters in the rural districts of the east was more than matched by the SPD's intimidation of shopkeepers, artisans and non-Socialist voters in the cities of the west. In the end Bethmann concluded that he had little choice but to withdraw the bill entirely, because it would not attract the support of any parties of the middle or Left.

The failure of Prussian franchise reform in 1910 displayed many features of earlier battles between the Conservatives and the government. (It also bore a remarkable similarity to the struggle for reform of the Saxon Landtag franchise, which had been resolved in the liberals' favour one year earlier.)[17] First, the Conservatives were throughly disunited. There was little communication between Conservatives in the Herrenhaus and in the House of Deputies, and even in the upper chamber the line of demarcation between moderates and die-hards was obscured until the final vote. However, Heydebrand's tactical genius left the liberals with nothing to show for their effort. Second, there was bitter disagreement among Conservative members of parliament, provincial spokesmen and newspaper editors about the need to accept any reform at all.[18] As in so many other crises, some Conservatives believed that a stand-fast policy was essential precisely because it might bring in its train a violent confrontation with parliament or the masses. Others, however, recognized that the best chance for legislating a palatable reform was to participate in the process and thereby avoid a more revolutionary solution. Third, the government displayed considerable uncertainty about Heydebrand's motives in accepting secret voting, and for a time it was hamstrung by doubts about whether Heydebrand's caucus colleagues would follow him.[19] Some members of Bethmann's administration hoped that enlightened Conservatism would carry the day. The State Secretary of the Interior noted that the Conservatives' decision to abandon the 'dogma' of public balloting might successfully defuse 'the charge of narrow-minded reaction . . . [and] give the party's policy a modern character'. But others were aware that the Conservatives were in the driver's seat and were unlikely to go beyond the appearance of making compromises with the Left.

Finally, this failure revealed Bethmann's own inability to confront the Conservatives directly. Bethmann pointedly observed after the crisis that the Conservatives had 'succeeded in focusing everyone's disgust and dissatisfaction against the three-class suffrage, which is generally seen as an expression of Junker predominance'.[20] But soon Bethmann came to see the limits to his own power. When the Prussian state ministry was considering another franchise reform bill in December 1913, Bethmann remarked that any reform must be enacted 'as far as possible in agreement with the Conservatives'.[21] And when he proposed to appoint Loebell as Prussian Minister of the Interior, he had to promise Loebell that he would not be asked to initiate another reform attempt. Bethmann had come to recognize the impossibility of proceeding decisively against the self-proclaimed protectors of Prussian interests.

The Farmers' League provided crucial assistance to the Conservative Party in the battle for votes under franchises neither the Left nor the Right was powerful enough to change. The results the BdL achieved were impressive. But it has already been noted that the agrarians' success at political mobilization prompted doubts in moderate Conservative circles as to whether the cost of participation in the new politics was worth the price. The historian Friedrich Meinecke wrote in 1911 that 'one's heart breaks to see how the Farmers' League has debased the propaganda of the parties to the level of machine work'. Writing about the style of politics, Meinecke referred in one breath to Heydebrand's 'desperado politics' and to the BdL's reliance on 'professional gladiators'.[22] Meinecke clearly expressed here the mood of a growing number of Wilhelmine conservatives after 1909, not all of them outside the DKP. Many of those within the Conservative Party who hoped to limit the impact of the BdL's style of politics on the DKP looked fondly back to a time when interest politics was not the order of the day and when Conservative sages, not sabre-rattlers, sat in parliament. A writer in the *Konservative Monatsschrift*, for example, argued in July 1912 against the imperative mandate, 'interest parties' and the 'mistrust' of authority.[23] Mirbach similarly regretted that the introduction of salaries for Reichstag deputies had reduced the influence of 'respected large estate owners with broad horizons' and had advanced 'little people with narrow vision, who are in a position to promise everything under the sun' and who 'ignore the interests of those with larger fortunes'.[24]

This remarkably persistent Conservative disinclination to descend to the level of political demagogy helps explain differences in the campaign style of the Conservatives and the Farmers' League. Where inequitable franchises allowed a more aloof posture, as in elections to state Landtage, the Conservatives took their pledges to the BdL programme far less seriously than in Reichstag elections, and they pursued their campaigns with far less financial and agitational assistance from the BdL. This was perhaps most notable in elections to the Saxon Landtag. As the Prussian envoy in Dresden reported in 1910: 'The Conservative leaders [in Saxony] are men of the old school who are opposed to any demagogic cultivation of the electorate and who, like Mehnert and [Rudolf] Hähnel, won their political experience in a time when the Social Democrats as yet played no role in Landtag elections.'[25]

The Saxon example, to be sure, was not wholly typical. Other statistics yield rather different conclusions about the impact of the Farmers' League on the Conservative Party.[26] They show, for instance, that every single Conservative who won a Reichstag seat between 1898 and 1912 was pledged to the BdL's agrarian programme. The same could be said for the vast majority of Conservatives who won Prussian Landtag seats. Rather fewer Conservative deputies were formally members of the League – in 1908, 122 of 152 Landtag deputies – because simply declaring in favour of the BdL's platform sufficed to win agitational assistance at campaign time. These figures also indicate that typically about one-third of Conservative deputies in the Reichstag caucus were higher functionaries in the BdL; that about one-fifth of Conservative deputies in the Prussian House of Deputies caucus were BdL functionaries; that roughly half of all constituency chairmen in the BdL organization (1897) were large estate owners; that between one-half and two-thirds of the BdL's functionaries were noble; that the percentage of non-noble BdL functionaries (or their relatives) sitting in the Conservative caucuses rose significantly;[27] and that BdL functionaries were represented even in the Prussian Herrenhaus.

Nevertheless, the sociological make-up of the DKP's parliamentary caucuses was only minimally altered by the advent of the BdL. Appendix 2 indicates that the Reichstag caucus was thoroughly dominated by large estate owners and landholders of other ranks both before and after 1893. Many other social groups also retained roughly the same representation. This suggests that whatever assistance the Farmers' League and other auxiliary associations provided the Conservatives was much more significant in electing Conservative candidates than in shifting the social balance within the caucus. It also reflects the failure of calls at Tivoli for a greater representation of the *Mittelstand* in parliament. The one clear shift was the rapid decline in the number of Prussian officials in the Reichstag caucus after 1893. The disciplining of pro-canal political officials in 1899 accelerated this trend.

There are three other groups of Conservatives for which a sociological analysis yields special rewards. These are the DKP caucus in the Prussian House of Deputies, the Committee of Fifty and the Committee of Twelve (the post-1900 variant of the Committee of Eleven).[28] The social make-up of the DKP caucus in the Prussian House of Deputies is especially significant because in the selection of their candidates for Landtag elections local Conservative *Vereine* could choose party men who closely represented their interests and those of the district. Far less weight than in Reichstag elections had to be put on the selection of candidates who would appear to be 'popular', since Conservative nominees less often faced large and hostile blocks of voters. The Committee of Fifty is also very revealing. Its meetings were private, and the Conservatives made no public noise about its social composition. Therefore the committee conducted its business, and regional Conservative *Vereine* nominated its members, without any great pressure to appear popular; there was little need to pad its ranks with token representatives of social groups to which the DKP hoped to appeal. This made the Committee of Fifty quite a different forum for policy-making than the party congresses, which assumed a much higher political profile and were directed mainly to embellishing the DKP's image as a *Volkspartei*. Finally, the importance of the Committee of Twelve needs little explanation. After 1900 it assumed the main decision-making power in the DKP, and it needed to solicit the Committee of Fifty's approval only from time to time.

Appendix 3 provides a rough sociological profile of the DKP's Prussian House of Deputies caucus. In 1903, 126 Conservative deputies represented east-Elbian constituencies and seventeen represented west-Elbian ones. Of the former group ninety were owners of large estates (that is, members of the agrarian élite), twenty-three came from the propertied middle classes in the city and countryside, nine were from the 'new' *Mittelstand*, including many bureaucrats, and four came from other business, professional or administrative élites. A total of sixty-seven aristocrats faced forty-nine commoners (if we include in the latter category men who were ennobled during their lifetime). Of the ninety large estate owners from east Elbia, forty-two had joined the officers corps of the Prussian army. Of these forty-two officers, twenty-six were career officers, three were retired generals and the remaining thirteen had retired to their estates after only a few years of military service. A further twenty-two of the ninety east-Elbian estate owners had entered the higher civil service after a university preparation, while twenty-five had pursued no outside career after their education, going directly into agriculture. This group included most of those who were born non-noble, hardly surprising considering the advantages that nobles enjoyed in receiving promotion in all the service branches. The educational background of eighty-four of these ninety east-Elbian estate owners is known. Exactly half had attended university. Finally, if we say (as contemporaries did) that a fortune of two million marks or more was the patent of a *grand seigneur*, while less implied inclusion in the lesser nobility or Junker class, then the Junker class clearly dominated the caucus in 1903. This domination was eventually to be extended to the highest reaches of the party.

The average age of these 126 east-Elbian Conservatives in 1903 was 55, approximately the same as the average for the Committee of Fifty. Yet the range of ages was very large indeed, and so was the age of initial entry into parliament. This reflects the many intangibles of local prestige, allowing some deputies to begin parliamentary careers early in life and forcing others to pursue other careers first. One hundred of these 126 east-Elbian Conservatives were members of the Farmers' League; six belonged to the BdL directorate, and twelve were BdL constituency chairmen. Many Conservative deputies also participated in the semi-autonomous administrative and co-operative associations of Prussian agriculture.

As with the Reichstag caucus, it is difficult to judge exactly how the social composition of the Conservative House of Deputies caucus was changed by the Farmers' League. The BdL did not win many new seats for the DKP in east Elbia, although it certainly helped them retain those they had. Of 126 east-Elbian seats won in 1903, 120 had been held since 1885 by either the DKP or another right-wing deputy. On the other hand, the proportion of nobles to commoners[29] in the eastern ranks of the caucus was noticeably reduced; in 1885 nobles had outnumbered non-nobles by a ratio of 2.3 to 1. In 1903 the ratio was 1.37 to 1.

Most of the seventeen Conservative seats from Prussian provinces west of the Elbe in 1903 had also been in Conservative hands since Bismarck's time. Naturally the role of the agrarian élite here was much less important than in the east. Only five deputies owned landed estates; all of these were noble and all could be classed as Junkers (by value of estate if not by geography). The other twelve deputies were all from the old and new *Mittelstand*. The influence of the BdL was most apparent in the provinces of the Rhineland and Hanover, but otherwise only nine of seventeen Conservative deputies from western Prussia were members of the League.

When we consider similar statistics from the years before and after 1903 we find that the long-term changes in the Conservative House of Deputies caucus were few. The agrarian élite always constituted roughly two-thirds of the east-Elbian contingent. The aristocracy of birth continued to predominate here, although there was also a large body of non-noble or newly ennobled Conservatives. Junkers outnumbered owners of great latifundia from 1903 onwards. In the east, the landed middle classes declined gradually up to 1914; the urban middle classes remained fairly steady; and the new middle class, led by civil servants, gained. None the less, the new *Mittelstand* continued to contribute less than one-fifth of the eastern Prussian delegation. In the west, the balance remained roughly equal between the agrarian élite, the new *Mittelstand* and the propertied bourgeoisie; but some gains were registered by the last.

The Committee of Fifty actually numbered some sixty-four members and thirty-five alternates in 1910.[31] Twenty-three members sat on the committee by virtue of nomination from one of the DKP's three Berlin caucuses. Forty-one were delegates from provincial party *Vereine*. Of the latter, thirty normally came from Prussian provinces and thirteen from non-Prussian states.

Six of eight delegates from the Prussian House of Deputies were landed estate owners; all of them were noblemen. Six of eight also represented eastern or central Prussian districts. All seven representatives from the Herrenhaus were east-Elbian aristocratic landowners. Four might be called *grands seigneurs* in every sense, while three were more in the Junker mould. Seven of eight Reichstag delegates were landed proprietors, including five nobles and two non-nobles. Interestingly, no representation in the Committee of Fifty was given to the eight non-Prussian members of the Conservatives' Reichstag caucus. However, agricultural interest groups of various sorts were well represented here (even though many of the titles borne by the Herrenhaus members were entirely honorary). Of these twenty-three delegates, only three belonged to the middle classes. Malkewitz surely owed his standing to his lengthy work as a BdL functionary and Conservative editor; the other two were from Minden-Ravensberg.

The representatives from eastern Prussian *Vereine* and the Mecklen-burgs generally bore a remarkable similarity in background and social status to their colleagues in the House of Deputies caucus and in the Committee of Twelve. Although three lawyers belonged to this group, as did two current or former DKP secretaries from Brandenburg, the remaining nineteen eastern provincial leaders were all owners of landed estates, and seventeen of these were aristocrats by birth. There were nevertheless some significant differences between this and other groups in the DKP leadership. First, the provincial party chiefs were on the whole richer. The wealthiest were two men from Schleswig-Holstein, the first and fourth largest landowners in the province, with estates worth 12.5 and 9 million marks. Three other full members and two alternates had property worth an estimated 5 million marks or more. Second, the leaders of the east-Elbian provincial *Vereine* were also younger than their colleagues; their mean age was 58, six years younger than that of the parliamentary delegates. Third, agrarian interest groups were less fully represented here than among the Committee of Twelve or the caucus representatives. There were only five higher BdL functionaries among the forty east-Elbian provincial delegates and alternates. Overall, then, this eastern delegation was dominated by rich, noble landowners, who were somewhat wealthier, younger and perhaps slightly more moderate agrarians than those among the Committee of Twelve and the parliamentarians.

Among delegates from west-Elbian DKP *Vereine* we find a social structure that is dramatically different. Reflecting the much weaker Conservative following in the west, the dominant feature of this delegation was the sharing of power between an agrarian élite, a professional (urban) élite and members of the new *Mittelstand*. Among delegates from the strong Conservative *Landesverein* in the Kingdom of Saxony, professionals and members of the business élite were strongly represented. Although there were five large estate owners among the nine-man Saxon delegation, three of these were non-noble, and two of these three were lawyers, including Mehnert. Further west, the social background of Rhenish, Westphalian and other delegates indicated that Catholics or other particularists drew the allegiance of the most eminent social leaders, leaving a different group to fill the top provincial posts in the DKP organization. Among the western Prussian delegates there were only two noble landowners and one lawyer (Klasing) who could be considered truly upper class; by contrast, six representatives came from the middle classes. In the Thuringian states, in Bavaria and in south-west Germany, the weak Conservative organizations sent to the Committee of Fifty other 'generals' who had even fewer troops behind them. Two delegates from Baden and Bavaria were *grands seigneurs*. Otherwise, the chairman of the Württemberg party was a Stuttgart lawyer, and others came from various administrative élites. Overall, then, of thirty-one delegates and alternatives from regions west of the Elbe, the landed élite sent only eleven delegates to the Committee of Fifty. Commoners outnumbered nobles by birth by a wide margin, eighteen to eleven. Thus the eastern and western provincial delegations shared few common socioeconomic traits. It is perhaps unsurprising, in light of this, that the Committee of Fifty was convened only infrequently to decide on large issues of party policy; the different interests, outlooks and backgrounds represented in this body complicated the formulation of a coherent Conservative policy.

A few words about the evolution of the Committee of Twelve are in order before we consider its social composition. During the 1890s this committee theoretically represented different geographic areas. The inclusion of Klasing from Westphalia was clearly designed to give Minden-Ravensbergers and other west German Conservatives a feeling that their views were being represented. When Stöcker resigned from the Committee of Eleven in 1896 he was replaced by another representative of Berlin and Brandenburg Conservatives, a former high-school teacher and later *Kreuzzeitung* staff member, Bernhard Irmer. Due to a change in the laws of association, the German Conservative *Wahlverein* was reorganized in December 1902; it now became the Central Association (*Hauptverein*) of German Conservatives. At the same time, the Committee of Eleven expanded to Twelve, and, more importantly, the stipulation that the three Berlin caucuses had to be represented by a fixed number of delegates was abandoned in practice. Henceforth the Committee of Twelve co-opted its own members, although changes in the composition of the committee occurred very rarely. The 1902 reorganization also introduced a special member of the Committee of Five (*engerer Vorstand*) who was charged with the task of attending to the organizational and financial consolidation of the party.[31] The first such member was Loebell, who had been elected to the Reichstag in 1898 and who had quickly risen to prominence in Brandenburg and then in national Conservative circles.[32] Loebell was also to manage the business affairs of the executive and to maintain contact with both the general party secretary (August Strosser) and the editor of the *Conservative Correspondenz* (Albert Clar), neither of whom sat on a top executive body. This arrangement underwent further change when Loebell was appointed to head Bülow's chancellory in 1904 and when Strosser was forced to resign his secretariat in 1905 because he advocated construction of the *Mittelland* canal. The Committee of Three from 1895 – Manteuffel, Mirbach and Limburg – had been transformed by 1905 into a Committee of Five with these three men plus Normann (head of the Reichstag caucus), Heydebrand (head of the House of Deputies caucus) and, in affiliate status, the new party secretary, Karl Stackmann. The fact that the overall party chairman, Manteuffel, was obliged to convene the Committees of Fifty and Twelve only once per year suggests how the Committee of Five was beginning to take over the day-to-day management of party affairs.

The structure of the party leadership was not changed again until reforms were introduced in the period 1910–12. The party statutes of 1912 gave the Committee of Twelve a number of new prerogatives. These included the right to expel heterodox *Vereine* or individuals from the party; the right to decide when official party congresses would be convened; and most importantly, the right to determine, at the beginning of each Reichstag legislative period, how many representatives each of the parliamentary caucuses and regional organizations would send to the Committee of Fifty. It appears that the Committee of Twelve could also decide matters concerning membership dues, and could issue urgent (i.e. all important) party directives. In practice, the Committee of Five often assumed these tasks, and had done so even before the new statutes sanctioned such procedures. At the same time, the Committee of Three was effectively revived when Manteuffel stepped down as overall head of the party in February 1911. His successor was Wedel-Piesdorf, formerly president of the Reichstag, informal Conservative leader (and in 1913–14 President) of the Herrenhaus and member of the Committee of Fifty. Wedel eminently fulfilled Heydebrand's criteria for a Conservative Party chairman:[33] 'a man highly distinguished through large landownership [and] a superior position, with strong ties to court, the army and the highest officials; but one, on the other hand, who despite such connections would lay great weight on maintaining his uncompromised political independence'.

Wedel was in fact little more than a figurehead; he rarely chaired meetings of the Committee of Five. By 1913 it was clear where the locus of real power lay in the top ranks of the party. Stackmann and the official general secretary of the party, Bruno Schröter, continued to handle the business and organizational affairs, in close consultation with Westarp. The members of the BdL directorate, Roesicke, Wangenheim and Hahn, continued to discuss important political matters with the top DKP men. But the single *de facto* leader was Heydebrand. The existing party correspondence from the years 1913–18 confirms the view that Heydebrand, although not disinclined to consult with these other Conservatives, directed DKP policy with a firm authoritarian hand.[34]

In both 1903 and 1910–14 nine members of the Committee of Twelve were noble estate owners. In 1903 the average age was 59, while by 1910 the average age had risen to 64. Only one representative, Klasing, was not a parliamentarian. Finally, the influence of the BdL in the Committee of Twelve was certainly less than dominant. True, sixteen of eighteen members who sat in the committee between 1900 and 1914 were formally members of the BdL. But only three held honorary offices of any sort in the League, and of these three – Manteuffel, Erffa and Mirbach – only the last could be counted as a close associate of Roesicke and Wangenheim. The others' legislative records, social standing and long history of party service made them close to untouchable politically.

The day-to-day affairs of caucus life are rather more difficult to penetrate. We know, for instance, that a complex selection process lay behind the choice of Conservative speakers and committee members, but this process was by no means always well thought out or consistent.[35] Sometimes certain DKP nominees for Landtag committee work were eminently qualified for their duties; Kropatschek, for example, was frequently selected to serve on the standing house committee on school instruction because of his training as an educator. Non-noble Conservatives with legal training were regularly selected to sit on the committee overseeing judicial affairs. The rationale behind other nominations, however, when the Conservative appointee had no qualifications for committee work that required considerable expertise and experience, remains obscure. Another opaque feature of caucus life was the mixture of sympathies that motivated famous 'guests' of the caucus (*Hospitanten*). If such men were outraged by the presumption of party chairmen, caucus whips and others who enforced discipline among the Conservative parliamentarians, and if some of them (such as Alexander zu Hohenlohe, the chancellor's son) regarded their colleagues as 'frowsy assessors' and as the most 'agrarian, conservative and narrow' types imaginable, why did they decide to join the Conservative caucus in the first place?[36] Even full members of the caucus found themselves selected to deliver speeches on political issues where their personal opinions diverged from those of the caucus majority.[37] It is clear that many Conservative notables chafed under their sentence to sit as lesser lights in a parliament they opposed in principle. Yet they looked in vain to the second rank of party leaders as alternative sources of authority from which to secure their own legitimization and self-aggrandizement.[38]

The nature of party life in the formal sense was determined in large part by the corps of party secretaries and organizational managers who were entrusted with the task of implementing major reforms in the DKP. These men, too, remained shadowy figures in the small circle of Conservative luminaries. Leo von Seckendorff, August Strosser, Karl Rabe von Pappenheim, Josef Kaufhold, Friedrich von Loebell, Richard Kunze, Karl Stackmann and Bruno Schröter, not to mention the provincial party secretaries, all played significant intermediary roles between different centres of authority in the top party ranks. When one includes other Conservative leaders who were interested in adapting the party to new political circumstances, the question of why the party assented to virtual one-man rule by 1914 becomes even more compelling. The Committee of Twelve, after all, included in 1903 such personalities as Durant, Klasing, Mehnert and Loebell; why were these men unable to raise a stronger voice against top party leaders who prevented the establishment of internal party democracy? It was not simply that they were shut out of party affairs. They and other would-be reformers, including Julius Werner, Wolfgang Eisenhart and Georg von Below, were given prominent propaganda roles in the final years before the war. Factionalism, dissent and efforts for reform within the DKP, so strong in the nineteenth century and during the *Kreuzzeitung*-group episode in the 1890s, lived on. But in the face of a personality like Heydebrand, earlier rebellions could not be repeated.

The following chapters make apparent the consequences of this petrification of the DKP leadership. It constrained efforts to refashion the party as a *Volkspartei*; it perpetuated the conflict between Conservatives, Free Conservatives and National Liberals; and it prevented the reestablishment of close relations between the Conservative Party and the government. In each of these developments the personal authority of Heydebrand was immensely significant.

*

Heydebrand was a superstar in the ranks of Wilhelmine politicians. A common thread running through contemporary descriptions of Heydebrand is the single-minded commitment with which he worked to preserve the power and prestige of the Conservative Party and of his native Prussia.[39] Sydow recalled that one question was repeatedly asked in the Prussian state ministry when domestic policy was discussed: 'What does von Heydebrand say about this?'[40] Eugen Schiffer, a leading right-wing National Liberal who met secretly with Heydebrand from time to time, provided what remains probably the most compelling portrait of Heydebrand:

> He is actually called, not without reason, the uncrowned king of Prussia. In parliament and in the government he is known as 'the little one', also not without justification. For he is remarkably small of stature, and therefore never stands behind, but rather beside, the speaker's podium. Naturally on the right-hand side, in order to remain close to his *gardes du corps* and as far as possible from the Left. There . . . he formulates his phrases, which are often more like a throne speech than a parliamentary one. Time and again he addresses the government benches and upbraids the men sitting there, sometimes with condescension, sometimes in a challenging or even threatening way; or he hurls lightning-bolts upon the Left, which are accompanied by the thunder of applause from his myrmidons.

Bethmann Hollweg once described Heydebrand's attitude within the party as 'dictatorial'.[41] Did there exist a real possibility that the governmental Conservatives within the DKP might have moderated or even disavowed Heydebrand's policies? The evidence suggests that Bethmann was deluding himself. Sontag noted that Heydebrand headed an 'absolutist regime' in the party executive; he always carried the day because the party was aware that it had no '*Führer* personality of comparable rank'. Schiffer observed once that contacts between the DKP, FKP and NLP were unlikely to come to much as long as Heydebrand's 'permanent dictatorship' (*Dauerdiktatur*) persisted.

To party insiders the larger consequences of Heydebrand's intransigence were evident even before 1914. This is one reason why so many Pan-Germans and other radical nationalists turned away from the party in the years after 1909. One observation must serve to convey the sense of alienation felt by right-wing activists who believed that Heydebrand's unassailable position left them no scope for action within the DKP. As a rising star in the new generation of wartime Conservatives, Albrecht von Graefe wrote to Westarp in 1915 to complain about the liabilities of anti-democratic attitudes as they had come to determine internal party relations:[42]

I fear that in the 'state of Denmark' of our so-called Conservative organization there is something rotten everywhere! . . . I see the root of this evil in that our party – perhaps also the caucus – is not ruled altogether constitutionally, but rather is still afflicted with absolutist tendencies!

By the end of 1918 the bankruptcy of Heydebrand's personal war on democracy was open to world view.

NOTES

1 Cf. Teipel, *Graf von Westarp. Der Parlamentarier wider den Parlamentarismus.*
2 In the following, 'universal' or 'Reichstag' franchise serves as a shorthand description of the Reichstag's universal, equal, secret and direct manhood suffrage.
3 See, for example, Wangenheim to his wife, 21.1.04, in Wangenheim, *Wangenheim*, p. 79; BAK, Kl. Erw. 455 (Reck), f. 50, Reck to Caprivi (draft), 4.8.92; the following illustrate the continuity in Conservative thought: Hubrich, *Diätenfrage* (1902); DKP *Ratgeber* [1903], p. 80; Leo, *Wahlrecht und Berufsstände* (1907); Gerlach, *Geschichte* (1908); Below, *Wahlrecht* (1909); Heinz, *Entwicklung* (1913), pp. 22 f.; Schiele, *Erneuerung* (1917); Dewitz, *Demokratisierung* [1919]; cf. Stillich, *Konservativen*, pp. 72–85; Wulff, 'Deutschkonservativen'.
4 Hamerow, *Social Foundations*, p. 211; Stillich, *Konservativen*, p. 79; cf. Hamerow, 'Origins'.
5 Heinz, *Entwicklung*, p. 23.
6 Below, *Wahlrecht*, pp. 21 ff.; Stegmann, *Erben*, p. 126; *DAB*, 6.11.10; BAK, NL Bülow, 105, f. 43, Mirbach to Loebell, 10.2.15; *KM*, 76, April 1919, pp. 468–74; *Rkz.* 1788–90; ZStA I, RLB/BdL press archive, 5849–52.
7 Oertel, *Konservatismus*, p. 60; Wulff, 'Deutschkonservativen', p. 84; Stillich, *Konservativen*, pp. 84 f.; *KM*, 63, 1906, pp. 739 f.
8 Fully documented in Stegmann, *Erben*, pp. 120–8; cf. Daun, 'Innenpolitik', pp. 80 ff.
9 Cited in Gerlach, *Geschichte*, p. 188.
10 See generally Gagel, *Wahlrechtsfrage.*
11 See Zmarzlik, *Bethmann*, p. 56 (original emphasis).
12 Prussian state ministry meeting protocol, ZStA II, Rep. 90a, B, III, 2, b, No. 6, Vol. 158, f. 200 f., 14.7.09; hereafter cited as ZStA II, St. Min., Vol., folio, date; cf. my 'Road to Philippi'.
13 Cf. Wulff, 'Deutschkonservativen', pp. 117–82; Huber, *Verfassungsgeschichte*, Vol. 4, pp. 368–84; Jarausch, *Chancellor*, pp. 74–9.
14 First reading, 10–12.2.10; second reading 11–14.3.10; the bill was withdrawn in the last week of May.
15 *Rb*, 24.2.10; *DTZ*, 24.2.10; *KZ*, 3.3.10; *KnZ*, 14.3.10.
16 See ZStA II, St. Min., Vol. 162, f. 192 ff., 31.12.13; and Westarp to Heydebrand, 9.6.11, from the archive of Baron Hiller von Gärtringen, Heydebrand–Westarp *Korrespondenz* (transcription); hereafter cited as Gärtringen, Heydebrand–Westarp *Korrespondenz.*
17 Cf. Oppe, 'Reform'; Pache, *Geschichte*; Tödter, 'Klassenwahlrechts', pp. 100 ff.
18 See *NZ*, 6.3.10; *Ger*, 10.3.10; *DTZ*, 15.4.10; *KnZ*, 3.5.10; Wulff, 'Deutschkonserva- tiven', *passim*; *Rb*, 23.3.10; *CC*, 29.3.10; *KM*, 67, August 1910.
19 ZStA II, St. Min., Vol. 159, f. 57–78, 26.2.10, 7.3.10.
20 Jarausch, *Chancellor*, pp. 78 f., 445; cf. the enlightening remarks in Spitzenberg, *Tagebuch*, pp. 518 ff.
21 ZStA II, St. Min., Vol. 162, f. 192 ff., 31.12.13; cf. ZStA II, NL Valentini, 2, f. 8, Valentini to Bethmann, 2.5.12; and, for the following, BAK, NL Loebell, 26, 'Erin- nerungen'.
22 GStA Berlin (Dahlem), NL Meinecke, 90, *Straßburger Post*, 18.12.11.

23   *KM*, 69, 1912, pp. 979–86, 'Niedergang des Parlamentarismus'.
24   BAK, NL Bülow, 105, f. 35, Mirbach to Bülow, 10.7.13.
25   PA AA Bonn, I, A, Sachsen (Königreich) 60, Vol. 8, letter of 25.4.10.
26   See mainly Puhle, *Interessenpolitik*, pp. 165–84, 213–25.
27   The ratio of nobles to non-nobles had changed from 10:5 in 1898 to 10:10 in 1907 for the Reichstag caucus, and from 22:6 in 1898 to 16:7 in 1908 for the House of Deputies caucus.
28   At this point the work of Charles Bacheller must be explicitly credited: 'Class and Conservatism', PhD thesis, 1976; the following account relies largely on Bacheller's data and analysis, although these have been supplemented with material from parliamentary handbooks and other reference works.
29   Again, also including newly ennobled Conservatives in this category.
30   Westarp, *Konservative Politik*, Vol. 1, p. 397, reports that it grew to about eighty members after a reorganization in 1912.
31   *CC*, 1.12.02.
32   BAK, NL Leobell, 26, 'Erinnerungen', chs. 1–4.
33   Westarp, *Konservative Politik*, Vol. 1, p. 396.
34   ZStA I, NL Westarp, 98, 'Berichte des Hauptvereins der Deutsch-Konservativen an v. Heydebrand, März 1914–November 1918'; Gärtringen, Heydebrand–Westarp *Korrespondenz*.
35   For the following, see the *Stenographische Berichte über die Verhandlungen des Hauses der Abgeordneten*, Vols. 342, 355, 365, 384, 424, 477, 530, 610, 'Übersichte', 'Drucksachen' and 'Verzeichnisse der Kommissionen und deren Mitglieder' (1889 to 1915), in GStA Berlin (Dahlem).
36   BAK, NL C. zu Hohenlohe, 1611, f. 101, A. zu Hohenlohe to C. zu Hohenlohe, 23.4.99; cf. other materials in BAK, NL A. zu Hohenlohe; and A. zu Hohenlohe, *Aus Meinem Leben*, pp. 187, 358 and especially 386 f.
37   Including Gustav Hüpeden, Alfred von Goßler and Joachim von Winterfeldt-Menkin; BAK, Kl. Erw. 227 (Hüpeden); BA–MA, NL Goßler, N 98/1, 'Lebenserinnerungen', f. 42; Winterfeldt-Menkin, *Jahreszeiten*, p. 136.
38   Cf. accounts of caucus life by Goßler, Hüpeden, Sontag, Loebell, Kapp and others; Winterfeldt-Menkin, *Jahreszeiten*, pp. 138–41; Oldenburg, *Erinnerungen*, pp. 61–7.
39   BAK, NL 'Alter', 6, 'Kampfjahre der Vorkriegszeit', pp. 27 f.; Riezler, *Tagebücher*, pp. 168, 172; Wolff, *Tagebücher*, Vol. 1, pp. 160, 350; BA–MA, NL Goßler, 1, 'Lebenserinnerungen', f. 43; cf. my 'Road to Philippi'.
40   Sydow in Thimme (ed.), *Front wider Bülow*, p. 126; for the following, BAK, NL Schiffer, 1, 'Memorien', Heft I, f. 34–47.
41   Full references in my 'Road to Philippi'.
42   Graefe to Westarp, 15.6.15, cited in Wallraf, 'Politik', pp. 215 f.

PART IV

The Siege Mentality, 1909–18

13

The Quest for the Conservative Volkspartei

After July 1909 the Conservative Party was regarded by many Germans as merely a chauvinistic agrarian party with no friends except the Centre. By 1912 a siege mentality had set in which turned Conservative attention further away from the masses and towards co-operation with other anti-governmental groups on the Right known as the 'nationalist opposition'. This reorientation was indeed a revolutionary reaction to political decline. However, new *völkisch* appeals gained acceptance only slowly within Conservative ranks. When we examine how Conservatives themselves believed they could renew the party and give it a broad base of support, we find that party members proposed a number of other strategies which had little to do with radical nationalist appeals.

The appearance of a new Conservative journal in 1905 signalled a revived interest in party organization. The trial issue of *Unsere Partei*[1] announced in its subtitle that it would be a 'Journal for the Technique of Political Organization and Agitation'. *Unsere Partei* had three main aims: to disseminate information on the art of practical politics; to inform Conservatives of the activities of other DKP *Vereine*; and to interest youth in Conservative affairs. In one article entitled 'Experiences in the Mass Distribution of Printed Materials', Conservatives were informed of the fastest way to seal envelopes. Examples were given of programme speeches, and a large number of quotations from the opposition press were provided in a section headed 'For the Armoury'. Reports 'From the Party' painted a very gloomy picture of the Conservatives' existing organization, listing the number of Conservative constituency *Vereine* which could be 'traced' in each region of Germany. It was claimed that in many provinces sickness and old age afflicted the *Verein* leaders, as did the disruption of frequent changes of chairmanship. The recommended remedy was the assignment of a business manager to the *Verein* executive.

Although *Unsere Partei* never achieved regular publication, other Conservatives began making similar observations about the sterility of party life after 1905. When the Conservative leader in West Prussia reported to Loebell that a new Conservative *Verein* had been founded in his province, due mainly to local initiative, he wrote: 'You know as well as I how much we need a younger leadership in place of the unhelpful central

179

executive. Perhaps Manteuffel will make a little more effort this winter?'[2] In the spring of 1906 the Conservative Central *Verein* for the suburban Berlin constituencies of Teltow, Beskow, Storkow and Charlottenburg demanded a general party congress to debate programme reform. The *Kreuzzeitung* and the party leadership, however, did not want a repeat of Tivoli's proceedings. Therefore, although a full party congress had not been held since February 1898, they assented to only a delegates' congress. In preparation for this congress, which was finally held on 30 November 1906,[3] Berlin Conservatives offered some lengthy and unorthodox proposals for amendments to the Tivoli programme. These proposals had in common a desire to attract *Mittelstand* voters in the outskirts of Berlin; the wish to protect these voters from intimidation by the SPD; and the belief that a stronger Conservative commitment to the nationalist programme of such groups as the Pan-German League would help win elements of the *Mittelstand* and nationalist workers to the party. After that, the reform plans diverged radically. The Conservative *Verein* in Groß-Lichterfelde pushed the party leadership to take a stand against rising meat prices. A Charlottenburg lawyer, Willy Hahn, sent the chancellor a draft programme, numbering fourteen pages, which offered a particularly odd mixture of progressivism and reaction; weighty issues like anti-Socialism and anti-Semitism lay side by side with points about the combating of syphilis and the expansion of Prussian water reservoirs.[4]

At the 1906 delegates' congress the Conservative leadership did not have everything its own way, although its fear of another Tivoli débâcle did not materialize either. At one point an East Prussian lawyer, Edwin Meyer-Tilsit, made a celebrated call for the inclusion of more non-aristocrats in the DKP; he also advocated a moderate revision of the Prussian franchise. The main onslaught against the party leadership, however, was led by a retired lieutenant in Charlottenburg, who insisted that a committee be established to revise the Tivoli programme. In the end a compromise was worked out whereby the Committee of Five would accept proposals for programme revision, co-opt members to a programme committee and submit another proposal to a subsequent general party congress. Once again there is no record of such a committee being convened or any such revised proposal.

Although programme reform was not, as the Committee of Five wished, removed from the party agenda, in the years ahead organizational reform was heralded as a more pressing matter. In March 1907 the Committee of Fifty established yet another 'organizational committee', and plans were set in gear for further congresses. It was recognized that these congresses, as long as they could be controlled, were an effective way of breaking Conservatives from their agitational slumber between elections. The *Kreuzzeitung* called for particular effort from the rank and file. District and provincial party congresses had to prepare the ground and bring party members in touch with each other; 'then the activity "from above" can begin in a useful way'.[5] Meanwhile certain Saxon Conservatives were finding that they shared some of the Berliners' dissatisfaction with the DKP programme. In April 1907 a meeting of Dresden's Conservative *Verein* was presided over by Otto Beutler, mayor of Dresden and member of the Committee of Twelve after 1909. Beutler himself argued that Conservatives' anti-industrial viewpoint limited their popularity in Saxony and elsewhere. Other proposals included the 'modernization of schools', revived social reform and even a Conservative endorsement of the Reichstag franchise. Nevertheless, the tangible results of this new interest in organization were few. The report on DKP organization which the party secretary presented to the 1907 delegates' congress was confidential, but there was surely little to say.[6]

The finance reform crisis prompted a rank-and-file rebellion against the DKP leadership in the summer and autumn of 1909.[7] Many Conservative parliamentarians made hurried trips back to their constituencies to pre-empt open revolt. Disaffection with the party leadership was especially prevalent among pastors, officials, retired army officers, *Mittelstand* representatives and Conservatives from urban or semi-urban areas. Even before Bülow left office there was talk of forming a Young Conservative Party, and almost every week from July 1909 onwards there were notices of Conservatives, both prominent and obscure, who formally withdrew from the party in protest against the outcome of the finance reform.[8]

One Conservative group which wished neither to defend the Reichstag caucus leadership nor to break entirely from the Conservative Party was the Conservative *Verein* in Groß-Lichterfelde, headed by a retired army major, Arthur von Loebell (brother of Bülow's chancellory chief).[9] The meeting of twenty-two Conservative *Bürgervereine* in Berlin on 14 July 1909 was the first opportunity for the rebels around Loebell to publicize their criticism of the DKP's Reichstag caucus. Local representatives claimed their *Vereine* had lost 25 per cent of their membership in the last months. Among the *Bürgervereine* most strongly represented in Loebell's rebellion were those from the Berlin suburbs of Moabit, Charlottenburg and the district which lent its name to this 'movement', Pankow.

In early August the Pankowers formed a Free Conservative Union under the leadership of a small retailer, Herbert Schmidt. They issued a founding declaration which called for greater representation of non-aristocratic elements within the DKP and for 'the renewal of Conservatism'.[10] The Union's programme was even more neatly summed up in a proclamation from November 1909:[11]

> More contact with the people!
> Independence from the Farmers' League!

Equity between city and country!
Away from the Centre Party!
Back to the Bloc concept against Social Democracy!
Then the Conservative Party will become a Volkspartei!

The Conservative Union was criticized by many DKP notables because it provided a focus for dissent against the finance reform. Engel on the other hand advised the DKP leadership to admit that errors of policy had been made. Conservatives in Silesia, Saxony and elsewhere concurred.[12]

The Pankowers met on 8 December and formally constituted their Union as 'an organization within the Conservative Party'. Paul Bredereck, a Berlin lawyer, was elected chairman; Herbert Schmidt became managing chairman; the treasurer was Pastor Julius Koch. Interestingly, the Pankowers were willing to accept the Committee of Twelve's offer of an opportunity to present their views at a general party congress three days later, but only if a speech by Bredereck were followed by a discussion opened by Koch.[13] As it happened, the Conservative Party congress of 11 November 1909 succeeded in parading a host of supporters of DKP finance policy before the public; its organizers successfully deflected the Pankowers' direct attack. Yet the congress did little to resolve the broader questions of Conservatism's 'renewal' which had raged since July. No practical consideration was given to the Conservatives' grass-roots organization or their regional press. Subsequently, the leaders of the Conservative Union began to carry their message to *Vereine* in different regions of Germany. This in turn compelled DKP leaders to inspire local resolutions or press articles expressing faith in the DKP's Reichstag caucus. Heydebrand abandoned much of his former disinclination to speak at provincial rallies. However, these attempts to quell the controversy succeeded only in part.[14]

The Pankow rebellion was associated with a drive to expand Conservative influence in the west of Germany. In December 1909 the *Kreuzzeitung* published a letter from Cologne which noted that most western Germans believed liberal demonologies of reactionary, boorish, east-Elbian Junkers. Therefore the author recommended the nomination of as many DKP test-candidates as possible. The Conservatives could not at first hope to win majorities in western Reichstag elections. But the rising demographic importance of the west, the substantial Protestant population there and the growth of dissatisfaction with Young Liberalism all argued for an increased Conservative commitment to expand the party's agitation in these provinces.[15]

By February 1910 Heydebrand had announced in his travels that party secretariats were to be established for both Westphalia and the Rhine Province. The political press discussed this organizational drive in articles with titles like 'Conservatives on the March' and 'The Step across the Elbe'. The 'westernization' of the Conservative Party was also considered necessary to undermine the arguments of the Pankowers about DKP one-sidedness and unpopularity.[16] Heydebrand declared at a party congress in Hanover that the Conservatives needed 'to get closer to the cities', since a 'Conservative Party that cannot understand this has no right to play a leading role in our nation'. The Conservatives staged a large party congress in Cologne in May 1911. On this and other occasions, however, opponents heaped scorn on the DKP's achievements in this westward drive. The *Schwäbischer Merkur* noted that whatever impression the Cologne extravaganza made was due mainly to 'the carnivalistic tendencies of the Cologne public'. After the 1912 Reichstag elections the liberal press had even more concrete data with which to chronicle DKP failure in the west.[17]

The 'Step across the Elbe' was accompanied by a wider debate about the role of Conservatism in an urbanizing society and the function of the DKP as a 'party of all interests and classes'. The concept of 'urban Conservatism' developed not only from the organizational initiatives taken in 1910 but also from the intellectual debates introduced in 1911 under the banner of 'cultural Conservatism'. In mid-1912 writers in the *Reichsbote* and the *Konservative Monatsschrift* suggested that the DKP programme required amendment to address urban interests. But others writing in the *Kreuzzeitung* and the *Deutsche Tageszeitung* disagreed.[18] The Conservatives, they said, could not risk losing their roots in the countryside to win 'uncertain ground' in the cities. In any case, the liberals were once again able to point to the DKP's notable lack of success in winning votes in the large cities.[19] In the 1912 Reichstag elections the Conservatives' share of the vote in cities of over 10,000 inhabitants shrank to only 3 per cent.

Conservative efforts in the cities did not end with the set-backs of 1912. In November 1913 the former Christian Social pastor, Julius Werner, now a prominent party speaker, was involved with plans to formulate a 'municipal programme' for the Conservatives. It had been discovered through a party circular that no Conservative *Verein* in the entire country had a concrete programme with which to contest municipal elections. In March 1914 Werner addressed a meeting of the Committee of Fifty on 'the possibility and necessity of Conservatism in the large cities'. In its May 1914 issue the *Konservative Monatsschrift* returned to the theme of 'Conservative Movements in the West'. Then, on 12 June 1914, Werner addressed the Committee of Twelve, again on urban Conservatism; subsequently a committee was established to study the question further. Nothing is known of this committee's later activity. But at least one report was written for the DKP by Wolfgang Kapp's associate, Georg Schiele, a physician and publicist from Naumburg. Schiele outlined the necessity of winning recruits among the urban middle classes if the Conservative Party were to survive. Thus, despite its near-total failure in electoral terms, urban Conservatism remained an important aspect of the DKP's strategy for popularity after 1909.[20]

A number of proposals in the period 1909–14 sought to increase the intellectual appeal of the Conservative Party. In early 1911 *Der Tag* published two articles by Dr Adolf Grabowsky, entitled 'Cultural Conservatism' and 'The Conservative *Weltanschauung* and the Conservative Party'.[21] In the first of these articles Grabowsky contrasted worldly and culturally refined English conservatives with their German counterparts, whose anti-literary and anti-intellectual bias divorced them from the broadly educated milieu in German society. As Grabowsky wrote, 'the educated man longs to be able to call himself Conservative, but the word sticks in his throat when he thinks of the Conservative Party'. A broadening of Conservative horizons was the basic element of Grabowsky's cultural Conservatism, but he also believed it could re-establish the DKP's 'national' credentials. Eventually Grabowsky advocated a new parliamentary alliance of right-wing forces whose common bond was an anti-democratic élitism but which was also based on Conservative open-mindedness.[22]

The reaction to Grabowsky's ideas from Conservative circles was, in the main, strongly negative. The *Kreuzzeitung* criticized Grabowsky's faith in 'the sham culture of the superficially educated'. The BdL directorate preferred to support such enterprises as the *Politisch-Anthropologische Revue*, which was designed to reach the 'urban so-called intellectuals'.[23] Even the *Konservative Monatsschrift* was critical. Given this reaction, it is no wonder that by early 1912 Grabowsky's tone had changed to one of disillusionment and alienation.[24] Labelling the DKP as much a 'class party' as the SPD, Grabowsky wrote that the Conservatives were 'antediluvian': 'Millions [of Germans] see how a little band of parochial agrarians pursue particularist politics at the expense of the people, under the name of Conservatism.'

Through 1912 Grabowsky found that his lack of success with the DKP was assuaged by an increasingly warm reception in the Free Conservative Party; this led to his appointment as chief editor of *Das neue Deutschland*. During the war Grabowsky continued to emphasize the distinction between 'real' and 'unyielding' Conservatism.[25] However, most Conservative leaders did not deign to debate cultural Conservatism after Grabowsky had left their camp.

There were reports as early as 1909 that Conservative women were organizing themselves. In March 1912 the *Kreuzzeitung* printed a letter from an unnamed Conservative countess who claimed that previous Reichstag elections would have turned out very differently if Conservative women had been more active in politics.[26] Conservatives were discovering too late that educated women from the upper classes had a duty to work among the women of other circles, in order to counter Social Democratic attacks on 'everything which is holy to mankind'. As this countess observed, many of the 110 Social Democratic deputies in the 1912 Reichstag had had bad mothers.

On 17 November 1912 Werner told a Committee of Fifty meeting that the Conservative Party must face its responsibilities on women's demands. In this report, Werner advocated improved educational opportunities for women and women's work, although 'within natural limits'. Any demand for *political* equality and the franchise for women, however, he rejected as 'neither necessary nor beneficial'.[27] Werner's comments did not receive unanimous approval within the Conservative Party, since many members felt that all women's demands should be condemned. A Conservative Women's Union was nevertheless founded on 9 April 1913. Again reactions were mixed. As the *Kreuzzeitung* observed, although politics was 'without doubt a hateful business', the 'new age demands new comrades-in-arms'. In any case, as Conservatives embraced their new allies, they found new unfamiliar faces among them. The chairwoman of the Union was Bertha von Kröcher; the secretary was Elisabeth Stackmann; other prominent figures included Frau von Heydebrand, Frau von Normann and Countess von Schwerin-Löwitz.[28]

Doubts were also soon expressed about the reliability of the Union as a bulwark against women's emancipation. Critics were most disturbed by the presence in the Union's executive of Paula Müller, chairwoman of another women's league which offered only very ambiguous opposition to the extension of the franchise to women. Such criticism prompted a more defensive posture from Bertha von Kröcher, who declared that any 'opening to the Left' was 'firmly bricked shut'.[29] By the beginning of the war, the majority of Conservatives probably believed that the organization of Conservative women had been only the opening of another Pandora's box full of modern, progressive, democratic spirits.

Much the same conclusion emerged from the shorter pre-war history of organized Young Conservatism. Like the Conservative women's group, the organization of young Conservatives was heralded long before it became a reality. But in July 1914 the founding of an Imperial Young Conservative Association was announced.[30] With its centre in Bonn, this 'organization' was little more than a collection of academic youths who wished somehow to gain attention for themselves within the Conservative Party. The Association's members were inspired by a curious mixture of anti-Semitism, *völkisch* nationalism and populism. They even had an odd conception of youth; membership was open to all Germans between 18 and 35 years of age. Otherwise, however, the Association signalled its desire to reach young artisans and retailers as well as students.[31]

Although the Conservatives' general secretary had apparently been in touch with the Bonn group in April 1914, Heydebrand and Westarp were faced with a disturbing *fait accompli* in early July. The liberal press linked the group's manifesto directly to earlier calls from Christian Socials, Pankow rebels and cultural Conservatives for a broader DKP commitment to urban, academic and non-agrarian groups. Therefore, although the *Reichsbote* and the *Kreuzzeitung* initially welcomed the 'spontaneous' appearance of young Conservatism, Heydebrand was very upset.[32] In a letter to Westarp he criticized Schröter for having lost his usual political tact and he noted the failure of Rhineland Conservative leaders to steer these upstarts into safe political channels.[33] Although Westarp showed himself to be marginally more tolerant than Heydebrand in 'putting a good face' on the affair, their was little chance that Young Conservatism would ever be accepted by the Conservative leadership. By 1914 the returns from such popular appeals were too slim and the dangers too large.

Before 1908 neither individual journalists nor Conservative delegates entrusted with the task of expanding the party press had accomplished much in the way of practical reform. When the Conservative Press Association met in Berlin in early October 1908, a number of striking deficiencies in the DKP press were discussed.[34] Delegates criticized the fact that press agitation was still regarded as a *quantité négligeable* within Conservative ranks. But in the wake of the finance reform crisis, more and more Conservatives realized that the success of liberal attacks on their party could be ascribed to the lack of a truly popular press. A number of different viewpoints were advanced.[35] Some Conservatives believed a new, inexpensive urban newspaper should be founded, or an already established non-Conservative newspaper should be purchased and adapted to DKP aims. Others believed that more effort was needed in rural areas, not Berlin. At the DKP's 1909 party congress, Karl Stackmann and the leader of Berlin Conservatives, Ulrich, both delivered reports on the need to found a 'popular' Conservative daily. The *Kreuzzeitung* remained dubious, noting that the 'little man' in the party would have to cancel his subscription to his local DKP newspaper if he were to do his duty and subscribe to the new organ.

Through 1910–11 liberals reported on failed Conservative newspapers almost as often as Conservatives celebrated the establishment of new ones. Meanwhile changes were being introduced to limit the possibility of dissent within the party. The party leadership successfully exploited Heinrich Engel's death in late 1911 to bring the troublesome *Reichsbote* closer to the DKP, financially and politically, by placing its editorial staff under the direction of a Conservative Party collegium. The *Konservative Monatsschrift* had already been reined in to the degree that Westarp had taken over responsibility for writing its monthly political reviews. Even the *Kreuzzeitung* suffered disruption and scandal due to the efforts of the DKP executive to enforce party discipline.[36] After these sensations the *Kreuzzeitung* staff stood under the influence of Schröter, Stackmann (chairman of the *Kreuzzeitung* board of governors) and Westarp, whose access to the columns of the newspaper was contractually assured. Similar action was taken to quiet dissent at the local level.[37]

In 1913 interest in the Conservative press quickened. Conservatives stepped up their efforts to solicit government patronage and agrarian assistance for struggling Conservative newspapers, though with only limited success.[38] Even Grabowsky turned his attention to the deficiencies of the DKP press. He claimed that Conservatives resorted too often to political polemics and included only 'superficial' or 'entertaining' literary articles. But the real issue was the popularity of the Conservative press in general. In response the *Conservative Correspondenz* argued that 'the press must not be judged by quantity but rather by quality'. Steps were also taken to dispel the anti-intellectual image of Conservative journalism. In June 1914 Conservatives staged a large exhibition of their press and its history in Leipzig. Here they tried to stress the dynamism of the 'eager pens' and the 'roaring presses' spreading the Conservative message through Germany.[39]

In truth, however, the Conservatives never overcame their inclination to dismiss the press as either an ineffective or an undignified means for influencing public opinion. Adam Röder, who had established the *Süddeutsche Conservative Correspondenz* in 1913, wrote in 1914 that it was wrong to believe 'that the people could be influenced in a decisive way *politically* by mass newspapers'. He also noted that the farmer abandoned newspaper reading completely for a good third of the year, 'for he has *important* things to do'.[40] Most clearly of all, the dynamic picture of Conservative journalism cultivated at the Leipzig exhibition stood in obvious contradiction to the reality of a still-dormant Conservative press, as illustrated by Sontag's description of the *Kreuzzeitung*'s editorial offices at this time. For here the mood was 'quiet' and 'subdued'; it was 'saturated with tradition and filled with a cool aloofness which regarded all haste as taboo, as plebeian bad conduct'.

Count Westarp recalled in his memoirs that lack of money was 'the greatest hindrance to a strong organization and propaganda in the Conservative Party'.[41] Around 1909 the annual budget of the DKP's *Hauptverein* was about 100,000 marks, that is, approximately one-tenth the budget of both the SPD and the BdL. Interest from accumulated capital and private contributions, Westarp claimed, were the central office's principal sources of income. Little is known of contributions to the *Hauptverein* by the regional and provincial organizations. In 1913 the Silesian Conservatives raised their annual contribution to the central party 'war chest' from 5,000 to 7,000 marks. But at that point the Silesians – along with the East Prussians – were considered to have the healthiest finances in the party.[42]

After the general interest in organizational reform was reawakened around 1905, the Conservative press occasionally devoted articles on the need to rationalize the party's finances. In practice these were usually little more than calls for greater individual sacrifice. The *Kreuzzeitung* spoke in 1906 of a 'party political savings bank' to which party members would make deposits between elections and from which the cost of election campaigns would be met; but no action was taken. Instead, the effort to accumulate campaign funds simply began further in advance of elections (if possible); or else funding drives were launched for a specific purpose, such as providing the salary for a new party secretary in one province.[43] Over time, the central leadership played a larger part in co-ordinating regional campaigns and outlays of party funds. But the individual party patron remained extremely important.[44]

The Conservatives' effort to build their organizational structure on a sound financial basis was also hindered by the unwillingness of the Farmers' League's leaders to use their own money to fund Conservative organizations. The fees demanded of farmers by the League prevented Conservatives from tapping this wider base of financial support, since commitment to the general BdL–DKP cause would be weakened if financial sacrifice were demanded twice. Westarp was unsuccessful in his bid to persuade Roesicke to share some of the BdL's 'harvest' in dues with the DKP. The League's strict financial independence from the Conservative Party went so far that Roesicke at one point gave his approval to Kaufhold to travel to East Prussia to address a Conservative meeting only if the DKP met Kaufhold's travel costs. In 1910 a *Landrat* in Poznan reported to Roesicke that a new Conservative *Verein* had been established in the province. Adding that this *Verein* could be expected to bring farmers back to the BdL fold, the *Landrat* requested that the BdL contract to pay a party secretary for the province. Roesicke wanted no part of this. Wangenheim agreed, writing: 'I find the demand somewhat naïve that we should pay the Conservatives for a secretary; we can do the work ourselves.'[45]

These difficulties prompted the DKP leaders to turn more attention to tapping all possible sources of revenue from sympathetic industrialists.[46] After 1910 the Conservatives showed more willingness to tailor their speeches to win support from industrial audiences, as when Heydebrand spoke to Westphalians in 1910 or to the new Conservative *Verein* in Hamburg in 1912. A Saxon Conservative Union of Industrialists was established under the leadership of Max Wildgrube in late 1913, although the influence of this group remained small. The question of Conservative relations with industry was closely tied up with the attempt of the DKP after 1912 to draw away the right wing of the National Liberal Party. Therefore these efforts to win financial support from industrialists became a major topic of discussion in the political press. From what is known about industrial contributions to DKP finances before the war, it appears that the need to reform the party's fiscal situation was the main impetus behind the celebration of the Conservatives' alleged 'friendliness to industry'.[47] Thus, when Westarp reported to Heydebrand in July 1914 that plans were under way to commit as many Conservatives as possible to contribute at least 100 marks annually, he noted that industrialists were not to be canvassed with undue pressure at this point. Instead, their irregular but larger contributions were to be held in reserve for when a fund was established specifically for election campaigns or for trade treaty agitation. Shortly before the war Conservative leaders were forced to contemplate relinquishing some of their personal control over central party funds. Heydebrand was aware that some reform would be efficacious in terms of making the party *appear* more democratic. Otherwise, however, he believed that any money a finance committee transferred into the general DKP account 'must, as *heretofore*, remain at the free disposal of the Committee of Five'.

After 1909 the Conservative leadership substantially increased its efforts to refine the agitational style of the party. The importance placed on agitational expertise was especially recognizable in the *Mitteilungen aus der konservativen Partei* (Reports from the Conservative Party), which appeared after February 1908.[48] In August 1910 the *Mitteilungen* were already urging party members to begin grass-roots organization and activity for the next Reichstag election, warning that '*in no constituency, no matter how secure it may appear, is one safe from surprises*'. A seven-point check-list was even provided for discussion of local party readiness.[49] Another issue of the *Mitteilungen* outlined in similar detail how a non-local agitator should make himself familiar with the constituency to which he was sent. Upon this groundwork, it was suggested, successful political agitation could be built. Later in the year the Saxon party secretary was co-opted by the central Berlin office to lead new speakers' courses.

After January 1912 the DKP's *Mitteilungen* printed articles by Conservatives who sought to identify the reasons for the DKP defeat. One of the most prominent of these writers was Wolfgang Eisenhart, an experienced right-wing propagandist and later leader of the Prussian League (Preußenbund, or Pb) in 1913. The similarity between these evaluations of Conservative agitation and those offered decades earlier was striking. These articles continued to rely on military vocabulary to describe the methods of 'mobilization' against the Social Democrats. In February 1912 Eisenhart described how the SPD achieved such success: 'With the coming of war – that is, elections – only the mobilization order is required, and the well-trained troops stand there, ready like a well-outfitted and disciplined army.' Such appeals, however, merely provided other parties with ammunition for their attacks on the DKP's 'press gang' tactics. They did not yield marked gains for the Conservatives at the polls, nor did they inspire Conservative leaders to break decisively with *Honoratioren* politics. Characteristically, Westarp's reflections on the deficiencies of the DKP were summed up in the casual observation that 'organization, and especially propaganda, was not the strongest side of the party'.[50]

In short, the party failed after 1909 to maintain the fiction that it was a *Volkspartei*. The inability of the Conservatives to expand their following in geographical, social, intellectual or organizational terms was clear before the outbreak of war. Yet this fact seemed to elicit from Heydebrand and his propagandists only sharper and louder affirmations that the DKP was, indeed, a party of the people. When the Conservatives met for a general party congress in mid-March 1913, the *Volkspartei* theme dominated all speeches and subsequent commentaries in the Conservative press. The *Kreuzzeitung* claimed that Conservatives now faced 'the time of renewal and self-awareness', and that 'there is no longer any "going back"'. A celebratory Conservative pamphlet reinforced the theme of *Volkstümlichkeit*, stating: 'We were and we are a true *Volkspartei* which has set out to be the choice of the entire people, and are independent from top to bottom.'[51] The slow progress of organizational expansion in the provinces and the ouflanking manoeuvres of radical nationalists soon showed the hollowness of this claim.

NOTES

1 'Our Party'; first issue, 1.11.05; *Rkz.* 1573, f. 21, Reimar Hobbing to Loebell, 7.11.05.
2 *Rkz.* 1391/5, f. 145, Dohna-Finckenstein to Loebell, 6.12.07.
3 *Stenographischer Bericht* printed in *CC*, 30.11.06–11.12.06; cf. Stillich, *Konservativen*, pp. 212, 253 ff.; Nipperdey, *Organisation*, pp. 256 f.
4 *Rkz.* 1391/5, f. 100 ff., Friedrich Wegener to Loebell, 5/6/10.11.06, and Loebell to Manteuffel, 19.11.06; Wegener, *Deutschkonservative Partei*.
5 *KZ*, 3–6.12.06, 25.3.07, 25.5.07, 5.8.07; *DTZ*, 14.4.07; *CC*, 11.11.07.
6 See *KM*, 63, 1906, pp. 1125–34; Beutler in *Das Vaterland*, 14, 1907; *DTZ*, 9/14.4.07, 30.10.07, 2.11.07, 10.5.08; congress *Stenographischer Bericht* in *CC*, 11–16.12.07.
7 The best overviews are in *Ger*, 22.8.09; *KnZ*, 16.8.09; *BT*, 2.7.09; *CC*, 16.8.09; cf. the NLP's 28-page brochure, *Konservative unter sich*.
8 *Die Post*, 5.7.09; *LeipZ*, 8.8.09; *Konservative unter sich*, p. 20; cf. *KZ*, *CC* and *Rb*, all 22.9.09; *NAZ*, 12.9.09; the Baden Conservatives' *Reichsfinanzreform 1909*; ZStA II, 2.2.1, 667, f. 53, Justus Hermes (*KZ* editor) to Valentini, 6.10.09.
9 Cf. *Rkz.* 1391/5, f. 166, F. W. von Loebell to Heydebrand, 16.5.09, defending his brother; Stegmann, *Erben*, pp. 48, 196 f.
10 *Rb*, 7.8.09, 'Die konservative Volkspartei'; *KZ*, 8.8.09.
11 *Aufruf*, 'Konservative Männer in Stadt und Land!', 13.11.09.
12 *Rb*, 26.8.09, 22.9.09, 29.10.09; *KnZ*, 25.8.09; *KZ*, 27.10.09; *DTZ*, 1.9.09; *DresdN*, 26.9.09; Wallraf, 'Politik', p. 156.

13 *Rb*, 9.12.09; *CC*, 9.12.09; *DTZ*, 20.12.09; *KZ*, 14/16.11.09; for the following, *DTZ*, 4/16.2.10; *Rb*, 11.2.10; *KZ*, 10.2.10; *DtRp*, 11.2.10; *OstprZ*, 17.2.10.

14 Westarp, *Konservative Politik*, Vol. 1, p. 397 f.; ZStA I, NL Westarp, 55, f. 36–71, and 1, f. 12 ff.; *DtRp*, 8.1.10; *KZ*, 17.1.10; *MecklN*, 6.2.10; *DTZ*, 2.4.10.

15 *KZ*, 14.12.09.

16 *Ger*, 23.1.10, 6.2.10; *NZ*, 11.7.10; *DTZ*, 16.2.10; *KZ*, 10.2.10.

17 *KZ*, 9.5.11; *CC*, 9.5.11; *SchwMerkur*, 10.5.11; *FkZ*, 27.1.14.

18 *KM*, 69, 1912, pp. 1083–92; *Rb*, 13.8.12; *DTZ*, 9.8.12.

19 *FsZ*, 31.10.13, 10.3.14; cf. Friesen, *Schwert*, p. 269.

20 ZStA I, NL Westarp, 1, f. 178, and 2, f. 72, *Hauptverein* report, 4.11.13, and circular, 23.6.14; *KZ*, 15/17.3.14; Peck, *Radicals*, p. 137; ZStA II, NL Kapp, D V 13, G. Schiele, 'Konservative Partei und städtisches Bürgertum', n.d.

21 *Der Tag*, 19, 22.1.11, and 31, 5.2.11; on Grabowsky cf. Thierbach (ed.), *Grabowsky*, especially Mende, 'Kulturkonservatismus'; and Grabowsky, *Kulturnotwehr* (1907), pp. 10–14; on DKP anti-intellectualism see Stillich, *Konservativen*, pp. 184–202.

22 Cf. Grabowsky's *Kulturnotwehr*, p. 6, and *Kulturkonservatismus*, pp. 5 ff.

23 Roesicke to Oertel (1913) cited in Stegmann, 'Neokonservatismus', p. 212.

24 *KZ*, 5.2.11, 4.5.11; *FsZ*, 7.5.11; *CC*, 11.7.11; *KM*, 68, 1911, pp. 586–8; Westarp, *Konservative Politik*, Vol. 1, p. 402; Puhle, *Interessenpolitik*, p. 277.

25 Cf. *NeueDtland*, 5.10.12, pp. 6–10; O. A. Schmitz, 'Kann ein moderner Mensch konservativ sein?', *Die Zukunft*, 78, 1912, pp. 153–7; Werner, 'Kulturpolitische Notwendigkeit'; Röder, *Zukunftspolitik*; Röder, *Konservatismus*; Mende, 'Kulturkonservatismus'.

26 *VossZ*, 9.2.09; *KZ*, 4/8/11.3.12; *FsZ*, 9.3.12, 12.7.12; *DTZ*, 15.11.12; cf. Nathusius-Ludom, 'Frauenfrage', pp. 1–22; Werner, *Geschichte der Frauenbewegung*; Westarp, *Konservative Politik*, Vol. 1, pp. 398 f.; ZStA I, RLB/BdL press archive, 7984.

27 CC cited in *KVZ*, 28.11.12.

28 *PommRp*, 20.12.12; *KZ*, 9.5.13; *Rb*, 16.5.13; *DTZ*, 17/24.5.13.

29 *NeueDtland*, 23.11.12, pp. 91 f., and 16.8.13, pp. 570–3; *DTZ*, 14.7.13, 6/16/26.9.13; *KZ*, 5.10.13, 14.2.14, 18.7.14; *SCC*, 1.1.14.

30 *Die Gegenwart*, 51, 1897, pp. 396 f., 'Jungconservativ'; *LeipNN*, 8.8.09; ZStA I, RLB/BdL press archive, 9023; ZStA I, NL Westarp, 2, f. 75 ff., statutes and G. Siegesmund to Westarp, 4.7.14; Peck, *Radicals*, pp. 143 f.; *DtRp*, 12.2.13.

31 Stegmann, 'Neokonservatismus', p. 211.

32 *Rb*, 8/10.7.14; *DTZ*, 13.7.14; *Die Hilfe*, 16.7.14; *KZ*, 26.7.14.

33 Gärtringen, Heydebrand–Westarp *Korrespondenz*, Heydebrand to Westarp, 4/21.7.14; Westarp to Heydebrand, 8/15.7.14.

34 *Rkz*. 1391/5, f. 157, meeting protocol and Clar to [Loebell], 29.10.08; cf. *KdBdL*, 17.11.08; *Rb*, 14.7.08.

35 *KZ*, 1.8.09; *DTZ*, 2.8.09; *KZ*, 19.12.09, 4.2.10.

36 ZStA I, RLB/BdL press archive, 2274.

37 *KZ*, 27.10.12, 24/25.4.13; *BT*, 25.4.13; *Vw*, 28.4.13; *KVZ*, 3.5.13.

38 For DKP–government correspondence see *Rkz*. 1572–8, *passim*; detailed references in my 'Reformist Conservatism', pp. 319 f.; for BdL attitudes see ZStA I, NL Wangenheim, 5, f. 17, Wangenheim to Roesicke, 17.1.10, and, on a new newspaper for Württemberg, ibid., 8, f. 63 f., Schmid-Platzhof to Roesicke, 3.7.13; ZStA I, NL Roesicke, 58b, f. 56, Roesicke to Felix Telge, 13.10.12; and ZStA I, NL Westarp, 20, f. 119, Heinrich Kraut to Westarp, 28.7.17.

39 *NeueDtland*, 8.11.13; *DTZ*, 10.11.13; *CC*, 11.11.13; *Rb*, 12.11.13; *Die Post*, 13.6.14.

40 *SCC*, 14.7.14 (original emphasis); for the following, BAK, NL 'Alter', 6, 'Kampfjahre', p. 12.

41 Westarp, *Konservative Politik*, Vol. 1, pp. 399 ff., and for the following.

42 *FsZ*, 9.12.13; *Mitteilungen*, 1913, p. 794.

43 *KZ*, 7.6.06, 5.3.11; *Das Vaterland*, 21.12.07.

44 Nipperdey, *Organisation*, pp. 263 f.; see also ZStA I, NL Roesicke, 3, f. 29, Ferdinand von Grumme-Douglas to Wangenheim, 14.1.14.

45 ZStA I, NL Wangenheim, 5, f. 33 ff., Roesicke–Wangenheim correspondence of April–June 1910.

46 See Wallraf, 'Politik', pp. 173–80; Stegmann, *Erben, passim*.

47 *DTZ*, 24.11.10; *Rb*, 8.8.12; Nipperdey, *Organisation*, p. 263; Peck, *Radicals*, p. 137; Schiele, 'Konservative Partei und städtisches Bürgertum'; *Die 'Industriefreundlichkeit' der Konservativen*; ZStA I, RLB/BdL press archive, 6764; for the following, Gärtringen, Heydebrand–Westarp *Korrespondenz*, pp. 8 ff., Westarp to Heydebrand, 1.7.14, and reply, 3.7.14.

48 Cf. such parliamentary reports as *Konservative Politik im Reichstage* (1908) and the annual *Konservativer Kalender*.

49 *Mitteilungen*, 20.8.10 (original emphasis); for the following, *Mitteilungen*, 3.2.12, 23.8.13, 21.2.14.

50 *VossZ*, 10.10.11; Westarp, *Konservative Politik*, Vol. 1, p. 397.

51 *KZ*, 16/22.3.13; *DTZ*, 25.3.13; *Rb*, 13.3.13; *Mitteilungen*, 29.4.13; Pfister, *Deutsch-Konservativ*, p. 18.

14

Organizational Initiatives
in the Provinces

The organizational expansion of regional Conservative *Vereine* was as uneven after 1900 as it had been under Hammerstein and Stöcker. In fact shortly before the war there was probably more diversity than ever in the institutional structure, social composition and political orientation of these *Vereine*. (See Appendix 4.) In some provinces, it is true, Conservative efforts appeared to have laid the groundwork for future success, as with the establishment of active party secretariats. On the whole, however, Conservatives failed to keep pace with the accelerating tempo and sophistication of political activity pursued by the other parties and interest groups.

Persisting gaps in party organization and propaganda initially increased the authority of Berlin party leaders, most notably Heydebrand and Westarp. Only they seemed to have the national perspective and political connections required to mitigate continuing inadequacies in the provinces. Thus the 1911–12 Reichstag election campaign saw the Berlin party leadership impose its tactical alliances and electoral slogans on the local constituency organizations as never before. Yet Heydebrand's peculiarly inflexible tactics in the Reichstag failed to solve the essential problem of Conservative isolation. By 1913 a number of regional provincial activists, in tandem with BdL leaders, had begun to disavow Heydebrand's sterile siege mentality. The nationalist allies they cultivated and the political strategies they adopted changed the face of right-wing politics fundamentally in the years ahead. Yet the sharp divisions that emerged within the DKP during the war had their genesis in the multiplicity of responses to the party's desperate plight in the period 1909–14. Along the way regional DKP chairmen found that their influence on national party policy remained very limited, whether they followed Heydebrand or one of his critics.

By 1914 East Prussian Conservatives had erected a *Verein* organization characterized by strong central leadership, good internal communication and healthy finances. There remained major weaknesses, however. In the city of Königsberg, for instance, the local Conservative *Verein* was no match for SPD or left-liberal opponents. East Prussia also included some constituencies where overwhelming Conservative majorities delayed the

193

founding of local *Vereine* until as late as 1914. Concern to fill gaps in the provincial party organization grew as the National Liberals and ˋFree Conservatives began to consider East Prussia as fruitful territory for their own geographical expansion.[1]

Since its founding the East Prussian Conservative *Verein* had a strong history of governmentalism. In late 1893 seven of sixteen executive members belonged to the Prussian Herrenhaus.[2] Paradoxically, the Conservatives in the province were also very closely associated with the Farmers' League. Yet an independent organizational structure and the predominance of notable estate owners in the Conservative *Verein* allowed the East Prussians a good deal of latitude in their politics. This freedom was reinforced by the strength of provincial party propaganda issued by the *Ostpreußische Zeitung*'s publishing house in Königsberg. As early as 1908 the East Prussians were in the unique position of being able to produce a handsome booklet documenting the full organizational structure of the provincial *Verein* and listing its local delegates. In 1909 the delegates' assembly, which prepared the annual general members' assembly, attracted two hundred constituency and press delegates.

The financial situation and circulation of the *Ostpreußische Zeitung* stagnated somewhat in the decade before the war, but other press initiatives in East Prussia enjoyed more success. In 1906 a press committee managed in only four months to collect over 10,000 marks. In 1910 an East Prussian circular suggested that local *Vereine* should sponsor subscriptions to the DKP's *Mitteilungen* for all members. By the end of 1911 East Prussian Conservatives had their own delegates' journal, and local *Vereine* were sending representatives to speakers' courses in Königsberg. The provincial *Verein* had a yearly income and expenditure of roughly 15,000 marks (1908), though the party secretary also asked twice for 100 mark contributions during the Reichstag elections in early 1912. This favourable financial situation, however, dissolved in the first week of the war, as it did for the DKP *Hauptverein* itself.[3]

In both West Prussia and Poznan 'national' considerations placed restrictions on the development of an independent German Conservative organization; but progress in this direction was unmistakable. From its founding shortly after the turn of the century, the Union of West Prussian Conservatives registered steady growth in membership, allegedly from seventy in 1903 to more than 3,000 in 1912.[4] The provincial party treasury reportedly rose from 4,500 marks in 1909 to 32,000 marks just before the 1912 Reichstag elections. Although it stood at 12,000 marks after the campaign, this figure was more than doubled by the end of the year.

An independent DKP organization to Poznan never aroused much enthusiasm, again due principally to the Polish threat. In 1910 the *Conservative Correspondenz* happily contrasted a Conservative *Verein* in the city of Poznan, which allegedly numbered 1,000 members, with a local

National Liberal *Verein*, numbering only two hundred. However, when Westarp's election agent sought to alter the 'two-thirds Conservative, one-third [National] Liberal' arrangement for local electoral committee membership, he found that most Conservatives believed that independent DKP *Vereine* would merely antagonize national allies while producing few electoral gains.[5] Thus, when the chairman of the Conservative Central *Verein* in Poznan welcomed Conservatives to their first provincial party congress in November 1912, he noted that an independent DKP organization was still 'a step in the dark'.[6]

In Silesia the distinction between German Conservatives and Free Conservatives was only a little clearer. Both conservative groups tended to coalesce around provincial grandees rather than work for comprehensive *Verein* organization.[7] General assemblies of the *Verein* were held in 1880, 1891 and 1895. After 1909, due partly to the efforts of two party secretaries, these rallies became more regular. Conservatives in Lower Silesia established their own regional *Verein* in April 1912 and staged a congress in December 1913; they reportedly had four party secretaries active before the war. Progress was also made in the city of Breslau. The Conservative *Verein* there numbered only 750 members in 1905, but five years later it had risen to over 1,100, where membership stagnated until the war.[8] In 1910 the Breslau *Verein* had a reported annual income and expenditure of some 2,000 marks.

Pomeranian Conservatives were among the most impassioned of those who supported Stöcker in 1896. Ten years later there was little evidence of this social conscience. Instead, the pragmatic and moderately pro-BdL style of Normann, a Pomeranian himself, was now ascendant. As Reichstag elections became critical for the DKP in its old preserves, more attention was paid to local organization. On balance, the provincial *Verein* remained amorphous; but Nearer and Further Pomerania were divided into separate organizational districts in 1912, and concerted efforts were made to expand the party's appeal to the *Mittelstand*. The latter task was taken up by Malkewitz and by the editor of the DKP's *Fürstentumer Zeitung*.[9] After January 1912 ten Pomeranian deputies in the Reichstag constituted almost one-quarter of the Conservative caucus.[10]

The executive of the Brandenburg Conservative *Verein* (excluding Berlin) was dominated by two groups: members of the Berlin professional and academic élites, and large estate owners from the countryside.[11] When the Free Conservatives established their own organization, secretary and party newspaper in Brandenburg in early 1908, the executive committee of the provincial *Verein* noted that it would continue to be comprised of representatives from both conservative parties. The appointment of the BdL's Brandenburg representative as chairman of the Conservatives' provincial *Verein* in 1910 strained this alliance, as did the Conservatives' willingness to employ anti-Semites like Böckel as travelling party speakers. None the less the obvious co-operation between Conservatives, leaders of the Imperial League against Social Democracy and other patriotic groups in the province facilitated right-wing unity. In many districts these groups shared a local notable to chair their meetings.[12]

The proximity to Berlin contributed to easy communication between provincial and central *Hauptverein* leaders, and the Brandenburgers were often able to attract the party's biggest names to speak at their provincial congresses. For the month of January 1908 Party Secretary W. Mannes could report that twenty-two rallies or executive meetings had been held, that he had travelled 900 kilometres visiting six localities, and that there had been 98 incoming pieces of correspondence and 295 outgoing.[13] Later that year, when the Patiotic *Verein* in Eberswalde established its own speakers' course, it was modelled on one already inaugurated by the Conservatives. The Brandenburg Conservatives also began publication of their *Amtliche Mitteilungen* in February 1908. These reports informed the party at large about the Brandenburgers' own organizational accomplishments until the *Mitteilungen* became a party-wide news-sheet two years later.

After the Conservative *Landesverein* for Both Mecklenburgs was formed in 1894 there was no major organizational initiative taken until May 1912, when a proper central leadership was first established. Dietrich von Oertzen recalled in his memoirs that during his tenure as editor of the *Mecklenburger Nachrichten* he had to balance the opposing views of pastors and larger estate owners in Mecklenburg. Oertzen's tribulations did not end the difficulties in establishing Conservative newspapers and party *Vereine* in the two grand duchies. The *Mecklenburger Nachrichten* remained reasonably strong, but the smaller *Mecklenburger Warte* was less reliable. On occasion it caused the BdL leaders considerable consternation because it threatened to divide Conservatives and adherents of the Farmers' League.[14] Reflecting the lack of distinction between shades of Conservatism, the Mecklenburg *Landesverein* opened its ranks to both conservative parties, although it formally affiliated itself with the DKP *Hauptverein*. In Rostock a Conservative *Verein* was founded only in 1912; it then hosted a 'Conservative week' of public lectures in 1913. There was no Conservative *Verein* in Schwerin until 1913. If there existed a party secretary, his efforts were neither heralded nor well paid, for the Mecklenburgers suffered from a chronic lack of funds. In May 1912 the party account stood at under 600 marks.[15]

The complexities of political and administrative boundaries in middle Germany produced a confusing picture of DKP organization, again characterized primarily by DKP–FKP co-operation and local successes rather than by a comprehensive organizational structure. In the Prussian province of Saxony, large Conservative *Vereine* existed in Merseburg,

Magdeburg and Halle. The Halle *Verein* reportedly grew from about 800 members in 1909 to more than 1,200 in 1912; in 1911 it had an income of about 3,000 marks. Halle also supplied the Conservatives' party secretary for the province and the Grand Duchy of Anhalt. Since Prussian Saxony was sometimes referred to as comprising an organizational unit (for the DKP) with Anhalt, sometimes with the Thuringian states in general, it is doubtful whether a firm regional *Verein* structure ever existed. In any case, the overall Conservative Party chairman, Wedel-Piesdorf, chaired the joint Saxon–Anhalt *Verein*. He presided over a party congress in Halberstadt in February 1911 which attracted over 1,000 participants. By July 1912 the Conservative *Landesverein* in Anhalt had constituted itself independently; it applied to both DKP and FKP leaders in Berlin to support it in plans for a regional party secretariat.[16]

In the Thuringian states only the Union of Rightist Men in Reuß appears to have achieved regular activity, particularly after the 1912 elections.[17] A Conservative *Verein* also existed in Erfurt. Otherwise, the main vehicle for BdL and DKP agitation was the yearly General Thuringian Peasants' Congress.[18] A Conservative *Verein* in Weimar was the focus of Conservative organization in the Grand Duchy of Saxe-Weimar. In the Principality of Lippe the DKP organization was also relatively well developed.[19] In December 1911 a large regional party congress was attended by over four hundred Conservatives, and committees were established to organize electoral agitation and press affairs. The Conservative *Verein* in Schaumburg-Lippe also made organizational progress, although most of its activity consisted of executive meetings. In 1908 it numbered roughly 1,200 members, with about 2,000 marks in party funds.[20]

In the Hanseatic cities of Hamburg, Bremen and Lübeck, urban Conservatism yielded few tangible results. When it was founded in 1912 the Hamburg Conservative Union stated that it wished to pursue a 'healthy Conservative policy' with both conservative parties. It also wrote that it wished to maintain the support of Hamburg's trade, shipbuilding, and commercial circles.[21] By 1914 the Union's membership was reported as over 1,200. A high profile in Conservative affairs for the Union was deliberately cultivated. Both Werner and Heydebrand spoke to it on the DKP's municipal policy, and Westarp met with the representative of Hamburg seamen. Organizationally, however, and electorally, little progress was made. Much the same could be said of the Conservative *Verein* in Lübeck, founded with the aid of Conservatives from Schleswig-Holstein and Hamburg. The Conservative Party in Bremen was supported mainly by Hahn and other Hanoverian agrarians.[22]

In Oldenburg the Prussian envoy reported in 1903 that the BdL had representatives in only one constituency and was not a factor in elections.[23] The Oldenburgers considered themselves part of the DKP–FKP organization in Schleswig-Holstein. In the Grand Duchy of Brunswick a right-wing *Wahlverein* had been established in 1907 but had to be revived by a congress in May 1912, when the call was issued for renewed co-operation between the DKP, FKP and NLP.[24] When the Association of German and Free Conservatives for Schleswig-Holstein was founded in 1911, provincial administrators and BdL functionaries played a prominent role, though the Conservatives' *Mittelstand* spokesman, August Pauli, gave the main speech of the day. When Schleswig-Holstein Conservatives staged their first party congress in March 1913, their chairman was able to report that relations with the National Liberals were good. In January 1912, however, both parties had lost the last of their seats in the province.[25]

Hanoverian attempts to found a provincial Conservative *Verein* had sputtered repeatedly between the 1870s and mid-1890s.[26] A new step was taken when a joint Conservative Union for the province was founded on 17 December 1898.[27] Rather than the older *Hannoversche Post* the Union chose the *Hannoversche Tages-Nachrichten* as its official party newspaper, and rather than one of the regional luminaries it chose a more obscure estate owner as its chairman. These Conservatives displayed a notable sympathy towards the Guelphs' legitimist aims – which was not reciprocated[28] – and sought no conflict with either the Free Conservatives or the Farmers' League. The National Liberals were the main villains, and the Conservatives' attempt to break their hold on Hanoverian seats in the Reichstag coloured the subsequent history of the Union. In 1899 the Union spokesmen decried the fact that 'national' and 'National Liberal' had become synonymous, and they claimed their action was a response to the NLP's drive to the east. They were also clearly worried that the provincial BdL supported mainly National Liberal candidates. So both urban and rural recruits were sought, as the district governor, Konstantin zu Stolberg-Wernigerode, wrote to the Prussian Minister of Cultural and Ecclesiastical Affairs in 1899.[29] Stolberg reported that the Conservatives were filling a large gap left by National Liberal inadequacies. He approved of the new Union, noting that recent NLP torpidity had created the need for a new anti-Socialist force. He also believed that Hanover's nobility and a large part of the clergy already regarded the Conservative Union as a welcome alternative to both the National Liberals and the Guelphs. Stolberg predicted that the Union, though presently small, would continue to gain new members at a steady pace.

By 1903 the Conservatives and National Liberals opposed each other in sixteen of nineteen Hanoverian Reichstag constituencies,[30] and by 1908 the district and provincial governors reported that Hanoverians were turning to the DKP in even greater numbers.[31] The Imperial League against Social Democracy was giving much greater support to the Conservatives than to National Liberals, and officials, artisans, farmers and large industrialists seemed to be following suit. One local NLP leader reportedly said that the National Liberals 'would have to anoint themselves with a drop of conservative oil' to survive in the province. The Conservative Union's cause was further boosted when a Conservative provincial congress was held in Hildesheim in February 1910. Although Free Conservatives were declared welcome, this event had a strongly anti-National-Liberal tone. Soon more *Vereine* sprang up in former NLP preserves such as Stade, Celle and East Friesland, and Hanoverian Party Secretary Max Kubel began his extensive pre-war travels addressing Conservative assemblies in north-central Germany. Nevertheless, the 1912 Reichstag elections illustrated the limits to Conservative influence in the province.[32]

In both the Grand Duchy of Hesse and the Prussian province of Hesse-Nassau, Conservative activity relied on the talents of only a few individuals. A province-wide *Verein* existed in Hesse-Nassau, but party efforts were concentrated in Wiesbaden and Frankfurt. When the chairman of the Conservative Union for the Administrative District of Wiesbaden attended a provincial rally in 1907 he argued for co-operation with the Free Conservatives. He spoke against the founding of Conservative *Vereine* in small towns and villages, claiming that he preferred the looser system of delegates. Pappenheim on the other hand called for more independence from the FKP; he argued that one could still socialize with one's conservative colleagues outside the organizational structure of the party.[33] The Conservative Union in Frankfurt, despite Werner's efforts there in the 1890s, stagnated until it was refounded in 1910. Werner helped stage a large rally in October 1910, but little enthusiasm remained for the Reichstag election campaign a year later.[34]

In Westphalia competition between Conservatives, Christian Socials and BdL agrarians continued to plague attempts to maintain the party organization after 1900. Conservatives also steadily lost ground to Catholic and left-wing opponents.[35] Another start was made in 1910 when the Conservative Union for the Province of Westphalia was founded under Klasing and when a very active party secretary, Wilhelm Albers, was appointed.[36] Albers attempted to recruit industrialists in the province as part of the Conservatives' drive westward, and helped establish a German Conservative Union for the Industrial District shortly before the war. The fate of this Union, however, is unknown.

In the Rhineland the combined efforts of German Conservatives, Free Conservatives, Christian Socials and agrarians produced equally meagre results. The single seat won in the district of Koblenz in 1907 and 1912 was counted as Christian Social, allowing the CSP to claim that it represented the sole conservative presence in the province. Few DKP *Vereine* displayed regular activity, and after the founding of the German Conservative *Verein* in the wake of Tivoli another provincial rally was not held until October 1910, in Duisburg.[37] Conservatives in Wetzlar, Elberfeld-Barmen and Mörs-Rees held occasional rallies after 1909, and in 1910–11 new *Vereine* were founded in Cologne, Bonn, Mühlheim and Koblenz-St-Goar.[38] The relative strength of the party in the Westerwald was due largely to Party Secretary Grund; but even he was far less active than his colleagues in other provinces.

In Alsace-Lorraine, despite claims that the Conservative Party had a significant role to play there as a 'Christian *Volkspartei*', electoral success declined rapidly after 1893.[39] The DKP's negative stand on constitutional rights for the *Reichsland* in 1911 made any propaganda in the region extremely difficult.

Berlin Conservatives had a history of stormy dissent out of all proportion to their electoral weight within Conservative ranks.[40] Never willing to admit defeat, they bristled whenever DKP leaders advised them simply to withhold their votes in elections. They needed to believe that Conservative work in the capital had a future and a purpose. Among the many Conservative *Bürgervereine* in Berlin the best organized and most influential was the Conservative Central *Verein* for the Constituency of Teltow-Beeskow-Storkow-Charlottenburg, in Germany's most populous Reichstag constituency. In the social complexion of its executive committee, the Central *Verein* was characteristic of most Conservative *Bürgervereine*; retired officers, officials, teachers, minor church officials and *Mittelstand* groups in general dominated. It was also fairly typical in its special concerns: the combating of department stores and consumer co-operatives; rising meat prices; the 'physical, national and moral education' of urban youth; protection of the right to work; and the usual catalogue of anti-Semitic demands.

The Conservative *Bürgerverein* in Charlottenburg could boast in 1908 that its own *Mitteilungen* had been published for five years.[41] *Verein* membership numbered over six hundred in 1908, and at its general assembly, a report reviewed very active *Verein* life over the past year. In early 1908 a *Verein* of National Voters was also established in Beeskow. Its name reflected the wish to attract National Liberal voters who lacked their own organization (Conservatives in Rixdorf had already tried the same tactic). Around the same time, the Brandenburg provincial office was establishing better contact with these *Bürgervereine*. The Brandenburg party secretary was closely involved in helping arrange party speakers to suit local circumstances, while local *Bürgervereine* functionaries reciprocated with information about their scheduled rallies, election results and organizational plans.

Activism brought rebellion in its wake. The *Bürgervereine* attempted in 1907 to propose a number of their leaders as delegates to the Conservative provincial *Verein* for Brandenburg. The Central *Verein* in Teltow-

200

Beeskow pointedly informed the Brandenburgers that its contribution of 400 marks for the year was conditional upon one of its representatives finding a seat on the provincial Conservative executive.[42] In February 1909 it was further proposed that the individual Conservative *Bürgervereine* unite formally. At a meeting of the Teltow-Beeskow Central *Verein* this proposal was defeated. At the same meeting, however, Arthur von Loebell tabled motions in favour of Conservative compromise on the Prussian franchise question and for a moderate inheritance tax. When these were also defeated, Loebell declared that his *Verein* 'would never again elect a parliamentary deputy who did not favour an improvement of the franchise'.[43] By the end of the year, Loebell's rebellion was a national embarrassment for the Conservative leadership.

Bavarian Conservatives were caught up in the tumultuous history of various peasant leagues in the 1890s, partly because the BdL leaders in Berlin did not advocate participation in Bavarian Landtag elections until 1899.[44] By the beginning of the war, estimates place the number of BdL members in Bavaria at roughly 16,000 to 17,000. This readership was enough to support not only older Conservative newspapers but also a special edition of the *Bund der Landwirte für Bayern* and a parliamentary correspondence entitled *Bavaria*. A Free Union (*Freie Vereinigung*) of agrarians, Conservatives and some National Liberals was constituted in the Bavarian Landtag after 1899, achieving a united strength of twenty deputies. In the Landtag elections of 1912, however, this Union was reduced to nine members.[45]

The evolution of the Bavarian Conservative *Wahlverein* proceeded along somewhat different paths. Having overcome internal dissension in 1905–6, Friedrich Beckh and other leaders of the *Wahlverein* were able to stage general assemblies of their state organization in April of 1910 and 1911. By mid-1911, however, a movement was afoot to 'refound' a Bavarian Conservative Union, based in Munich.[46] As the Prussian envoy reported to Bethmann Hollweg from Munich, about sixty conservative men met to establish a 'patriotic *Mittelpartei*'. In this group were former liberals, imperial councillors, inactive officers, writers and professors, led by the Director of the Bavarian Agricultural Bank and regional representative of the German Society of Nobles, Baron Karl von Cetto. This 'party' was finally constituted as the Bavarian Conservative Union at a meeting in Munich on 20 October 1911. The sixty attendants were evenly divided between nobles and non-nobles, while officials and Protestant pastors were in abundance. However, industrialists and commercial leaders remained steadfastly aloof; they eventually founded their own Bavarian Reichspartei or Free Conservative Union, which, the Prussian envoy noted, was 'conservative in name only'.[47]

At first there was some doubt about whether the Bavarian Conservative Union wished to ally with Beckh's group. However, when the Union held its first party congress in mid-December 1911, Diederich Hahn was invited to speak, and one of the Union's members was elected to the DKP's Committee of Fifty. When the group around Beckh held their own congress in April 1912, Cetto was a welcome guest. Beckh announced plans to amalgamate his own executive with that of the Union, and by 1912 the Bavarian Conservative *Landesverband* (state association) had been established.[48] Nevertheless, the Prussian envoy reported immediately after the January 1912 Reichstag elections that the Black–Blue bloc in Bavaria now had an 'extremely slim blue component'; the Conservatives had not even been surprised at the disastrous outcome of the elections. The party's 'monstrous difficulties' (arising from the natural constellation of parties in the state) were compounded by 'artificial' ones, stemming from a dearth of suitable personalities. To these were added desperate financial circumstances and the competition of the Bavarian Reichspartei. In August 1913 the envoy concluded: 'No matter how the crisis is resolved, it is indicative of the minimal interest with which purely Conservative efforts here are greeted.'

'The Conservative Organization in the Kingdom of Saxony' was the title of a long article (probably written by Oertel) which appeared in 1892.[49] According to this report, the Conservative *Landesverein* in Saxony had only 2,000 members, partly due to its high membership fees.[50] The total membership of the fifty local *Vereine* in the kingdom, however, allegedly totalled some 20,000. Of the twenty-three Reichstag constituencies, only one had no Conservative *Verein*. The largest individual *Vereine* were in Dresden and Leipzig, with roughly 2,000 and 1,500 members respectively; five *Vereine* had between 500 and 1,000 members, while only two had under 100. In 1892 these *Vereine* allegedly still recognized no distinction between German Conservatives and Free Conservatives, although the FKP had already staged one independent rally a few months earlier.

After the Saxon Conservatives' flirtation with anti-Semitism ended abruptly in 1894 the *Landesverein* was led by a highly respected but politically indolent industrialist from Leipzig. The tasks of Consul-General Dr Schober and his successors were mainly defensive, including the preservation of Conservative ascendancy in the Saxon Landtag; close relations with the government; Kartell alliances in elections; a healthy Conservative press; cordial relations with the Farmers' League; unity between different occupational groups within the state organization; and an advantageous Saxon Landtag franchise. On each count the success of Saxon Conservatives was very mixed.[51]

Only after Mehnert had taken over as regional party chairman was there a strong impulse for greater organizational independence and activity. Most notably Mehnert worked closely with Ludwig Fahrenbach, a higher functionary in the Saxon *Mittelstand* Association.[52] As well as the Union of Industrialists, a 'committee on officials' within the *Landesverein* met after 1910.[53] At the Saxon Conservative congress in December 1912, Mehnert reported that the number of individual *Vereine* in the state had risen since 1910 from 72 to 104. In 1913 the *Landesverein* gained an alleged 4,000 new members. This put its total membership at about 20,000, that is, exactly the same number reported in 1892. The Dresden *Verein* grew by only 142 members in 1911–12, and new faces did not appear in the *Landesverein*'s executive committee either; all twelve members were re-elected in 1912.[54] Prussian trends, in short, were not as foreign to the Kingdom of Saxony as many Conservatives might have wished. In the 1912 Reichstag elections Conservatives won only one of Saxony's twenty-three seats.

Even more than in Bavaria, the Conservative organization in Württemberg was integrated with the BdL's regional affiliate, the Peasants' League (Bauernbund).[55] Friedrich Schrempf, for example, was not only the Conservatives' party secretary after 1890 and editor of the *Deutsche Reichspost*, but also a leading functionary and publicist in the Peasants' League. In 1895 the Conservative–BdL coalition made its first appearance in the Landtag, with two deputies who designated themselves members of the Peasants' League, and one Conservative.[56] By the Reichstag elections of 1898 the Prussian envoy in Stuttgart reported that only the BdL and the SPD seemed really active in the state.[57] Although the Conservatives and the BdL offered separate election manifestos[58] in the Landtag campaign of November 1912, their twenty elected deputies subsequently formed a united caucus dominated by small farmers, village mayors, lawyers, teachers, party functionaries and editors.[59] The Württembergers also sent two or three deputies to the Reichstag from 1898 onwards. Nevertheless, thoroughly independent Conservative *Vereine* existed only in some areas of the Black Forest and in the large cities. The Stuttgart *Verein* was headed by Rudolf Behringer, a wealthy business man who later chaired the local chapter of the German Fatherland Party.

In 1912 the *Württembergischer Bauernfreund* illustrated the direction of Conservative–BdL propaganda in literal terms. On its cover it depicted a farmer and a tradesman meeting on a country road, surrounded by peasants, vintners, bee-keepers and urban artisans. The espousal of a *mittelständisch*, anti-Semitic, agrarian and vaguely oppositional policy by Conservatives and the BdL in Württemberg recast the balance of state politics. Most notable were the affinities between the agrarian Conservatives and the Centre Party, not only in their political agendas but also in their agitational styles.[60] By 1912 the regional manifestation of the Black–Blue bloc held more than half of the seats in the Landtag.

The Conservatives in Württemberg were atypical in one respect, for their organizational expansion slowed after 1909. Between 1895 and 1904 the Peasants' League in Württemberg grew in membership from about

1,500 to over 20,000, organized in about nine hundred local units. But after 1904 the membership figures stagnated. From 1900 to 1906 the Conservative–League Landtag deputies increased from six to fifteen, but this rate of increase then dropped off. In 1910 six newspapers served the Conservatives and agrarians, but subsequently this figure was not improved upon.[61] The *Süddeutsche Zeitung* was founded in Stuttgart in 1913, but this arose from collaboration between members of both conservative parties, the BdL and the Pan-Germans. Like the radical nationalists themselves, the *Süddeutsche Zeitung* was very serious about following its own call to arms – 'The Fatherland above the Party!'[62]

In the State Committee (*Landesausschuß*) of Baden Conservatives, *Honoratioren* politics persisted after 1900 almost unchanged. At the local level few permanent *Vereine* were established, and election campaigns continued to be the responsibility of the individual candidate almost entirely.[63] Party delegates were recruited as volunteers; when they failed to turn out to distribute propaganda, a wage of two to three marks had to be paid to those willing to do the work. This system prevailed in outline throughout the Second Reich. After 1900, however, a chronic lack of funds further constrained agitation.[64]

After the disruptions of the mid-1890s the Baden Conservatives had begun to view co-operation with the NLP sceptically. In 1903 a turning-point was reached. At that time Otto von Stockhorn sent a letter to the Baden Conservative executive committee arguing for a closer alliance with the Centre.[65] Stockhorn's appeal elicited no clear response from the Baden Conservative leadership. The chairman's reply refused to commit the party to one course or the other, and no executive statement of policy was issued.[66] This did not prevent Stockhorn from stating his case in correspondence with other Baden Conservatives. But the matter was soon taken out of Conservative hands. In 1905 the National Liberals and Socialists for the first time concluded an electoral agreement to support each other's candidates in Landtag elections. This was the genesis of the Grand Bloc in Baden, which the Left in Germany vainly hoped might become the model for a nationwide parliamentary alliance 'from Bassermann to Bebel'. In response a partnership was slowly consolidated between Centre Party members and Conservatives in Baden.[67] In this *Rechtsblock* the DKP–BdL deputies, who called themselves the Rightist Union, were similar in background to their colleagues elsewhere in the south-west. Small farmers, small business men, mill-owners, town mayors and lawyers predominated – hardly a *Volkspartei*, but then again hardly reflective of the exclusively aristocratic leadership of the Baden Conservative Party itself.[68] As well as bringing them some modest electoral success, the new alliance induced the Conservatives to redouble their organizational efforts. This task was all the more urgent once the FKP and NLP established their own party secretariats in the state. Soon the Conservatives' dauntless party secretary, Wilhelm Schmidt of Heidelberg, was busy organizing a Union of Young German Conservative Men in Karlsruhe.[69] By September 1913, at the height of the Landtag election campaign, the Conservatives were able to stage a large party rally, the first in twenty years.[70]

By that point Baron Udo von La Roche-Starkenfels, the Baden party co-chairman, had long been decrying the Grand Bloc. But some observers felt the Baden Conservatives had brought this misfortune on themselves. Eisendecher spoke of 'the complete incompetence and unsuitability' of these men.[71] Even the BdL leaders were very dissatisfied with the attitude of La Roche and colleagues. As Roesicke wrote to Wangenheim in 1908, at election time the Baden Conservative leaders wanted 'to bring in the League secondarily, in order to exploit the fruits of the League's organization for merely party-political ends'. Roesické also noted that these leaders were 'still motivated by the desire to see the League suspend its agitation wherever the Conservatives can expect success and proceed with it wherever such success is absolutely impossible'.[72]

And so Conservative isolation increased. When La Roche wrote to the chancellory in 1910 he indicated that unless the Grand Duke of Baden disavowed his government's flirtation with the Grand Bloc, 'the work of the right-wing parties will be completely paralysed'. He then aded: 'We are not "feudal Conservative" here in the narrow Prussian sense, but rather more Christian-Conservative, through the drawing-in of the Christian-national workers and with the wish to include in our ranks the right-wing elements of the National Liberals.' By that point nothing could disguise the fact that Baden politics had become bisected into liberal and anti-liberal blocs. The Baden prototype of an alliance from Bassermann to Bebel was only the most obvious manifestation of Conservatives' larger isolation in Reich politics.

NOTES

1 On the NLP see materials in BAK, R45 I, *Nationalliberale Partei*, 4; ZStA I, RLB/BdL press archive, 6222–4; Mundle, *National Liberal Party*, chs. 1 and 4; on FKP reorganization see Stegmann, *Erben*, pp. 316–23.
2 *Rb*, 9.1.94; for the following, see materials in ZStA II, NL Kapp, C VIII, 3, 'Konservativer Verein', *passim*; Nipperdey, *Organisation*, p. 251.
3 ZStA I, NL Westarp, 98, f. 29 ff., 59.
4 *Rkz.* 1391/5, f. 145, Dohna-Finckenstein to Loebell, 6.12.07; *KZ*, 20.12.09; *Danziger Allgemeine Zeitung*, 17.12.10, 13.12.11, 20.12.12; *Mitteilungen*, 1912, p. 841.
5 *CC*, 24.5.10, 29.6.10; *NAZ*, 29.5.10; *Posener Tageblatt*, 1/15.5.10; ZStA I, NL Westarp, 1, f. 19, Landrat Kley to Westarp, 8.9.10, 13.10.10.
6 *Posener Tageblatt*, 24.11.12; provincial executive listed in *Mitteilungen*, 1912, pp. 428, 778.
7 Executive (1895) listed in BAK, ZSg 1, 70/1 (17); it included one bookseller, one factory owner and two educators among an overwhelmingly noble seventeen-man committee.

8 *SchlMZ*, 18.11.06; *KZ*, 28.3.13, 5.2.14; *Mitteilungen*, 1912, pp. 242, 259, 777; 1913, p. 93; *SchlZ*, 9.4.11; *Vw*, 20.4.12.
9 *CC*, 1.12.10; *FsZ*, 28.3.12, 6.1.14; *DTZ*, 31.10.11, 29.6.12, 23.1.14; *Pommersche Tagespost*, 7.3.13; *Fürstentumer Zeitung*, 7.3.13; DKP, *Parteitag des Konservativen Provinzialvereins für Pommern* [1910]; *Mitteilungen*, 1910, pp. 322, 466; 1911, p. 305; 1912, pp. 139, 461, 638, 698.
10 Provincial executive listed in *Mitteilungen*, 1914, p. 27.
11 *Mitteilungen*, 1909, p. 49.
12 See *Mitteilungen*, 1908, p. 84 and *passim*, on the strong Patriotic *Verein* in Eberswalde.
13 *Mitteilungen*, 1908, pp. 3–4, 150.
14 ZStA I, NL Wangenheim, 5, f. 30.
15 *MecklN*, 24.5.12; *Mitteilungen*, 1912, pp. 355, 732; 1913, p. 731; 1914, p. 296.
16 Executive listed in *Mitteilungen*, 1912, p. 637; *Hallesche Zeitung*, 27.1.10, 3.5.10, 26.6.10, 24.2.12; *DTZ*, 13.2.11; *Mitteilungen*, 14.1.11, 24.6.11, 9.3.12, 6.7.12, 14.3.14.
17 *Vereinigung der rechtsstehenden Männer in Reuß*; *Mitteilungen*, 1912, pp. 219 ff., 461; 1913, p. 711 (LT *Wahlaufruf*); 1914, pp. 331, 423.
18 PA AA Bonn, Deutschland 125, 3, Vol. 16, Dönhoff to Bülow, 13/15.6.03.
19 *Wahlaufruf* in GStA Berlin (Dahlem), XII Hauptabteilung IV, 172, f. 44.
20 *Rb*, 18.9.94, 24.3.12; *Vk*, 23.2.96; *Weimarer Zeitung*, 3.7.13; *SCC*, 7.7.14; *KZ*, 21.11.10; *Lippesche Tageszeitung*, 24.11.08, 13–16.12.11, 7.12.12; *Mitteilungen*, 1910, p. 387; 1913, p. 329; 1914, p. 157.
21 Executive listed in *Mitteilungen*, 1912, p. 276, including seven 'academics' (doctors, lawyers, judges, teachers), three officials, six retailers, three tradesmen and artisans, and two farmers.
22 *DTZ*, 9/10.3.12, 5/23.6.12, 18.12.12; *Die Post*, 9.6.12; *HN*, 5.10.13; *NeueDtland*, 22.2.13; ZStA I, NL Westarp, 2, f. 33; *Mitteilungen*, 1912, pp. 181, 308 f.; 1914, p. 109.
23 PA AA Bonn, Deutschland 125, 3, Vol. 16, Henckel to Bülow, 22.5.03.
24 *Mitteilungen*, 1912, p. 309; *Hoyaer Zeitung*, 11.3.13.
25 *DTZ*, 27.3.11; *Rb*, 15.3.13; *Mitteilungen*, 1913, p. 588.
26 See the copious materials in Staatsarchiv Aurich, NL Edzard zu Inn- und Knyphausen (provincial BdL chairman), Dep. IV, III q, 30 and 35.
27 Full report in *HannTN*, 2/19.3.99; large and small estate owners dominated the executive, which also included two factory owners, a lawyer and a cobbler.
28 Cf. Backhaus, *Wer sind die Conservativen Hannovers?*
29 GStA Berlin (Dahlem), NL Bosse, 14, f. 51, Stolberg to Robert Bosse, 14.4.99.
30 Cf. Ehrenfeuchter, 'Willensbildung'; Franz, *Wahlen*.
31 *Rkz*. 1081, f. 215 ff., von Philipsborn and Dr Wentzel, both to the Minister of the Interior, 5/8.6.08.
32 *HannTN*, 5.2.10, 4.4.10, 15.3.11, 10.10.11; *Mitteilungen*, 1910, pp. 119, 322; 1911, p. 773; 1912, pp. 153–5, 443; 1913, p. 43; *TR*, 22.2.13; *Rb*, 13.3.14; *DTZ*, 23.6.14.
33 Report in *CC*, 15.4.07; cf. *Nassauer Zeitung*, 4.4.10; elections to the executive committee in *Mitteilungen*, 1912, p. 373; also materials in BAK, Sg F, 46.
34 *Mitteilungen*, 1910, pp. 309 ff.; *DAB*, 1910, pp. 373 ff., 385 ff.; *Rb*, 2.6.12.
35 See Möller-Gütersloh to Reck, 2.2.03, cited in Hoener, 'Christlich-konservative Partei', p. 103; on the provincial BdL, ZStA I, NL Roesicke, 39, Baron von Stietencron to Roesicke, 24.1.94.
36 *DAB*, 1910, pp. 607 ff.; cf. *DTZ*, 26.4.10, listing the provincial executive; *Mitteilungen*, 1910, pp. 135, 244; 1911, pp. 102–6; 1912, p. 457; 1914, p. 364; Albers, *Verderben*; Albers, *Besiegten*, especially pp. 17–19.
37 *Mitteilungen*, 1910, p. 119; *DAB*, 1910, pp. 557 f.
38 *Mitteilungen*, 1910, pp. 403, 435 ff.; 1911, p. 341; 1912, pp. 260, 841; *Westdeutsches Tageblatt*, 11/13.5.10; 10/11.9.10; 25.10.10.
39 *Mitteilungen*, 1912, pp. 119, 837; *DTZ*, 12.12.12.
40 For the following, except where noted, see materials in ZStA I, 60 Pa 2, 'Konservativer Verein für die Provinz Brandenburg'.
41 *Mitteilungen des konservativen Bürgervereins zu Charlottenburg*, 3, April 1908.
42 *Landrat* Röthe to Treskow, 24.5.07; letter to the Brandenburg executive, 6.4.07.
43 See Bruno Schröter to Sigismund von Treskow, 18.2.09.

44 For details see mainly Heller, 'Bund', pp. 6–17, 36–42; also Farr, 'Populism'; Puhle, *Interessenpolitik*, pp. 172 f.; *SddLp*, 22.2.95.

45 Biographies in the Bavarian LT *Handbücher*; election materials in the Bayrische Staatsbibliothek, 2° J.publ.g. 355 dd and 2° Bavar. 526 ae.

46 For the following see reports in PA AA Bonn, Bayern, 61, Vols. 5 and 6, *passim*; Deutschland 125, 3, Vol. 25; *Mitteilungen*, 1911, *passim*.

47 *Bayerische Reichspartei*; cf. materials in Bayrische Staatsbibliothek, 4 Bavar. 3297.

48 Puhle, *Interessenpolitik*, p. 276; executive listed in *Mitteilungen*, 1912, p. 811.

49 *Rb*, 31.7.92 by 'G.O.'.

50 The figure given by the *DtRp*, 7.4.80, was 414.

51 See reports in PA AA Bonn, I A Sachsen (Königreich), 48, Vols. 17–20, *passim*; I Deutschland 125, 3, Vols. 14–16, *passim*; I A Sachsen (Königreich), 60, Vol. 8; cf. *DTZ*, 12.7.07, 31.8.07; *DresdN*, 20.6.12, 9.12.13; *Mitteilungen*, 1910, pp. 194 ff., 209.

52 Stegmann, 'Neokonservatismus', pp. 206 ff.

53 *Mitteilungen*, 1912, p. 213; 1913, p. 795.

54 In 1909 the wider executive reportedly included 58 members of the legal profession, 20 other officials, 13 educators, 6 doctors, 6 retired officers, 3 independents, 19 industrialists, 1 artisan and 31 farmers; *DTZ*, 21.4.09.

55 The BdL initially tried to establish a German Economic Party in Württemberg; ZStA I, NL Roesicke, 40, f. 5 ff., including Rudolf Schmid to Roesicke, 15.2.95, 15.3.95; for the following see mainly Körner, *Schmid*; Hunt, *People's Party*, ch. 6; Hunt, '"Egalitarianism"'; Blackbourn, *Class*, ch. 7.

56 *Wahlaufruf* in BAK, NL Friedrich Payer, 18, f. 165 ff.

57 Reports in PA AA Bonn, Deutschland 125, 3, Vols. 15 (1898) and 25 (1912).

58 Both in the *Schwäbischer Landmann*, 25.10.12.

59 Biographies in *Der württembergische Landtag* (1913), pp. 74–96.

60 Cf. Grube, *Landtag*, pp. 549–54; Kraut's speech in the Württemberg Conservatives' *Landesversammlung*, pp. 2–8; Körner, *Kann der Bauer Sozialdemokrat sein?*; *Schwäbischer Landmann*, 1912, pp. 151 ff.; Hunt, *People's Party*, pp. 97–110; and especially Blackbourn, *Class*, pp. 210 f.

61 The *DtRp* ceased publication on 1.10.13.

62 *SddZ*, 16.9.13.

63 Karlsruhe *Verein* executive listed in *DtRp*, 25.4.12; for details below see Sepaintner, *Reichstagswahlen*, pp. 72–80; GLA Karlsruhe, NL Stockhorn, 69h, *passim*.

64 Documented in *Rkz*. 1391, f. 86 ff., Baron Udo von La Roche-Starkenfels to Wahnschaffe, 7.10.10.

65 Letter (concept), 26.7.03, cited in Sepaintner, *Reichstagswahlen*, p. 77.

66 *CC*, 29.2.04.

67 Cf. Thiel, *Großblockpolitik*; Kremer, *Mitt Gott*; Wacker, *Warum*; Zangerl, 'Baden's Opening', pp. 114 ff., 156 ff., 218 ff.

68 Biographies in Rapp, *Landtags-Abgeordneten*.

69 *Mitteilungen*, 1911, p. 372; cf. Schmidt, *Wohin steuern wir?*; Schmidt, 'Großblock'.

70 *SddZ*, 21–23.9.13.

71 PA AA Bonn, Deutschland 125, 3, Vol. 14 Eisendecher to Hohenlohe, 9.2.97, 4.3.97; cf. other reports in Vols. 15–16.

72 ZStA I, NL Wangenheim, 3, f. 53 ff., Roesicke to Wangenheim, 31.7.08.

15

Radicalism, War and Collapse

In a climate of public opinion unprecedentedly hostile to their party, Conservatives after 1909 were at last forced to yield much of their traditional independence and outlook. Efforts to resurrect close ties with the National Liberals and Free Conservatives succeeded only in part. This, together with Bethmann Hollweg's perceived weakness in foreign policy, pushed the Conservatives (as the chancellor saw it) 'down demagogic paths'. At the same time, the numerical strength and programmatic extremism of the nationalist opposition were growing. As these forces became more potent their attractiveness for the Conservatives increased. The self-marginalization of Heydebrand further opened the door for radical Pan-Germans to state their case within the DKP. In these processes August 1914 marked no caesura (although the war obviously changed the political context in which they occurred). Irresolution characterized the party's response to the dilemmas of popular mobilization in peace and war. Yet only the events of November 1918 revealed how unsuccessfully the DKP had adjusted to new realities in a period of violent political upheaval. As the Conservative Party was consumed in war and revolution, it finally revealed itself as Hellmut von Gerlach once referred to it – as an anti-*Volkspartei*.[1]

From the previous two chapters it might appear that Conservatives attempted to rejuvenate their party after 1909 exclusively through autonomous organizational activity. However, another Conservative campaign ran parallel with this effort. It too was designed to allow the party to overcome the legacy of the finance reform. But it sought to make the Conservative Party influential again primarily through the establishment (or re-establishment) of political ties at the highest level of politics. It was by means of a new constellation of forces on the Right, rather than through an increase in the DKP's own popular capability, that some Conservatives wanted to revive their party's fortunes.

Bethmann for one was hopeful in 1909 that the Conservatives could be brought back into a 'natural' constellation of state-supporting parties. He formulated legislation in both the Prussian Landtag and the Reichstag which could foster co-operation between the NLP, FKP and DKP. The failure of this strategy was revealed not only by the abortive franchise reform of 1910 but also by other bills in the next two years. These bills introduced a Reich capital gains tax and revised workers' insurance programmes; a constitution was also finally provided for the *Reichsland* of Alsace-Lorraine. On each occasion, however, Conservative intransigence contributed to the DKP's parliamentary isolation.[2]

In 1910–11 there were signs that the heavy industrialists on the right wing of the National Liberal Party were moving towards a closer relationship with the leaders of the BdL and DKP.[3] In this complex process both Bethmann and the Conservative leadership played important roles. Yet ambivalence and lack of resolve on all sides undermined their efforts. Bethmann for instance complained about the National Liberals' 'unreliability' and 'radicalism' but he also criticized Heydebrand's 'intractable dictatorial strain' and his clear intention to turn his back on the NLP.[4]

In late 1911 the right-wing parties and the government were driven further apart. The story of Germany's unsuccessful diplomacy in the second Moroccan crisis is well known. By November 1911 Bethmann had suffered humiliation and public outrage when the *Panthersprung* failed to win significant concessions from the French. On 9 November 1911 Bethmann defended his final settlement in the Reichstag. It was on this occasion that Heydebrand chose to indicate that the DKP was indeed a 'nationally minded' party. He charged that Bethmann's 'yieldings' would not secure peace; 'only our good German sword can do that'. The significance of Heydebrand's speech was not lost on anyone. It was recognized that for the first time the Conservatives' pugilistic attitude – towards England, but more notably towards the chancellor himself – rivalled what Pan-German agitators had been saying for years.[5]

Shortly after this exchange another shock was provided by the Reichstag elections of January 1912.[6] There were many reasons for the leftist victory: the reverberations of the 1909 finance reform, rising consumer prices, right-wing disunity and Bethmann's failure to provide a national rallying-cry. More crises ensued in 1912, as right-wing deputies were forced to face the implications of sitting in a parliament where Socialists now formed the largest caucus. There are nevertheless good reasons not to overemphasize the discontinuity of January 1912. The following years saw only a more determined defence of positions first assumed in the period 1909–12. As vehemently as ever, Bethmann claimed he could steer a diagonal course, enlighten the Conservative Party and avoid his own demise. And just as vehemently, the Conservatives claimed that their policy of 'no compromise' with liberalism had been the correct one, in 1909 and afterwards. The government was forced to include the SPD in its legislative equations, but the Conservatives now spoke of the inevitable show-down between the 'Red 110' (Socialists) and the 'Iron 54' (Conservatives).[7]

Just as tension characterized the relationship between Conservative estate owners in the east and the Society for the Eastern Marches, it also coloured relations between the DKP and other nationalist pressure groups. The most important of these organizations were the Pan-German League, the Navy League (founded 1898), the Imperial League against Social Democracy (1904), the German Union (Deutsche Vereinigung, 1908), the Defence League (Wehrverein, 1911) and the Prussian League (1913). What was the source of these conflicts? What type of radical nationalist tended to endorse the Conservative Party, and what type tended to define himself in opposition to it? Conversely, which Conservatives were more likely to offer their services to these nationalist groups, and which remained aloof?

Social status was one important factor. In general, greater enthusiasm for these nationalist groups was displayed by non-aristocratic Conservatives, those who lived in cities, those with military or bureaucratic backgrounds and those with connections to the world of business. Less interested were Conservatives in the Herrenhaus, those from isolated east-Elbian estates and those with close ties to court. This was partially due to the fact that the nationalist groups recruited the bulk of their members from middle-class and urban circles. Otherwise a logical process of self-selection prevailed whereby retired officers tended to drift towards the defence leagues, *Mittelstand* representatives towards the anti-Socialist groups and Conservative aristocrats towards any group eager to have a dignitary on its executive committee.

Second, the nationalist groups found their greatest resonance in what might generally be considered prime National Liberal territory, that is, in middle Germany and areas west of the Elbe, the perimeter of old Prussia. Conservative chairmen of *Vereine* in these regions, together with those who supported Kartell alliances, were especially prone to join these associations. Thus in 1891 the executive committees of the Pan-German League[8] included Mehnert (Saxony), Plettenberg-Mehrum (Rhineland), Thüngen-Roßbach (Bavaria), Douglas (Baden) and Helldorff (Prussian Saxony). Mehnert in fact was a good example of the kind of Conservative most likely to participate in radical nationalist enterprises. He was not particularly enamoured of the Farmers' League, and did not have to rely on its assistance at election time; he faced a potent Socialist threat in his homeland; his name was known nationally; and he believed that the Right had a duty to bury its party-political differences. This background qualified Mehnert to serve as a liaison between the DKP's Committee of Five and the Navy League, the Imperial German *Mittelstand* Association (Reichsdeutscher Mittelstandsverband, or RDMV), the Bismarckdank Foundation[9] and, later, the German Fatherland Party (Deutsche Vaterlands-Partei, or DVP).

Third, a number of factors inclined some activists to serve as functionaries in the patriotic societies, and others to devote their energies to the cause of the Conservative Party *per se*. Among Conservatives who preferred the non-party forum, journalists like Heinrich Oberwinder, associational organizers like Ludwig Weber and disaffected parliamentarians like Alexander zu Hohenlohe found no home within the Conservative Party in the 1890s; they each discovered greater fulfilment in the nationalist *Verbände*. Soon these men were joined by hundreds more who experienced similar disappointment with the interest politics and national equivocation of the right-wing parties. By 1900 they had begun to define a nationalism which corresponded more closely to their conception of the *Volk* and less closely to that of the Conservatives. They defined Germany's national goals (and the symbols that represented them) in their own, rather than their betters', terms. Most broadly of all they endorsed the further consolidation of the nation with an essentially optimistic perspective on the future, rather than fearful reliance on the symbols of nationhood and techniques of repression established by Bismarck. These, then, were the radicals who were inclined to accuse the Conservatives of 'debilitating caution, social élitism, blindness to Germany's national needs and a refusal to obey the dictates of the new mass politics'.[10] Such accusations represented perhaps the greatest blow to the political prestige and popular capability of the Conservative Party, and the one with the widest implications.

There were, however, many nationalists who had made their reputations outside the party sphere but who later contributed to the new, aggressive tone in Conservative propaganda or sat for the party in parliament. Although a number of these men made no distinction between German Conservatism and Free Conservatism, they provided extremely important personal and ideological links between the DKP and the nationalist *Verbände*, especially after 1911. First, they wrote a steady stream of programmatic articles for such major DKP journals as the *Kreuzzeitung*, the *Mitteilungen*, the *Konservative Monatsschrift* and the *Deutsches Adelsblatt*. Second, they contributed to Conservative pamphlet series, which grew in number during the war.[11] Third, they travelled widely among Conservative *Vereine* in the provinces, giving practical expression to the growing community of interest between radical nationalism and Conservatism.[12] These patrioteers were joined by a younger generation of radical nationalist Conservatives who were elected to parliament or became party insiders in the final years before the war. Among the most outspoken were Wolfgang Kapp, Georg Schiele, Ferdinand von Grumme-Douglas, Prince Otto von Salm-Horstmar, Albrecht von Graefe and Walter Graef. Certainly the commitment of these men to the Conservative Party was highly problematic. Their endorsement of official DKP policy was given grudgingly or not at all. Also, the Free Conservative Party was emerging in the immediate pre-war years as the pace-setter among the parties attempting to adapt themselves to the nationalist agenda. So by sponsoring such individuals, DKP *Vereine* and

211

journals were effectively repudiating Heydebrand and the isolation he seemed to prefer. Nevertheless, the DKP's reputation on nationalist issues was less tarnished than it might have been had such men refused to contribute to Conservative propaganda or join Conservative caucuses in parliament.

The failure of the Pan-German League to win over the Conservative leadership before 1911 was due to deep-seated differences of outlook. These differences had also led to considerable antagonism between the DKP and other nationalist groups. An example was provided in 1907 when the *Conservative Correspondenz* condemned the radical anti-governmental line which the Navy League had recently adopted in its agitation:[13]

[The Navy League] has been able to make its valuable contribution only so long as it has proceeded with its business without noise, without political airs and without defying those who disagree with it . . . Among the vast majority of the population – this must be said loudly and clearly – one has had enough of the chauvinistic, Pan-German agitation which parades itself in the Navy League.

The Imperial League against Social Democracy made the Conservatives fear for their organizational independence. When it was founded in early 1904 the RvgSD was initially endorsed by many prominent DKP parliamentarians and provincial chairmen. By 1905, however, the *Conservative Correspondenz* was already condemning the League's efforts to win recruits and collect financial contributions at Conservative *Verein* meetings.[14] These fears were fuelled when the League unleashed its considerable propaganda talents in the Reichstag elections of January 1907 by forming patriotic workers' associations, wooing German farmers and establishing branch organizations in the rural east. The Conservatives now warned the RvgSD to abandon its 'quite monstrous plan to create an organization embracing all the parties or, more accurately, swallowing them up'. Even on the eve of the war the Conservatives disapproved of the 'insubordinate posture' of most nationalist pressure groups. Although the founding of the Defence League in December 1911 was naturally welcomed by Conservatives, the *Kreuzzeitung* declared that it went against 'the Prussian grain to have to resort to organized pressure-group activity' to meet Germany's military requirements.[15] Quite understandably, then, the particularist and highly reactionary Prussian League elicited a much more enthusiastic Conservative response upon its founding in mid-1913.[16] The battle-cries of aristocratic Conservative spokesmen in the Prussian Herrenhaus, not those of demagogic bourgeois nationalists outside, were used to legitimize the Prussian League's efforts. There was little chance here of confusing top hats and street clothes.

Despite these many reservations about the radical nationalists' style and
programme, a subtle shift in Conservative attitudes was registered as early
as mid-1909 when the *Reichsbote* postulated the identity of 'popular' and
'nationalist' politics:[17]

> The Conservative Party must . . . abandon its reserved, dignified
> bearing . . . [It] has contributed much to the happy development of the
> nation's strength and prosperity through the protection of national
> work, social reform, naval expansion and colonies . . . A fresh, happy
> confirmation of its national feeling would give the Conservative Party a
> popular stamp.

The *Reichsbote* did not represent the DKP leadership, however. The
Pan-Germans found after 1908 that their relations improved much more
quickly with the other nationalist *Verbände*, with the National Liberals
and with the Free Conservatives than with the German Conservatives.[18]

The first decisive change in this relationship came in 1911. Early in the
year Heydebrand met with Heinrich Claß, chairman of the ADV.
Although Claß reported boldly to Alfred Hugenberg that he was now in
'personal touch' with Heydebrand, these discussions hardly yielded the
desired results on the Pan-German side. Heydebrand suggested that if the
Pan-German leaders hoped to improve their relations with the Conservative Party they should devote their energies to establishing local Conservative *Vereine* in western and central Germany. By year's end, however, a
new Conservative attitude seemed to be emerging. Immediately after
Heydebrand's Morocco speech the Pan-Germans began to believe that
they could take heart from 'the Conservatives' exceedingly welcome and
sharp posture' against the government.[19] Yet almost two years elapsed
before the nascent Conservative–Pan-German *rapprochement* yielded
tangible results.

As the Pan-German star rose, the fortunes of the Conservative Party
seemed to reach their nadir. Four decisive shifts in the Conservatives'
political position preceded an understanding with the Pan-Germans. The
first and most conspicuous development occurred in the winter of
1911–12; a harsher tone infected Conservative foreign-policy statements,
and the party suffered disaster at the polls. Second, the Conservatives
became less reserved with their attacks on Jews and more forthright in
their campaigns against the universal franchise.[20] Third was the growing
isolation of the Conservative Party in the Reichstag. To be sure, the
Conservatives joined with the National Liberals and Free Conservatives in
passing large army increases in March 1912.[21] However, Conservatives
would not accept an inheritance tax to cover the army expenses. Bethmann
spent more than a year trying to help the Conservatives remove the
'hatred' and 'demagogy' that had been directed against them during the

Reichstag election campaign because of their fiscal policies.[22] In the end a tax on the increase of property values was legislated in June 1913 as a one-time levy, described as a 'national sacrifice'. Such attractive packaging did nothing to bring Conservatives into the final sale. After having accepted his soldiers from a right-wing majority the year before, Bethmann was forced to pass the tax bill with a majority that excluded the Conservatives. For the first time in its history, the Reichstag had passed a major fiscal bill against the determined opposition of the DKP.

The opening of an unbridgeable chasm between Heydebrand and Bethmann did not simultaneously close all remaining differences between the DKP and the Pan-Germans. Thus the fourth and final prerequisite for a new direction to Conservative politics was the determination of Roesicke and Wangenheim to lead the BdL and DKP together into a new constellation on the Right. Once the divisive tax issue was removed, common patriotic fervour could more easily bring the BdL and ADV together on a platform of anti-Semitism, anti-Socialism and opposition to the government. After mid-1913 the Pan-German League agreed to serve 'more or less as specialist' to the Farmers' League in questions of foreign policy and other national issues. The BdL, conversely, was to 'advise' the ADV on the domestic political situation and on purely economic matters. The BdL also secured the ADV's promise that it would cease its criticism of large estates in the east and would support higher grain tariffs.

None of these plans was realized immediately. It required a series of meetings during the summer of 1913 to give them practical form. In June 1913 Claß met with Wangenheim for the first time; he made a 'very good impression'.[23] Claß was simultaneously establishing contact with a Franconian estate owner and member of the Conservative *Verein* in Munich, Konstantin von Gebsattel. When Gebsattel wrote to Claß in June 1913 he reported that he knew little of the Pan-Germans' activities because the *Kreuzzeitung* rarely published reports on them.[24] Gebsattel subsequently put his efforts behind overcoming the Conservative leadership's fears of independent Pan-German action. Since others were working towards the same end, Claß could report in July 1913 that success seemed imminent.[25]

The final block which apparently cemented the new pre-war constellation on the Right was put in place in August 1913 with the public founding of a so-called Kartell of Productive Estates.[26] The BdL, the CvdI and the Union of Christian Peasants' Associations joined the third annual congress of the Imperial German *Mittelstand* Association in Leipzig on 24 August 1913. There they proclaimed the solidarity of agriculture, industry and the old *Mittelstand* in the face of the Social Democratic threat. Even before the congress, the NLP leader, Ernst Bassermann, accurately described the essential ingredients of the Kartell's programme: 'high protection, watertight tariffs, anti-Socialist laws, no franchise reform in Prussia, at first an unobtrusive struggle against the Reichstag franchise, struggle against everything liberal, struggle against Bethmann-Delbrück, the hope for the strong man'.[27] These demands coincided almost exactly with Pan-German plans at this time. Both Wangenheim and Claß appear to have believed that the Pan-German League would soon be incorporated formally into the Kartell. On the face of it, then, this was an impressive gathering. It seemed to mark an entirely new start on the Right.

In fact there is good reason to be cautious about proclaiming any practical breakthroughs in right-wing politics in August 1913. This is especially true when discussing the position of the Conservative Party itself, as distinct from its traditional or would-be allies. First, as Bassermann's appraisal would suggest, the Kartell of Productive Estates did nothing to re-establish good relations between Conservatives and either the National Liberals or the government. Second, the Kartell did not include the most prominent nationalist *Verbände*. Thus, neither the older political élites nor the newer mass cadres of radical nationalists were involved in this 'rallying' of the Right. Third, Conservative (as opposed to BdL) involvement in the Leipzig congress was minimal. As Gebsattel wrote to Claß in February 1914, 'A new party now is probably still impossible', because Heydebrand and Westarp (and in fact 'the Conservative Party as a whole') had yet to be won.[28] Fourth, there was a good possibility that the agrarians and the Conservatives might soon play the role of the sorcerer's apprentice. The leader of the CvdI, for one, believed in October 1913 that industry could exploit the Kartell and assume leadership of it.[29] In short, although some Conservatives were certainly thinking more seriously about how to win popular support, Heydebrand and his officers had not really found their troops.[30] The prospects for Conservative leadership of the Wilhelmine Right on the eve of the war resembled less those of Henry V before Agincourt, and more those of Captain Bligh before the launching of HMS Bounty.

The outbreak of war in August 1914 and the proclamation of the *Burgfriede* fundamentally changed the way Conservatives influenced political decision-making in the Reich. Suddenly the political struggle had to be fought with new rules and, for the most part, on a different plane. No general elections were held, few debates about grain tariffs occupied parliamentary deputies, the press was strictly censored, and the struggle against Social Democracy had to be muted in order to ensure the co-operation of workers in war industries. Later in the war the Kaiser's heavy hand on policy was replaced by those of Generals Paul von Hindenburg and Erich Ludendorff.

Yet it has already been noted that certain features of the dynamic of 1911–14 persisted after the outbreak of war.[31] The broad developments that most centrally determined the fate of the Conservative Party were:

(1) The continuing drift towards a radical nationalist and Pan-German consensus embracing all right-wing groups, centring on the determination to conclude a victorious peace with annexations in both the east and west.

(2) The rejection of any plans to democratize the Reich, involving resistance to reform of the Prussian three-class franchise, preservation of monarchical institutions and the continued exclusion of Social Democracy from the political establishment.

(3) The effort to establish a truly mass party of the Right. This included plans to recruit workers and salaried employees, attempts to discover a more popular name for such a party, concentration on anti-Semitic and other *völkisch* appeals to popularize it and strategies to translate wartime unity into more transcendent political strength.

(4) Finally, other attempts to counter the increasing strength of the Left, especially in parliament. By 1916 these efforts had led to virtual unanimity on the need to topple Bethmann – or any other German leader who could not effectively resist these forces.

The roles of the Farmers' League and the Conservative Party also remained essentially those of the pre-war years. On the one hand, the leaders of the BdL frequently criticized the tempo or radicalism with which these aspirations were pursued, but in general they fully endorsed the anti-parliamentary, anti-governmental, anti-Socialist and anti-Semitic features of the right-wing programme being worked out in these years. Roesicke and Wangenheim contributed significantly to each of these crusades, and this assisted them in their effort to place the Farmers' League at the centre of any right-wing *Sammlung*. On the other hand, the Conservative leadership around Heydebrand displayed a consistent tendency to prevaricate as each new strategy was taken up. As one bastion of Conservative strength after another fell, this required constant political compromise on the part of the DKP leaders, which came no more easily than before. Heydebrand and colleagues, however, were far less successful than even the BdL leaders in preventing the new nationalist agenda from supplanting traditional Conservative concerns with 'revolutionary' ones. This contributed to a marked increase in criticism of Heydebrand's leadership within the party, something that seemed hardly imaginable in 1911.

In September 1914 the Pan-Germans and other radical nationalists were already calling for extensive annexations.[32] At first out of touch on his Silesian estate, Heydebrand did not endorse these demands. After the disappointment of the Battle of the Marne, the Conservative leadership was even more determined to limit annexationist agitation and to deflect it into purely economic demands.[33] In November 1914 the Pan-Germans and Hugenberg drew up more detailed plans, for instance over the fate of

Poland, and by July 1916 the Independent Committee for a German Peace had illustrated the breadth of the war-aims movement. But even now Heydebrand held back. Westarp was the only high-ranking DKP signatory to the Independent Committee's manifesto. Heydebrand would not commit his party publicly to the anti-Bethmann Fronde, fearing in wartime circumstances that this could further undermine the authority of the German state. This gave the impression of further prevarication and 'pig-headedness', which was denounced by the Pan-Germans, the BdL leaders and rank-and-file Conservatives far more emphatically than it was welcomed by Bethmann. By August 1916 the same Pan-German Conservatives who were using the Independent Committee to consolidate their conspiracy against Bethmann were conducting a secret war against Heydebrand. According to one such Conservative who wrote to Westarp, Heydebrand was 'now leader in name only'.[34] Although this pronouncement was premature, these developments and the shock of the Reichstag's peace resolution of July 1917 finally pressed Heydebrand to the wall on war aims. Thereafter he allowed DKP speakers to express greater Conservative enthusiasm (if not precision) on the war-aims issue. Until the end of the war, the Conservatives maintained this position. By then, however, war aims were not the leading concern of Pan-Germans. Hardship and unrest on the home front had turned attention to other more pressing campaigns against the leftist threat.

What was the significance of this Conservative reluctance to join in the extreme war-aims movement? First, Heydebrand remained aloof for both substantive and tactical reasons. On 31 December 1914 he wrote to Westarp that the plans of Claß and Hugenberg 'go much too far and for the most part are in practice neither realizable nor useful'.[35] Heydebrand maintained this posture for many more months. Yet he and Westarp also resisted the entreaties of subordinates like Grumme-Douglas and Gebsattel with a classic defence of the party's parliamentary independence. 'If it came to peace negotiations', Westarp wrote later, it would be 'much less satisfactory for the party and the caucus, which had to debate responsibly in parliament, to be bound to previous demands than for the representatives of public opinion outside parliament'. This helps explain why Heydebrand and Westarp continued to enjoy the confidence of certain sectors of a Conservative Party which was, by 1917, deeply divided. When the Committee of Fifty met on 18 February 1917, the Conservatives with Pan-German sympathies took a predictable line in attacking Heydebrand's hesitant attitude. But most Conservatives in the Herrenhaus were solidly behind the DKP chairman. One of them declared that the party leaders had acted correctly in not participating 'in the cheap fireworks of a Fronde' against Bethmann.[36]

Second, Conservatives were much more interested in directing national antagonism against Britain than against Russia. This brought them into conflict with the Pan-Germans and others who envisioned large annexations in the east.[37] Third, Heydebrand's attitude was a major reason for BdL–DKP tension during the war. In April 1915 Roesicke wrote to Wangenheim concerning war aims: 'I had the impression that Heydebrand is very determined not to let us get too big because we are the determining ones in this area. I am therefore concerned that we in the League agree on a plan.' A few months later Wangenheim reported that Heydebrand was becoming less recalcitrant; but in October, Roesicke felt that he was being excluded from Conservative debates in the Reichstag and that Heydebrand was not eager for contact with him. Even after the founding of the Independent Committee for a German Peace, Roesicke remained pessimistic about Heydebrand: 'He will give advice, but not act.'[38]

Fourth and finally, Conservatives were always motivated by the desire to harness Pan-German expansionist sentiment to enhance their own economic and political position at home. In his retrospective account of Conservative politics after 1914, Westarp devoted chapter after chapter to the wartime economy.[39] The titles to these chapters illustrated how important the traditional economic concerns of the Conservative Party remained during the war: 'The Grain Economy', 'Implementation and Expansion of the Controlled Economy', 'Our Criticism and Co-operation', 'Failure of the Food Production Economy' and 'Finances and Natural Resources'. These chapters, moreover, were sandwiched between others on the *Burgfriede*, Social Democracy, the peace resolution of 1917, Prussian franchise reform, and revolution. They thereby indicated how central the issues of economic mobilization and social control were to larger questions about the course of political reform.[40]

Certainly all groups on the Right criticized the government for its willingness to allow Social Democratic politicians and trade-union leaders to participate in directing the wartime economy. Conservatives and Pan-Germans alike refused to recognize political emancipation as the corollary to economic mobilization. However, Bethmann recognized the DKP's cynical motives when he wrote in 1915 that the Conservatives 'portray the need for the old, unchanged position of conflict against the Social Democrats as a requirement of national conviction'.[41] As Bethmann indicated, it was more a matter of Conservatives deflecting movements on the Right they could not control than initiating such developments themselves. In fact, the Conservative resistance to challenges from both the Left and the Right defined their essentially defensive posture as a whole. Therefore, although the Conservatives undertook a determined but vain defence of the Prussian three-class franchise after April 1917,[42] one can speak of Conservative attempts at mass *mobilization* during the war only in a limited sense. It might be better to ask: How did Conservatives react to plans formulated by groups *outside* the party to recruit a mass following?[43]

The German Fatherland Party has been described as pre-fascist, proto-fascist and the first truly mass movement of the German Right.[44] Some doubt remains whether this party actually mobilized the masses, merely manipulated them, or sought to shut them out of the political nation entirely. There are, moreover, major quantitative and qualitative differences, which are too often overlooked, between these 'pre-fascist' movements and truly fascist ones. Nevertheless, the prehistory, founding and development of the Fatherland Party illustrated that the whole concept of party politics was being radically redefined in ways which consigned DKP leaders to the role of impotent observers.

The first decisive step towards a reconstitution of the Right was taken when Wolfgang Kapp drew up his so-called May Promemorium in 1916, entitled 'The Nationalist Circles and the Reich Chancellor'.[45] Only three hundred copies of this document were produced; they were distributed among leading nationalists, including high government officials and military officers. Without citing the Pan-German programme, Kapp suggested that only a victorious peace would facilitate the 'concentration and reformation of the political parties' and restore 'our fractured party life' to health. Kapp also attacked the government of Bethmann Hollweg on both its domestic and foreign policy, and demanded that the chancellor be replaced. Such a sensational document by a member of the Prussian administration could not remain secret, and Bethmann soon responded. In the Reichstag he condemned the 'secret writings and brochures' of the nationalist opposition and labelled their authors the 'pirates of public opinion'.[46] Bethmann also ensured that Kapp was not reappointed as East Prussian *Generallandschaft* Director at the end of June.

Convinced by August 1916 that Heydebrand was impossible to move, Wangenheim wrote to Kapp that the rallying of the nationalist opposition had to bypass the DKP and constitute itself as a 'movement' which would stand above the party struggle. Pan-Germans and radical Conservatives offered their own prescriptions, ranging from a 'New Conservative Party' (Schiele) to a 'Conservative *Mittelstand* Party' or 'Conservative Burgher Party' (Gebsattel).[47] Despite the rising democratic tide after the Easter Message of 1917, Heydebrand had rejected Free Conservative overtures to participate in a 'closer alliance of the right-wing parties in the Reichstag' which would be labelled the 'Allied Right' or *Bundespartei*. He also remained aloof from efforts to mobilize public opinion outside parliament. Thus the Pan-German wing within the DKP finally concluded that another 'clean break' had to be made with the vestiges of governmentalism and 'false' monarchism that lived on within the Conservative Party. As Ernst von Hertzberg-Lottin wrote to Westarp in July 1917: 'The Conservative Party has missed its opportunity to become a *Volkspartei*, on the one hand for tactical reasons, but in the main due to a false royalism, which cannot distinguish between the person of the monarch and the monarchical idea of the state.'[48] This conviction was strengthened by the Reichstag's peace resolution of 19 July 1917 and the refusal of Bethmann's successor, Georg Michaelis, to crush the Left. These developments compelled radical nationalist Conservatives to participate in the founding of the Fatherland Party.

Early proposals for the name of the new party reflected the degree to which domestic political considerations were central to the whole conception of the DVP. Many of the names proposed and rejected bore a remarkable similarity to those entertained when the National Party was conceived in 1892–3; all of them reflected the wish to overcome the narrowness reflected in the word 'Conservative'. These names included: 'Hindenburg Party', 'Bismarck Party', 'Bismarck League against Party Strife in Wartime' and 'German Unity Party'. Controversy also arose over whether the new organization should be designated a 'party' or a 'league'. The initial DVP manifesto of 2 September 1917 declared: 'Partisan action to obtain power for the political parties cannot be allowed to tear the Empire asunder.' In particular it condemned 'the pernicious party spirit of which Otto von Bismarck complained'. In the end, however, designation as a 'league' was considered too tentative and passive.[49] Instead the DVP stressed the *Volkspartei* theme. Its *Katechismus* stated that 'The German Fatherland Party is a people's league (*Volksbund*) of men and women from all classes and callings, from all party tendencies and religious creeds.'

The rapid expansion of the Fatherland Party's regional organization and propaganda was impressive by any standards. By the summer of 1918 it had more than 800,000 members, supplemented by corporate memberships that brought the total to over 1,250,000.[50] Heydebrand, Westarp and their inner circle could only attempt once again to put a good face on a bad business.[51] Westarp greeted the Fatherland Party in the *Kreuzzeitung*, but without much enthusiasm, and the party press in the provinces remained reserved. Only in November did the *Kreuzzeitung* express more hope for this 'popular movement', thereby falling into line with the more positive reviews of the *Konservative Monatsschrift*, the *Deutsches Adelsblatt* and the *Deutsche Tageszeitung*. The Committee of Fifty endorsed the DVP on 19 October 1917, and soon Protestant pastors, *Landräte*, local police officials and town mayors began to work for the Fatherland Party's *Vereine* with more dedication than they had ever supported formal Conservative organizations. Even more noteworthy was the number of Conservatives in the Herrenhaus who now supported the new enterprise. On every front, it seemed, Heydebrand and Westarp were in retreat.

In the final months and weeks of the war Heydebrand and Westarp fought as much for the Conservatives' independence on the political Right as for their power in the state. These leaders even launched a counter-offensive of their own. They attempted to mobilize such extra-parliamentary movements as the Prussian League, which they revived in 1917, and the League of Imperial Loyalists (Bund der Kaisertreuen).[52] They supplemented these plans with new appeals to industrial and banking circles to stand together against the 'state-socialist' tendencies of the planned economy. They even managed to wring sufficient financial assistance from these sources to revive the long-dormant party news-sheet, *Unsere Partei*, in April 1918.

Heydebrand was unable to conceal his disillusionment. At a provincial party rally in June 1918 he spoke of the transformation of the authoritarian state into a *Volksstaat*. Westarp and other Conservatives were particularly fearful of the political consequences of demobilization.[53] Yet the total demise of the Conservative Party, even at this point, was not pre-ordained. Reflecting the volatile political situation, and in part because hostility had arisen between the Pan-Germans and the Fatherland Party, plans for a new political party continued to evolve. In August 1918 a Pomeranian estate owner suggested to Claß that the Conservatives had to give up their name and become a 'great national party' which could rally all 'levels of the population who stand on a national-*völkisch* basis, including workers and low-level bureaucrats'.[54] Claß, however, believed the Conservatives still had 'much to learn' before this would be possible. Subsequent proposals from these circles included a '*Sammlungspartei* of the Right' (Schiele in mid-October 1918), a *Bürger- und Bauernbund* (Schiele in November) and a new, 'resolute national party' which would pursue the 'ruthless struggle against Jewry' (Claß, in early October).[55] Around the same time, the Pan-German sympathizers were circulating a memorandum within the DKP which asked the question: 'How can we build a more purposeful and fruitful organization in the German Conservative Party?' These men answered their own question: 'through the organization of a General Staff; for we have two Generals but no General Staff'.[56] Finally, the situation regarding franchise reform in Prussia remained extremely fluid. Although they defied reform as long as they could, by October 1918 the two Conservative caucuses in the Prussian Landtag had had to recognize the impossibility of further resistance. Members of the majority (left-wing) parties in the Reichstag had been invited to join the cabinet of Prince Max of Baden. Catastrophe at the front added to the crisis atmosphere.

The 'revolutionary' franchise reform which was implemented against the Conservatives' helpless protests in the last month of the empire found its analogue in eleventh-hour proposals to change the Conservative Party's name and programme. Apparently inspired by a letter of 6 October from Otto Hoetzsch, foreign editor of the *Kreuzzeitung*, Westarp attempted to meet these challenges in a number of ways. (Heydebrand was again isolated on his Silesian estate.) First, he convened a programme committee to consider revisions to the Tivoli programme; its five members, however, produced no workable proposal before 6 November. Second, negotiations were undertaken with the anti-Semitic parties in the Reichstag. Third, the Conservatives made the cynical and transparent promise to double the salary of troops returning from the front; they also tried to display their new egalitarian convictions by arguing that all ranks should receive equal room and board. Finally, Westarp reviewed three crucial memoranda which proposed the final dismantling of the Conservative Party.

The first of these was from a Dr Richard Fuß, about whom little is known.[57] Fuß's main points were that the DKP had to retain what it could from the political collapse; that the fight against the SPD had to be abandoned; that the Conservatives must support a 'people's monarchy'; and that the party could no longer successfully oppose a tax on property. The second memorandum came from an equally obscure Baron von Hammerstein, who also feared the consequences of demobilization. The third and most comprehensive memo was by Hoetzsch, dated 5 November 1918.[58] Hoetzsch reviewed the full range of dilemmas facing the DKP: its confrontation with democracy; its relationship with the other parties of the Right; its role as a party of opposition; the social make-up of the party, particularly its aristocratic core; its agrarian basis; its failure to win urban recruits; its *Mittelstand* policies; its foreign policy; its organization; and finally its entire *Weltanschauung*. What is perhaps most remarkable about Hoetzsch's appeal is that his formulas for popularizing and enlightening Conservatism had not appeared earlier. Other Conservatives, it is true, had offered equally profound reappraisals of Conservative policy during the war years.[59] However, it was consistent with earlier Conservative history that these counsels of reason were not heard until the collapse was unavoidable.

It is not known whether Westarp failed to answer Hoetzsch's memorandum because he disapproved of its proposals or because he was overwhelmed by the pace of revolutionary events of 8–9 November.[60] We do know that Westarp's prodding was very likely instrumental in leading the DKP's programme committee to issue a statement on 8 November that it would participate in negotiations leading to the union of all right-wing parties in Germany. The hope was to 'secure a place for the [Conservative] Party in the future of Germany'. However, on the day of the Allied–German armistice, 11 November 1918, Westarp recognized that the Conservative Party's future was of no immediate concern to the German masses. It seemed that Westarp's presence in Berlin was not needed. He wrote to Heydebrand that 'as a result of the news I have received, I am going on vacation for a while. There is nothing that the Conservative Party can do.'[61]

After 1918 Heydebrand refused to disband the Conservative *Hauptverein* and secretly hoped for a renaissance of the old DKP. This indicated how truly 'reactionary' the Conservative leadership had become.[62] Not even

222

inclusion in a new 'national *Volkspartei*' provided Conservatives with the means to prevent more dynamic movements from overwhelming their traditional conception of party politics. As radical parties on both the Left and the Right grew during the Weimar Republic, Conservatives found themselves either condemning the demagogy they had helped to introduce or retreating into a world of political obscurity. Yet their failure to reconcile popular and élitist brands of conservatism contributed to the political whirlwind reaped by all Germans. In 1932 Franz von Papen's 'cabinet of barons' confronted the same dilemmas Conservatives had faced decades before. As Edgar Jung wrote from the perspective of 1933: 'Von Papen had the last opportunity to eliminate, from above, the pluralistic forces (the parties and the economic interests) and restore the purity of the state without mobilizing the masses.'[63] The moral and political bankruptcy of Papen's political strategy represented only the culmination of a long process whereby Conservatives had lost objectivity and influence both 'above' and 'below'. No longer assured of their traditional place in political society, Conservatives had become willing to express their disillusionment with the direction of German politics in radical terms. In the 1930s and 1940s disillusionment was not sufficient to prevent the final demise of either *Honoratioren* politics or the Junker class itself.

Looking ahead too earnestly can make us lose sight of the more immediate implications of Conservatism's political misadaptation after 1871. Even in the Second Empire ambivalence and factionalism helped prevent the emergence of a clear division between progressive and reactionary forces within the Conservative Party and within the political nation as a whole. Although many tensions arose between Berlin leaders and provincial spokesmen, between the Conservatives and the government, even between the DKP and BdL, all too few 'clean breaks' occurred. Tension within the DKP, generated by the challenges of political adaptation, had its analogue in the conflicting pressures for modernization and stabilization in the *Kaiserreich*. The fact that so many reformist Conservatives remained loyal to an anti-*Volkspartei* in the 1890s had its parallel in the belief among government figures that conservatism was the only option for Germany's rulers. As Hohenlohe asked in 1899: 'How would His Majesty be expected to work with a liberal ministry?'

The dilemmas of Conservatism, in short, were many and profound. They did not always appear so. After his dismissal from office Bismarck remarked that Conservatives regarded politics and parliament as 'mere sport':[64] 'One enjoys living a few months in Berlin, going to breakfast in the House, and, when the bell for a division rings, quickly wiping one's mouth, rushing into the chamber, and asking, "How do we vote?"' This was wishful thinking. A more candid appraisal was provided a few years later by Mirbach:[65]

Eminent statesmen . . . have often expressed to me the wish to resurrect a Conservative Party as it once existed. Indeed, gentlemen, we would be exceedingly happy to allow ourselves this retired life (*Stilleben*), if this universal, equal and secret franchise had not grown so hot under our feet. Now every party is more or less dependent on the large masses and must reckon with them, whether or not it wants to, whether or not it finds it comfortable to do so.

For Conservatives in the twentieth century, caught between the demands of political exclusivity and mass mobilization, politics was anything but 'mere sport'. Rather it was a hard-headed enterprise designed to preserve cherished ideals, privileges and interests. It was debilitated by a deep ambivalence towards the means for generating popular support; but it was deadly serious business. Arguably it had never been anything else.

NOTES

1 Specialists will recognize the degree to which nuance and detail have been squeezed out of this chapter due to limits of space. For rehydration see works listed in the notes below. A separate study of this period is planned by the author.
2 See Westarp, *Konservative Politik*, Vol. 1, *passim*; Barth, 'Innenpolitik', chs. I.3, I.5.
3 See *inter alia* Bueck, *Weshalb*; Kaelble, *Interessenpolitik*; Stegmann, *Erben*.
4 *Rkz.* 1391/5, f. 192 ff., Bethmann to Loebell, 16.8.11; cf. Mehnert to Loebell, 11.8.11; Loebell to Bethmann, 14.8.11.
5 *SBR*, Vol. 268, pp. 7721 ff., 7756 ff., 9/10.11.11; cf. the reactions to this speakers' duel in my 'Road to Philippi'.
6 See Bertram, *Wahlen*.
7 *Mitteilungen*, 1913, p. 803, presumably including the Free Conservatives.
8 In 1891 the ADV was still named the General German League; ADV *Aufruf* in *KZ*, 3.5.91.
9 BAK, NL Hugenberg, 10, f. 252 ff.
10 See Eley, *Reshaping*, pp. 190, 201; also Chickering, *We Men*, pp. 303 f.
11 Including the *Beiträge zur konservativen Politik und Weltanschauung*; *Schriften zur Tagespolitik*; and *Konservative Flugschriften*.
12 A partial list includes: Eduard von Liebert (RvgSD, DKP speaker), August Keim, (ADV, Navy League, Conservative Union speaker), Wolfgang Eisenhart (Pb, *KZ*, *Mitteilungen*, DKP speaker and pamphleteer), Ulrich von Hassell (DVP, *KM* editor), Max Wildgrube (ADV, *Mitteilungen*, DKP pamphleteer and speaker), Count Ernst zu Reventlow (ADV, *DTZ* foreign editor), Max Lorenz (RvgSD, DKP speaker), Otto von Pfister (German Union, *KZ*, *SddZ*, DKP pamphleteer), Franz Sontag (ADV, *KZ*, *Post*), and Georg von Below (*NeueDtland, Deutschlands Erneuerung, KZ, KM*, DVP).
13 *CC*, 16.12.07; *CC*. 18.12.07, 'Nationaler Terrorismus'.
14 *CC*, 5/12.1.05, 22.4.07, 6/27.5.07.
15 *KZ*, 22.12.11, cited in Eley, *Reshaping*, p. 330.
16 See the *Stenographischer Bericht* for the first *Preußen-Tag* (1914), p. 5; ZStA I, RLB/BdL press archive, 8173; cf. *Preußen-Bund*, 'Bismarck-Nummer', 7, March 1915, pp. 51–62.
17 *Rb*, 15.8.09.
18 For this and the following, ZStA I, 60 Ve 1, Alldeutscher Verband (hereafter ADV), 193, f. 306–10, Max von Klitzing to Normann, 27.7.09; 194, f. 66 ff., Klitzing to Heinrich Claß, 28.1.10 to 15.2.10, *passim*; reply, 29.1.10; Claß to *KZ Schriftleitung*, 4.2.10; 195, f. 42, Stössel to Claß, 4.2.11; BAK, NL Hugenberg, 10, f. 290, Claß to Alfred

Hugenberg, 18.3.11; for Claß's revealing assessment of Heydebrand, see 'Frymann', *Wenn ich der Kaiser wär'* (1912), pp. 207–16; cf. Chickering, *We Men*, pp. 185–207, 279–91; Stegmann, *Erben*, pp. 317 ff.

19 ZStA I, ADV 195, f. 400, Stössel to Claß, 12.11.11.

20 *KM*, 70, December 1912, pp. 197–204; Albers, *Besiegten*, p. 17; Stegmann, *Erben*, pp. 325 f.; *KZ*, 29.1.12; ZStA I, RLB/BdL press archive, 9024; BAK, NL Bülow, 108, f. 59, A. von Huhn to Bülow, 27.1.12.

21 See Westarp, *Wehr- und Deckungsvorlagen*.

22 St. Min., Vol. 161, f. 25, 4.3.12; Vol. 162, f. 36, 24.2.13; cf. the SPD's *Worte and Taten der Konservativen*, pp. 21, 38 f.

23 Wangenheim to Roesicke, 27.6.13, cited in Chickering, *We Men*, p. 281.

24 ZStA I, NL Gebsattel, 1, f. 15 ff., Gebsattel to Claß, 10.6.13; cf. letter of 20.8.13, and replies of 16.6.13, 22.8.13; on the Kartell of Productive Estates and further contacts before the war see ibid., f. 37 ff., Claß to Gebsattel, 28.8.13, 23.9.13; and f. 115 f., 140, Gebsattel to Claß, 12.2.14, 5.5.14; Gebsattel to Liebert, 26.6.14; and Gebsattel to Claß, 23.7.14, 30.8.14; General [Georg] von Kleist to Gebsattel, 21.7.14; ZStA I, ADV 197 (1913), *passim*; ADV 198, f. 54, 83, Grumme-Douglas to Claß, 20.4.14, Gebsattel to Baron Friedrich Kress von Kressentin, 18.1.14; ADV, 246, f. 132 ff., Sontag to Claß, 10/14.7.13; and ADV 90, f. 6, 'Sitzung des Geschäftsführenden Ausschusses', 5.9.13.

25 ZStA I, ADV 246, f. 139, Claß to Klitzing, 29.7.13; cf. Chickering, *We Men*, p. 282, n. 174.

26 *Kartell der schaffenden Stände*, which the Left defamed immediately as the Kartell of Grasping Hands (*Kartell der raffenden Hände*); congress report reprinted in Steitz (ed.), *Quellen*, pp. 454 ff.

27 Cited in Stegmann, *Erben*, p. 365.

28 Gebsattel to Claß, 12.2.14, cited above.

29 BAK, NL Hugenberg, 31, f. 79, Henry Axel Bueck to Hugenberg, 15.10.13.

30 Cf. Eley, *Reshaping*, p. 319.

31 On the breakdown of the *Burgfriede* cf. reports on DKP meetings and congresses (1914–19) in ZStA I, RLB/BdL press archive, 4328, f. 39 ff.

32 See ZStA I, NL Westarp, 3, f. 10 ff., Gebsattel to Westarp, 4.9.14.

33 Cf. Kaufhold's comprehensive documentary account: *Konservative Partei und der Weltkrieg*; also Kube, *Kriegsziele*; Westarp, *Konservative Politik*, Vol. 2, *passim*; Westarp, *Deutschlands Zukunft*; Westarp, *Zwei Gedenktage*; Westarp, *Regierung des Prinzen Max von Baden*.

34 See Peck, *Radicals*, p. 190 and ch. 8.

35 For this and the following, Westarp, *Konservative Politik*, Vol. 2, pp. 43 ff., 309 ff. and *passim*.

36 Cited in Peck, *Radicals*, p. 203.

37 Committee of Twelve declaration (20.9.15) in Kaufhold, *Konservative Partei*, pp. 33 f.

38 NL Wangenheim, 10, f. 98, 181, 264, letters of 17.4.15, 23.6.15, 25.10.15; 11, f. 116, 155, Roesicke to Wangenheim, 9.8.16, 29.9.16; cf. Wangenheim to Kapp, 4.8.16, cited in Stegmann, *Erben*, p. 467.

39 Westarp, *Konservative Politik*, Vol. 2, pp. 365–463.

40 Cf. Kocka, *Facing Total War*, especially pp. 126 ff.

41 ZStA II, NL Valentini, f. 15 ff., Bethmann to Valentini, 9.12.15.

42 For this campaign see Westarp, *Konservative Politik*, Vol. 2, pp. 505–25; Dewitz, *Demokratisierung*; Schiele, *Erneuerung*; Patemann, *Kampf*.

43 On attempts to establish a Conservative Workers' Party during the war, see ZStA I, NL Westarp, 12, f. 131, Oskar Kresse to Westarp, 22.7.16; 19, f. 118 ff., Gustav von Halem to Westarp, 13.4.17, 15.5.17; reply, 18.5.17; 20, f. 50 ff., Kresse to Westarp, 28.4.17, 12/19.5.17; replies, 30.4.17, 24.5.17; 21, f. 53 ff., Baurat Linde to Westarp, 13.11.17; reply, 19.11.17; cf. 99, memorandum from Richard Fuß (discussed below); Stegmann, 'Zwischen Repression' and 'Neokonservatismus'.

44 Cf. *inter alia* Puhle, *Agrarkrise*; Wehler, *German Empire*, p. 216; Peck, *Radicals*, p. 210; Stegmann, 'Neokonservatismus', pp. 199 f., 229 f.

45 'Die nationalen Kreise und der Reichskanzler', 20.5.16, especially pp. 44–6; copy (and press reactions) in BAK, NL Traub, 51.

46 *SBR* Vol. 307, pp. 1509–12, 5.6.16; other materials in ZStA, II, NL Valentini, 25.
47 Wangenheim to Kapp, 4.8.17, cited in Stegmann, 'Neokonservatismus', p. 215; ZStA I, NL Wangenheim, 11, Wangenheim to Roesicke, 29.9.16; cf. Stegmann, *Erben*, pp. 494 f.
48 ZStA I, NL Westarp, 19, f. 152, 3.7.17.
49 Etue, 'Fatherland Party', p. 67; Wortmann, 'Vaterlands-Partei', p. 28; Peck, *Radicals*, p. 212; cf. materials in ZStA II, NL Kapp; BAK, NL Traub; and BAK, ZSg1, 252, including *Mitteilungen der Deutschen Vaterlands-Partei*; *Deutsche Ziele, passim*.
50 *MdDVP*, 21.9.18; Etue, 'Fatherland Party', pp. 85 ff.; cf. Below, *Gute Recht*, and materials in GStA Berlin (Dahlem), NL Meinecke, 69 and 84, and BAK, NL Delbrück, 44.
51 For the following, Stegmann, 'Neokonservatismus', pp. 220 f.
52 On the Pb and the *Bund der Kaisertreuen*, ZStA I NL Westarp, 20, f. 184 ff.
53 Limburg to Westarp, 3.6.18, in Peck, *Radicals*, pp. 224 f.
54 ZStA I, ADV 204 (formerly 245/1), f. 268, R. Pretzell-Dübzow to Claß, 6.7.18.
55 Cited in Stegmann, 'Neokonservatismus', pp. 223 f.; ZStA I, ADV 204, f. 689, Claß to Rösch, 3.10.18.
56 Cited in Peck, *Radicals*, p. 226.
57 ZStA I, NL Westarp, 99, 'Die Konservativen und die politische Lage nach dem Kriege. Wirkungen des Krieges auf die Politik' (15 pp.); Peck cites a letter of 5.11.18 in NL Westarp, 26; see *Radicals*, pp. 229 f. for this and the following.
58 Full text in Witt, 'Denkschrift'; cf. Voigt, *Hoetzsch*, p. 122.
59 Oertzen, 'Konservative Partei und der soziale Staat' (1916); Friedrich Thimme, 'Drei offene Briefe an Herrn von Heydebrand' (1917) and other materials in *Rkz.* 1392; Röder, *Zukunftspolitik* (September 1918).
60 Cf. Westarp, *Ende der Monarchie*.
61 Gärtringen, Heydebrand–Westarp *Korrespondenz*, Westarp to Heydebrand, 11.11.18.
62 Cf. Flemming, 'Konservatismus'; Flemming, 'Bewaffnung'; Muth, 'Entstehung'; Weißbecker, 'Monarchistische Organisationen'; and works on the DNVP by Thimme, Hertzman and Liebe.
63 Cited in Struve, 'Elites', p. 209.
64 Comments made at Friedrichsruh in 1891, cited in *FkZ*, 6.4.95.
65 *Stenographische Berichte über die Verhandlungen des Preußischen Herrenhauses* (Berlin, 1896), Vol. 1, p. 132, 26.3.96.

Appendices

APPENDIX 1

Structure and Leadership of the German Conservative Party, 1876–1918

```
┌─────────────────┐
│ Party Chairman  │
└─────────────────┘
         ↑
┌───────────────────────────┐
│ Committee of Three or Five │
└───────────────────────────┘
         ↑
(party chairman + caucus chairmen + party secretary)


┌────────────────────────────┐
│ Committee of Eleven or Twelve │
└────────────────────────────┘
         ↑
(RT reps + PAH reps + PHH reps + Kingdom of Saxony rep)


┌──────────────────────┐
│ Committee of Fifty   │
└──────────────────────┘
         ↑
(RT reps + PAH reps + PHH reps + regional reps + alternates + party
                        secretary)
```

DKP Chairmen

Helldorff, 1876–92
Manteuffel, 1892–1911
Wedel, 1911–13
Heydebrand, 1913–18

DKP Committee of Three or Five (C-3, C-5)

1892: Helldorff, Levetzow, Rauchhaupt (before 27 May)
      Manteuffel, Mirbach, Rauchhaupt (after 27 May)

1895: Manteuffel, Mirbach, Limburg
1902: Manteuffel, Mirbach, Limburg, Heydebrand, Loebell
1910: Heydebrand, Normann, Stackmann (secretary)
1912: Heydebrand, Normann (replaced by Mehnert, November 1912), Stackmann, Wedel, Klasing

DKP Committee of Eleven or Twelve (C-11, C-12)

1892: Manteuffel, Schlieben, Klinkowström (PHH); Rauchhaupt, Erffa, Limburg (PAH); Helldorff, Mirbach, Levetzow, Kleist-Schmenzin (RT); Friesen (Saxony)
1903: Manteuffel, Durant, Klasing, Levetzow, Mirbach, Limburg, Mehnert, Klinkowström, Irmer (replaced Stöcker, February 1896), Schlieben, Kröcher
1912: Wedel, Heydebrand, Beutler, Buch, Erffa (died June 1912), Klasing, Kröcher, Limburg, Mehnert, Mirbach, Normann (died October 1912), Pappenheim, Westarp

Chairmen of the Conservative Parliamentary Caucuses

Prussian Herrenhaus 'Caucus'
Kleist-Retzow, 1876–92
Manteuffel, 1892–7
Kurt Wilmowski (Chief of the Reich Chancellory under Hohenlohe)
Wedel
Leopold von Buch, 1911–18

Prussian House of Deputies Caucus
Rauchhaupt (with interruptions), 1876–93
Limburg, 1893–1905
Heydebrand and Erffa, December 1905–6
Heydebrand, 1906–18

Reichstag Caucus
Helldorff, 1876–81
Minnigerode, 1881–4
Helldorff, 1884–92
Manteuffel, 1892–February 1897
Levetzow, 1897–1902
Normann, 1902–12
Kanitz, 1912–13
Westarp, 1913–18

DKP Party Secretaries

Carl Wilmanns and Martin Anton Niendorf, 1876–7
Hermann von Busse–Neustettin, 1877–81
Baron Leo von Seckendorff, treasurer and secretary, 1881–1902
August Strosser, party secretary, 1902–5
Karl Stackmann, secretarial member C-12 after 1905 and C-3 after 1910
Bruno Schröter, general party secretary, 1 October 1907–18
Karl Rabe von Pappenheim, 'honorary secretary' of the PAH caucus
Josef Kaufhold, informal secretary to the RT caucus, 'on loan' from BdL
Richard Kunze, second party secretary after 1910; former secretary in
   Prussian Saxony

APPENDIX 2

Social Composition of the DKP Reichstag Caucus, 1871–1912

	1871	1874	1877	1878	1881	1884	1887	1890	1893	1898	1903	1907	1912
Total DKP seats (actual)	57	22	40	59	50	78	80	73	72	56	54	60	43
Total DKP seats (Kremer calculation)	54	21	40	59	50	78	80	71	68	56	52	62	45
Large estate owner (*Rittergutsbesitzer*)	30	16	23	38	28	40	42	35	36	29	26	27	24
(Retired *Landräte*) (*RGB-Landrat z.D./a.D.*)	(8)	(4)	(7)	(9)	(3)	(8)	(11)	(7)	(4)	(5)	(3)	(4)	(3)
Estate owner (*Gutsbesitzer*)	1	0	1	0	1	2	3	4	4	5	7	7	5
Farmer (*Landwirte*)	0	0	1	1	1	3	2	1	4	3	3	5	5
Tenant farmer (*Pächter*)	1	1	1	1	1	2	1	1	4	2	2	3	0
Landholders subtotal	32	17	26	40	31	47	48	41	48	39	38	42	34
(% of caucus)	59	81	65	68	62	60	60	58	71	70	73	68	76
Minister (*Minister*)	2	0	1	2	1	1	0	0	0	0	0	0	0
Provincial governor (*Ober-Präsident*)	6	3	6	6	4	4	5	4	3	0	0	1	0
Superior privy councillor (*Wirkl. Geheim-Rat*)	1	1	2	2	2	2	1	2	0	0	1	1	0
Administrative officer (*Regierungsrat*)	2	0	0	0	0	0	2	0	0	1	2	2	0
Landrat	4	0	2	2	3	8	7	4	4	3	1	2	1
Retired officials (*Beamte a.D.*)	1	0	1	1	1	2	1	3	0	0	0	0	0
Administrative officials subtotal	16	4	9	13	10	17	16	13	7	4	4	6	1
(% of caucus)	30	19	23	22	20	22	20	18	10	7	8	10	2

	(German)	1871	1874	1877	1878	1881	1884	1887	1890	1893	1898	1903	1907	1912
Chief justice	(Gerichtspräsident)	2	0	1	0	0	0	1	1	0	0	0	0	0
Judicial councillor	(Gerichtsräte)	1	0	0	1	0	1	2	3	1	1	1	4	3
State prosecutor	(Staatsanwälte)	0	0	2	2	3	2	2	1	0	0	0	0	0
Lawyer	(Rechtsanwälte)	1	0	2	1	1	1	0	2	0	1	1	1	1
Justice officials subtotal		4	0	3	4	4	4	5	7	1	2	2	5	4
(% of caucus)		7	0	8	7	8	5	6	10	1	4	4	8	9
General, officer	(Generale, Offiziere)	1	1	2	3	3	2	2	5	1	0	1	1	0
Landowners' representative	(Landschaftsdirektor)	2	1	0	1	0	0	0	0	1	2	2	2	1
Mayor	(Bürgermeister)	0	0	0	0	0	0	1	0	1	0	0	0	1
Forest master	(Forstmeister)	0	0	0	0	1	1	1	0	0	0	0	0	0
Merchant, businessman	(Kaufmann)	0	1	2	0	1	1	1	1	0	0	1	0	0
Factory owner	(Fabrikbesitzer)	0	0	0	1	1	1	1	1	1	0	1	1	0
Chairman of agricultural credit association	(Vorsitz. d. landwirt-schaftl. Creditvereine)	0	0	0	0	0	0	1	1	0	0	0	0	0
Pres., bd of directors	(Aufsichtsratpräsident)	0	0	0	0	0	0	1	1	0	0	0	0	0
Brewery owner	(Brauereibesitzer)	0	0	0	0	0	0	0	0	2	0	1	1	1
Printing-house owner	(Buchdruckereibesitzer)	0	0	0	0	0	0	0	0	0	1	1	2	1
Associational director	(Verbandsdirektoren)	0	0	0	0	0	0	0	0	0	1	2	1	1
Rentier	(Rentner)	0	0	0	0	0	0	0	0	0	1	1	0	0
University professor	(Uni.-Professoren)	0	0	0	1	0	1	0	0	0	0	0	0	0
High-school teacher	(Studienrat)	0	0	0	0	1	0	1	0	0	0	0	0	0
Preacher	(Prediger)	0	0	0	1	0	1	1	1	0	0	0	0	1
Author	(Schriftsteller)	0	0	0	2	2	1	1	1	3	3	0	0	0
City treasurer	(Kämmerer)	0	0	1	0	0	2	2	1	0	0	0	0	0
Building master	(Baumeister)	0	0	0	0	1	0	0	0	0	0	0	0	0
Artisan, craftsman	(Handwerker)	0	0	0	0	0	0	0	1	3	2	1	1	1

Source: Willy Kremer, 'Der soziale Aufbau der Parteien des Deutschen Reichstages von 1871–1918' (Ph.D. thesis, Cologne, 1934), pp. 4–5.

APPENDIX 3

Social Composition of the DKP Prussian House of Deputies Caucus, 1893–1913

	1893		1898		1903		1908		1913	
	No.	%	No.	%	No.	%	No.	%	No.	%
Active administrative officials (including z.D.)	32	22.5	29	20.0	9	6.3	25	16.5	25	16.9
Active judicial officials	7	4.9	7	4.8	2	1.4	2	1.3	3	2.0
Active officers (including à la suite and z.D.)	0	0	2	1.4	3	2.1	2	1.3	5	3.4
Retired (a.D.) state officials and officers	2	1.4	1	0.7	2	1.4	3	2.0	0	0
Communal and municipal officials	0	0	2	1.4	8	5.6	1	0.7	1	0.7
University professors, teachers	2	1.4	3	2.1	1	0.7	2	1.3	6	4.1
Protestant clergy	2	1.4	1	0.7	3	2.1	3	2.0	2	1.4
Catholic clergy	0	0	0	0	0	0	0	0	0	0
Lawyers	1	0.7	1	0.7	2	1.4	2	1.3	3	2.0
Business men, merchants	1	0.7	0	0	0	0	0	0	0	0
Private officials	0	0	0	0	1	0.7	2	1.3	2	1.4
Farmers (including landowning officials and officers a.D.)	92	64.8	93	64.1	96	67.1	99	65.1	88	59.5
Craftsmen, industrialists	1	0.7	3	2.1	6	4.2	7	4.6	5	3.4
Physicians	0	0	0	0	0	0	0	0	0	0
Authors, journalists (1913, including private scholars)	1	0.7	0	0	2	1.4	0	0	1	0.7
Rentiers	1	0.7	3	2.1	8	5.6	4	2.6	7	4.7
Total	142	100	145	100	143	100	152	100	148	100

Source: Zeitschrift des Königlich Preussischen Statistischen Bureaus (Berlin), 17. Ergänzungsheft, 1895; Jg. 40 (3), 1900; 23. Ergänzungsheft, 1905; 30. Ergänzungsheft, 1909; 43. Ergänzungsheft, 1916.

APPENDIX 4

Provincial and State DKP Vereine, *1876–1918*

The following information has been gathered from sources too numerous to list here; the most important were ZStA I, RLB/BdL press archive, 6147–51, on local Conservative assemblies, and the DKP's *Mitteilungen*, 1908–18. (See also the notes to Chapters 5 and 14.) Only a small selection of provincial Conservative newspapers are listed; circulation figures are approximate, with dates referring to the year reported.

East Prussia

Founded: December 1881
Chairmen:
    Auer (1881–)
    Count zu Dohna-Schlodien (1884–)
    Burggrave and Count Friedrich zu Dohna-Lauck (*c.* 1890–)
        (Deputy chairman: Landrat (ret.) Max von Batocki-Bledau)
        (Treasurer: Kommerzienrat Adolf Siebert)
    Prince Richard zu Dohna-Schlobitten (*c.* 1909–)
Party secretaries:
    Schulze (1883–)
    Captain Reissert (1908–)
    Gottfried Bluhm (1909–)
    P. Hildenhagen (1911–)
    Fischer-Lyck, for the Administrative District of Allenstein (1912–)
Press:
    Mitteilungen des Ostpreußischen Konservativen Vereins an seine Vertrauensmänner

Ostpreußische Zeitung	(1892: 4,000)
Preußischer Volksfreund	(1892: 2,000)
Preußisch-Littauische Zeitung	(1892: 1,250)

West Prussia

Founded: 1903 (FKP–DKP); December 1911 (DKP)
Chairmen:
    Count Georg zu Dohna-Finckenstein (1903–12)
    Count von Keyserlingk-Neustadt (1912–)

Party secretaries:
  Sennecke (1909–)
  Direktor Brunzen (1910–)
Press:
  Danziger Allgemeine Zeitung   (1892: 2,500)
  Elbinger Zeitung (Elbinger Anzeiger)   (1892: 7,400–8,300)
  Thorner Presse   (1892: 1,700–1,800)

Brandenburg

Founded: 1897
Chairmen:
  Dr Hermann Kropatschek (1897–1906)
  Sigismund von Treskow-Friedrichsfelde (1906–December 1910)
    (Vice-chairman: Major (ret.) August Strosser)
  Wolf von Dallwitz-Tornow (December 1910–)
Party secretaries:
  W. Mannes, editor of the Brandenburgers' *Amtliche Mitteilungen*
    (1907–)
  Lieutenant (ret.) Heinrich Meyer (died February 1914)
  Konrad Döring-Berlin, former editor of the *Staatsbürger Zeitung*
Press:
  Amtliche Mitteilungen des Konservativen Vereins für die Provinz
    Brandenburg, founded 1908
  Potsdamer Tageszeitung (Potsdamer Intelligenzblatt)   (1914: 14,500)
  Prenzlauer Zeitung und Kreisblatt   (1892: 3,285)

Berlin

Founded: 1881; refounded 1894
  Conservative General Representation (*Gesamt-Vertretung*), 1881–94
  Wahlverein of German Conservatives in Berlin, January 1894–
Chairmen:
  Blume (1881–94)
  Dr Bernhard Irmer (1894–5)
  Colonel (ret.) von Krause (1895–7)
  Baron von Langen (1897–8)
  Major General (ret.) Arthur von Loebell (1898–)
  Ulrich, lawyer (*c.* 1909–)
Press:
  Mitteilungen des konservativen Bürgervereins zu Charlottenburg
  (See also Berlin DKP press)

Pomerania

Chairman:
  Landrat (ret.) Eugen Heinrich von Brockhausen
Party secretaries:
  Willy Ohm (–1912), editor of the *Pommersche Tagespost*
  Pfotenhauer-Stettin
  Küntzel
  Jordan
  Sachße-Stralsund (Nearer Pomerania)
  Kindervater-Greifswald (Nearer Pomerania)
Press:
  Pommersche Reichspost, founded 1882   (1895: 2,500)
    (replaced in 1911 by . . .)
  Pommersche Tagespost
  Zeitung für Hinterpommern (Stolper Wochenblatt)
                                                     (1895: 5,600)
  Norddeutsche Presse. Zeitung für Pommern und Westpreußen
                                                     (1895: 2,150)
  Fürstentumer Zeitung

Poznan

Founded: *c.* 1908 (DKP–FKP); refounded 1910 (DKP)
Chairmen:
  Ludwig von Staudy (–1909)
  Sigismund von Dziembowski (1909–12)
  von Klitzing (1912–   )
Party secretary:
  Professor Huver
Press:
  Posener Tageblatt (Ostdeutsche Zeitung) (DKP–FKP)   (1883: 3,420)
  Bromberger Tageblatt
  Ostdeutsche Warte (German nationalist)   (1913: 20,000)

Silesia

Founded: October 1880
Chairman:
  Baron Hans von Durant-Baranowitz (1880–   )
  Count Leopold von Harrach (*c.* 1893–   )
  Count Ernst von Seidlitz-Sandreczki (*c.* 1915–   )
Party secretaries
  Dr Nitschke, editor of the *Schlesische Morgenzeitung* (*c.* 1906–   )

Breslau office and second secretariat established 1911
Koop-Liegnitz
Neumann-Breslau
Strack
Press:
Schlesisches Morgenblatt, founded 1880
(continued after 1893 as . . .)
Schlesische Morgenzeitung   (1913: 11,000)
Stadt- und Landbote. Conservative Zeitung für Niederschlesien
Schlesische Zeitung (DKP–FKP)   (1895: 17,550)

Prussian Saxony and the Thuringian States

Vereine:
Conservative *Landesverein* in Anhalt, founded *c.* 1912
Conservative *Verein* for Saxony and Anhalt
Union of Rightist Men in Reuß, founded 1911
Conservative Party in the Principality of Lippe
Conservative *Verein* in the Principality of Schaumburg-Lippe, 1897
Chairman:
Wilhelm von Wedel-Piesdorf, for Prussian Saxony and Anhalt
Party secretaries:
Thiede-Dessau, Anhalt
Richard Kunze, Province of Saxony (–1910)
Kurt Plehwe, Province of Saxony and Anhalt
Secretariat for the Principality of Lippe, December 1912
Press:
Hallesche Zeitung   (1883–4: 6,000; 1895: 8,475)
Neue Erfurter Zeitung (DKP–FKP)
(continued after 1880 as . . .)
Thüringer Post. Conservative Zeitung für Mitteldeutschland
Thüringer Volksfreund. Conservatives Volksblatt für Stadt und Land
Thüringer Landeszeitung   (1912: 4,000–5,000)
Weimarische Zeitung   (1895: 1,700)

Schleswig-Holstein

Founded: March 1911 (DKP–FKP)
Chairman:
Count von Waldersee-Neverstorff
Party Secretaries:
von Kries (Kiel)
Ludwig Schaper (Kiel)

Press:
  Norddeutsche Reichspost, founded *c.* 1878   (1881: 1,200)

Hansa Cities and other North-German Vereine

Hamburg
Founded: March 1912
Chairman: Dr Andreas Koch
Press: *Hamburger Neueste Nachrichten*

Lübeck
Founded: June 1912

Duchy of Brunswick
Founded: 1907; refounded 1912
Chairman: Count Matthias von der Schulenburg-Nordsteimke
Press: *Hannoversche Tages-Nachrichten*

Grand Duchy of Oldenburg
Founded: April 1911

Hanover

Founded: 1884–5; refounded 1892 and December 1898
Chairmen:
  Kammerherr Baron von Bothmar-Bennemühlen (1885–)
  Baron Gebhard von Marenholtz (–1898 and *c.* 1909–)
  von Alten-Goltern (1898–)
  Landeshauptmann von der Wense (May 1917–)
Party secretaries:
  Georg Windewald (1899–)
  F. Hupfer, editor of the *Hannoversche Tages-Nachrichten* (1908–)
  Max Kubel, editor of the *Hannoversche Tages-Nachrichten* (1910–)
Press:
  Hannoversche Post (after 1892, DSP)   (1883–4: 2,800)
  Hannoversche Tages-Nachrichten

Westphalia (Minden-Ravensberg)

Founded:
  Christian Conservative Party of Minden-Ravensberg, *c.* 1854
  Conservative Union for the Province of Westphalia, April 1910
Chairmen:
  Karl Strosser (*c.* 1854–72)

239

Pastor Theodor Schmalenbach (1872–1902)
Pastor Möller-Gütersloh (1902–   )
August Klasing (1910–   )
Party secretaries:
Julius Werner
Wilhelm Albers (1910–   )
Press:
  Conservativer Volksfreund, founded 1862   (1892: 1,000)
  Neue Westfälische Volkszeitung, founded 1877
                                              (1883: 2,600; 1913: 4,500)
  Mindener Post   (1895: 1,000)

The Grand Duchy of Hesse and the Prussian Province of Hesse-Nassau

Chairmen:
  Pastor Hermann Dietz (later editor of the *NWVZ*) (1870s), Hesse
  Count Friedrich zu Solms-Laubach (1880s), Hesse
  Manufacturer C. Schäfer, Hesse-Nassau
  Karl Rabe von Pappenheim, Hesse and Waldeck
  Justice of the County Court, Dr Hermann Weihe, Hesse and Waldeck
  Lieutenant-Colonel (ret.) Heinrich Wilhelmi, Conservative Union for
    the Administrative District of Wiesbaden (founded 1880)
  Dr Ludwig Ziehen, Conservative *Verein* in the city of Frankfurt a.M.
    (refounded 1910) (–1911)
  Gerhard Kropatschek, editor of the *Reichsbote*, city of Frankfurt
    (1911–   )
Party secretaries:
  Gustav Hüpeden
  Julius Werner
  Dr Hermann Weihe
  Albersmeyer
Press:
  *Deutscher Volksfreund. Organ der deutsch-conservativen Partei in
    Hessen*, founded 1871   (1895: 600)
  Rheinische Kurier
  Wiesbadener Presse
  Oberhessische Zeitung   (1880: 1,200)
  Hessisches Tageblatt
    (continued after 1880 as . . .)
  Kasseler Journal. Konservatives Organ für Mitteldeutschland
                                                    (1883–4: 2,100)

Rhineland

Chairmen: .
  Baron Gustav von Plettenberg-Mehrum (early 1880s–1893)
  Dr Georg Burckhardt (1893–   )
  Baron Friedrich von der Leyen-Blömersheim (late 1890s–   )
Party secretary
  Grund (*c.* 1910)
Press:
  *Das conservative Volksblatt. Organ des conservativen Vereins für
    Duisburg, Mühlheim a.d.R. und Essen* (1880s)
  Rheinisch-Westfälische Post (DKP–FKP)
  Westdeutsche Zeitung
  Westdeutsches Tageblatt (*c.* 1909–11)

Kingdom of Bavaria

Founded:
  Wahlverein of Bavarian Conservatives, 1881
  Bavarian Conservative Union, 1911
  Bavarian *Reichspartei* (Free Conservative Union), 1911
  Landesverband of Bavarian Conservatives, 1912
Chairmen:
  Friedrich Pfaff (1881–4)
  Erbgraf Friedrich Reinhard von Rechteren-Limpurg (1884–died 1893)
  Friedrich Beckh-Rathsburg (1894–1912)
  Phillip Seuffert, Bavarian Conservative Union (1911–12)
  Seuffert and Beckh, *Landesverband* of Bavarian Conservatives
    (1912–   )
  (Deputy chairman: Baron Karl von Cetto)
Party secretary: 1912–
Press:
  Süddeutsche Landpost, founded 1874   (1895: 3,000)
  Bayrischer Landbote. Deutsch-konservative Bürgerzeitung
                                                    (1880: 1,500)
  Bayerischer Volksfreund, founded 1904
  Bavaria, founded 1909
  Fränkische Boten
  Nürnberger Volksfreund. Conservatives Volksblatt

Kingdom of Saxony

Founded:
  German *Reichsverein*, February 1874
  Conservative *Landesverein* in the Kingdom of Saxony, May 1878

Chairmen:
 Justizrat Strödel (1870s)
 Baron von Burgk-Roßthal (–1880)
 Kammerherr Baron von Fink-Nöthnitz (1880–3)
 Baron Heinrich von Friesen-Rötha (1883–May 1894)
  (Vice-chairman: Carl Ackermann)
 Consul-General Schober (1894–1904)
 Major-General Sachse, Professor Gravelius and Dr Friedrich Wagner
  (together 1904–*c.* 1907)
 Paul Mehnert (*c.* 1907–   )
Party secretaries:
 Curt Fritzsche, general secretary of the *Landesverein*
 von Litsow
 Kretzschmar
 Baron o Byrn (treasurer)
Press:
 Neue Reichszeitung
  (continued after 1879 as . . .)
 Sächsischer Volksfreund. Conservatives Wochenblatt und
  Organ der conservativen Vereine Sachsens   (1880: 4,000)
 Dresdner Nachrichten   (1912: 40,000)
 Sächsische Politische Nachrichten
 Conservatives Vereinsblatt
  (continued after 1888 as . . .)
 Das Vaterland. Organ des konservativen Landesvereins im Königreich
  Sachsen   (1895: 3,000; 1912: 4,900)
 Sächsische Landeszeitung
 Dresdner Tageblatt

Kingdom of Württemberg

Founded: 1895
Chairmen:
 Oberfinanzrat Klaiber (1895–7)
 Heinrich Kraut (1897–   )
Party secretary:
 Friedrich Schrempf, editor of the *Deutsche Reichspost*, (1890–   )
Press:
 Süddeutsche Reichspost (Augsburg)
  (continued after 1876 as . . .)
 Deutsche Reichspost (Württembergische Landpost)
     (1895: 2,400)
 Süddeutsche Tageszeitung   (1912: 2,000)

Südddeutsche Zeitung, founded 1913 (DKP–FKP–ADV)

(1914: 10,000)

Der schwäbische Landmann (DKP–BdL)
Der württembergische Bauernfreund (DKP–BdL)

Grand Duchy of Baden

Founded: 1878
Chairmen:
  Baron Ernst August Göler von Ravensburg (1878–October 1885)
  Baron Emil von Stockhorn (1885–1903)
  Superior Court Judge Baron Albrecht Rüdt von Collenberg-Bödigheim
    (1903–8)
  Prince Alfred zu Löwenstein-Wertheim-Freudenburg and Baron Udo
    von La Roche von Starkenfels (1908–   )
Party secretaries:
  Wilhelm Schlehbach (1878–   ), chairman of the Karlsruhe Conservative
    Verein
  Wilhelm Schmidt (*c.* 1907–13)
Press:
  Badische Landpost, founded 1877   (1881–3: 2,000)
    (continued after 1901 as . . .)
  Badische Post (amalgamated with the *Deutsche Reichspost*, 1906)
  Badische Warte, founded 1909
  Süddeutsche Conservative Correspondenz, founded 1913 (1913: *c.* 350)

The Grand Duchies of Mecklenburg-Schwerin and Mecklenburg-Strelitz

Founded: 1894
Chairmen:
  Theodor von Oertzen-Kotelow and
    Lieutenant-General von Häseler-Schwerin (1894–1912)
  Hermann von Bernstorff (1912–   )
Party secretaries: none known
Press:
  Mecklenburgische Landesnachrichten, founded 1878
    (continued after 1887 as . . .)
  Mecklenburger Nachrichten   (1895: 4,050; 1913: 8,700)
  Mecklenburger Warte, founded 1907

APPENDIX 5

Reichstag Elections (DKP National Summary), 1871–1912

Year	Total turn-out (%)	DKP votes	DKP % of vote	DKP candidates	Seats won	DKP % of seats won	Run-off Elections Contested	Won	By-election years	By-elections Contested	Won
1871	51.0	548,877	14.1	165	57	14.9	14	4	1871–4	8	3
1874	61.2	359,959	6.9	124	22	5.5	17	6	1874–7	4	3
1877	60.6	526,039	9.7	166	40	10.1	20	7	1877–8	3	2
1878	63.4	749,494	13.0	175	59	14.9	20	7	1878–81	14	10
1881	56.3	830,807	16.3	222	50	12.6	33	8	1881–4	7	7
1884	60.6	861,063	15.2	192	78	19.6	24	11	1884–7	6	4
1887	77.5	1,147,200	15.2	132	80	20.2	17	9	1887–90	11	10
1890	71.6	895,103	12.4	174	73	18.4	28	18	1890–3	14	7
1893	72.5	1,038,353	13.5	164	72	18.1	47	22	1893–8	16	7
1898	68.1	859,222	11.1	144	56	14.1	47	17	1898–1903	7	5
1903	76.1	948,448	10.0	136	54	13.6	37	21	1903–7	3	2
1907	84.7	1,060,209	9.4	119	60	15.1	30	17	1907–12	6	5
1912	84.9	1,126,270	9.2	166	43	10.8	45	16	1912–18	14	10

Source: G. A. Ritter and M. Niehuss, *Wahlgeschichtliches Arbeitsbuch* (Munich, 1980), pp. 38–42, 121, 125, 128; *Statistik des Deutschen Reichs*, Vol. 250, Heft 3 (Berlin, 1913), table 2.

APPENDIX 6

Reichstag Elections in the Administrative Districts (Regierungsbezirke, RB) of Germany, 1871–1912

DKP percentage of vote/number of seats won

District (seats available)		1871	1874	1877	1878	1881	1884	1887	1890	1893	1898	1903	1907	1912
Kingdom of Prussia														
East Prussia														
RB Königsberg	(% of vote)	43.9	27.3	33.6	36.9	30.1	48.9	54.0	41.3	47.7	35.5	35.2	42.4	30.3
(10)	(No. of seats)	6	2	5	6	3	7	7	7	6	6	6	6	5
RB Gumbinnen	(% of vote)	51.4	32.1	42.1	69.1	55.5	72.6	80.3	64.3	65.4	63.1	69.1	77.7	44.4
(7)	(No. of seats)	4	1	2	7	5	7	7	7	6	6	7	7	4
West Prussia														
RB Danzig	(% of vote)	15.7	12.6	7.1	15.9	18.6	25.2	19.2	16.7	19.9	19.0	18.2	19.8	14.2
(5)	(No. of seats)	2	1	0	1	1	2	2	1	1	1	1	1	1
RB Marienwerder	(% of vote)	22.9	19.4	20.4	26.8	14.6	27.3	16.9	15.2	34.2	9.5	1.9	15.3	6.8
(8)	(No. of seats)	2	2	3	4	2	3	2	1	2	1	0	2	1
Brandenburg														
Berlin	(% of vote)	10.1	5.2	0.1	3.9	27.7	28.5	17.4	14.4	14.4	5.2	12.4	7.3	3.2
(6)	(No. of seats)	0	0	0	0	0	0	0	0	0	0	0	0	0
RB Potsdam	(% of vote)	59.1	31.7	19.6	26.0	33.3	39.4	45.2	29.4	32.7	35.1	27.8	20.2	13.0
(10)	(No. of seats)	7	1	2	3	2	5	6	5	5	6	4	3	2
RB Frankfurt	(% of vote)	52.3	29.1	43.4	46.6	43.1	44.5	49.0	41.2	36.6	36.4	25.1	20.8	24.9
(10)	(No. of seats)	6	2	7	8	5	6	8	7	6	3	3	4	3

APPENDIX 6 – continued

DKP percentage of vote/number of seats won

District (seats available)		1871	1874	1877	1878	1881	1884	1887	1890	1893	1898	1903	1907	1912
Pomerania														
RB Stettin	(% of vote)	57.9	31.8	45.8	59.5	53.4	62.4	63.3	50.4	47.1	37.9	41.6	44.9	37.5
(7)	(No. of seats)	5	4	4	6	5	6	6	6	5	5	5	5	5
RB Köslin	(% of vote)	88.9	52.5	61.0	73.0	70.8	73.1	80.8	69.3	55.1	51.2	55.0	66.4	58.6
(5)	(No. of seats)	5	5	3	5	5	5	4	5	4	4	5	5	5
RB Stralsund	(% of vote)	0.0	13.6	7.4	0.0	28.1	0.0	0.0	0.0	20.9	54.8	26.1	23.8	42.7
(2)	(No. of seats)	0	0	0	0	0	0	0	0	1	2	1	0	0
Poznan														
RB Poznan	(% of vote)	21.2	3.6	0.3	15.9	8.5	6.6	7.4	8.9	14.7	10.8	11.2	20.0	18.2
(10)	(No. of seats)	0	0	0	0	0	0	0	0	0	0	1	1	1
RB Bromberg	(% of vote)	14.3	13.7	21.5	29.3	32.7	25.7	26.5	23.6	14.1	15.3	30.0	27.0	22.4
(5)	(No. of seats)	1	1	1	2	1	2	2	2	1	0	1	1	1
Silesia														
RB Breslau	(% of vote)	21.4	12.4	8.4	9.9	12.4	10.2	16.8	10.3	21.8	24.1	29.5	27.6	22.9
(13)	(No. of seats)	2	1	1	1	1	2	3	2	5	6	6	7	5
RB Liegnitz	(% of vote)	28.9	22.9	23.7	34.9	32.4	20.5	11.0	11.4	18.0	22.2	20.6	15.2	21.6
(10)	(No. of seats)	3	1	3	2	2	0	0	1	1	2	1	2	1
RB Oppeln	(% of vote)	5.8	0.0	1.4	4.9	5.3	8.4	18.4	9.6	10.0	9.4	4.7	7.1	2.4
(12)	(No. of seats)	1	0	0	0	0	1	1	1	1	1	1	1	1
Prussian Saxony														
RB Magdeburg	(% of vote)	37.9	14.1	20.3	16.1	23.9	22.6	18.7	14.6	11.1	10.8	14.9	14.1	16.5
(8)	(No. of seats)	2	0	1	1	1	2	2	2	1	2	2	2	1
RB Merseburg	(% of vote)	41.4	21.9	16.9	4.8	22.9	17.3	18.1	19.2	4.3	4.0	9.0	8.5	13.1
(8)	(No. of seats)	3	0	1	1	0	2	3	2	1	0	1	1	0
RB Erfurt	(% of vote)	22.0	12.9	6.1	9.6	11.0	24.4	20.2	14.4	13.8	14.1	11.4	11.3	18.8
(4)	(No. of seats)	1	0	0	0	0	1	1	0	1	1	0	1	1

APPENDIX 6 – continued

DKP percentage of vote/number of seats won

District (seats available)		1871	1874	1877	1878	1881	1884	1887	1890	1893	1898	1903	1907	1912
Schleswig-Holstein (10)	(% of vote)	10.1	0.0	8.2	16.2	20.2	6.0	5.7	4.2	4.6	0.0	0.0	0.0	5.4
	(No. of seats)	0	0	1	1	1	1	1	1	1	0	0	0	0
Hanover (19)	(% of vote)	0.3	0.0	3.1	5.4	4.5	1.1	0.0	0.0	2.1	2.6	4.7	4.1	6.1
	(No. of seats)	0	0	0	0	0	0	0	0	1	0	1	2	0
Westphalia														
RB Münster (4)	(% of vote)	1.7	0.0	0.5	2.7	1.0	3.6	8.3	3.2	0.0	1.9	0.0	0.0	4.2
	(No. of seats)	0	0	0	0	0	0	0	0	0	0	0	0	0
RB Minden (5)	(% of vote)	28.4	18.2	40.3	37.7	37.0	39.0	45.7	34.0	35.6	24.7	19.0	19.2	11.3
	(No. of seats)	2	0	3	2	3	3	3	2	2	1	2	1	0
RB Arnsberg (8)	(% of vote)	2.4	0.7	7.2	3.7	5.4	11.3	8.1	4.8	4.0	0.0	0.2	0.0	0.0
	(No. of seats)	0	0	0	0	0	2	1	1	0	0	0	0	0
Province of Hesse-Nassau														
RB Kassel (8)	(% of vote)	10.5	4.1	7.5	12.4	39.9	32.7	38.4	21.0	16.5	7.3	7.0	1.8	2.0
	(No. of seats)	1	0	0	1	3	5	3	3	2	0	0	0	0
RB Wiesbaden (6)	(% of vote)	8.7	3.6	3.3	5.1	9.3	4.3	0.0	0.0	0.0	0.0	0.0	0.0	5.6
	(No. of seats)	1	0	0	0	0	0	0	0	0	0	0	0	0
Rhine Province														
RB Koblenz (6)	(% of vote)	5.1	2.1	7.9	2.6	8.3	8.8	17.8	0.0	5.7	0.0	4.2	13.0	10.2
	(No. of seats)	1	0	0	0	1	1	1	0	0	0	0	0	0
RB Düsseldorf (12)	(% of vote)	2.9	0.1	0.0	0.0	10.6	0.1	0.0	0.7	5.0	0.0	0.0	0.0	0.8
	(No. of seats)	0	0	0	0	0	0	0	0	1	0	0	0	0
RB Cologne (6)	(% of vote)	6.6	0.8	0.0	0.1	0.1	0.2	16.4	0.2	0.1	0.0	0.0	0.0	0.4
	(No. of seats)	0	0	0	0	0	0	0	0	0	0	0	0	0
RB Trier (6)	(% of vote)	7.9	0.0	0.0	0.0	0.0	0.0	2.6	1.0	0.0	0.0	0.3	0.0	0.3
	(No. of seats)	1	0	0	0	0	0	0	0	0	0	0	0	0
RB Aachen (5)	(% of vote)	6.8	1.1	0.0	0.0	3.4	0.4	4.5	0.0	0.0	0.1	0.0	0.0	0.0
	(No. of seats)	0	0	0	0	0	0	0	0	0	0	0	0	0

APPENDIX 6 – continued

DKP percentage of vote/number of seats won

District (seats available)		1871	1874	1877	1878	1881	1884	1887	1890	1893	1898	1903	1907	1912
RB Hohenzollern-Sigmaringen (1)	(% of vote)	0.0	0.0	0.0	0.0	0.0	0.0	0.0	0.0	34.5	0.0	0.0	0.0	0.0
	(No. of seats)	0	0	0	0	0	0	0	0	0	0	0	0	0
Total Prussia (236)	(% of vote)	20.8	10.0	12.4	16.0	20.0	19.7	20.2	15.1	16.2	13.7	13.3	13.2	11.5
	(No. of seats)	56	21	37	50	42	63	63	55	54	45	48	52	37
Bavaria (48) (DKP/BdL)	(% of vote)	1.0	0.9	2.8	4.0	3.2	1.3	0.5	1.3	2.5	1.9	1.4	1.8	4.5
	(No. of seats)	0	0	0	0	0	0	0	1	1	2	3	4	3
(including . . . .) (RB Middle Franconia) (6)	(% of vote)	0.0	7.7	13.7	14.4	14.4	7.8	0.0	7.0	10.8	14.0	14.0	11.3	12.3
	(No. of seats)	0	0	0	0	0	0	0	1	1	1	2	2	1
Saxony (23)	(% of vote)	5.2	7.2	17.4	16.2	24.3	22.7	24.0	22.6	21.5	18.1	10.1	7.7	8.0
	(No. of seats)	0	1	4	4	5	8	8	10	5	5	0	2	1
Württemberg (DKP/BdL/WV) (17)	(% of vote)	1.6	0.0	0.1	1.1	3.7	1.2	1.6	0.4	2.4	4.6	11.7	10.8	5.8
	(No. of seats)	0	0	0	0	0	0	0	0	0	1	2	3	2
Baden (14) (DKP/BdL)	(% of vote)	3.7	0.7	7.8	14.6	9.8	13.1	14.6	11.0	8.9	3.0	0.7	6.4	4.1
	(No. of seats)	0	0	1	2	1	3	3	3	2	0	0	1	1
Hesse (9) (DKP/BdL)	(% of vote)	0.4	0.0	4.6	5.8	2.3	0.0	0.0	0.0	0.4	1.6	0.0	5.1	0.0
	(No. of seats)	0	0	0	0	0	0	0	0	0	0	0	1	0
Mecklenburg-Schwerin (6)	(% of vote)	37.2	34.2	29.9	46.0	47.2	49.0	39.4	29.2	35.6	25.1	29.2	30.5	30.1
	(No. of seats)	0	0	0	1	2	3	4	3	5	3	4	3	2

DKP percentage of vote/number of seats won

District (seats available)		1871	1874	1877	1878	1881	1884	1887	1890	1893	1898	1903	1907	1912
Mecklenburg-Strelitz (1)	(% of vote)	47.9	40.8	46.7	51.7	48.2	55.4	85.9	44.1	52.6	0.0	0.0	0.0	0.0
	(No. of seats)	0	0	0	1	0	1	1	1	1	0	0	0	0
Oldenburg (3)	(% of vote)	0.0	14.1	0.0	0.0	0.2	0.0	0.0	0.0	0.0	0.0	0.0	0.0	0.0
	(No. of seats)	0	0	0	0	0	0	0	0	0	0	0	0	0
Brunswick (3)	(% of vote)	0.0	0.0	2.2	5.4	0.0	0.1	0.0	0.0	6.8	0.0	0.0	0.0	0.0
	(No. of seats)	0	0	0	0	0	0	0	0	0	0	0	0	0
Anhalt (2)	(% of vote)	0.2	0.0	0.0	0.0	16.3	0.0	0.0	5.9	10.3	7.6	0.0	0.0	7.6
	(No. of seats)	0	0	0	0	0	0	0	0	0	0	0	0	0
Waldeck, Lippe and Schaumburg-Lippe (3)	(% of vote)	11.6	14.5	21.1	31.1	36.5	39.2	24.0	20.8	36.8	22.9	11.6	13.9	0.0
	(No. of seats)	0	0	0	0	0	1	1	0	1	0	0	0	0
Thuringian States[1] (12)	(% of vote)	6.7	1.3	2.8	8.9	9.6	5.1	0.8	1.0	2.0	5.0	8.5	2.9	5.5
	(No. of seats)	1	0	0	1	0	0	0	0	0	0	0	1	0
Lübeck (1)	(% of vote)	0.0	0.0	0.0	0.0	23.5	0.0	0.0	0.0	0.0	0.0	0.0	0.0	0.0
	(No. of seats)	0	0	0	0	0	0	0	0	0	0	0	0	0
Bremen (1)	(% of vote)	0.0	0.0	0.0	0.0	8.9	0.0	0.0	0.0	0.0	0.0	0.0	0.0	0.0
	(No. of seats)	0	0	0	0	0	0	0	0	0	0	0	0	0
Hamburg (3)	(% of vote)	0.0	0.0	0.0	1.2	0.9	0.0	0.0	0.0	0.5	0.0	0.0	0.0	0.0
	(No. of seats)	0	0	0	0	0	0	0	0	0	0	0	0	0
Alsace-Lorraine (15)	(% of vote)	—	0.0	0.0	0.2	2.8	0.0	0.0	12.5	14.7	10.0	4.8	0.0	0.0
	(No. of seats)	—	0	0	0	0	0	0	1	3	1	1	0	0

[1]Thuringian states: Saxe-Weimar, Saxe-Meiningen, Reuß (Older Line), Reuß (Younger Line), Saxe-Altenburg, Saxe-Coburg-Gotha, Schwarzburg-Sonderhausen and Schwarzburg-Rudolstadt.

Source: G. A. Ritter and M. Niehuss, *Wahlgeschichtliches Arbeitsbuch* (Munich, 1980), pp. 67–96.

APPENDIX 7

Prussian House of Deputies Elections, 1898 and 1913

| | DKP percentage of vote/number of seats won | | | | | | | |
| | 1898 | | | | 1913 | | | |
Province	Total % turn-out	DKP % of vote	Total seats available	DKP no. of seats	Total % turn-out	DKP % of vote	Total seats available	DKP no. of seats
East Prussia	17.2	67.0	32	23	22.4	50.8	32	24
West Prussia	39.7	17.3	22	6	52.1	22.3	22	5
Berlin	17.4	18.1	9	0	53.3	1.0	12	0
Brandenburg	16.0	53.9	36	28	35.3	22.2	38	18
Pomerania	11.3	67.9	26	24	17.2	49.5	26	24
Poznan	46.8	20.5	29	8	62.4	21.5	29	9
Silesia	20.4	33.2	65	24	24.7	26.9	66	26
Saxony	14.0	45.6	38	17	27.2	26.1	38	19
Schleswig-Holstein	17.7	10.4	19	2	35.6	5.7	19	2
Hanover	11.4	4.9	36	1	27.5	8.8	36	6
Westphalia	13.2	9.2	31	4	31.6	3.8	34	6
Hesse-Nassau	13.0	17.6	26	6	26.2	9.1	26	8
Rhineland	16.7	2.0	62	2	31.2	2.2	63	1
Hohenzollern	10.9	1.7	2	0	15.4	0	2	0
Total Prussia	18.4	25.3	433	145	32.7	14.8	443	148

Source: G. A. Ritter and M. Niehuss, *Wahlgeschichtliches Arbeitsbuch* (Munich, 1980), p. 148.

APPENDIX 8

The DKP Press in Berlin (Selected Titles), 1876–1918

Official Party News-Sheets, Newspapers and Journals

	Founded (ceased publication)	Approximate circulation (year reported)	Editors
Mitteilungen des Wahlvereins der Deutsch-Konservativen (continued as . . .)	1876		L. v. Seckendorff, 1876–
Conservative Correspondenz	c. 1883	Distributed as a supplement to 200 newspapers in 1884	L. v. Seckendorff, c. 1883– E. v. Ungern-Sternberg and M. Griesemann, 1880s A. Clar, c. 1890–1910
Der Deutsche Patriot	July 1881 (1881)	160,000 printed	O. de Grahl
Unsere Partei	1905 (1905)		R. Hobbing (publisher)
Amtliche Mitteilungen des Konservativen Vereins für die Provinz Brandenburg (continued as . . .)	1908		W. Mannes
Mitteilungen aus der konservativen Partei	1910 (1912)	4,000	Hauptverein der Deutsch-Konservativen

Conservative-Affiliated Newspapers and Journals

Neue Preußische (Kreuz-) Zeitung	1848	5,000–6,500 (1850s–1860s)	H. Wagener, 1848–54; T. Beutner, 1854–72; P. v. Nathusius-Ludom, 1872–6; B. v. Niebelschütz, 1876–81
		8,600–10,000 (1881–1914)	W. v. Hammerstein, 1881–95; H. Kropatschek, 1895–1906; J. Hermes, 1906–12; T. Müller-Fürer, 1912–13; H. Wendland, 1913–18; G. Foertsch, 1913–14, 1918–
Der Reichsbote	1873	11,000–13,000 (1876–1914)	H. Engel, 1873–1911; G. Kropatschek, 1911–13
Das Volk	1888 (1898)	8,000 (1890)	H. v. Gerlach and H. Oberwinder, 1888–96; D. v. Oertzen, 1896–8
Deutsches Adelsblatt	1883	2,000–2,200 (1899–1912)	P. v. Roëll, 1883–6; R. v. Mosch, 1886–c. 1905; G. v. Sass, c. 1905–11; H. v. Wedel, c. 1911–
Volksblatt für Stadt und Land (continued as . . .)	1843		P. v. Nathusius, 1849–72; M. v. Nathusius, 1872–9
Allgemeine Konservative Monatsschrift für das christliche Deutschland (Leipzig)	1879	2,300 (1879) 1,700 (1896)	M. v. Nathusius, 1879–1904; D. v. Oertzen, 1882–96

(continued as . . .) *Monatsschrift für Stadt und Land*	1898	1,500 (1898)	U. v. Hassell, 1896–1905
(continued as . . .) *Konservative Monatsschrift für Politik, Literatur und Kunst*	1905	14,000 (1902–8)	R. Hobbing, 1905– H. v. Berger, c. 1915– H. Wendland, c. 1918–
Deutsches Tageblatt	1881 (1891)		J. Cremer, 1880s M. Griesemann
Konservatives Wochenblatt	1890 (1893)		O. v. Helldorff *et al.*

Agrarian News-Sheets, Newspapers and Journals

Deutsche Landes-Zeitung	1870 (1881)	4,500 (1881)	M. A. Niendorf
Bund der Landwirte (with regional editions for East Prussia, Pomerania, south-west Germany, Bavaria and Württemberg)	1893	167,000 (1893) 247,000 (1912)	
Deutsche Tageszeitung	1894	33,000–42,000 (1894–6) 36,000 (1913–14)	G. Oertel, 1894–1916 P. Bäcker, 1916–
Korrespondenz des Bundes der Landwirte (MS)	1895	2,000 (1896–7) 3,209 (1911)	J. Hoffmann, 1894–7 B. Schoultz, 1897–9 O. Kastner, 1897–

253

APPENDIX 8 – continued

Mitteilungen des Bundes der Landwirte	1896		
Berliner Blatt	1897		
Deutsche Agrarzeitung	1898		E. Klapper
Zeitschrift für Agrarpolitik	1903	1,850 (1912)	Prof. Dr Dade
Agrarpolitische Wochenschrift	1908		

Glossary

Aufruf: proclamation or manifesto, especially for elections or party foundings.
Bauern(bund): peasants/farmers (league of).
Botschaft: royal message or proclamation.
Bund: league.
Bürgerverein(e): burgher association(s) (in Berlin).
Burgfriede: domestic truce (among parties), dating from August 1914.
Deklaranten: Conservative opponents of Bismarck, after February 1876.
Erlass: royal or governmental decree.
Flugblatt/Flugschrift: (electoral) flyer.
Hauptverein: central association.
Honoratioren (politik): (the politics of) notables.
Hospitant(en): guest(s) (of a parliamentary caucus).
Kartell: (Bismarckian) cartel (of parties).
Kreisblatt: (semi-official) county newspaper.
Landesverband: state association.
Landesverein: state association.
Landrat(-̈e): county councillor(s) (in the Prussian administration).
Landtag: state parliament.
Landwirt: farmer.
Machtpolitik: power politics, politics of force.
(Amtliche) Mitteilung(en): (official) report(s).
Mittelpartei: (Bismarckian) (right-wing) middle party.
Mittelstand(s)(politik): (policies in aid of the) middle estate, middle classes.
Oberpräsident: provincial governor.
Preussisches Abgeordnetenhaus: House of Deputies, lower chamber of the Prussian Landtag.
Preussisches Herrenhaus: House of Lords, upper chamber of the Prussian Landtag.
Preussisches Staatsministerium: Prussian state ministry.
Probenummer: trial edition of a newspaper or journal.
Regierungsbezirk: administrative district.
Regierungspräsident: district governor.
Regierungsrat: government councillor.
Rittergut(s)(besitzer): large estate (owner).
Sammlung: rallying together (of parties and/or economic interests).

255

Sozialpolitik: social policy (on the workers' question).
staatserhaltend: state-supporting.
Staatsstreich: *coup d'état* from above.
Stand/Stände/ständisch: (social) estate/estates/estate-oriented.
Verein(e): association(s).
Vereinigung: union.
Volk: people.
völkisch: nationalist, racialist, ethnic.
Volkspartei: people's party.
Volkstümlich(keit): popular(ity).
Wahlverein: electoral association.
Wirtschaftliche Vereinigung: Economic Union, in the Reichstag, dating from 1893.
Zeitung: newspaper.

Select Bibliography

ARCHIVAL SOURCES, NEWSPAPERS
AND JOURNALS

Zentrales Staatsarchiv I, Potsdam (ZStA I)
  NL K. v. Gebsattel
  NL O. Hammann
  NL M. Liebermann v. Sonnenberg
  NL R. Mumm
  NL F. Naumann
  NL G. Roesicke
  NL H. Wagener
  NL C. v. Wangenheim
  NL K. v. Westarp

  Alldeutscher Verband (61 Ve 1)
  Konservativer Verein für die Provinz Brandenburg (60 Pa 2)
  Preußenbund (61 Pr 1)
  Reichskanzlei-Akten
  Reichslandbund/BdL Pressearchiv (61 Re 1)
  Reichsministerium des Innern

Zentrales Staatsarchiv II, Merseburg (ZStA II)
  NL A. Bovenschen
  NL W. Kapp
  NL O. Tippel
  NL R. v. Valentini
  NL A. v. Waldersee

  Hausarchiv (Rep. 53 J, 53 E)
  Pr. Abgeordnetenhaus (Rep. 169c)
  Pr. Finanzministerium (Rep. 151)
  Pr. Geheimes Zivilkabinett (2.2.1.)
  Pr. Ministerium des Innern (Rep. 77)
  Pr. Staatsministerium (Rep. 90a)

Bundesarchiv Koblenz (BAK)
  NL 'J. Alter' (F. Sontag)
  NL O. v. Bismarck (microfilm)
  NL K. v. Bötticher
  NL B. v. Bülow
  NL H. Delbrück
  NL P. Eulenburg
  NL K. v. Fechenbach
  NL M. Harden
  NL A. zu Hohenlohe
  NL C. zu Hohenlohe
  NL A. Hugenberg
  NL F.W. v. Loebell
  NL F. Payer
  NL F. v. Rottenburg
  NL E. Schiffer
  NL R. Seeberg
  NL G. Traub

  Kl. Erw. 329 (W. Abegg)
  Kl. Erw. 319 (R. Hepke)

Kl. Erw. 536 (Erinnerungen an Dr v. Heydebrand und der Lasa)
Kl. Erw. 227 (G. Hüpeden)
Kl. Erw. 455 (W. v. d. Reck)
Kl. Erw. 584-1 (K. Riezler)
Kl. Erw. 230 (G. Roesicke)
Kl. Erw. 393 (G. Schiele, E. v. Reventlow)
Kl. Erw. 701 (T. Schiemann)
Kl. Erw. 341 (R. v. Valentini)

R 45 I, Nationalliberale Partei
Reichskanzlei-Akten
Sammlung Fechenbach
Zeitgeschichtliche Sammlung, 1 and 2

Alldeutsche Blätter
Badische Landpost
Deutsche Reichspost
Deutscher Volksfreund
Mitteilungen der deutschen Vaterlands-Partei
Nationalliberale Blätter
Das neue Deutschland
Neue Preußische (Kreuz-) Zeitung
Neue Westfälische Volkszeitung
Schlesisches Morgenblatt

Bundesarchiv-Militärarchiv, Freiburg i.B. (BA-MA)
NL A. v. Goßler

Politisches Archiv des Auswärtigen Amtes (PA AA), Bonn
NL K. v. Eisendecher

Geheimes Staatsarchiv Preußischer Kulturbesitzes (GStA), Berlin, (Dahlem)
NL R. Bosse
NL F. Meinecke
NL T. Schiemann

Pr. Staatsministerium (Rep. 90)
XII. Hauptabteilung IV: Flugblätter und Plakate (Konservative Partei)

Staatsarchiv Aurich
NL E. zu Inn- und Knyphausen

Generallandesarchiv (GLA) Karlsruhe
NL O. v. Stockhorn (materials provided courtesy of H.-J. Kremer)

Privatarchiv Dr Friedrich Freiherrn Hiller von Gaertringen, Gärtringen
Heydebrand–Westarp *Korrespondenz*, 1911–18 (transcription)

Staatsbibliothek Preußischer Kulturbesitz (W. Berlin)
(Allgemeine) Konservative Monatsschrift
Conservative Correspondenz
Deutsche Agrarzeitung
Deutsches Adelsblatt
Fürstentumer Zeitung

Notables of the Right

    Mecklenburger Nachrichten
    Mitteilungen aus der konservativen Partei

Deutsche Staatsbibliothek (Berlin – GDR)
    Conservative Correspondenz
    Der Reichsbote

Pfälzische Landesbibliothek, Speyer
    Badische Post

Bayerische Staatsbibliothek, Munich
    Bayerische Landbote
    Bayrischer Volksfreund
    Deutsches Adelsblatt
    Konservativer Kalender
    Süddeutsche Landpost

Württembergische Landesbibliothek, Stuttgart
    Deutsche Reichspost
    Der schwäbische Landmann
    Süddeutsche Zeitung
    Der württembergische Bauernfreund

Stadtbibliothek Hannover
    Hannoversche Post
    Hannoversche Tages-Nachrichten

Stadtarchiv und Landesgeschichtliche Bibliothek, Bielefeld
    Conservativer Volksfreund
    Neue Westfälische Volkszeitung

University of California at Berkeley
    (Allgemeine) Konservative Monatsschrift

Hoover Institution, Stanford
    Conservative Correspondenz

University of Alberta, Edmonton
    Neue Preußische (Kreuz-) Zeitung

CONTEMPORARY SOURCES, MEMOIRS AND REFERENCE WORKS

Ahlwardt, Hermann, *Judenflinten* (Dresden, 1890).
Albers, Wilhelm, *Die Besiegten von Philippi! Ein Wort zu den Reichstagswahlen von 1912* (Bielefeld, [1912]).
Albers, Wilhelm, *Vom Verderben zurück! Ein ernstes Wort zur Konsumvereins-frage* (Bielefeld, n.d.).
Almanach für den Bayerischen Landtag, ed. C. Luthardt (Munich, 1881).
Altkonservativ. Versuch einer Zusammenstellung und Begründung altkonserva-tiver Forderungen (Berlin, 1897–8).
Altrock, Walther von, *Gedanken über die Reichserbschaftssteuer vom Standpunkt des ländlichen Grundbesitz* (Berlin, 1908)

Amtliches Handbuch der Kammer der Abgeordneten des Bayerischen Landtags, ed. Bureau der Kammer der Abgeordneten (Munich, 1900, 1906, 1908).

Amtliches Reichstagshandbuch (Berlin, 1890–).

Die Antisemiten im Reichstag (Berlin, 1903).

Arendt, Otto, and Stall, Bernhard, *Die Wahrungsfrage* (Berlin, 1893).

Arnim, Hans von, and Below, Georg von (eds.), *Deutscher Aufstieg. Bilder aus der Vergangenheit und Gegenwart der rechtsstehenden Parteien* (Berlin, 1925).

Backhaus, R., *Wer sind die Conservativen Hannovers? Rede des Herrn R. Backhaus in der V. Landesversammlung der deutsch-hannoverschen Partei am 29. Mai 1899 in Verden* (Hanover, 1899).

Barth, Theodor, *Das Reichsschiff im Schlepptau von Zentrum und Konservativen* (Berlin, 1904).

Bauer, Bruno, *Vollständige Geschichte der Parteikämpfe in Deutschland während der Jahre 1842–1846*, reprint (Berlin, 1964).

Bauer, Erwin, *Graf Caprivi und die Konservativen*, 2nd edn (Leipzig, 1894).

Die Bayerische Reichspartei 1911–1913 (Munich, 1914).

Bayerischer Landtags-Almanach vom Jahre 1887 (Elberfeld, 1887).

Becker, Bernhard, *Die Reaktion in Deutschland gegen die Revolution von 1848*, 3rd edn (Brunswick, 1873).

Below, Georg von, *Das parlamentarische Wahlrecht in Deutschland* (Berlin, 1909).

Below, Georg von, 'Die Anfänge einer Konservativen Partei in Preußen', *Internationale Wochenschrift*, vol. 5, (1911), pp. 1089–1102, 1121–34.

Below, Georg von, 'Deutschkonservative und Reichspartei', in *Handbuch der Politik* (1912–13), Vol. 2, pp. 1–11.

Below, Georg von, *Das gute Recht der Vaterlandspartei. Eine Antwort an Prof. H. Delbrück* (Berlin, [1917]).

Berger, H. von, *Der Konservatismus und die Parteien* (Berlin, [1910]).

Bericht über die Tagung der freikonservativen Partei am 26. Mai 1910 in Elberfeld (n.p., [1910]).

Beta, O., *Wir und die Conservativen. Mit einem Tableau der Bodenbesitzreform* (Leipzig, 1893).

Bethmann Hollweg, Theobald von, *Betrachtungen zum Weltkrieg*, 2 vols. (Berlin, 1919–22).

Bettelheim, A. (ed.), *Biographische Blätter*, continued as *Biographisches Jahrbuch und Deutscher Nekrolog* (Berlin, 1895–).

Bismarck, Otto von, *Gedanken und Erinnerungen*, 2 vols. (Stuttgart, 1898).

Bismarck, Otto von, *Die gesammelten Werke*, 15 vols. (Berlin, 1924–35).

Blumenthal, Werner von, *Wer geht mit? Wider den Umsturz! Für den Mittelstand!* (Dresden, 1894).

Bodelschwingh, Franz von, *Konservativ und Sozial* (Berlin, 1903).

Bodewig, H., *Geistliche Wahlbeeinflussungen in ihrer Theorie und Praxis dargestellt* (Munich, 1909).

Böck, A., *Die Berufsgliederung der Reichstagswahlkreise* (Meiningen, 1911).

Böhme, Dr, 'Ein Fraktionsgemeinschaft der Rechten', *Das nationale Deutschland*, vol. 26 (1908), pp. 798–802.

Böttger, Hugo, *Die Sozialdemokratie auf dem Lande. Ein Beitrag zur deutschen Agrarpolitik* (Leipzig, 1900).

Bonin-Bahrenbusch, B. von, *25 Jahre Landrat* (Neustettin, 1924).

Born, K. E., Henning, H.-J., and Schick, M. (eds.), *Einführungsband, Quellensammlung zur Geschichte der Deutschen Sozialpolitik 1867 bis 1914* (Wiesbaden, 1966).

Born, K. E., and Rassow, Peter (eds.), *Akten zur Staatlichen Sozialpolitik in Deutschland 1890–1914* (Wiesbaden, 1959).

Braun, Adolf, 'Die Reichstagswahlen von 1898 und 1903. Eine statistische Studie', *Archiv für soziale Gesetzgebung und Statistik*, vol. 18 (1903), pp. 539–63.

Braun, Max, *Adolf Stöcker* (Berlin, 1912).

Bueck, Henry Axel, *Der Centralverband Deutscher Industrieller und seine dreißigjährige Arbeit von 1876 bis 1906* (Berlin, 1906).

Bueck, Henry Axel, *Weshalb die Industrie der Rießer'schen Parole 'Kampf gegen Rechts' nicht folgen soll* (Berlin, 1911).

Bülow, Bernhard von, *Imperial Germany* (New York, 1914).

Bülow, Bernhard von, *Denkwürdigkeiten*, 4 vols. (Berlin, 1930–1).

Bund der Landwirte (BdL), 'Anleitung zur ersten Haupt-Organisation im Bunde der Landwirte' (Berlin, 1893).

BdL, *Stenographischer Bericht über die konstituirende Versammlung des Bundes der Landwirte am 18. Februar 1893 im Salle der Tivoli-Brauerei zu Berlin* (Berlin, 1893).

BdL, *Stenographischer Bericht über die Versammlung des Bundes der Landwirte zu Posen am 24. März 1893* (Berlin, 1893).

BdL, *Kurzer Bericht über die Versammlung des Bundes der Landwirte in Süddeutschland am 25 März in der Stadthalle zu Mainz* (n.p., [1893]).

BdL, *Ausführlicher Bericht über die Versammlung der Landwirte im Tivolisaale zu Weimar am 23. April 1893* (Berlin, n.d.).

BdL, *Stenographischer Bericht der General-Versammlung des Bundes der Landwirte am 18. Februar 1895 zu Berlin* (Berlin, 1895).

BdL, *Stimmen aus dem agrarischen Lager* (Berlin, 1896).

BdL, *Agrarisches Handbuch* (Berlin, 1898; 2nd edn, 1903; 3rd edn, 1911).

BdL, *Kritik und Vorschläge des Bundes der Landwirte zum neuen preußischen Schulgesetzentwurf* (Berlin, 1906).

'Caliban', 'Die conservative Volkspartei', *Die Gegenwart* (1896), pp. 155–7.

'Caliban', 'Jungconservativ', *Die Gegenwart* (1897), pp. 396–7.

Christlicher Zeitschriftenverein, *Vom Senfkorn zum Baume. Geschichte der ersten 25 Jahre des christlichen Zeitschriftenvereins in Berlin* (Berlin, 1905).

Claß, Heinrich, *Wider den Strom* (Leipzig, 1932).

Die Conservativen als Partei der verpaßten großen Gelegenheiten (Marburg, 1890).

Crümpelmann, August, *Was hat der Landmann von der Sozialdemokratie zu erwarten?* (Leipzig, 1893).

Curtius, Paul, *Der Weg zum Frieden. Denkschrift über die social-conservativen Bestrebungen* (Berlin, 1881).

Deetjen, Ernst, *Freikonservativ! Die nationale Mittelpartei* (Breslau, 1913).

Deutsche Ziele. Reden bei der ersten öffentlichen Partei-Kundgebung von Herzog Johann Albrecht zu Mecklenburg, Großadmiral von Tirpitz (Berlin, [1917]).

Deutsches Biographisches Jahrbuch (Berlin/Leipzig, 1925–   ).

Deutschkonservative Partei (DKP), *Die konservative Partei im Abgeordneten-haus. Session 1882/83. In Auszügen aus den Reden ihrer Mitglieder* (Marburg, 1883).

DKP, *Konservatives Handbuch* (Berlin, 1892; 2nd edn, 1894; 3rd edn, 1898 [all-DKP–FKP]; 4th edn, 1911 [DKP]).

DKP, *Die Konservativen im Kampfe gegen die Uebermacht des Judentums und für die Erhaltung des Mittelstandes*, ed. Konservativer Landesverein im Königreich Sachsen (Leipzig, 1892).

DKP, *Stenographischer Bericht über den Allgemeinen konservativen Parteitag, abgehalten am 8. Dezember 1892 zu Berlin* (Berlin, 1893).

DKP, *Die Ungiltigkeit von Reichstagsmandaten und deren Verhütung. Ratgeber bei der Abhaltung von Wahlversammlungen und Wahlen für den Reichstag* (Berlin, [1897]).

DKP, *Unkorrigierter stenographischer Bericht über die Verhandlungen des Allgemeinen konservativen Parteitages zu Dresden am 2. Februar 1898* (Berlin, 1898).

DKP, *Ratgeber für die Konservativen im Deutschen Reich* (n.p., [1903]).

DKP, *Wahlbüchlein (Vademecum) zur Reichstags-Wahl 1903* (Berlin, [1903]).

DKP, *Stenographischer Bericht über die Verhandlungen des Delegiertentages der Deutsch-Konservativen Partei am 30.11.1906* (Berlin, 1906).

DKP, *Bericht über die Verhandlungen der Delegierten-Versammlung der deutsch-konservativen Partei am Mittwoch, den 11. Dezember 1907* (Berlin, 1908).

DKP, *Organisation des Ostpreußischen Konservativen Vereins*, ed. Ostpreußischer Konservativer Verein (Königsberg, 1908; 2nd edn, 1910).

DKP, *Ordentliche Generalversammlung des Ostpreußischen Konservativen Vereins vom 22. Feb. 1908/vom 18. Jan. 1909*, ed. Ostpreußischer Konservativer Verein (Königsberg, 1908–9).

DKP, *Konservative Politik im Reichstage. XII. Leg. Per., 1. Session. 19. Feb. 1907–7. Mai 1908* (Berlin, 1908).

DKP, *Die politischen Parteien und das Handwerk. Mit besonderer Berücksichtigung der Stellungnahme der konservativen Partei zu den Wünschen und Forderungen des Handwerks* (n.p., [1909]).

DKP, *Protokoll von einer Delegiertenversammlung des ostpreußischen Konservativen Vereins, 14. Mai 1909*, ed. Ostpreußischer Konservativer Verein (n.p., [1909]).

DKP, *Zur Steuer der Wahrheit. Gedanken über die innerpolitische Lage nach dem Zustandekommen der Reichsfinanzreform*, von einem ostpreußischen Konservativen (Königsberg, 1909).

DKP, *Die Reichsfinanzreform 1909 im Lichte der Oeffentlichkeit*, ed. Generalsekretariat der Konservativen Partei Badens, 2nd edn (Karlsruhe, [1909]).

DKP, *Die Landesversammlung der konservativen Partei in Württemberg* (Stuttgart, 1910).

DKP, *Parteitag des Konservativen Provinzialvereins für Pommern am 30. November 1910* (n.p., [1910]).

DKP, *Vademecum zur Reichstagswahl 1912* (Berlin, [1911]).

DKP, *Stenographischer Bericht über die Versammlung rechtstehender Wähler im Kaisersaale der städtischen Tonhalle zu Düsseldorf am 17. Januar 1913*, ed. Konservativer Provinzialverein für die Rheinprovinz in Düsseldorf (Düsseldorf, 1913).

DKP, *Die preußischen Landtagswahlen 1913. Gedanken und Bemerkungen zur Wahlagitation*, ed. Bureau des Deutsch-konservativen Vereins für die Provinz Schlesien (Breslau, 1913).

DKP, *Konservativer Kalender (Kriegs-Kalender)* (Berlin, 1916).

Deutsch-konservative Parteitag in Linz am 22. November 1880 (Linz, 1880).

Dewitz, Hermann von, *Erbzuwachssteuer als Besitzsteuer. Eine Krönung der Reichsfinanzreform* (Berlin, 1912).

Dewitz, Hermann von, *Die Demokratisierung des preußischen Wahlrechts* (Berlin, n.d.).

Dewitz, Hermann von, *Von Bismarck bis Bethmann. Innenpolitischer Rückblick eines Konservativen* (Berlin, 1918).

Diederich, Nils, et al., *Wahlstatistik in Deutschland* (Munich, 1976).

Dumas, Georg, *Konservative Wirtschaftspolitik* ((Frankfurt a.M., 1913).

Eichhorn, K. von, *Konservativ-Nationalliberal oder Nationalliberal-Sozialdemokratisch? Ein Bild deutschkonservativer Politik* (Berlin, 1905).

Eichhorn, K. von, *Vorschlag einer Reichs-Gewinnzuwachssteuer* (Breslau, 1909).

Eisenhart, Wolfgang, *Königtum und politische Freiheit. Ein offenes Wort zu den bevorstehenden Wahlen über die Parteiverhältnisse Deutschlands* (Halle a.S., 1888).

Eisenhart, Wolfgang, *Liberal und Konservativ. Ein Kampf um deutsche Ideale in der Politik* (Naumburg a.S., 2nd edn, 1911).

Eisenhart, Wolfgang, *Zwanzig Jahre deutscher Politik seit Bismarcks Rücktritt* (Naumburg a.S., 1911).

Eisenhart, Wolfgang, *Deutschland, erwache!* (Leipzig, 1913).

Eisner, Kurt, *Eine Junkerrevolte. Drei Wochen preußischer Politik* (Berlin, 1899).

Eisner, Kurt, *Der Zukunftsstaat der Junker: Manteuffeleien gegen die Sozialdemokratie im preußischen Herrenhaus am 11. und 13. Mai 1904* (Berlin, 1904).

Endemann, W., *Der deutsche Mittelstand und die politischen Parteien. Ein politisches Programm* (n.p., n.d.).

Engels, Friedrich, *The Role of Force in History: A Study of Bismarck's Policy of Blood and Iron*, ed. E. Wangermann (New York, 1968).

Eulenburg, Philipp, *Philipp Eulenburgs politische Korrespondenz*, 3 vols., ed. John C. G. Röhl (Boppard a.R., 1976–83).

Eynern, E. von, *Zwanzig Jahre Kanalkämpfe* (Berlin, 1901).

[Fechenbach-Laudenbach, Karl Reichsfreiherr von], *Die Ursachen der Entstehung und Weiterentwicklung der Sozialdemokratie*, von einem praktischen Bürger (Berlin, 1880).

Fechenbach, Karl von, *Gouvernmental und conservativ oder die Partei Bismarck sans phrase* (Osnabrück, 1885).

Fechenbach, Karl von, *Noch einmal: 'Die Partei Bismarck sans phrase'* (Augsburg, 1885).

Fechenbach, Karl von, *Fürst Bismarck und die 'deutsch'-conservative Partei oder eine politische Abrechnung* (Frankfurt a.M., 1887).

Fechenbach, Karl von, *Die Kaiserliche Erlasse vom 4. Februar 1890* (Frankfurt a.M., 1890).

Fechenbach, Karl von, *Die Bedeutung der heutigen Sozialdemokratie für Staat und Gesellschaft* (Frankfurt a.M., 1895).

Fechenbach, Karl von, *Der Kaiser ruft!*, 3rd edn (Berlin, 1896).

Fechenbach, Karl von, *Soll man die Sozialdemokratie zur akuten Revolution, zu Strassenkämpfen zwingen?* (Berlin, 1896).

Flaischlen, Markus, and Grieben, P., *Verzeichnis der in der Provinz Sachsen und dem Herzogtum Anhalt erscheinenden Zeitungen* (Halle a.S., 1894).

Fontane, Theodor, *Der Stechlin* (Frankfurt a.M., 1982).

Frank, Walter, 'Aus der Vorgeschichte von Bismarcks Sturz. Unveröffentlichtes aus dem Nachlasse des Hofpredigers Stöcker', *Süddeutsche Monatshefte* (August 1927), pp. 319–34.

Frantz, Constantin, *Der Untergang der alten Parteien und die Parteien der Zukunft* (Berlin, 1878).

Friesen-Rötha, Heinrich Freiherr von, *Conservativ! Ein Mahnruf im letzter Stunde* (Leipzig, 1892).

Friesen-Rötha, Heinrich Freiherr von, *Schwert und Pflug* (Berlin, 1907).

'Frymann, Daniel' (pseud. for Heinrich Claß), *Wenn ich der Kaiser wär'* (Leipzig, 1912).

Für unsere Landarbeiter. Eine freundliche Bitte an Besitzer und Geistliche (Stettin, 1895).

Gageur, Karl, *Reform des Wahlrechts im Reich und in Baden* (Freiburg i.B., 1893).

Gasteiger, Michael, *Die christliche Arbeiterbewegung in Süddeutschland* (Munich, 1908).

Gerlach, Hellmut von, 'Die sogenannte Wahlurne', *Die Nation*, vol. 22 (1904–5), pp. 692–4.

Gerlach, Hellmut von, *Die Geschichte des preußischen Wahlrechts* (Berlin, 1908).

Gerlach, Hellmut von, *Erinnerungen eines Junkers* (Berlin, [1924]).

Gerlach, Hellmut von, *Von rechts nach links* (Zurich, [1937]).

Gesamtverzeichnis Deutschsprachiger Zeitschriften und Serien in Bibliotheken der Bundesrepublik Deutschland einschließlich Berlin (West), 2 vols. (Munich, 1978).

Göhre, Paul, *Die evangelisch-soziale Bewegung, ihre Geschichte und ihre Ziele* (Leipzig, 1896).

Goldschmidt, Dr, *Zur Reichstagswahl vom 21. Februar und 2. März 1887* (Berlin, 1887).

Goltz, Dr Theodor Freiherr von der, *Die ländliche Arbeiterfrage und ihre Lösung*, 2nd edn (Danzig, 1874).

Goltz, Dr Theodor Freiherr von der, *Die Lage der ländlichen Arbeiter im deutschen Reich* (Berlin, 1875).

Goltz, Dr Theodor Freiherr von der, *Die ländliche Arbeiterklasse und der preußische Staat* (1893), reprint (Frankfurt a.M., 1968).

Goßler, Alfred von, *Die Konservativen vor den Landtagswahlen 1913* (Breslau, 1913).

Grabowsky, Adolf, *Kulturnotwehr. An den Liberalismus in letzten Stunde!* (Berlin, 1907).

Grabowsky, Adolf, *Der Kulturkonservatismus und die Reichstagswahlen* (Berlin, 1912).

Graf, Armin, *Herrenhaus redivivus. Der Fall Paasch im preußischen Herrenhause am 1. April 1892 . . . nebst einem Anhang über die Verjudung unserer Aristokratie* (Berlin, 1892).

Grisshammer, Ferdinand, *Konservative Politik und Evangel. Tagespresse, eine Notwendigkeit für das Wohl unseres Volkes*, 2nd edn (Nuremberg, [1912]).

Grosse, C., and Raith, C., *Beiträge zur Geschichte und Statistik der Reichstags- und Landtagswahlen in Württemberg seit 1871* (Stuttgart, 1912).

Groth, Otto, 'Die politische Presse Württembergs', (PhD thesis, Eberhard-Karl University, Tübingen, 1915).

Habermann, Gustav, *Wider den Reichsboten. In Sachen des Evangeliums und der Freiheit* (Leipzig, 1893).

Hagelweide, Gert, *Deutsche Zeitungsbestände in Bibliotheken und Archiven* (Düsseldorf, 1974).

Hagelweide, Gert (ed.), *Zeitung und Bibliothek. Ein Wegweiser zu Sammlungen und Literatur* (Munich, 1974).

Halt – mehr rechts! Ein Wort zur Abwehr unwürdiger Fremdherrschaft, von einem niederdeutschen Bauern, 2nd edn (Dresden, 1892).

Hammerstein, Baron Wilhelm von, *Zur Judenfrage. Vortrag gehalten auf der evangelisch-lutherischen Conferenz, den 25. August 1881* (n.p., 1892).

Hammerstein, Baron Wilhelm von (ed.), *Briefe berühmter Zeitgenossen an Wilhelm Freiherrn von Hammerstein* (Zurich, 1892).

Handbuch der Politik, Vol. 2, *Die Aufgaben der Politik* (Berlin/Leipzig, 1912–13).

Handbuch des Alldeutschen Verbandes, 9th edn (Munich, 1915).

Handbuch Deutscher Zeitungen 1917 (Nachtrag 1918), ed. O. Michel (Berlin, 1917–18).

Handbuch für das preußische Abgeordnetenhaus, ed. R. Plate (Berlin, 1894–   ).

Handbuch für das preußische Herrenhaus, eds. Dr Meitzel and A. Reißig (Berlin, 1891–   ).

Handbuch über den Königlichen Preußischen Hof und Staat (Berlin, 1890–   ).

265

Heinz, Reinhold von, *Ueber konservative Entwicklung. Ein Vortrag* (Hanover, 1913).

Helldorf-Bedra, Otto von, 'Die heutigen Konservativen in England und Deutschland', *Deutsche Revue*, vol. 22 (1897), pp. 285–307.

Helldorff-Bedra, Otto von, 'Der Fall des Sozialistengesetzes', *Deutsche Revue*, vol. 25 (1900), pp. 41–3, 273–84.

Herr, Erich, 'Die Entwicklung der Konservativen Partei in Deutschland' *Akademische Blätter*, vol. 18 (1903–4), pp. 223–7.

Die Herrenhaus-Junker und die Arbeiter (Berlin, 1897).

Hertling, Georg Graf von, *Briefwechsel Hertling-Lerchenfeld 1912–1917*, Part 2, ed. E. Deuerlein (Boppard a.R., 1973).

Hertzberg, Adolf von, *Das Programm der Deutsch-Konservativen Partei im Lichte des Christentums* (Frankfurt a.O., 1893).

Heydebrand und der Lasa, Ernst von, 'Beiträge zu einer Geschichte der konservativen Partei in den letzten 30 Jahren (1888 bis 1919)', *Konservative Monatsschrift*, vol. 77 (1920), pp. 497–504, 539–45, 569–75, 605–11, 638–44.

Hintze, Otto, 'Die Epochen des evangelischen Kirchenregiments in Preußen', *Historische Zeitschrift*, vol. 97 (1906), pp. 67–118.

Historische Forschungen in der DDR 1970–1980. Analysen und Berichte (Berlin, 1980).

Hohenlohe-Schillingsfürst, Alexander zu, *Aus Meinem Leben* (Frankfurt a.M., 1925).

Hohenlohe-Schillingsfürst, Chlodwig zu, *Denkwürdigkeiten*, 2 vols. (Stuttgart, 1907).

Hohenlohe-Schillingsfürst, Chlodwig zu, *Denkwürdigkeiten der Reichskanzlerzeit*, ed. K. A. Müller (Stuttgart, 1931).

Hohorst, G., Kocka, J., and Ritter, G. A. (eds.), *Sozialgeschichtliches Arbeitsbuch*, Vol. 2, 2nd edn (Munich, 1978).

Huber, Victor Aimé, *Über die Elemente, die Möglichkeit oder Notwendigkeit einer konservativen Partei in Deutschland* (Marburg, 1841).

Huber, Victor Aimé, *Die Opposition. Ein Nachtrag zu der konservativen Partei* (Halle, 1842).

Huber, Victor Aimé, *Bruch mit Revolution und Ritterschaft* (Berlin, 1852).

Huber, Victor Aimé, *Die Machtfülle des altpreußischen Königthums und die conservative Partei* (Bremen, 1862).

Huber, Victor Aimé, 'Grundzüge eines konservativen Programms', in Huber, *Hubers Ausgewählte Schriften* [1894], ed. Munding.

Huber, Victor Aimé, 'Die konservative Presse' (1846), in Huber, *Hubers Ausgewählte Schriften* [1894], ed. Munding.

Huber, Victor Aimé, *V. A. Hubers Ausgewählte Schriften über Socialreform und Genossenschaftswesen*, ed. K. Munding (Berlin, [1894]).

Hubrich, Eduard, *Die Diätenfrage im Reichstag und das allgemeine Wahlrecht. Vom Standpunkt eines Conservativen* (Königsberg, 1902).

Hugenberg, Alfred, *Streiflichter aus Vergangenheit und Gegenwart*, 2nd edn (Berlin, 1927).

'Ignotus', *Die Kreuzzeitungs-Politik und die Ära Hammerstein-Stöcker*, 3rd edn (Berlin, 1895).

Die 'Industriefreundlichkeit' der Konservativen (Leipzig, 1914).

Jacoby, Julius, *Die antisemitische Bewegung in Baden* (Karlsruhe, 1897).

Jöhlinger, Otto, *Bismarck und die Juden* (Berlin, 1921).

Jordan, E., *Die Entstehung der konservativen Partei und die preußische Agrarverhältnisse von 1848* (Munich, 1914).

Kaeller, Reinhard, 'Die konservative Partei in Minden-Ravensberg, ihre Grundlagen, Entstehung und Entwicklung bis zum Jahre 1866', PhD thesis, Ruprecht-Karl University, Heidelberg, 1912.

Im Kampfe für Deutschlands Zukunft! (Berlin, 1911).

Kanitz-Podangen, Hans Graf von, *Die Heeresvorlage und die Silberfrage* (Pr. Holland, 1893).

Kanitz-Podangen, Hans Graf von, *Die neuen Handelsverträge* (Pr. Holland, 1894).

Kann Hofprediger Stöcker Parteiführer sein?, von einem Eingeweihten (Berlin, 1896).

Kardorff, Wilhelm von, *Gegen den Strom! Eine Kritik des Handelspolitik des deutschen Reichs* (Berlin, 1875).

Kaufhold, Josef, *Die konservative Partei und die Reichstagswahlen 1907* (Berlin, 1907).

Kaufhold, Josef, *Die Fürsorge der konservativen Partei für den Mittelstand*, ed. Hauptverein der Deutsch-Konservativen (n.p., 1908).

Kaufhold, Josef, *Die Geschichte des deutschen Parteiwesens* (Berlin, n.d.)

Kaufhold, Josef, *Die konservative Partei und der Weltkrieg. Die gradlinige Kriegszielpolitik der Deutsch-Konservativen* (Berlin, [1918]).

Kiesenwetter, Otto von, *Fünfundzwanzig Jahre wirtschaftspolitischen Kampfes. Geschichtliche Darstellung des Bundes der Landwirte* (Berlin, 1918).

Klapper, Edmund, *Kornhäuser und Kleinbahnen* (Berlin, 1896)

Klapper, Edmund, *Zur Neugestaltung des deutschen Schlachtvieh-Marktverkehrs* (Berlin, 1896).

Klein, Albert, *Preußens Eigenart – Deutschlands Stärke!*, 2nd edn (Berlin, [1918]).

Die konservative Presse, von einem konservativen Journalisten (Berlin, 1885).

Konservative unter sich (Berlin, 1909).

Körner, Theodor, *Kann der Bauer Sozialdemokrat sein?* (Stuttgart, 1911).

[Körner, Theodor], *Oekonomierat Rudolf Schmid. Ein Lebensbild eines württembergischen Bauernführers* (Stuttgart, 1927).

Krafft, Rudolf, *Wider Junkertum* (Nuremberg, 1897).

Krause, Oberst z.D. von, *Zum Austritt Stöckers aus der konservativen Partei* (Berlin, 1896).

Kube, W., *Unsere Kriegsziele. Vortrag* (Breslau, 1917).

Kuhn, Axel (ed.), *Deutsche Parlamentsdebatten*, Vol. 1 (Frankfurt a.M., 1970).

Kürschners Deutscher Reichstag (Der Neue Reichstag) (Stuttgart/Berlin, 1890–   ).

Kunze, Dr Johannes, *Die Stellung des Liberalismus zu Christentum und Königtum*, ed. Hauptverein der Deutsch-Konservativen (Berlin, [1911]).

'Kynades, L.', *Herkules am Scheideweg, oder Stöcker und die konservative Fraktion* (Leipzig, 1896).

Lagarde, Paul de, *Programm für die konservative Partei Preußens* (Göttingen, 1884).

Längin, Georg, *Zur Charakteristik der kirchlich-konservativen Partei in Baden* (Karlsruhe, 1892).

Leo, Erich, *Wahlrecht und Berufsstände. Ein Beitrag zur Reform des preußischen Landtagswahlrechts* (Berlin, 1907).

Leser, Guido, *Untersuchungen über das Wahlprüfungsrecht des Deutschen Reichstags* (Leipzig, 1908).

Leuß, Hans, *Wilhelm Freiherr von Hammerstein. 1881–1895 Chefredakteur der Kreuzzeitung* (Berlin, 1905).

Limburg-Stirum, Friedrich Wilhelm Graf von, *Aus der konservativen Politik der Jahre 1890/1905* (Berlin, 1921).

Loebell, Arthur von, *Das Deutsche Heer* (Berlin, [1908]).

Lucius von Ballhausen, Robert Freiherr, *Bismarck-Erinnerungen* (Stuttgart, 1921).

Luthardt, August Emil, *Mein Werden und Wirken im öffentlichen Leben* (Munich, 1901).

Maier, Hans, *Die Konservativen* (Munich, 1910).

Mann, Heinrich, *Man of Straw (Der Untertan)* (Harmondsworth, 1984).

Martin, Rudolf, *Deutsche Machthaber*, 3rd edn (Berlin, 1910).

Massow, Conrad von, *Reform oder Revolution!* 2nd edn (Berlin, 1895).

Massow, Conrad von, 'Die Reform der konservativen Partei!', *Deutsches Adelsblatt*, 28 July–11 August 1895.

Massow, Conrad von, *Die Reform unseres politischen Parteilebens* (Berlin, 1895).

Massow, Conrad von, *Die soziale Frage vom konservativen Standpunkt* (Stuttgart, 1898).

Massow, Wilhelm von, *Die deutsche innere Politik unter Kaiser Wilhelm II.* (Stuttgart, 1913).

Mehring, Franz, *Herr Hofprediger Stöcker der Sozialpolitiker* (Bremen, 1882).

Meyer, Rudolph, *Was heißt konservativ sein? Reform oder Restauration?* (Berlin, 1873).

Meyer, Rudolph (ed.), *Briefe und Socialpolitische Aufsätze von Dr Robertus-Jagetzow*, Vol. 1 (Berlin, [1880]).

Meyer, Rudolph, *Hundert Jahre Conservativer Politik und Literatur*, Vol. 1 (Vienna/Leipzig, [1895]).

Meyer-Tilsit, Edwin, *Einige Vorträge und Aufsätze* (Tilsit, 1915).

Michels, Robert, 'Zum Problem der zeitlichen Widerstandsfähigkeit des Adels', in R. Michels, *Probleme der Sozialphilosophie* (Leipzig/Berlin, 1914), pp. 132–58.

Michniewicz, Bernhard, 'Stahl und Bismarck', PhD thesis, University of Berlin, 1913.

Mirbach-Sorquitten, Julius Graf von, *Der Fortfall des Identitätsnachweises beim Getreideexport* (Berlin, 1888).

Mirbach-Sorquitten, Julius Graf von, *Die für Preußen und für das Deutsche Reich vorgeschlagenen Steuern* (Königsberg, 1909).

Mommsen, Wilhelm (ed.), *Deutsche Parteiprogramme* (Munich, 1960).

Müller, Eduard, *Der Großgrundbesitz in der Provinz Sachsen. Eine Agrarstatistische Untersuchung* (Jena, 1912).

Mumm, Reinhard, *Der christlichsoziale Gedanke* (Berlin, 1933).

Müsebeck, Ernst, *Die ursprünglichen Grundlagen des Liberalismus und Konservatismus in Deutschland* (Berlin, 1915).

Muser, Gerhard, 'Statistische Untersuchung über die Zeitungen Deutschlands 1885–1914', PhD thesis, University of Leipzig, 1918.

Nathan, Dr Paul, *Der jüdische Blutmord und der Freiherr von Wackerbarth-Linderode* (Berlin, 1892).

Nathusius-Ludom, Philipp von, *Zur 'Frauenfrage'* (Halle, 1871).

Nathusius-Ludom, Philipp von, *Conservative Partei und Ministerium* (Berlin, 1872).

Nathusius-Ludom, Philipp von, *Conservative Position* (Berlin, 1876).

Needon, Richard, *Georg Oertel. Ein Lebensbild* (Berlin, 1917).

Neues Sündenregister der Konservativen. Zum Gebrauch für die Reichstagswahlen (Berlin, 1884).

Neumann-Hofer, Dr, *Konservative im Wahlkampf! Ein Nachwort zur Landtagswahl im 6. Wahlkreise* (Detmold, 1913).

Oberwinder, Heinrich, *Sozialismus und Sozialpolitik* (Berlin, 1887).

Oberwinder, Heinrich, *Weltmachtpolitik und Socialpolitik* (Berlin, 1900).

Oelze, Friedrich, *Konservative Partei und Beamtenschaft*, Konservative Flugschriften, No. 3 (Berlin, [1918]).

Oertel, Georg, *Der Konservatismus als Weltanschauung* (Leipzig, 1893).

Oertzen, Dietrich von, *Konservativ oder christlich-sozial? Oder beides?* (Siegen i.W., 1900).

Oertzen, Dietrich von, 'Erinnerungen eines Zeitungsschreibers', *Konservative Monatsschrift für Stadt und Land*, vol. 60 (1903), Hefte 1–6, pp. 42–571.

Oertzen, Dietrich von, *Von Wichern bis Posadowsky. Zur Geschichte der Sozialreform und der christlichen Arbeiterbewegung*, 2nd edn (Hamburg, 1908).

Oertzen, Dietrich von, *Adolf Stöcker*, 2 vols., 2nd edn (Berlin, 1911).

Oertzen, Dietrich von, *Erinnerungen aus meinem Leben* (Berlin-Lichterfelde, [1914]).

Oertzen, Dietrich von, 'Die konservative Partei und der soziale Staat', in Friedrich Thimme (ed.), *Vom inneren Frieden des Deutschen Volkes* (Leipzig, 1916), Vol. 2, pp. 375–85.

Oldenburg-Januschau, Elard von, *Erinnerungen* (Leipzig, 1936).

Oncken, Hermann, *Rudolf von Bennigsen*, 2 vols. (Stuttgart, 1910).

Opitz-Treuen, Hugo, 'Soll die Industrie konservativ oder liberal sein', *Konservative Monatsschrift*, vol. 63 (1906), pp. 1125–34.

Oppe, E., 'Die Reform des Wahlrechts für die II. Kammer·der Ständeversammlung im Königreich Sachsen', *Jahrbuch des öffentlichen Rechts der Gegenwart*, Vol. 4 (1910), pp. 374–409.

Pache, Alfred, *Geschichte des sächsischen Landtagswahlrechts von 1831–1907* (Leipzig, 1919).

Pachnicke, H., *Führende Männer im alten und neuen Reich* (Berlin, [1930]).

Parisius, Ludolf. *Deutschlands politische Parteien und das Ministerium Bismarck* (Berlin, 1878).

Die Partei der Zukunft, von einem Deutschen (Leipzig, 1914).

Perthes, Otto, *Die deutsch-konservative Partei und das höhere Schulwesen. Eine Bitte an den Vorstand der deutsch-konservativen Partei* (Bielefeld, 1892).

Pestalozzi, J., *Herr Hofprediger Stöcker und die christlich-soziale Arbeiterpartei* (Halle, 1885).

Petersdorff, Hermann von, 'Ein Programm Bismarcks zur Gründung einer konservativen Zeitung', *Forschungen zur Brandenburgischen und Preußischen Geschichte*, vol. 17 (1904), pp. 240–6.

Petersdorff, Hermann von, *Kleist-Retzow. Ein Lebensbild* (Berlin, 1907).

Pfister, Otto von, *Deutsch-Konservativ* (Berlin, 1913).

Pfister, Otto von, *Ein monarchisches oder parlamentarisches Deutschland?* (Berlin, 1914).

Philipps, Wilhelm, 'Konservativ und christlich-soziale', *Die Reformation*, vol. 9 (1910), pp. 810–12.

Pittius, Erich, 'Die politische Tagespresse Schlesiens', PhD thesis, Sorau N.-L., 1914.

Pommer, Otto, *Die Konservativen* (Berlin-Schöneberg, 1912).

Poschinger, Dr H. Ritter von, *Fürst Bismarck und die Parlamentarier*, 3 vols. (Breslau, 1894–6).

Preisliste der durch das Kaiserliche Postamt in Berlin und die Kaiserlichen Postanstaltungen des Reichs-Postgebiets im Jahre 1912 zu beziehenden Zeitungen, Zeitschriften u.s.w. (Berlin, 1912).

Das preußische Abgeordnetenhaus, eds. J. Kürschner *et al.* (Stuttgart, 1888–   ).

'Die preußischen Landtagswahlen des Jahres 1903/1908/1913 und frühere Jahre', by G. Evert, H. Höpker *et al.*, in *Zeitschrift des Königlich Preussischen Statistischen Bureaus/Landesamtes (Ergänzungshefte)* (Berlin, 1903–   ).

Der Prozess Ahlwardt. Ein Zeichen der Zeit und eine lehrreiche Studie, von einem Deutsch-Nationalen (Berlin, n.d.)

Die Publicistik der Gegenwart, Hefte 1–6, *Die Presseverhältnisse in Hessen/Baden/*

Württemberg / Schweiz / Bayern / Oesterreich-Ungarn / Preußen (Würzburg / Vienna, 1879–81).

Reck, Wilhelm Friedrich Freiherr von der, *Laien-Gedanken über den Culturkampf* (Lübbecke, 1879).

'Die Reichstagswahlen von 1912', in *Statistik des Deutschen Reichs*, Vol. 250, Hefte 1–3 (Berlin, 1912–13).

Reichsverband gegen die Sozialdemokratie, *Handbuch für nichtsozial-demokratische Wähler*, 3rd edn (Berlin, 1911).

Reuß, Eleonore Fürstin, *Philipp von Nathusius. Das Leben und Wirken des Volksblattschreibers* (Neinstedt a.H., 1900).

Reventlow, Ernst Graf von, *Die Reichsfinanzreform eine nationale Frage* (Leipzig, 1908).

Richter, Eugen, *Gegen die Konservativen* (Berlin, 1898).

Richter, Otto, *Geschichte der Stadt Dresden in den Jahren 1871 bis 1902*, 2nd edn (Dresden, 1904).

Richthofen, Elisabeth von, 'Über die historischen Wandlungen in der Stellung der autoritären Parteien zur Arbeiterschutzgesetzgebung und die Motive dieser Wandlungen', PhD thesis, Ruprecht-Karl University, Heidelberg, 1901.

Riezler, Kurt, *Tagebücher, Aufsätze, Dokumente*, ed. K. Erdmann (Göttingen, 1972).

Ritter, Gerhard A., with Niehuss, M., *Wahlgeschichtliches Arbeitsbuch. Materialen zur Statistik des Kaiserreichs 1871–1918* (Munich, 1980).

Robert, Elmer, *Monarchical Socialism in Germany* (New York, 1913).

Röder, Adam, *Der Austritt Stöckers aus der konservativen Partei* (Karlsruhe, 1896).

Röder, Adam, *Reisebilder aus Amerika* (Berlin, 1906).

Röder, Adam, *Kulturkonservatismus* (Stuttgart, 1911).

Röder, Adam, *Konservative Zukunftspolitik. Ein Mahnwort an die Konservativen Deutschlands* (Karlsruhe, 1918).

Röder, Adam, *Der deutsche Konservatismus und die Revolution* (Gotha, 1920).

Rohmer, Friedrich, *Lehre von den politischen Parteien*, ed. H. Schultheß (Nördlingen, 1885).

Roon, Albrecht Graf von, *Denkwürdigkeiten aus dem Leben des Generalfeldmarschalls Kriegsminister Graf von Roon*, 2 vols. (Breslau, 1892).

Rosenmund, Dr Richard, *Die Kaiserliche Erlasse, die Parteien und die Reichstagswahl* (Berlin, 1890).

Rossi, Walter, 'Die Entwicklung der ländlichen Polizeiverwaltung in den östlichen preußischen Provinzen', PhD thesis, University of Rostock, 1916.

Roth, Paul, *Die Programme der politischen Parteien und die politische Tagespresse in Deutschland* (Halle, 1913).

Ruhland, Gustav, *Grundsätze einer vernunftgemässen Getreidepreispolitik* (Berlin, 1896).

Ruhland, Gustav, *Zur Aufhebung der Blanko-Termingeschäfte in Getreide* (Berlin, 1896).

Ruhland, Gustav, *Zur Ausführung des ... Börsengesetzes vom 22. Juni 1896* (Berlin, 1896).

Sächsischer Landtags-Almanach vom Jahre 1887 (Elberfeld, [1887]).

Salomon, Felix (ed.), *Die Deutschen Parteiprogramme*, 2 Hefte, 2nd edn (Leipzig, 1912).

Schacht, H., 'Statistische Untersuchungen über die Presse Deutschlands', *Jahrbücher für Nationalökonomie und Statistik*, Vol. 70 (1898), pp. 503–25.

Schiele, Georg, *Die Erneuerung des preußischen Wahlrechts* (Berlin, 1917).

Schmidt, Dr R., and Grabowsky, Dr A. (eds.), *Die Parteien. Urkunden und Bibliographie der Parteienkunde*, Vol. 1 (Berlin, 1912).

Schmidt, Fr. W., 'Karl August Mühlhäußer', *Badische Biographieen*, Vol. 3 (Karlsruhe, 1881), pp. 109–14.

Schmidt, Wilhelm, *Wohin steuern wir? Ein politisches Stimmungsbild vor den badischen Landtagswahlen 1909* (Karlsruhe, [1908]).

Schmidt, Wilhelm, *'Großlock' oder 'bürgerlicher Block'? Ein politischer Wegweiser für alle rechts-stehenden Wähler in Baden* (Heidelberg, [1911]).

Schneidewin, Max, 'Briefe des Reichskanzlers v. Caprivi', *Deutsche Revue*, vol. 47/2 (1922), pp. 136–47, 247–58.

Schöller, Leopold, *Ueber die Staffeltarife* (Breslau, 1894).

Schön, Max, *Die Geschichte der Berliner Bewegung* (Leipzig, 1889).

Schubert, Ernst, *Die evangelische Predigt im Revolutionsjahr 1848* (Gießen, 1913).

Schücking, Lothar, *Die Reaktion in der inneren Verwaltung Preußens* (Berlin, 1908).

Schücking, Lothar, *Die Mißregierung der Konservativen unter Wilhelm II.* (Munich, 1909).

Schulte, F. von, 'Adel im deutschen Offizier- und Beamtenstand. Eine soziale Betrachtung', *Deutsche Revue*, vol. 21 (1896), pp. 181–92.

Schultheß' Europäischer Geschichtskalender (Munich, 1876–   ).

Schultz, Albert, *Wie hilft der Sozialdemokrat, wie der Landwirt, dem ländlichen Tagelöhner?* (Leipzig, 1895).

Schultz, Fritz, 'Die politische Tagespresse Westpreußens', PhD thesis, Ruprecht-Karl University, Heidelberg, 1913.

Schwarz, Max, *MdR. Biographisches Handbuch der Reichstage* (Hanover, 1965).

Schwerin-Löwitz, Dr Hans Graf von, *Aufsätze und Reden. Aus Anlaß seiner 10-jährigen Präsidentschaft* (Berlin, 1911).

Die socialdemokratische Presse, Zeitfragen des Vaterlands-Vereins, Heft 1 (Berlin, 1896).

Specht, Fritz, and Schwabe, Paul, *Die Reichstagswahlen, 1867–1907*, 3rd edn (Berlin, 1908).

Sperlings Zeitschriften- und Zeitungs-Addressbuch, ed. H. O. Sperling, Vols. 32, 36, 47, (Stuttgart, 1891, 1895, 1912).

Spitzemberg, Hildegard von, *Das Tagebuch der H. Baronin von Spitzemberg*, ed. R. Vierhaus (Göttingen, 1963).

Staats-, Hof- und Kommunal-Handbuch des Reichs und der Einzelstaaten, ed. J. Kürschner (Berlin, 1888–   ).

Statistik des Deutschen Reichs (with *Monats-* and *Vierteljahreshefte*) (Berlin, 1874–   ).

Stenographische Berichte über die Verhandlungen des Preußischen Abgeordneten-hauses (Berlin, 1871–   ).

Stenographische Berichte über die Verhandlungen des Preußischen Herrenhauses (Berlin, 1876–   ).

Stenographische Berichte über die Verhandlungen des Reichtages (Berlin, 1871–   ).

Stenographischer Bericht über die Verhandlungen des Ersten Preußen-Tages am 18. Januar 1914 zu Berlin im Hause der Abgeordneten (Hanover, 1914).

Stephan, F., *Die 25jährige Tätigkeit der Vereinigung der Steuer- und Wirtschafts-reformer (1876 bis 1900)* (Berlin, 1900).

Stillich, Oskar, *Die politischen Parteien in Deutschland*, Vol. 1, *Die Konservativen* (Leipzig, 1908).

Stöcker, Adolf, *Die Bewegungen der Gegenwart im Lichte der christlichen Weltanschauung* (Heidelberg, 1881).

Stöcker, Adolf, *Christlich-Sozial. Reden und Aufsätze*, 2nd edn (Berlin, 1890).

Stöcker, Adolf, *Sozialdemokratie und Sozialmonarchie* (Leipzig, 1891).

Stöcker, Adolf, *Dreizehn Jahre Hofprediger und Politiker* (Berlin, 1895).

Stöcker, Adolf, 'Warum ich als Pfarrer Politik treibe?', in Ludwig Weber (ed.), *Deutsch-Evangelisches Jahrbuch für 1899* (Berlin, 1899), pp. 113–34.

Stöcker, Adolf, *Reden und Aufsätze von Adolf Stöcker*, ed. R. Seeberg (Leipzig, 1913).

Stöcker, Adolf, *Reden im Reichstag. Amtlicher Wortlaut*, ed. R. Mumm (Schwerin, 1914).

Stratz, Rudolph, *Schwert und Feder. Erinnerungen aus jungen Jahren* (Berlin, 1925).

Thiel, Friedrich, *Die Fusion des Dt. Tageblatt mit der Kreuzzeitung* (Berlin, 1891).

Thimme, Friedrich (ed.), *Front wider Bülow. Staatsmänner, Diplomaten und Forscher zu seinen Denkwürdigkeiten* (Munich, 1931).

Thüngen-Roßbach, Karl Freiherr von, *Thüngen contra Caprivi. Verteidigungsschrift*, 6th edn (Würzburg, 1894).

Tönnies, Ferdinand, *Community and Society*, ed. C. Loomis (East Lansing, MI, 1957).

Treue, Wolfgang (ed.), *Deutsche Parteiprogramme, 1861–1956*, 4th edn (Göttingen, 1968).

U., H. R. von, *Das Recht auf Arbeit. Eine Wahlflugschrift* (Leipzig, 1884).

Uechtritz, Oldwig von, *Der Adel in der Christlich-Soziale Bewegung der Gegenwart*, Zeitfragen des Christlichen Volkslebens, Vol. 9, Heft 7 (Frankfurt a.M., n.d.)

Umsturz und Sozialdemokratie. Verhandlungen des Deutschen Reichstags am 17. Dezember 1894 und 8.–12. Januar 1895 (Berlin, 1895).

Valentin, Conrad, *Der Kaiser hat gesprochen. Wie haben wir Conservativen uns jetzt zu verhalten?* (Berlin, 1889).

Vater, Otto, *Zur Organisation der konservativen Partei in Preußen* (Hirschberg, 1887).

Vorster, Julius, *Der Socialismus der Gebildeten Stände* (Cologne, 1894).

Wacker, Theodor, *Warum sollen Zentrumswähler Konservative Landtagskandidaturen unterstützen? Was soll dabei vermieden werden?* (Karlsruhe, 1909).

[Wagener, Hermann], *Grundzüge conservativer Politik. In Briefen conservativer Freunde über conservative Partei und Politik in Preußen* (Berlin, 1868).

[Wagener, Hermann], *Ein sozialpolitisches Programm*. Separat-Abdruck aus der *Deutschen Landes-Zeitung* (n.p., n.d.)

Wagener, Hermann, *Erlebtes. Meine Memorien aus der Zeit von 1848 bis 1866 und von 1873 bis jetzt* (Berlin, 1884).

Wagener, Hermann, *Die kleine aber mächtige Partei* (Berlin, 1885).

Wagener, Hermann, *Die Mängel der Christlich-sozialen Bewegung* (Minden, 1885).

Wagener, Hermann (ed.), *Aus Rodbertus' Nachlaß* (Minden, 1886).

Wagner, Hans, 'Der Zusammenbruch der konservativen Kolonialpolitik', *Koloniale Zeitschrift*, vol. 22 (1902), pp. 407–9.

Die Wahl im Ostpreußischen Landwirtschaftlichen Centralverein zu Königsberg am 18. Dezember 1883 und die Conservativen Ostpreußens (Königsberg, 1884).

Wahlbeeinflussungen (Elbing-Marienburg) und Hetze der Kartellparteien gegen die Krone (Berlin, 1888).

Waldersee, Alfred Graf von, *Denkwürdigkeiten des Generalfeldmarschalls Alfred Grafen von Waldersee*, 3 vols., ed. H. O. Meisner (Stuttgart, 1922–3).

Waldersee, Alfred Graf von, *Aus dem Briefwechsel des Generalfeldmarschalls Alfred von Waldersee*, ed. H. O. Meisner (Stuttgart, 1928).

Wangenheim-Klein-Spiegel, Conrad Freiherr von, 'Bund der Landwirte', in *Handbuch der Politik* (1912–13), Vol. 2, pp. 58–61.

Weber, Ludwig, *Praktische Anweisungen zur Begründung und Leitung Evangelischer Arbeitervereine* (Leipzig, 1890).

Weber, Ludwig, 'Christlich-Soziale', in *Handbuch der Politik* (1912–13), Vol. 2, pp. 11–14.

Weber, Max, *From Max Weber: Essays in Sociology*, eds. H. H. Gerth and C. Wright Mills (New York, 1965).

Weber, Max, *Gesammelte Politische Schriften*, 3rd edn (Tübingen, 1971).

Weber, Max, 'Beamtenherrschaft und politisches Führertum', in Weber, *Gesammelte Politische Schriften* (1971), pp. 320–50.

Weber, Max, 'Der Nationalstaat und die Volkswirtschaftspolitik', in Weber, *Gesammelte Politische Schriften* (1971), pp. 1–25.

Wegener, Dr Friedrich, *Die deutschkonservative Partei und ihre Aufgaben für die Gegenwart* (Berlin, 1908).

Welcker, Viktor Hugo, *Die nationalen und sozialen Aufgaben des Antisemitismus* (Ulm, [1892]).

Wen wählen wir? Ein Mahnwort an die ländliche Bevölkerung (Berlin, 1898).

Wer ist's? Wer ist wer?, ed. H. Degener (Leipzig, 1905–   ).

Werner, Julius, *Sozialrevolution oder Sozialreform?*, 2nd edn (Halle a.S., 1891).

Werner, Julius, *Soziales Christentum. Vorträge und Aufsätze über die grossen Fragen der Gegenwart*, 2nd edn (Dessau, 1897).

Werner, Julius, *Die Geschichte und der gegenwärtige Stand der Frauenbewegung* (Berlin, 1899).

Werner, Julius, *Der deutsche Protestantismus und das öffentlichen Leben* (Hagen i.W., [1906]).

Werner, Julius, 'Die kulturpolitische Notwendigkeit des Konservatismus für Staat und Gesellschaft', *Deutschvölkischen Hochschulblättern*, Heft 1, Sonderabdruck, 1914.

Werner, Julius, *Was ist konservativ?* Konservative Flugschriften, No. 2, 3rd edn (Berlin, [1917]).

Westarp, Kuno Graf von, *Die Wehr- und Deckungsvorlagen des Jahres 1913 und die konservative Partei*, (Berlin, 1913).

Westarp, Kuno Graf von, *Rede . . . in der öffentlichen Versammlung des Konservativen Vereins zu Leipzig am 28. Februar 1914* (n.p., n.d.)

Westarp, Kuno Graf von, *Deutschlands Zukunft. Vortrag . . . gehalten am 11. November 1916 im Industrie-Club, Düsseldorf* (Düsseldorf, [1916]).

Westarp, Kuno Graf von, 'Preußens Verwaltung und Verfassung als Grundlage seiner Führerstellung im Reiche', in *Preußen. Deutschlands Vergangenheit und Deutschlands Zukunft. Vier Vorträge*, 2nd edn (Berlin, 1916).

Westarp, Kuno Graf von, *Zwei Gedenktage in schwerer Zeit* (Berlin, 1916).

Westarp, Kuno Graf von, *Die Regierung des Prinzen Max von Baden und die konservative Partei* 2nd edn (Berlin, [1928]).

Westarp, Kuno Graf von, 'Die Konservative Partei und das Ende des Bülowblocks', *Süddeutsche Monatshefte*, vol. 28/6 (March 1931), pp. 411–34.

Westarp, Kuno Graf von, *Am Grabe der Parteiherrschaft. Bilanz des deutschen Parlamentarismus von 1918–1932* (Berlin, 1932).

Westarp, Kuno Graf von, *Konservative Politik im letzten Jahrzehnt des Kaiserreiches*, 2 vols. (Berlin, 1935).

Westarp, Kuno Graf von, *Das Ende der Monarchie am 9. November 1918*, ed. W. Conze (Berlin, 1952).

Wie steht die Nationalliberale Partei zur Reichsfinanzreform? (Berlin, 1909).

Wiechel, Hugo, *Berufsklassen-Wahlkreise. Vorschläge zur Umgestaltung des*

Sächsischen Landtagswahlrechtes und zur Neuabgrenzung des Reichstagswahl-kreise (Dresden-Neustadt, 1903).

Wildgrube, Max, *Der Konservatismus im Kampfe für das föderative Prinzip. Vortrag gehalten am 8. Dezember 1913 in Dresden* (Dresden, [1913]).

Wilhelm II. und die Revolution von Oben (Zurich, 1896).

Wilmowsky, Tilo Freiherr von, *Rückblickend möchte ich sagen . . .* (Oldenburg, 1961).

Winterfeldt-Menkin, Joachim von, *Jahreszeiten des Lebens* (Berlin, 1942).

Wippermann, Karl (ed.), *Deutscher Geschichtskalender* (Leipzig, 1890–   ).

Witte, Hermann, 'Bismarck und die Konservativen. Briefen aus Trieglaff', *Deutsche Rundschau*, vol. 149 (1911), pp. 372–87.

Wittenberg, Hans, *Was bietet die Sozialdemokratie dem Landarbeiter?* (Leipzig, n.d.)

Wittwer, Max, 'Das deutsche Zeitungswesen in seiner neueren Entwicklung', PhD thesis, Friedrich University, Halle-Wittenberg, 1914.

Wolff, Theodor, *Tagebücher 1914–1919*, 2 vols., ed. B. Sösemann (Boppard a.R., 1984).

Wolfstieg, August, 'Die Anfänge der freikonservativen Partei', in E. Daniels *et al.* (eds.), *Hans Delbrück Festschrift. Gesammelte Aufsätze* (Berlin, 1908), pp. 313–36.

Wolfstieg, August, and Meitzel, Dr K., *Bibliographie der Schriften über beide Häuser des Landtages in Preußen* (Berlin, 1915).

Worte und Taten der Konservativen. Material zur Bekämpfung der konservativen Parteien, ed. Parteivorstand der Deutschen Sozialdemokratie (Berlin, 1911).

Der Württembergische Landtag 1912–1917 (Stuttgart, 1913).

Zedlitz-Trützschler, Count Robert, *Twelve Years at the Imperial German Court* (London, 1924).

Zeitschrift des Königlich Preussischen Statistischen Bureaus/Landesamts (with *Ergänzungshefte*), vol. 34–   (Berlin, 1894–   ).

Zeitschrift des Königlich Sächsischen Statistischen Bureaus/Landesamts, vol. 49– (Dresden, 1903–   ).

Zeitungs-Katalog, Verlag von Rudolf Mosse, vols. 19 and 28 (Berlin, 1883–4, 1895).

Zeitungs-Katalog für das Jahre 1913, Daube & Co. (Berlin, 1913).

Der Zerfall der konservativen Partei im Kampfe Preußens gegen Deutschland (Zurich, 1898).

Zwanzig Jahre alldeutscher Arbeit und Kämpfe, ed. Hauptleitung des Alldeut-schen Verbandes (Leipzig, 1910).

SECONDARY LITERATURE

The following provides a selection of works directly relevant to the history of German Conservatism from 1800 to 1945. English translations are included where possible, except in some cases where the original German was cited in the text.

Aandahl, Friedrich, 'The Rise of German Free Conservatism', PhD thesis, Princeton University, 1955.

Albers, Detlef, *Reichstag und Außenpolitik von 1871–1879* (Berlin, 1927).

Albertin, Lothar, and Link, Werner (eds.), *Politische Parteien auf dem Weg zur parlamentarischen Demokratie in Deutschland* (Düsseldorf, 1981).

Allen, David, 'From Romanticism to *Realpolitik*: Studies in Nineteenth-Century German Conservatism', PhD thesis, Columbia University, 1971.

Anderson, Margaret, *Windhorst. A Political Biography* (Oxford, 1981).

Anderson, Margaret, and Barkin, Kenneth, 'The Myth of the Puttkamer Purge and the Reality of the Kulturkampf: Some Reflections on the Historiography of Imperial Germany', *Journal of Modern History*, vol. 54 (1982), pp. 647–86.

Anderson, Pauline R., *The Background of Anti-English Feeling in Germany, 1890–1902* (New York, 1969).

Angel-Volkov, Shulamit, 'Popular Anti-Modernism: Ideology and Sentiment among Master-Artisans during the 1890s', *Jahrbuch des Instituts für Deutsche Geschichte* (Tel Aviv), vol. 3 (1974), pp. 203–25.

Apitzsch, Friedrich, *Die deutsche Tagespresse unter dem Einfluß des Sozialistengesetzes* (Leipzig, 1928).

Bacheller, Charles R., 'Class and Conservatism: The Changing Social Structure of the German Right, 1900–1928', PhD thesis, University of Wisconsin-Madison, 1976.

Bade, Klaus, 'Massenwanderung und Arbeitsmarkt im deutschen Nordosten von 1880 bis zum Ersten Weltkrieg', *Archiv für Sozialgeschichte*, vol. 20 (1980), pp. 265–323.

Bade, Klaus, 'Politik und Ökonomie der Ausländerbeschäftigung im preußischen Osten 1885–1914', in Puhle and Wehler (eds.), *Preußen im Rückblick* (1980), pp. 273–99.

Bade, Klaus, '"Kulturkampf" auf dem Arbeitsmarkt: Bismarcks "Polenpolitik" 1885–1890', in Pflanze (ed.), *Innenpolitische Probleme* (1983), pp. 121–42.

Barkin, Kenneth, *The Controversy over German Industrialization 1890–1902* (Chicago, 1970).

Barkin, Kenneth, 'Conflict and Concord in Wilhelmian Social Thought', *Central European History*, vol. 5/1 (1972), pp. 55–71.

Barth (née Haberland), Brigitte, 'Die Innenpolitik des Reiches unter der Kanzlerschaft Bethmann Hollwegs 1909–1914', PhD thesis, Christian-Albrecht University, Kiel, 1950.

Behnen, Michael, *Das Preußische Wochenblatt (1851–1861)* (Göttingen, 1971).

Beidler, F. W., 'Der Kampf um den Zolltarif im Reichstag 1902', PhD thesis, University of Berlin, 1929.

Berdahl, Robert, 'The Transformation of the Prussian Conservative Party, 1866–1876', PhD thesis, University of Minnesota, 1965.

Berdahl, Robert, 'Conservative Politics and Aristocratic Landowners in Bismarckian Germany', *Journal of Modern History*, vol. 44/1 (1972), pp. 1–20.

Berdahl, Robert, 'Preußischer Adel: Paternalismus als Herrschaftssystem', in Puhle and Wehler (eds.), *Preußen im Rückblick* (1980), pp. 123–45.

Berghahn, Volker R., *Germany and the Approach of War in 1914* (London, 1973).

Bergmann, Klaus, *Agrarromantik und Großstadtfeindlichkeit* (Meisenheim, 1970).

Bertram, J., *Die Wahlen zum Deutschen Reichstag vom Jahre 1912* (Düsseldorf, 1964).

Bialke, Waltraud, 'Die Kanalvorlage des Jahres 1899 und die konservative Partei Preußens', PhD thesis, University of Berlin, 1944.

Blackbourn, David, 'The *Mittelstand* in German Society and Politics, 1871–1914', *Social History*, vol. 4 (1977), pp. 409–33.

Blackbourn, David, *Class, Religion and Local Politics in Wilhelmine Germany. The Centre Party in Württemberg before 1914* (New Haven, Conn., 1980).

Blackbourn, David, 'Roman Catholics, the Centre Party and Anti-Semitism in Imperial Germany', in Kennedy and Nicholls (eds.), *Nationalist and Racialist Movements* (1981), pp. 106–29.

Blackbourn, David, 'Peasants and Politics in Germany, 1871–1914', *European History Quarterly*, vol. 14 (1984), pp. 47–75.

Blackbourn, David, 'The Politics of Demagogy in Imperial Germany', *Past and Present*, no. 113 (1986), pp. 152–84.

Blackbourn, David, and Eley, Geoff, *The Peculiarities of German History. Bourgeois Society and Politics in Nineteenth-Century Germany* (Oxford, 1984).

Blasius, Dirk, 'Konservative Sozialpolitik und Sozialreform im 19. Jahrhundert', in Kaltenbrunner (ed.), *Rekonstruktion des Konservatismus* (1972), pp. 469–88.

Blasius, Dirk (ed.), *Preußen in der deutschen Geschichte* (Königstein/Ts., 1980).

Bleyberg, Derek M., 'Government and Legislative Process in Wilhelmine Germany: The Reorganisation of the Tariff Laws under Reich Chancellor von Bülow, 1897–1902', PhD thesis, University of East Anglia, 1980.

Bock, Eberhard, 'Die Konservativen in der Provinz Sachsen und die soziale Frage in den Jahren 1848 bis 1870', PhD thesis, Friedrich University, Halle-Wittenberg, 1932.

Böhme, Helmut, *Deutschlands Weg zur Großmacht. Studien zum Verhältnis von Wirtschaft und Staat während der Reichsgründungszeit 1848–1881* (Cologne, 1966).

Bonham, Gary, 'Bureaucratic Modernizers and Traditional Constraints: Higher Officials and the Landed Nobility in Wilhelmine Germany, 1890–1914', PhD thesis, University of California–Berkeley, 1986.

Boog, Horst, 'Graf Ernst zu Reventlow (1869–1943). Eine Studie zur Krise der deutschen Geschichte seit dem Ende des 19. Jahrhunderts', PhD thesis, Ruprecht-Karl University, Heidelberg, 1965.

Booms, Hans, *Die Deutschkonservative Partei. Preußischer Charakter, Reichsauffassung, Nationalbegriff* (Düsseldorf, 1954).

Borell, Adolf, 'Die soziologische Gliederung des Reichsparlaments als Spiegelung der politischen und ökonomischen Konstellationen', PhD thesis, Hessische Ludwig University, Gießen, 1933.

Bottomore, T. B., *Elites and Society* (Harmondsworth, 1964).

Bowen, Ralph, *German Theories of the Corporative State* (New York, 1947).

Bowman, Shearer Davis, 'Antebellum Planters and *Vormärz* Junkers in Comparative Perspective', *American Historical Review*, vol. 85/4 (1980), pp. 779–808.

Brakelmann, Günter, 'Adolf Stoecker und die Sozialdemokratie', in Brakelmann, Greschat und Jochmann, *Protestantismus* (1982), pp. 84–122.

Brakelmann, Günter, Greschat, Martin, and Jochmann, Werner, *Protestantismus und Politik: Werk und Wirkung Adolf Stoeckers* (Hamburg, 1982).

Bramsted, E. K., *Aristocracy and the Middle Classes in Germany. Social Types in German Literature 1830–1900* (Chicago, 1964).

Brose, Eric, *Christian Labor and the Politics of Frustration in Imperial Germany* (Washington, DC, 1985).

Broszat, Martin, 'Die antisemitische Bewegung im Wilhelminischen Deutschland', PhD thesis, University of Cologne, 1952.

Bruckmüller, Ernst, 'Bäuerlicher Konservatismus in Oberösterreich', *Zeitschrift für bayerische Landesgeschichte*, vol. 37/1 (1974), pp. 121–43.

Buchheim, Karl, 'Die Partei Gerlach-Stahl', in Alfred Herrmann (ed.), *Aus Geschichte und Politik, Festschrift zum 70. Geburtstag von Ludwig Bergstrasser* (Düsseldorf, 1954), pp. 41–56.

Burkhardt, Hans, 'Die politische Tagespresse des Königreiches Sachsen', PhD thesis, Freiberg in Sachsen, 1914.

Busch, Helmut, *Die Stöckerbewegung im Siegerland. Ein Beitrag zur Siegerländer Geschichte in der zweiten Hälfte des 19. Jahrhunderts* (Siegen, 1968).

Büsch, Otto, Wölk, Monica, and Wölk, Wolfgang (eds.), *Wählerbewegung in der deutschen Geschichte 1871–1933* (Berlin, 1978).

Buttlar, Madelaine von, *Die politischen Vorstellungen des F.A.L. v.d. Marwitz. Ein Beitrag zur Genesis und Gestalt konservativen Denkens in Preußen* (Frankfurt a.M., 1980).

Canis, Konrad, 'Der Wandel in der Funktion konservativer Organisationen 1848–1866', *Wissenschaftliche Zeitschrift der Friedrich-Schiller-Universität Jena*, Gesellschaft- und Sprachwissenschaftliche Reihe, vol. 14 (1965), pp. 223–4.

Canis, Konrad, *Bismarck und Waldersee* (Berlin, 1980).

Canis, Konrad, 'Verein für König und Vaterland 1848/49', in Fricke *et al.* (eds.), *Lexikon* (1983–6), Vol. 4, pp. 298–303.

Canis, Konrad, 'Verein zur Wahrung der Interessen des Grundbesitzes und Förderung des Wohlstandes aller Volksklassen 1848–1852', in Fricke *et al.* (eds.), *Lexikon* (1983–6), Vol. 4, pp. 403–7.

Cecil, Lamar, 'The Creation of Nobles in Prussia, 1871–1918', *American Historical Review*, vol. 75 (1970), pp. 757–95.

Černý, Jochen, and Fahlbusch, Lutz, 'Reichs-Landbund 1921–1933', in Fricke *et al.* (eds.), *Lexicon* (1883–6), Vol. 3, pp. 688–712.

Chickering, Roger, *We Men Who Feel Most German. A Cultural Study of the Pan-German League, 1886–1914* (Boston, 1984).

Coetzee, Frans, and Coetzee, Marilyn Shevin, 'Rethinking the Radical Right in Germany and Britain before 1914', *Journal of Contemporary History*, vol. 21 (1986), pp. 515–37.

Coetzee, Marilyn Shevin, 'The Mobilization of the Right? The Deutscher Wehrverein and Political Activism in Württemberg, 1912–14', *European History Quarterly*, vol. 15 (1985), pp. 431–52.

Cole, Terry F., 'The *Daily Telegraph* affair and its aftermath: the Kaiser, Bülow and the Reichstag, 1908–1909', in Röhl and Sombart (eds.), *Wilhelm II* (1982), pp. 249–68.

Craig, Gordon A., *Germany 1866–1945* (Oxford, 1981).

Crothers, George D., *The German Elections of 1907* (New York, 1968).

Dahrendorf, Ralf, *Society and Democracy in Germany* (New York, 1967).

Daun, Johannes, 'Die Innenpolitik der *Kölnischen Zeitung* in der Wilhelminischen Epoche 1890 bis 1914', PhD thesis, University of Cologne, 1964.

David, Erwin, 'Der Bund der Landwirte als Machtinstrument des ostelbischen Junkertums 1893–1920', PhD thesis, University of Halle-Wittenberg, 1967.

Deuerlein, Ernst (ed.), *Der Reichstag. Aufsätze, Protokolle und Darstellungen* (Bonn, 1963).

Dierks, Margarete, *Die preußischen Altkonservativen und die Judenfrage 1810/1847* (Rostock, 1939).

Dissow, Joachim von, *Adel im Uebergang. Ein kritischer Standesgenosse berichtet aus Residenzen und Gutshäusern* (Stuttgart, 1961).

Dittmar, Gerhardt, 'Zur Theorie und Praxis der Socialdemokratischen Landagitation unter den deutschen Kleinbauern in den 90er Jahren des 19. Jahrhunderts', PhD thesis, University of Rostock, 1964.

Diwald, Hellmut (ed.), *Von der Revolution zum Norddeutschen Bund. Politik und Ideengut der preußischen Hochkonservativen 1848–1866. Aus dem Nachlaß von Ernst Ludwig von Gerlach*, 2 parts (Göttingen, 1970).

Dorpalen, Andreas, 'The German Conservatives and the Parliamentarization of Imperial Germany', *Journal of Central European Affairs*, vol. 10 (1951), pp. 184–99.

Dreher, Ernst, 'Anfänge der Bildung politischer Parteien in Baden', PhD thesis, Albert-Ludwig University, Freiburg i.B., 1952.

Droz, Jacques, 'Préoccupations sociales et préoccupations religieuses aux origines du parti conservateur prussien', *Revue d'Histoire Moderne et Contemporaine*, vol. 2 (1955), pp. 280–300.

Dürr, Volker, Harms, Kathy and Hayes, Peter (eds.), *Imperial Germany* (Madison, Wis., 1985).

Duverger, Maurice, *Political Parties. Their Organization and Activity in the Modern State* (London, 1959).

Eckert, Hans-Gustav, 'Die Wandlungen der Konservativen Partei durch Bismarcks Innenpolitik. Ein Beitrag zur Geschichte der Konservativen Partei 1876–1890', PhD thesis, Christian-Albrecht University, Kiel, 1953.

Ehrenfeuchter, Bernhard, 'Politische Willensbildung in Niedersachsen zur Zeit des Kaiserreiches. Ein Versuch auf Grund der Reichstagswahlen von 1867 bis 1912, insbesondere seit 1890', PhD thesis, University of Göttingen, 1951.

Eley, Geoff, 'Sammlungspolitik, Social Imperialism and the Navy Law of 1898', *Militärgeschichtliche Mitteilungen*, vol. 15 (1974), pp. 29–63.

Eley, Geoff, 'Defining Social Imperialism: Use and Abuse of an Idea', *Social History*, vol. 1/3 (1976), pp. 265–90.

Eley, Geoff, 'Reshaping the Right: Radical Nationalism and the German Navy League, 1898–1908', *Historical Journal*, vol. 21/2 (1978), pp. 327–54.

Eley, Geoff, 'The Wilhelmine Right: How It Changed', in Evans (ed.), *Society and Politics* (1978), pp. 112–35.

Eley, Geoff, 'Recent Work in Modern German History' (review), *Historical Journal*, vol. 23/2 (1980), pp. 463–79.

Eley, Geoff, *Reshaping the German Right. Radical Nationalism and Political Change after Bismarck* (New Haven, Conn., 1980).

Eley, Geoff, 'Some Thoughts on the Nationalist Pressure Groups in Imperial Germany', in Kennedy and Nicholls (eds.), *Nationalist and Racialist Movements* (1981), pp. 40–67.

Eley, Geoff, 'What Produces Fascism: Preindustrial Traditions or a Crisis of a Capitalist State', *Politics and Society*, vol. 12 (1983), pp. 53–82.

Eley, Geoff, 'Army, State and Civil Society: Revisiting the Problem of German Militarism', in Eley, *From Unification* (1986), pp. 85–109.

Eley, Geoff, *From Unification to Nazism. Reinterpreting the German Past* (Winchester, Mass., 1986).

Eley, Geoff, 'Social Imperialism in Germany. Reformist Synthesis or Reactionary Sleight of Hand', in Eley, *From Unification* (1986), pp. 154–67.

Eley, Geoff, 'Anti-Semitism, Agrarian Mobilization, and the Crisis in the Conservative Party: Radicalism and Containment in the Foundation of the Bund der Landwirte, 1892–1893' (draft), forthcoming in Fout (ed.), *Politics, Parties and the Authoritarian State*.

Engelberg, Ernst (ed.), *Im Widerstreit um die Reichsgründung. Eine Quellensammlung zur Klassenauseinandersetzung in der deutschen Geschichte von 1849 bis 1871* (Berlin, 1970).

Engelmann, Hans, 'Die Entwicklung des Antisemitismus im XIX. Jahrhundert und Adolf Stöckers "Antijudische Bewegung"', PhD thesis, Friedrich-Alexander University, Erlangen, 1953.

Epstein, Klaus, *The Genesis of German Conservatism* (Princeton, 1966).

Etue, George Edward, Jr, 'The German Fatherland Party, 1917–1918', PhD thesis, University of California–Berkeley, 1959.

Evans, Richard (ed.), *Society and Politics in Wilhelmine Germany* (London, 1978).

Evans, Richard, and Lee, W. R. (eds.), *The German Peasantry. Conflict and Community in Rural Society from the Eighteenth to the Twentieth Centuries* (New York, 1986).

Everke, Karl Friedrich, *Zur Funktionsgeschichte der politischen Parteien* (Baden-Baden, 1974).

Farr, Ian, 'Populism in the Countryside: The Peasant League in Bavaria in the 1890s', in Evans (ed.), *Society and Politics* (1978), pp. 136–59.

Farr, Ian, 'Peasant Protest in the Empire – the Bavarian Example', in Moeller (ed.), *Peasants and Lords* (1986), pp. 110–39.

Farr, Ian, ' "Tradition" and the Peasantry: On the Modern Historiography of Rural Germany', in Evans and Lee (eds.), *German Peasantry* (1986), pp. 1–36.

Fehrenbach, Elisabeth, 'Bonapartismus und Konservatismus in Bismarcks Politik', *Francia*, Beiheft 6 (1977), pp. 39–55.

Femerling, Karl, 'Die Stellung der konservativen Partei zur gewerblichen Arbeiterfrage in der Zeit von 1848–1880', PhD thesis, University of Halle, [1927].

Fenske, Hans, *Konservatismus und Rechtsradikalismus in Bayern nach 1918* (Bad Homburg, 1969).

Fenske, Hans, 'Der Landrat als Wahlmacher. Eine Fallstudie zu den Reichstagswahlen von 1881', *Die Verwaltung*, 28, vol. 12/4 (1979), pp. 433–56.

Fischer, Fritz, 'Der Deutsche Protestantismus und die Politik im 19. Jahrhundert', *Historische Zeitschrift*, vol. 151 (1951), pp. 473–518.

Fischer, Fritz, *Germany's Aims in the First World War* (London, 1967).

Fischer, Fritz, *War of Illusions: German Politics from 1911 to 1914* (London, 1975).

Fischer, Fritz, *Bündnis der Eliten. Zur Kontinuität der Machtstrukturen in Deutschland 1871–1945* (Düsseldorf, 1979).

Fischer, Hubertus, 'Konservatismus von unten. Wahlen im ländlichen Preußen 1849/52 – Organisation, Agitation, Manipulation', in Stegmann, Wendt and Witt (eds.), *Deutscher Konservatismus* (1983), pp. 69–128.

Fischer-Frauendienst, Irene, *Bismarcks Pressepolitik* (Münster, 1963).

Flemming, Jens, 'Großagrarische Interessen und Landarbeiterbewegung. Überlegungen zur Arbeiterpolitik des Bundes der Landwirte und des Reichslandbundes in der Anfangsphase der Weimarer Republik', in H. Mommsen *et al.* (eds.), *Industrielles System und politische Entwicklung in der Weimarer Republik* (Düsseldorf, 1974), pp. 745–62.

Flemming, Jens, 'Landarbeiter zwischen Gewerkschaften und "Werkgemeinschaft". Zum Verhältnis von Agrarunternehmern und Landarbeiterbewegung im Übergang vom Kaiserreich zur Weimarer Republik', *Archiv für Sozialgeschichte*, vol. 14 (1974), pp. 351–418.

Flemming, Jens, *Landwirtschaftliche Interessen und Demokratie. Ländliche Gesellschaft, Agrarverbände und Staat 1890–1925* (Bonn, 1978).

Flemming, Jens, 'Die Bewaffnung des "Landvolks". Ländliche Schutzwehren und agrarischer Konservatismus in der Anfangsphase der Weimarer Republik', *Militärgeschichtliche Mitteilungen*, vol. 26/2 (1979), pp. 7–36.

Flemming, Jens, 'Obrigkeitstaat, Koalitionsrecht und Landarbeiterschaft. Zur Entwicklung des ländlichen Arbeitsrechts in Preußen zwischen Vormärz und Reichsgründung', in Puhle and Wehler (eds.), *Preußen im Rückblick* (1980), pp. 247–72.

Flemming, Jens, 'Konservatismus als "nationalrevolutionäre Bewegung". Konservative Kritik an der Deutschnationalen Volkspartei 1918–1933', in Stegmann, Wendt and Witt (eds.), *Deutscher Konservatismus* (1983), pp. 295–332.

Fout, John C., '"Protestant Christian Socialism in Germany 1848–1896. Wichern, Stöcker, Naumann: The Search for a New Social Ethic', PhD thesis, University of Minnesota, 1969.

Fout, John C. (ed.), *Politics, Parties and the Authoritarian State: Imperial Germany, 1871–1918*, 2 vols. (New York, forthcoming 1987).

Frank, Robert, *Der Brandenburger als Reichstagswähler*, Vol. 1, *1867/71 bis 1912/14* (Berlin, 1934).

Frank, Walter, *Hofprediger Adolf Stöcker und die christlichsoziale Bewegung*, 2nd edn (Hamburg, 1935).

Franz, Günther, *Die politischen Wahlen in Niedersachsen, 1867 bis 1949*, 3rd edn (Bremen, 1957).

Frey, Ludwig, 'Die Stellung der christlichen Gewerkschaften Deutschlands zu den politischen Parteien', PhD thesis, Julius-Maximilian University, Würzburg, 1931.

Fricke, Dieter, 'Der Reichsverband gegen die Sozialdemokratie von seiner Gründung bis zu den Reichstagswahlen von 1907', *Zeitschrift für Geschichtswissenschaft*, vol. 7 (1959), pp. 237–80.

Fricke, Dieter, *Bismarcks Prätorianer. Die Berliner politische Polizei im Kampf gegen die deutsche Arbeiterbewegung (1871–1898)* (Berlin, 1962).

Fricke, Dieter, 'Bund der Landwirte 1893–1920', in Fricke *et al.* (eds.), *Handbuch* (1968), Vol. 1, pp. 129–49.

Fricke, Dieter, 'Christlichsoziale Partei 1878–1918', in Fricke *et al.* (eds.), *Handbuch* (1968), Vol. 1, pp. 245–54.

Fricke, Dieter, 'Antisemitische Parteien 1879–1894', in Fricke *et al.* (eds.), *Lexikon* (1983–6), Vol. 1, pp. 77–88.

Fricke, Dieter, 'Christlichsoziale Partei 1878–1918', in Fricke *et al.* (eds.), *Lexikon* (1983–6), Vol. 1, pp. 440–54.

Fricke, Dieter, 'Gesamtverband evangelischer Arbeitervereine Deutschlands 1890–1933', in Fricke *et al.* (eds.), *Lexikon* (1983–6), Vol. 3, pp. 14–29.

Fricke, Dieter, 'Nationalsozialer Verein 1896–1903', in Fricke *et al.* (eds.), *Lexikon* (1983–6), Vol. 3, pp. 441–53.

Fricke, Dieter, 'Reichs- und freikonservative Partei 1867–1918', in Fricke *et al.* (eds.), *Lexikon* (1983–6), Vol. 3, pp. 745–72.

Fricke, Dieter, 'Reichsverband gegen die Sozialdemokratie 1904–1918', in Fricke *et al.* (eds.), *Lexikon* (1983–6), Vol. 4, pp. 63–77.

Fricke, Dieter, 'Sozialmonarchische Vereinigung 1890–1891', in Fricke *et al.* (eds.), *Lexikon* (1983–6), Vol. 4, pp. 135–6.

Fricke, Dieter, and Hartwig, Edgar, 'Bund der Landwirte 1893–1920', in Fricke *et al.* (eds.), *Lexikon* (1983–6), Vol. 1, pp. 241–70.

Fricke, Dieter, and Rößling, Udo, 'Deutsche Adelsgenossenschaft 1874–1945', in Fricke *et al.* (eds.), *Lexikon* (1983–6), Vol. 1, pp. 530–43.

Fricke, Dieter, *et al.* (eds.), *Die Bürgerliche Parteien in Deutschland. Handbuch der Geschichte der bürgerlichen Parteien und anderer bürgerlicher Interessenorganisationen vom Vormärz bis zum Jahre 1945*, 2 vols. (Berlin, 1968).

Fricke, Dieter, *et al.* (eds.), *Lexikon zur Parteiengeschichte. Die bürgerlichen und kleinbürgerlichen Parteien und Verbände in Deutschland (1789–1945)*, 4 vols. (Leipzig, 1983–6).

Gabler, Hans, 'Die Entwicklung der deutschen Parteien auf landwirtschaftlicher Grundlage von 1871–1912', PhD thesis, University of Berlin, 1934.

Gagel, Walter, *Die Wahlrechtsfrage in der Geschichte der deutschen liberalen Parteien 1848–1918* (Düsseldorf, 1958).

Gagliardo, J. G., *From Pariah to Patriot. The Changing Image of the German Peasant* (Lexington, Ky, 1969).

Gall, Lothar, 'Die partei- und sozialgeschichtliche Problematik des badischen Kulturkampfes', *Zeitschrift für die Geschichte des Oberrheins*, vol. 113 (1965), pp. 151–96.

Galos, A., Gentzen, F.-H., and Jacobczyk, W., *Die Hakatisten. Der Deutsche Ostmarkenverein 1894–1934* (Berlin, 1966).

Geis, Robert, *Der Sturz des Reichskanzlers Caprivi* (Berlin, 1930).

Geiss, Imanuel, and Wendt, Bernd-Jürgen (eds.), *Deutschland in der Weltpolitik des 19. und 20. Jahrhunderts* (Düsseldorf, 1973).

Gellately, Robert, *The Politics of Economic Despair: Shopkeepers and German Politics 1890–1914* (London, 1974).

Gerlach, Hans-Christian, 'Agitation und parlamentarische Wirksamkeit der deutschen Antisemitenparteien 1873–1895', PhD thesis, Christian-Albrecht University, Kiel, 1956.

Gerschenkron, Alexander, *Bread and Democracy in Germany* (New York, 1946).

Gerstenberger, H., *Der revolutionäre Konservatismus* (Berlin, 1969).

Gessner, D., *Agrardepression, Agrarideologie und konservative Politik in der Weimarer Republik* (Wiesbaden, 1976).

Gilbert, Ursula, *Hellmuth von Gerlach (1866–1935)* (Frankfurt a.M., 1984).

Gillis, John R., 'Aristocracy and Bureaucracy in Nineteenth-Century Prussia', *Past and Present*, vol. 40 (1968), pp. 103–29.

Görlitz, Walter, *Die Junker. Adel und Bauer im deutschen Osten* (Glücksburg, 1964).

Götting, Hildegard, 'Die sozialpolitische Idee in den konservativen Kreisen der vormärzlichen Zeit', PhD thesis, University of Berlin, 1920.

Gossweiler, Kurt, 'Junkertum und Faschismus', in Seeber and Noack (eds.), *Preußen in der deutschen Geschichte* (1983), pp. 290–302.

Gottwald, Herbert, 'Vormerkung', 'Bericht über die wissenschaftliche Konferenz "Konservative Politik und Ideologie" . . . am 21. und 22. März 1979 in Jena' and 'Zu einigen ausgewählten Problemen konservativer Politik und Ideologie im Zeitraum 1871–1914', *Jenaer Beiträge zur Parteiengeschichte*, vol. 44, special issue (Konservatismus), ed. H. Gottwald (1980), pp. 5–64.

Gottwald, Herbert, 'Deutscher Landwirtschaftsrat 1872–1933', in Fricke *et al.* (eds.), *Lexikon* (1983–6), Vol. 2, pp. 167–83.

Gottwald, Herbert, 'Kongress Deutscher Landwirte 1868–1893', in Fricke *et al.* (eds.), *Lexikon* (1983–6), Vol. 3, pp. 276–7.

Gottwald, Herbert, 'Preußenbund 1913–1934', in Fricke *et al.* (eds.), *Lexikon* (1983–6), Vol. 3, pp. 594–8.

Gottwald, Herbert, 'Reichsverband ländlicher Arbeitnehmer 1912–1933', in Fricke *et al.* (eds.), *Lexikon* (1983–6), Vol. 4, pp. 78–83.

Gottwald, Herbert, 'Sozialkonservative Vereinigung 1880–1882', in Fricke *et al.* (eds.), *Lexikon* (1983–6), Vol. 4, pp. 131–4.

Gottwald, Herbert, 'Vereinigung der Steuer- und Wirtschaftsreformer 1876–1928', in Fricke *et al.* (eds.), *Lexikon* (1983–6), Vol. 4, pp. 358–67.

Gourevitch, P., 'International Trade, Domestic Coalitions and Liberty: Comparative Responses to the Crisis of 1873–96', *Journal of Interdisciplinary History*, vol. 8/2 (1977), pp. 281–313.

Grebing, Helga, *et al.*, *Konservatismus – Eine deutsche Bilanz* (Munich, 1971).

Greiffenhagen, Martin, *Das Dilemma des Konservatismus in Deutschland* (Munich, 1971).

Greschat, Martin, 'Adolf Stoecker und der deutsche Protestantismus', in Brakelmann, Greschat and Jochmann, *Protestantismus* (1982), pp. 19–83.

Grube, Walter, *Der Stuttgarter Landtag 1457–1957* (Stuttgart, 1957).

Gutsche, Willibald, *Aufstieg und Fall eines kaiserlichen Reichskanzlers. Theobald von Bethmann Hollweg 1856–1921* (Berlin, 1973).

Hagen, William, 'National Solidarity and Organic Work in Prussian Poland, 1815–1914', *Journal of Modern History*, vol. 44/1 (1972), pp. 38–64.

Hagen, William, 'The Impact of Economic Modernization on Traditional Nationality Relations in Prussian Poland 1815–1914', *Journal of Social History*, vol. 6/3 (1973), pp. 306–24.

Hagen, William, *Germans, Poles, and Jews. The Nationality Conflict in the Prussian East, 1772–1914* (Chicago, 1980).

Hagen, William, 'The Junkers' Faithless Servants: Peasant Insubordination and the Breakdown of Serfdom in Brandenburg-Prussia, 1763–1811', in Evans and Lee (eds.), *German Peasantry* (1986), pp. 71–101.

Hahn, Adalbert, *Die Berliner Revue. Ein Beitrag zur Geschichte der konservativen Partei zwischen 1855 und 1875* (Berlin, 1934).

Hall, Alex, *Scandal, Sensation, and Social Democracy. The SPD Press and Wilhelmine Germany 1890–1914* (Cambridge, 1977).

Hamel, Iris, *Völklischer Verband und nationale Gewerkschaft. Der Deutschnationale Handlungsgehilfen-Verband 1893–1933* (Frankfurt, 1967).

Hamerow, Theodore S., *Restoration, Revolution, Reaction. Economics and Politics in Germany, 1815–1871* (Princeton, NJ, 1958)

Hamerow, Theodore S., *The Social Foundations of German Unification 1858–1871. Ideas and Institutions* (Princeton, NJ, 1969).

Hamerow, Theodore S., 'The Origins of Mass Politics in Germany 1866–1867', in Geiss and Wendt (eds.), *Deutschland in der Weltpolitik* (1973), pp. 105–120.

Handke, Horst, 'Einige Probleme der inneren Struktur der herrschenden Klasse in Deutschland vom Ende des 19. Jahrhunderts bis zum ersten Weltkrieg', in Klein (ed.), *Studien zum deutschen Imperialismus* (1976), pp. 85–114.

Hank, Manfred, *Kanzler ohne Amt. Fürst Bismarck nach seiner Entlassung 1890–1898* (Munich, 1977).

Hannay, Eberhard, 'Der Gedanke der Wiedervereinigung der Konfessionen in den Anfängen der konservativen Bewegung', PhD thesis, University of Berlin (Düsseldorf, 1936).

Harnisch, Hartmut, 'Probleme junkerlicher Agrarpolitik im 19. Jahrhundert', *Wissenschaftliche Zeitschrift der Universität Rostock*, vol. 21 (1972), Gesellschaft- und Sprachwissenschaftliche Reihe, Heft 1, Teil 2, pp. 99–117.

Hartmann, Hans-Georg, 'Die Innenpolitik des Fürsten Bülow 1906–1909', PhD thesis, Christian-Albrecht University, Kiel, 1950.

Hartwig, Edgar, 'Zu einigen Konzeptionen, taktischen Varianten, und Methoden des Bundes der Landwirte im Kampf gegen die revolutionäre Arbeiterbewegung (1893 bis 1910)', *Jenaer Beiträge zur Parteiengeschichte*, vol. 41 (1977), pp. 91–109.

Hartwig, Edgar, 'Deutscher Bauernbund 1885–1893', in Fricke *et al.* (eds.), *Lexikon* (1983–6), Vol. 2, pp. 29–32.

Hartwig, Edgar, 'Konservative Partei 1848–1918', in Fricke *et al.* (eds.), *Lexikon* (1983–6), Vol. 3, pp. 283–309.

Hauser, Oswald, *Zur Problematik 'Preußen und das Reich'* (Cologne, 1984).

Heckart, Beverly, *From Bassermann to Bebel. The Grand Bloc's Quest for Reform in the Kaiserreich, 1900–1914* (New Haven, Conn., 1974).

Heffter, Heinrich, *Die Kreuzzeitungspartei und die Kartellpolitik Bismarcks* (Leipzig, 1927).

Heffter, Heinrich, *Die Opposition der Kreuzzeitungspartei gegen die Bismarckische Kartellpolitik in den Jahren 1887 bis 1890* (Leipzig, 1927).

Heller, Karl, 'Der Bund der Landwirte bzw. Landbund und seine Politik mit besonderer Berücksichtigung der fränkischen Verhältnisse', PhD thesis, Bayr. Julius-Maximilian University, Würzburg (Kulmbach, [1936]).

Hellwig, Fritz, *Carl Ferdinand Freiherr von Stumm-Halberg 1836–1901* (Heidelberg, 1936).

Hertzman, Lewis, 'The Founding of the German National People's Party

(DNVP), November 1918–January 1919', *Journal of Modern History*, vol. 30/1 (1958), pp. 24–36.

Herzman, Lewis, *DNVP. Right-Wing Opposition in the Weimar Republic 1918–1924* (Lincoln, Nebr., 1963).

Herwig, Holger, '"Allens nur noch Seelenadel!" The Prussian Nobility and the Imperial German Navy 1888–1918', *Canadian Journal of History*, Vol. 15/2 (1980), pp. 197–205.

Herz, Hans, 'Kreuzzeitungspartei 1848–1867', in Fricke *et al.* (eds.), *Lexikon* (1983–6), Vol. 3, pp. 321–4.

Herz, Hans, 'Preußischer Volks-Verein 1861–1872', in Fricke *et al.* (eds.), *Lexikon* (1983–6), Vol. 3, pp. 599–603.

Hesse, Max, 'Die politische Haltung Ludwig von Gerlachs unter Bismarcks Ministerium 1862 bis 1877', PhD thesis, Marburg University, 1912.

Heuss, Theodor, *Friedrich Naumann* (Stuttgart/Berlin, 1937).

Hindelang, Sabine, *Konservatismus und soziale Frage. Victor Aimé Hubers Beitrag zum sozialkonservativen Denken im 19. Jahrhundert* (Frankfurt a.M., 1983).

Hoener, Erich, 'Die Geschichte der christlich-konservativen Partei in Minden-Ravensberg von 1866 bis 1896', PhD thesis, Westfälische Wilhelm University, Bielefeld, 1923.

Holldack, Heinz Georg, 'Untersuchungen zur Geschichte der Reaktion in Sachsen 1849–55', PhD thesis, University of Berlin, [1931]).

Holmes, Kim R., 'The Forsaken Past: Agrarian Conservatism and National Socialism in Germany', *Journal of Contemporary History*, vol.17 (1982), pp. 671–88.

Horn, Hannelore, *Der Kampf um den Bau des Mittellandkanals* (Cologne, 1964).

Huber, Ernst Rudolf, *Deutsche Verfassungsgeschichte seit 1789*, Vol. 4, *Struktur und Krisen des Kaiserreichs* (Stuttgart, 1969).

Hübner, Hans, 'Die ostpreußischen Landarbeiter im Kampf gegen junkerliche Ausbeutung und Willkür (1848–1914)', *Zeitschrift für Geschichtswissenschaft*, vol. 11 (1963), pp. 552–69.

Hübner, Hans, and Kathe, Heinz (eds.), *Lage und Kampf der Landarbeiter im ostelbischen Preußen*, Vol. 1, *Quellen* (Vaduz, 1977).

Hull, Isabel, *The Entourage of Kaiser Wilhelm II, 1888–1918* (Cambridge, 1982).

Hunt, James C., 'Peasants, Grain Tariffs, and Meat Quotas: Imperial German Protectionism Reexamined', *Central European History*, vol. 7/4 (1974), pp. 311–31.

Hunt, James C., 'The "Egalitarianism" of the Right: The Agrarian League in Southwest Germany, 1893–1914', *Journal of Contemporary History*, vol. 10 (1975), pp. 513–30.

Hunt, James C., *The People's Party in Württemberg and Southern Germany 1890–1914* (Stuttgart, 1975).

Hussain, Athar, and Tribe, Keith, *Marxism and the Agrarian Question*, Vol. 1, *German Social Democracy and the Peasantry 1890–1907* (London, 1981).

Hutton, Patrick H., 'Popular Boulangism and the Advent of Mass Politics in France, 1886–90', *Journal of Contemporary History*, vol. 11 (1976), pp. 85–106.

Jarausch, Konrad, *The Enigmatic Chancellor. Bethmann Hollweg and the Hubris of Imperial Germany* (New Haven, Conn., 1973).

Jarausch, Konrad, 'Illiberalism and Beyond: German History in Search of a Paradigm', *Journal of Modern History*, vol. 55/2 (1983), pp. 268–84.

Jochmann, Werner, 'Stoecker als nationalkonservativer Politiker und antisemitischer Agitator', in Brakelmann, Greschat and Jochmann, *Protestantismus* (1982), pp. 123–98.

Jonas, E., *Die Volkskonservativen 1928–1933* (Düsseldorf, 1965).

Jostock, Paul, *Der Deutsche Katholizismus und die Ueberwindung des Kapitalismus* (Regensburg, 1932).

Kaehler, Siegfried, 'Stöckers Versuch, eine christlich-soziale Arbeiterpartei in Berlin zu begründen (1878)', in Wentzcke (ed.), *Deutscher Staat* (1922), pp. 227–65.

Kaelble, Hartmut, *Industrielle Interessenpolitik in der Wilhelminischen Gesellschaft. Centralverband Deutscher Industrieller 1895–1914* (Berlin, 1967).

Kaltenbrunner, Gerd-Klaus (ed.), *Rekonstruktion des Konservatismus* (Freiburg, 1972).

Kampmann, Wanda, 'Adolf Stöcker und die Berliner Bewegung', *Geschichte in Wissenschaft und Unterricht*, vol. 13 (1962), pp. 558–79.

Kardorff, Siegfried von, 'Die Beziehungen des Fürsten Bismarck zur konservativen und zur nationalliberalen Partei (1866–1887)', in Kardorff, *Bismarck* (1930).

Kardorff, Siegfried von, *Bismarck. Vier Vorträge. Ein Beitrag zur Deutschen Parteigeschichte*, 2nd edn (Berlin, 1930).

Kardorff, Siegfried von, *Wilhelm von Kardorff. Ein nationaler Parlamentarier im Zeitalter Bismarcks und Wilhelms II. 1828–1907* (Berlin, 1936).

Kehr, Eckart, *Schlachtflottenbau und Parteipolitik 1894–1901* (Berlin, 1930).

Kehr, Eckart, *Economic Interest, Militarism, and Foreign Policy*, ed. G. A. Craig (Berkeley, Calif., 1977).

Kennedy, Paul, *The Rise of the Anglo-German Antagonism 1860–1914* (London, 1980).

Kennedy, Paul, 'The Pre-War Right in Britain and Germany', in Kennedy and Nicholls (eds.), *Nationalist and Racialist Movements* (1981), pp. 1–20.

Kennedy, Paul, and Nicholls, Anthony J. (eds.), *Nationalist and Racialist Movements in Britain and Germany Before 1914* (London/Oxford, 1981).

Kitchen, Martin, *The German Officer Corps 1890–1914* (Oxford, 1968).

Kitzel, Karlheinz, *Die Herrfurth'sche Landgemeindeordnung* (Stuttgart, 1957).

Klatte, Klaus, 'Die anfänge des Agrarkapitalismus und der preußische Konservatismus', PhD thesis, University of Hamburg, 1974.

Klawitter, Willy, *Die Zeitungen und Zeitschriften Schlesiens* (Hildesheim, 1978).

Klein, Fritz (ed.), *Politik im Krieg 1914–1918. Studien zur Politik der deutschen herrschenden Klassen im ersten Weltkrieg* (Berlin, 1964).

Klein, Fritz, (ed.), *Studien zum deutschen Imperialismus vor 1914* (Berlin, 1976).

Klemperer, K. von, *Germany's New Conservatism* (Princeton, NJ, 1957).

Knobel, Enno, *Die Hessische Rechtspartei. Konservative Opposition gegen das Bismarckreich* (Marburg, 1975).

Koch, Walter, 'Jungkonservative Bewegung und Jugendbewegung', in Thierbach (ed.), *Adolf Grabowsky* (1973), pp. 129–31.

Kocka, Jürgen, *Facing Total War. German Society 1914–1918* (Cambridge, Mass., 1984).

Kornhauser, William, *The Politics of Mass Society* (New York, 1959).

Koselleck, Reinhart, 'Altständische Rechte, außerständische Gesellschaft und Beamtenherrschaft im Vormärz', in Blasius (ed.), *Preußen in der deutschen Geschichte* (1980), pp. 219–36.

Koszyk, Kurt, *Deutsche Presse im 19. Jahrhundert* (Berlin, 1966).

Koszyk, Kurt, *Deutsche Pressepolitik im Ersten Weltkrieg* (Düsseldorf, 1968).

Kremer, Hans-Jürgen, *Mit Gott für Wahrheit, Freiheit und Recht. Quellen zur Organisation und Politik der Zentrumspartei und des politischen Katholizismus in Baden 1888–1914* (Stuttgart, 1983).

Kremer, Willy, 'Der soziale Aufbau der Parteien des Deutschen Reichstages von 1871–1918', PhD thesis, University of Cologne, 1934.

Kröger, Karl Heinz, 'Die Konservativen und die Politik Caprivis', PhD thesis, University of Rostock, 1937.

Küttler, Wolfgang, 'Nochmals zur Klassenposition des Junkertums während und nach der bürgerlichen Umwälzung', *Zeitschrift für Geschichtswissenschaft*, vol. 33/3 (1985), pp. 238–46.

Lambi, Ivo N., 'The Agrarian–Industrial Front in Bismarckian Politics 1873–1879', *Journal of Central European Affairs*, vol. 20/4 (1961), pp. 378–96.

Lambi, Ivo N., *Free Trade and Protection in Germany, 1868–1879* (Wiesbaden, 1963).

Land, Hanne-Lore, 'Die Konservativen und die preußische Polenpolitik (1886–1912)', PhD thesis, Free University, Berlin, 1963.

Langewiesche, Dieter, 'Die Anfänge der deutschen Parteien. Partei, Fraktion und Verein in der Revolution von 1848/49', *Geschichte und Gesellschaft* (1978), pp. 324–61.

Lebovics, Hermann, 'A Socialism for the Middle Classes. The Social Conservative Response to Industrialism, 1900–1933', PhD thesis, Yale University, 1964.

Lebovics, Hermann, ' "Agrarians" versus "Industrializers". Social Conservative Resistance to Industrialism and Capitalism in Late Nineteenth-Century Germany', *International Review of Social History*, vol. 12/1 (1967), pp. 31–65.

Lebovics, Hermann, *Social Conservatism and the Middle Classes in Germany, 1914–1933* (Princeton, NJ, 1969).

Lees, Andrew, 'Debates about the Big City in Germany, 1890–1914', *Societas*, vol. 5/1 (1975), pp. 31–47.

Lehmann, Hans Georg, *Die Agrarfrage in der Theorie und Praxis der Deutschen und internationalen Sozialdemokratie* (Tübingen, 1970).

Leopold, John A., *Alfred Hugenberg. The Radical Nationalist Campaign against the Weimar Republic* (New Haven, Conn., 1977).

Lerman, Katharine Anne, 'Bernhard von Bülow and the Governance of Germany 1900–1909', PhD thesis, University of Sussex, 1983.

Leupolt, Erich, *Die Außenpolitik in den bedeutendsten politischen Zeitschriften Deutschlands 1890–1909* (Leipzig, 1933).

Levy, Richard S., *The Downfall of the Anti-Semitic Political Parties in Imperial Germany* (New Haven, Conn., 1975).

Lewis, G., 'The Peasantry, Rural Change and Conservative Agrarianism. Lower Austria at the Turn of the Century', *Past and Present*, vol. 81 (1978), pp. 119–43.

Liebe, W., *Die Deutschnationale Volkspartei 1918–1924* (Düsseldorf, 1956).

Lindig, Ursula, 'Der Einfluß des Bundes der Landwirte auf die Politik des Wilhelminischen Zeitalters 1893–1914', PhD thesis, University of Hamburg, 1953.

Lougee, Robert W., 'The Anti-Revolution Bill of 1894 in Wilhelmine Germany', *Central European History*, vol. 15/3 (1982), pp. 224–40.

Maehl, William Harvey, 'Germany Social Democratic Agrarian Policy, 1890–1895, Reconsidered', *Central European History*, vol. 13/2 (1980), pp. 121–57.

Maltzahn, Christoph Freiherr von, *Heinrich Leo (1799–1878). Ein Politisches Gelehrtenleben zwischen Romantischem Konservatismus und Realpolitik* (Göttingen, 1979).

Martin, Alfred von, 'Der preußische Altkonservatismus und der politische Katholizismus in ihren gegenseitigen Beziehungen', *Deutsche Vierteljahrschrift für Literaturwissenschaft und Geistesgeschichte*, vol. 7 (1929), pp. 489–514.

Martin, Alfred von, 'Weltanschauliche Motive im altkonservativen Denken', in Ritter (ed.), *Deutsche Parteien vor 1918* (1973), pp. 142–64.

Massing, Paul W., *Rehearsal for Destruction. A Study of Political Anti-Semitism in Imperial Germany* (New York, 1949).

Mehnert, Gottfried, *Evangelische Presse* (Bielefeld, 1983).

Mende, Dietrich, 'Kulturkonservatismus und Konservative Erneuerungsbestrebungen', in Thierbach (ed.), *Adolf Grabowsky* (1973), pp. 87–128.

Meyer, Folkert, 'Das konservative Schulregiment in Preußen während der 80er Jahre', in Blasius (ed.), *Preußen in der deutschen Geschichte* (1980), pp. 271–92.

Meyer, Klaus, *Theodor Schiemann als politischer Publizist* (Frankfurt a.M., 1956).

Möckl, Karl, *Die Prinzregentenzeit. Gesellschaft und Politik während der Ära des Prinzregenten Luitpold in Bayern* (Munich, 1972).

Möhlmann, Günther, 'Fürst Edzard zu Innhausen und Knyphausen 1827–1908', *Niedersächsische Lebensbilder*, vol. 3 (Hildesheim, 1957), pp. 105–25.

Moeller, Robert G., 'Peasants, Politics and Pressure Groups in War and Inflation: A Study of the Rhineland and Westphalia, 1914–1924', PhD thesis, University of California–Berkeley, 1980.

Moeller, Robert G., 'Dimensions of Social Conflict in the Great War: The View From the German Countryside', *Central European History*, vol. 14 (1981), pp. 142–68.

Moeller, Robert G., 'Peasants and Tariffs in the Kaiserreich: How Backward were the Bauern?', *Agricultural History*, vol. 55/4 (1981), pp. 370–84.

Moeller, Robert G., 'Introduction: Locating Peasants and Lords in Modern German Historiography', in Moeller (ed.), *Peasants and Lords* (1986), pp. 1–23.

Moeller, Robert G. (ed.), *Peasants and Lords in Modern Germany. Recent Studies in Agricultural History* (Boston, 1986).

Mohler, A., *Die konservative Revolution in Deutschland 1918–1932* (Darmstadt, 1972).

Mommsen, Wilhelm, 'Bismarcks Sturz und die Parteien', in Wentzcke (ed.), *Deutscher Staat* (1922), pp. 266–93.

Mommsen, Wolfgang J., *Max Weber and German Politics 1890–1920* (Chicago, 1984).

Mosse, Werner (ed.), *Juden im Wilhelminischen Deutschland 1890–1914* (Tübingen, 1976).

Müller, Hugo, 'Der Preußische Volks-Verein', PhD thesis, University of Berlin, 1914.

Muncy, Lysbeth W., *The Junker in the Prussian Administration under William II, 1888–1914* (Providence, RI, 1944).

Muncy, Lysbeth W., 'The Prussian Landräte in the Years of the Monarchy: A Case Study of Pomerania and the Rhineland in 1890–1918', *Central European History*, vol. 6/4 (1973), pp. 299–338.

Mundle, George F., 'The German National Liberal Party, 1900–1914: Political Revival and Resistance to Change', PhD thesis, University of Illinois at Urbana-Champaign, 1975.

Muth, Heinrich, 'Die Entstehung der Bauern- und Landarbeiterräte im November 1918 und die Politik des Bundes der Landwirte', *Vierteljahrshefte für Zeitgeschichte*, vol. 21/1 (1973), pp. 1–38.

Neumann, Sigmund, *Die Stufen des preußischen Konservatismus* (Berlin, 1930).

Neumann, Wolfgang, 'Die Innenpolitik des Fürsten Bülow von 1900–1906', PhD thesis, Christian-Albrecht University, Kiel, 1949.

Nichols, J. Alden, *Germany After Bismarck. The Caprivi Era 1890–1894* (Cambridge, Mass., 1958).

Nichols, J. Alden, *The Year of the Three Kaisers. Bismarck and the German Succession, 1887–88* (Urbana and Chicago, Ill., 1987).

Nichtweiß, Johannes, *Die ausländischen Saisonarbeiter in der Landwirtschaft der östlichen und mittleren Gebiete des Deutschen Reiches* (Berlin, 1959).

Nipperdey, Thomas, *Die Organisation der deutschen Parteien vor 1918* (Düsseldorf, 1961).

Nipperdey, Thomas, 'Interessenverbände und Parteien in Deutschland vor dem Ersten Weltkrieg,' in Wehler (ed.), *Moderne deutsche Sozialgeschichte* (1973), pp. 369–88.

O'Donnell, Anthony J., 'National Liberalism and the Mass Politics of the German Right 1890–1907', PhD thesis, Princeton University, 1973.

Oehlmann, Horst, 'Studien zur Innenpolitik des Reichskanzlers Leo von Caprivi', PhD thesis, Albert-Ludwig University, Freiburg i.B., 1953.

Oertzen, F. W. von, *Junker. Preußischer Adel im Jahrhundert des Liberalismus* (Oldenburg, 1939).

Orr, William J., Jr, 'The Prussian Ultra Right and the Advent of Constitutionalism in Prussia', *Canadian Journal of History*, vol. 11/3 (1976), pp. 295–310.

Pack, Wolfgang, *Das parlamentarische Ringen um das Sozialistengesetz Bismarcks 1878–1890* (Düsseldorf, 1961).

Pacyna, Günther, *Gustav Ruhland. Ein Kämpferleben für eine bodengebundene Volksordnung* (Leipzig, [1943]).

Patemann, Reinhard, *Der Kampf um die preußische Wahlreform im Ersten Weltkrieg* (Düsseldorf, 1964).

Peck, Abraham J., *Radicals and Reactionaries: The Crisis of Conservatism in Wilhelmine Germany* (Washington, DC, 1978).

Perkins, J. A., 'The Agricultural Revolution in Germany, 1850–1914', *Journal of European Economic History*, vol. 10 (1981), pp. 71–118.

Perkins, J. A., 'Dualism in German Agrarian Historiography', *Comparative Studies in Society and History*, vol. 28/2 (1986), pp. 287–306.

Petzold, Joachim, *Konservative Theoretiker der deutschen Faschismus* (Berlin, 1978).

Pflanze, Otto (ed.), *Innenpolitische Probleme des Bismarck-Reiches* (Munich, 1983).

Plieninger, Martin, 'Die Württembergische Presse und die Wendung der Bismarckischen Innenpolitik 1876–1881', PhD thesis, Tübingen University, 1922.

Poepke, Arnold, 'Der christliche Sozialismus Adolf Stöckers', PhD thesis, University of Berlin (Würzburg, 1938).

Pogge von Strandmann, Hartmut, 'Staatsstreichpläne, Alldeutsche und Bethmann Hollweg', in I. Geiss and H. Pogge v. Strandmann, *Die Erforderlichkeit des Unmöglichen* (Frankfurt a.M., 1965), pp. 7–45.

Pogge von Strandmann, Hartmut, 'Nationale Verbände zwischen Weltpolitik und Kontinentalpolitik', in H. Schottelius and W. Deist (eds.), *Marine und Marinepolitik im kaiserlichen Deutschland 1871–1914* (Düsseldorf, 1972), pp. 296–317.

Pöls, W., *Sozialistenfrage und Revolutionsfürcht in ihrem Zusammenhang mit den angeblichen Staatsstreichplänen Bismarcks* (Lübeck, 1960).

Pollmann, Klaus E., *Landesherrliches Kirchenregiment und Soziale Frage. Der evangelische Oberkirchenrat der altpreußischen Landeskirche und die sozialpolitische Bewegung der Geistlichen nach 1890* (Berlin, 1973).

Popper-Lynkeus, Josef, *Fürst Bismarck und der Antisemitismus* (Vienna, 1925).

Puhle, Hans-Jürgen, *Agrarische Interessenpolitik und preußischer Konservatismus im wilhelminischen Reich 1893–1914. Ein Beitrag zur Analyse des Nationalismus in Deutschland am Beispiel des Bundes der Landwirte und der Deutsch-Konservativen Partei* (Hanover, 1966; 2nd edn, Bonn Bad-Godesberg, 1975).

Puhle, Hans-Jürgen, 'Parlament, Parteien und Interessenverbände 1890–1914', in Stürmer (ed.), *Kaiserliche Deutschland* (1970), pp. 340–77.

Puhle, Hans-Jürgen, *Von der Agrarkrise zum Präfaschismus. Thesen zum Stellenwert der Agrarischen Interessenverbände in der Deutschen Politik am Ende des 19. Jahrhunderts* (Wiesbaden, 1972).

Puhle, Hans-Jürgen, 'Radikalisierung und Wandel des deutschen Konservatismus vor dem Ersten Weltkrieg', in Ritter (ed.), *Deutsche Parteien vor 1918* (1973), pp. 165–86.

Puhle, Hans-Jürgen, *Politische Agrarbewegungen in kapitalistischen Industriegesellschaften* (Göttingen, 1975).

Puhle, Hans-Jürgen, 'Conservatism in Modern German History', *Journal of Contemporary History*, vol. 13/4 (1978), pp. 689–720.

Puhle, Hans-Jürgen, 'Preußen: Entwicklung und Fehlentwicklung', in Puhle and Wehler (eds.), *Preußen im Rückblick* (1980), pp. 1–42.

Puhle, Hans-Jürgen, 'Vom Programm zum Versatzstück. Zehn Thesen zum deutschen Konservatismus', in *Kursbuch*, vol. 73, *Konservatismus im Angebot* (1983), pp. 45–60.

Puhle, Hans-Jürgen, 'Lords and Peasants in the Kaiserreich', in Moeller (ed.), *Peasants and Lords* (1986), pp. 81–109.

Puhle, Hans-Jürgen, and Stürmer, Michael, *Two Lectures in Modern German History*, (Buffalo, NY, 1978).

Puhle, Hans-Jürgen, and Wehler, Hans-Ulrich (eds.), *Preußen im Rückblick* (Göttingen, 1980).

Pulzer, Peter G. J., *The Rise of Political Anti-Semitism in Germany and Austria* (New York, 1964).

Puttkamer, Albert von (ed.), *Staatsminister von Puttkamer. Ein Stück preußischer Vergangenheit, 1828–1900* (Leipzig, 1928).

Quabbe, Georg, *Tar a Ri. Variationen über ein konservatives Thema* (Berlin, 1927).

Ramlow, Gerhard, *Ludwig von der Marwitz und die Anfänge konservativer Politik und Staatsanschauung in Preußen* (Berlin, 1930).

Rapp, Alfred, *Die badischen Landtags-Abgeordneten 1905/1929* (Karlsruhe, 1929).

Rathmann, Lothar, 'Bismarck und der Uebergang Deutschlands zur Schutzzollpolitik (1873/75–1879)', *Zeitschrift für Geschichtswissenschaft*, vol. 4/5, (1956), pp. 899–949.

Rauh, Manfred, *Die Parlamentarisierung des Deutschen Reiches* (Düsseldorf, 1977).

Rejewski, H.-J., *Die Pflicht zur politischen Treue im preußischen Beamtenrecht (1850–1918)* (Berlin, 1973).

Remer, Gertraude, 'Deutsche Mittelstandsvereinigung 1904–1912/13', in Fricke *et al.* (eds.), *Lexikon* (1983–6), Vol. 2, pp. 17–22.

Retallack, James N., 'Reformist Conservatism and Political Mobilization: A Study of Factionalism and Movements for Reform within the German Conservative Party, 1876–1914', D.Phil. thesis, University of Oxford, 1983.

Retallack, James N., 'Social History with a Vengeance? Some Reactions to H.-U. Wehler's "Das Deutsche Kaiserreich"', *German Studies Review*, vol. 7/3 (1984), pp. 423–50.

Retallack, James N., 'Conservatives *contra* Chancellor: Official Responses to the Spectre of Conservative Demagoguery, from Bismarck to Bülow', *Canadian Journal of History*, vol. 20/2 (1985), pp. 203–36.

Retallack, James N., 'The Road to Philippi: The Conservative Party and Bethmann

Hollweg's "Politics of the Diagonal," 1909–1914', forthcoming in Fout (ed.), *Politics, Parties and the Authoritarian State* (1987), Vol. 2.

Rieger, Isolde, *Die Wilhelminische Presse im Überblick 1888–1918* (Munich, 1957).

Ritter, Gerhard, 'Die preußischen Konservativen in der Krise von 1866', PhD thesis, Ruprecht-Karl University, Heidelberg, 1913.

Ritter, Gerhard A. (ed.), *Die deutschen Parteien vor 1918* (Cologne, 1973).

Ritter, Gerhard A. (ed.), *Gesellschaft, Parlament und Regierung. Zur Geschichte des Parlamentarismus in Deutschland* (Düsseldorf, 1974).

Ritter, Gerhard A., *Die deutschen Parteien 1830–1914* (Göttingen, 1985).

Röhl, John C. G., 'The Disintegration of the Kartell and the Politics of Bismarck's Fall from Power, 1887–90', *Historical Journal*, vol. 9 (1966), pp. 60–89.

Röhl, John C. G., *Germany without Bismarck. The Crisis of Government in the Second Reich, 1890–1900* (London, 1967).

Röhl, John C. G., and Sombart, Nicolaus (eds.), *Kaiser Wilhelm II. New Interpretations* (Cambridge, 1982).

Roeske, Ulrich, 'Volkskonservative Vereinigung 1930–1933', in Fricke *et al.* (eds.), *Lexikon* (1983–6), Vol. 4, pp. 423–30.

Rogalla von Bieberstein, Johannes, *Preußen als Deutschlands Schicksal* (Munich, 1981).

Roper, Katharine Larson, 'The Urban Aristocracy in Novels of Imperial Germany: A Crisis of Honor and Means', paper read at the annual meeting of the German Studies Association, Denver, October 1984.

Rosenbaum, Louis, *Beruf und Herkunft der Abgeordneten in den deutschen und preußischen Parlamenten 1847–1919* (Frankfurt, 1923).

Rosenberg, Hans, 'The Rise of the Junkers in Brandenburg-Prussia, 1410–1653,' *American Historical Review*, vol. 49 (1943–4), pp. 1–22, 228–42.

Rosenberg, Hans, *Große Depression und Bismarckzeit. Wirtschaftsablauf, Gesellschaft und Politik in Mitteleuropa* (Berlin, 1967).

Rosenberg, Hans, *Probleme der deutschen Sozialgeschichte* (Frankfurt a.M., 1969).

Rosenberg, Hans, 'Die Pseudodemokratisierung der Rittergutsbesitzerklasse', in Wehler (ed.), *Moderne deutsche Sozialgeschichte* (1973), pp. 287–308.

Rosenberg, Hans, 'Political and Social Consequences of the Great Depression of 1873–1896 in Central Europe', in Sheehan (ed.), *Imperial Germany* (1976), pp. 39–60.

Rosenberg, Hans, *Machteliten und Wirtschaftskonjunkturen. Zur neueren deutschen Sozial- und Wirtschaftsgeschichte* (Göttingen, 1978).

Ruge, Wolfgang, 'Deutschnationale Volkspartei 1918–1933', in Fricke *et al.* (eds.), *Lexikon* (1983–6), Vol. 2, pp. 476–528.

Sagarra, Eda, *An Introduction to Nineteenth-Century Germany* (Harlow, 1980).

Saile, Wolfgang, *Hermann Wagener und sein Verhältnis zu Bismarck. Ein Beitrag zur Geschichte des konservativen Sozialismus* (Tübingen, 1958).

Saul, Klaus, 'Der "Deutsche Kriegerbund". Zur innenpolitischen Funktion eines "nationalen" Verbandes im kaiserlichen Deutschland', *Militärgeschichtliche Mitteilungen*, vol. 2 (1969), pp. 95–160.

Saul, Klaus, 'Der Staat und die "Mächte des Umsturzes". Ein Beitrag zu den Methoden antisozialistischer Repression und Agitation vom Scheitern des Sozialistengesetzes bis zur Jahrhundertwende', *Archiv für Sozialgeschichte*, vol. 12 (1972), pp. 293–350.

Saul, Klaus, *Staat, Industrie, Arbeiterbewegung im Kaiserreich* (Düsseldorf, 1974).

Saul, Klaus, 'Der Kampf um das Landproletariat. Sozialistische Landagitation,

Großgrundbesitz und preußische Staatsverwaltung, 1890 bis 1903', *Archiv für Sozialgeschichte*, vol. 15 (1975), pp. 163–208.

Saul, Klaus, 'Um die konservative Struktur Ostelbiens: Agrarische Interessen, Staatsverwaltung und ländliche "Arbeiternot". Zur konservativen Landarbeiterpolitik in Preußen-Deutschland 1889–1914', in Stegmann, Wendt and Witt (eds.), *Deutscher Konservatismus* (1983), pp. 129–98.

Schaaf, Fritz, *Der Kampf der deutschen Arbeiterbewegung um die Landarbeiter und werktätigen Bauern 1848–1890* (Berlin, 1962).

Schier, Rolf, *Standesherren. Zur Auflösung der Adelsvorherrschaft in Deutschland (1815–1918)* (Heidelberg, 1977).

Schilling, K., 'Beiträge zu einer Geschichte des radikalen Nationalismus 1890–1909', PhD thesis, University of Cologne, 1968.

Schissler, Hanna, *Preußische Agrargesellschaft im Wandel. Wirtschaftliche, gesellschaftliche und politische Transformationsprozesse von 1763 bis 1847* (Göttingen, 1978).

Schissler, Hanna, 'The Junkers: Notes on the Social and Historical Significance of the Agrarian Elite in Prussia', in Moeller (ed.), *Peasants and Lords* (1986), pp. 24–51.

Schlegelmilch, Margarete, 'Die Stellung der Parteien des Deutschen Reichstages zur sogenannten Daily-Telegraph Affäre', PhD thesis, University of Halle a.S., 1936.

Schmidt, Gustav, 'Parlamentarisierung oder "Präventative Konterrevolution"? Die deutsche Innenpolitik im Spannungsfeld konservativer Sammlungsbewegungen und latenter Reformbestrebungen 1907–1914', in Ritter (ed.), *Gesellschaft, Parlament und Regierung* (1974), pp. 249–74.

Schmitz, Josef Anton, 'Die christlich-soziale Bewegung und der Kampf gegen den Umsturz 1894–95', PhD thesis, University of Cologne, 1938.

Schöler, Gisela, 'Die Anfänge der konservativen Publizistik in Deutschland', PhD thesis, University of Berlin, 1945.

Schöne, Gerhard, 'Die Verflechtung wirtschaftlicher und politischer Motive in der Haltung der Parteien zum Bülowschen Zolltarif (1901/02)', PhD thesis, University of Halle a.S., 1934.

Schoeps, Hans-Joachim, 'CDU vor 75 Jahren. Die sozialpolitischen Bestrebungen des Reichsfreiherrn Friedrich Carl von Fechenbach (1836–1907)', *Zeitschrift für Religions- und Geistesgeschichte*, vol. 9 (1957), pp. 266–77.

Schoeps, Hans-Joachim, *Das andere Preußen. Konservative Gestalten und Probleme im Zeitalter Friedrich Wilhelms IV.* (Honnef a.R., 1957).

Schoeps, Hans-Joachim, 'Die preußische Konservativen', in Kaltenbrunner (ed.), *Rekonstruktion des Konservatismus* (1972), pp. 181–8.

Schorske, Carl, 'Politics in a New Key: An Austrian Triptych', *Journal of Modern History*, vol. 39 (1967), pp. 343–86.

Schröder, Wolfgang, 'Junkertum und preußisch-deutsches Reich. Zur politischen Konzeption des Junkertums und zu ihrer Widerspiegelung in der Kreuz-Zeitung 1871–1873', in H. Bartel and E. Engelberg (eds.), *Die großpreußisch-militaristische Reichsgründung 1871* (Berlin, 1971), Vol. 2, pp. 170–234.

Schüddekopf, Otto-Ernst, *Die deutsche Innenpolitik im letzten Jahrhundert und der konservative Gedanke* (Brunswick, 1951).

Schult, Richard, 'Partei wider Willen. Kalküle und Potentiale konservativer Parteigründer in Preußen zwischen Erstem Vereinigten Landtag und Nationalversammlung (1847/48)' in Stegmann, Wendt and Witt (eds.), *Deutscher Konservatismus* (1983), pp. 33–68.

Schulte, Engelbert, 'Die Stellung der Konservativen zum Kulturkampf 1870–1878', PhD thesis, University of Cologne, 1959.

Schulte, Wilhelm, 'Anfang und Entwicklung der politischen Parteien in Westfalen. Ein Überblick bis zur Jahrhundertwende', *Westfälische Heimatskalender* (1965), pp. 67–74.

Schumacher, Martin, *Land und Politik. Eine Untersuchung über politische Parteien und agrarische Interessen 1914–1923* (Düsseldorf, 1979).

Schumann, Hans-Gerd (ed.), *Konservatismus* (Cologne, 1974).

Schwentker, Wolfgang, 'Conservatism in Nineteenth- and Twentieth-Century German History', review article, *Bulletin of the German Historical Institute*, London, No. 23 (1986), pp. 3–15.

Seeber, Gustav, *et al.*, *Bismarcks Sturz* (Berlin, 1977).

Seeber, Gustav, and Hohberg, Claudia, 'Nationalliberale Partei 1867–1918', in Fricke *et al.* (eds.), *Lexikon* (1983–6), Vol. 3, pp. 403–36.

Seeber, Gustav, and Noack, Karl-Heinz (eds.), *Preußen in der deutschen Geschichte nach 1789* (Berlin, 1983).

Sepaintner, Fred L., *Die Reichstagswahlen im Großherzogtum Baden* (Frankfurt a.M. 1982).

Shanahan, William O., 'The social outlook of Prussian conservatism', *Review of Politics*, vol. 15 (1953), pp. 209–52.

Shanahan, William O., *German Protestants Face the Social Question*, Vol. 1, *The Conservative Phase 1815–1871* (Notre Dame, Ind., 1954).

Sheehan, James J. (ed.), *Imperial Germany* (London, 1976).

Sheehan, James J., *German Liberalism in the Nineteenth Century* (Chicago, 1978).

Sontheimer, K., *Antidemokratisches Denken in der Weimarer Republik* (Munich, 1968).

Stark, Gary, *Entrepreneurs of Ideology: Neoconservative Publishers in Germany, 1890–1933* (Chapel Hill, NC, 1981).

Stegmann, Dirk, *Die Erben Bismarcks. Parteien und Verbände in der Spätphase des Wilhelminischen Deutschlands* (Cologne, 1970).

Stegmann, Dirk, 'Zwischen Repression und Manipulation: Konservative Machteliten und Arbeiter- und Angestelltenbewegung 1910–1918', *Archiv für Sozialgeschichte*, vol. 12 (1972), pp. 351–432.

Stegmann, Dirk, 'Wirtschaft und Politik nach Bismarcks Sturz. Zur Genesis der Miquelschen Sammlungspolitik 1890–1897', in Geiss and Wendt (eds.), *Deutschland in der Weltpolitik* (1973), pp. 161–84.

Stegmann, Dirk, 'Vom Neokonservatismus zum Proto-Faschismus: Konservative Partei, Vereine und Verbände 1893–1920', in Stegmann, Wendt and Witt, (eds.), *Deutscher Konservatismus* (1983), pp. 199–230.

Stegmann, Dirk, 'Literaturbericht. Konservativismus und nationale Verbände im Kaiserreich. Bemerkungen zu einigen neueren Veröffentlichungen', *Geschichte und Gesellschaft*, vol. 10 (1984), pp. 409–20.

Stegmann, Dirk, 'Between Economic Interests and Radical Nationalism: Attempts to Found a New Right Wing Party in Imperial Germany 1887–1894' (draft), forthcoming in Fout (ed.), *Politics, Parties and the Authoritarian State* (1987).

Stegmann, Dirk, Wendt, Bernd-Jürgen, and Witt, Peter-Christian (eds.), *Deutscher Konservatismus im 19. und 20. Jahrhundert. Festschrift für Fritz Fischer* (Bonn, 1983).

Steitz, Walter (ed.), *Quellen zur deutschen Wirtschafts- und Sozialgeschichte* (Darmstadt, 1985).

Stern, Fritz, *The Failure of Illiberalism* (New York, 1972).

Stern, Fritz, *Gold and Iron. Bismarck, Bleichröder and the Building of the German Empire* (London, 1977).

Stern, Fritz, 'Prussia', in D. Spring (ed.), *European Landed Elites in the Nineteenth Century* (Baltimore, Md, 1977), pp. 45–67.

Stock, Erich, *Wirtschafts- und sozialpolitische Bestrebungen der deutsch-konservativen Partei unter Bismarck, 1876–1890* (Breslau, 1928).

Stolberg-Wernigerode, Otto Graf zu, *Die unentschiedene Generation. Deutschlands konservative Führungsschichten am Vorabend des Ersten Weltkrieges* (Munich, 1968).

Struve, Walter, 'Elites *versus* Democracy: The Conflict of Elite Theories with the Ideals of Political Democracy in Germany, 1918–1933', PhD thesis, Yale University, 1963.

Struve, Walter, *Elites against Democracy. Leadership Ideals in Bourgeois Political Thought in Germany, 1890–1933* (Princeton, NJ, 1973).

Stürmer, Michael, 'Staatsstreichgedanken im Bismarckreich', *Historische Zeitschrift*, vol. 209 (1969), pp. 566–615.

Stürmer, Michael (ed.), *Bismarck und die preußisch-deutsche Politik 1871–1890* (Munich, 1970).

Stürmer, Michael (ed.), *Das kaiserliche Deutschland. Politik und Gesellschaft 1870–1918* (Düsseldorf, 1970).

Stürmer, Michael, 'Konservatismus and Revolution in Bismarcks Politik', in Stürmer (ed.), *Kaiserliche Deutschland* (1970), pp. 143–67.

Stürmer, Michael, *Regierung und Reichstag im Bismarckstaat 1871–1880* (Düsseldorf, 1974).

Suval, Stanley, *Electoral Politics in Wilhelmine Germany* (Chapel Hill, NC, 1985).

Tal, Uriel, *Christians and Jews in Germany. Religion, Politics, and Ideology in the Second Reich, 1870–1914* (Ithaca, NY, 1975).

Teipel, Heinrich, *Graf von Westarp. Der Parlamentarier wider den Parlamentarismus* (Berlin, 1932).

Thiel, Jürgen, *Die Großblockpolitik der nationalliberalen Partei Badens 1905–1914* (Stuttgart, 1976).

Thierbach, Hans (ed.), *Adolf Grabowsky. Leben und Werk* (Cologne, 1973).

Thimme, Annelise, *Flucht in der Mythos. Die Deutschnationale Volkspartei und die Niederlage von 1918* (Göttingen, 1969).

Thränhardt, Dietrich, *Wahlen und politische Strukturen in Bayern 1848–1953* (Düsseldorf, 1973).

Tims, R. W., *Germanizing Prussian Poland. The H-K-T Society and the Struggle for the Eastern Marches in the German Empire 1894–1919* (New York, 1941).

Tirrell, Sarah, *German Agrarian Politics after Bismarck's Fall* (New York, 1951).

Tödter, Niels-Uwe, 'Die deutschen parlamentarischen Klassenwahlrechts im 19. und 20. Jahrhundert', PhD thesis, University of Hamburg, 1967.

Treude, Burkhard, *Konservative Presse und National Sozialismus. Inhaltsanalyse der 'Neuen Preußischen (Kreuz-) Zeitung' am Ende der Weimarer Republik* (Bochum, 1975).

Trumpener, Ulrich, 'Junkers and Others: The Rise of Commoners in the Prussian Army, 1871–1914', *Canadian Journal of History*, vol. 14/1 (1979), pp. 29–47.

Valjavec, Fritz, *Die Entstehung der politischen Strömungen in Deutschland 1770–1815* (Düsseldorf, 1978).

Viebig, K., *Die Entstehung und Entwicklung der Reichs- und Freikonservative Partei* (Weimar, 1920).

Vierhaus, Rudolf, 'Wahlen und Wählerverhalten in Ostwestfalen und Lippe untersucht an den Reichstags- und Landtagswahlen von 1867 bis 1912/13', *Westfälische Forschungen*, vol. 21 (1968), pp. 54–68.

Vogel, G., 'Die Konservativen und die Blockpolitik Bülows', PhD thesis, University of Berlin, 1925.

Voigt, Gerd, *Otto Hoetzsch 1876–1946. Wissenschaft und Politik im Leben eines deutschen Historikers* (Berlin, 1978).

Volkov, Shulamit, *The Rise of Popular Antimodernism in Germany. The Urban Master Artisans, 1873–1896* (Princeton, NJ, 1978).

Vossler, Otto, 'Bismarcks Sozialpolitik', *Historische Zeitschrift*, vol. 167 (1943), pp. 336–57.

Vossler, Otto, 'Bismarcks Ethos', *Historische Zeitschrift*, vol. 171 (1951), pp. 263–92.

Wallraf, Lothar, 'Deutschkonservative Partei 1876–1918', in Fricke *et al.* (eds.), *Handbuch* (1968), Vol. 1, pp. 673–701.

Wallraf, Lothar, 'Vereinigung der Steuer- und Wirtschaftsreformer 1876–1928', in Fricke *et al.* (eds.), *Handbuch* (1968), Vol. 2, pp. 775–83.

Wallraf, Lothar, 'Zur Politik der Deutschkonservativen Partei in den letzten Jahrzehnten ihres Bestehens (1898–1918) unter den Bedingungen der imperialistischen Epoche', PhD thesis, Friedrich-Schiller University, Jena, 1970.

Wangenheim, H. Freiherr von (ed.), *Conrad Freiherr von Wangenheim Klein-Spiegel* (Berlin, 1934).

Wawrzinek, Kurt, *Die Entstehung der deutschen Antisemitenparteien (1873–1890)* (Berlin, 1927).

Webb, Steven B., 'Agricultural Protection in Wilhelminian Germany: Forging an Empire with Pork and Rye', *Journal of Economic History*, vol. 62/2 (1982), pp. 309–26.

Wehler, Hans-Ulrich (ed.), *Moderne deutsche Sozialgeschichte* (Cologne/Berlin, 1973).

Wehler, Hans-Ulrich (ed.), *Sozialgeschichte Heute* (Göttingen, 1974).

Wehler, Hans-Ulrich, *The German Empire 1871–1918* (Leamington Spa, 1985).

Weißbecker, Manfred, 'Deutsche Vaterlandspartei 1917–1918', in Fricke *et al.* (eds.), *Lexikon* (1983–6), Vol. 2, pp. 391–403.

Weißbecker, Manfred, 'Monarchistische Organisationen 1918/19–1933/34', in Fricke *et al.* (eds.), *Lexikon* (1983–6), Vol. 3, pp. 384–7.

Weitowitz, Rolf, *Deutsche Politik und Handelspolitik unter Reichskanzler Leo von Caprivi 1890–1894* (Düsseldorf, 1978).

Wentzcke, Paul (ed.), *Deutscher Staat und Deutsche Parteien. Beiträge zur Deutschen Partei- und Ideengeschichte* (Munich, 1922).

Wertheimer, M., *The Pan-German League, 1890–1914* (New York, 1924).

White, Dan S., *The Splintered Party. National Liberalism in Hessen and the Reich, 1867–1918* (Cambridge, Mass., 1976).

Winkler, Heinrich August, 'From Social Protectionism to National Socialism: The German Small-Business Movement in Comparative Perspective', *Journal of Modern History*, vol. 48 (1976), pp. 1–18.

Winkler, Heinrich August, 'Der rückversicherte Mittelstand: Die Interessenverbände von Handwerk und Kleinhandel im deutschen Kaiserreich', in H. A. Winkler, *Liberalismus und Antiliberalismus* (Göttingen, 1979), pp. 83–98.

Witt, Peter-Christian, *Die Finanzpolitik des Deutschen Reiches von 1903 bis 1913* (Hamburg, 1970).

Witt, Peter-Christian, 'Eine Denkschrift Otto Hoetzschs vom 5. November 1918', in *Vierteljahrshefte für Zeitgeschichte*, vol. 21/3 (1973), pp. 337–53.

Witt, Peter-Christian, 'Der preußische Landrat als Steuerbeamter 1891–1918. Bemerkungen zur politischen und sozialen Funktion des deutschen Beamtentums', in Geiss and Wendt (eds.), *Deutschland in der Weltpolitik* (1973), pp. 205–19.

Witt, Peter-Christian, 'Konservatismus als "Überparteilichkeit". Die Beamten der Reichskanzlei zwischen Kaiserreich und Weimarer Republik 1900–1933', in Stegmann, Wendt and Witt (eds.), *Deutscher Konservatismus* (1983), pp. 231–80.

Witte, Hermann, *Die pommerschen Konservativen. Männer und Ideen 1810–1860* (Berlin, 1936).

Wortmann, Karl, 'Geschichte der Deutschen Vaterlands-Partei 1917–1918', PhD thesis, Friedrich University, Halle-Wittenberg, 1926.

Wulff, Kurt, 'Die Deutschkonservativen und die preußische Wahlrechtsfrage', PhD thesis, University of Greifswald, 1921.

Zangerl, Carl H. E., 'Baden's Opening to the Left: A Study of Regional Politics 1904–1909', PhD thesis, University of Illinois at Urbana-Champaign, 1974.

Zechlin, Egmont, *Staatsstreichpläne Bismarcks und Wilhelms II. 1890–1894* (Stuttgart, 1929).

Zeender, John K., 'German Catholics and the Concept of an Interconfessional Party 1900–1922', *Journal of Central European Affairs*, vol. 23/4 (1964), pp. 424–39.

Zeender, John K., *The Catholic Center Party 1890–1906*, Transactions of the American Philosophical Society (Philadelphia, 1976).

Zmarzlik, Hans-Günter, *Bethmann Hollweg als Reichskanzler 1909–1914* (Düsseldorf, 1957).

Zmarzlik, Hans-Günter, 'Der Antisemitismus im Zweiten Reich', *Geschichte in Wissenschaft und Unterricht*, vol. 14 (1963), pp. 273–86.

Index

295